I AM NOT A TRACTOR!

Also by the Author

Unconventional Warfare: Rebuilding U.S. Special Operations Forces

I AM NOT A TRACTOR!

How Florida Farmworkers Took On
the Fast Food Giants and Won

Susan L. Marquis

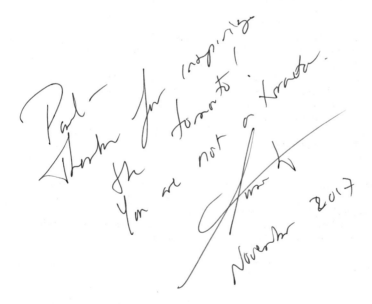

Paul—
thank you for inspiring
the toronto!
You are not a tractor.

November 2017

ILR PRESS
AN IMPRINT OF
CORNELL UNIVERSITY PRESS   **ITHACA AND LONDON**

First published 2017 by Cornell University Press

Printed in the United States of America

Library of Congress Cataloging-in-Publication Data
Names: Marquis, Susan L. (Susan Lynn), 1960– author.
Title: I am not a tractor! : how Florida farmworkers took on the fast food giants and won / Susan L. Marquis.
Description: Ithaca : ILR Press, an imprint of Cornell University Press, 2017. | Includes bibliographical references and index. |
Identifiers: LCCN 2017035097 (print) | LCCN 2017035883 (ebook) | ISBN 9781501714313 (pdf) | ISBN 9781501714306 (epub/mobi) | ISBN 9781501713088 (cloth : alk. paper)
Subjects: LCSH: Coalition of Immokalee Workers. | Agricultural laborers—Florida—Immokalee. | Agricultural laborers—Labor unions—Florida—Immokalee. | Food industry and trade—Florida—Immokalee—Employees.
Classification: LCC HD1527.F6 (ebook) | LCC HD1527.F6 M37 2017 (print) | DDC 331.88/130975944—dc23
LC record available at https://lccn.loc.gov/2017035097

Cornell University Press strives to use environmentally responsible suppliers and materials to the fullest extent possible in the publishing of its books. Such materials include vegetable-based, low-VOC inks and acid-free papers that are recycled, totally chlorine-free, or partly composed of nonwood fibers. For further information, visit our website at cornellpress.cornell.edu.

To Chris

Contents

Characters

Greg Asbed Cofounder of the Coalition of Immokalee Workers. A member of the CIW watermelon harvesting co-op crew that included Gerardo Reyes, Cruz Salucio, and Sean Sellers. Lead for the expansion of CIW's Worker-driven Social Responsibility (WSR) concept and program. Married to Laura Germino.

Lucas Benitez Cofounder of the Coalition of Immokalee Workers. Born and raised in the southwestern Mexican state of Guerrero. Widely recognized voice of the CIW and an active leader in the Campaign for Fair Food and of CIW's Worker Education Program and outreach efforts. Active early in CIW's antislavery efforts.

Jon Esformes Co-CEO of Pacific Tomato Growers, one of the largest tomato growers in Florida, with operations in Florida, Georgia, South Carolina, Virginia, California, and Mexico.

Laura Safer Espinoza Moved to Florida in 2010 after retiring as a justice on the New York State Supreme Court. Founding executive director of the Fair Food Standards Council.

Laura Germino Cofounder of the Coalition of Immokalee Workers. Director of the CIW's antislavery efforts and a recognized international leader in issues of forced labor. Married to Greg Asbed.

Steve Hitov Long-time social justice and human rights attorney. Began working with the Coalition of Immokalee Workers in the early 1990s. Instrumental in negotiating Fair Food agreements with retail giants including Taco Bell, McDonald's, and Walmart.

Gerardo Reyes Joined the Coalition of Immokalee Workers in the late 1990s soon after arriving in Florida from Zacatecas, Mexico. Active leader in the Campaign for Fair Food and a frequent CIW voice on television and other media. In addition to working in citrus and tomatoes, a member of the watermelon crew.

Leonel Perez Met Cruz, Gerardo, Sean, and Greg in 2006 when they were working in Georgia on the CIW watermelon crew. Moved to Immokalee in 2007. Leonel is on the Coalition of Immokalee Workers staff and has been a radio host on Radio Conciencia 107.9, known as La Tuya, given presentations during major actions as part of the CIW Campaign for Fair Food, and is an active leader on the CIW's worker education teams.

Silvia Perez Arrived in Immokalee in 1993 and was one of the Coalition of Immokalee Workers' earliest members, discovering the workers' group in 1994. One of the first members of CIW's Grupo de Mujeres and joined the staff in 2007. A leader in the CIW's worker education team, long-time radio host on La Tuya, and an active voice in the Campaign for Fair Food.

Nely Rodriguez Worked in Michigan's farm fields and then moved to Immokalee in 2000. Has been significantly involved in CIW's antislavery work and in the groundbreaking anti-sexual-harassment program.

Cruz Salucio Arrived in Immokalee from Huehuetenango, Guatemala, and learned of the Coalition of Immokalee Workers through La Tuya. An active leader in the Campaign for Fair Food, a long-time radio host on La Tuya, and a primary leader of the CIW's worker education teams.

Sean Sellers Initially interned at the Coalition of Immokalee Workers through the Student/Farmworker Alliance. Eventually led the SFA and later became a founding staff member of the Fair Food Standards Council. Long-time member of the watermelon harvesting crew.

David Wang Immigrated to the United States when he was fourteen, just after World War II. Graduated in engineering from Georgia Tech. In his career he has been a senior vice president at Union Carbide, a director at International Paper, and an operating partner at Atlas Holdings. Began supporting the Coalition of Immokalee Workers in the late 1990s.

Southwest Florida Farmworker Project: Precursor to the Coalition of Immokalee Workers. Founded in 1993 by farmworkers in Immokalee, Florida. The migrant workers worked in citrus and, most significantly, in tomatoes. Greg Asbed, Lucas Benitez, and Laura Germino are the three remaining cofounders active in the CIW.

Coalition of Immokalee Workers (CIW): The Southwest Florida Farmworkers Project formally incorporated as the Coalition of Immokalee Workers in 1995. Usually referred to as CIW but also as "the Coalition."

Student/Farmworker Alliance (SFA): Ally of the Coalition, established in the late 1990s by university students in Florida and now a national organization.

Campaign for Fair Food: The campaign launched by the CIW in 2001 beginning with a boycott against Taco Bell. The campaign called for fair wages and safe working conditions for farmworkers and for workers to have a "place at the table" when the Florida tomato industry made decisions that affected their work, pay, and safety.

Fair Food Program: The CIW established this program in 2010 when the Campaign for Fair Food achieved agreements with major retail buyers and producers (referred to as "growers"). The Fair Food Program includes the code of conduct, the "penny-per-pound" Fair Food premium, the Fair Food Standards Council and its audits and 24/7 complaint line, and CIW's Worker Education Program.

Fair Food Standards Council (FFSC): The oversight and monitoring nongovernmental agency for the Fair Food Program. Established in 2011.

Acknowledgments

Writers may write the books, but this writer at least could not have done so without support and encouragement from many, many people. As is always the case, their assistance was critical, and any errors are my own. I must begin my appreciation with David Wang, who introduced me to the members of the Coalition of Immokalee Workers. David is a generous philanthropist, and his support of the Pardee RAND Graduate School made it possible for me to visit Immokalee. His thoughtful insight was of great value, and David remained a touchstone throughout my research and writing.

This book is about not just the history of the CIW and the mechanics of the Fair Food Program but about the people of the CIW and the Fair Food Standards Council. They have shared their ideas and their lives with me for the past six years. I'd particularly like to thank those who were patient through many interviews and discussions, worked with me to schedule about a half-dozen visits to Immokalee, made it possible for me to observe and interview CIW worker education teams and FFSC audit teams, and took the time to walk me through the intricacies and nuances of Fair Food agreements, the code of conduct, and the Fair Food premium. In addition to those who participated in formal interviews and are acknowledged in the Note on Sources, I'd like to thank Marley Moynahan, Natalie Rodriguez, Daniel Cooper Bermudez, and Brian Kudinger from the CIW and the Student/Farmworker Alliance. Logistics, scheduling, translating, and photos: I could not have dived as deeply without your help.

I would not have written this book were it not for the work of Barry Estabrook and Eric Schlosser. Barry wrote the *Gourmet* article and then the masterful book *Tomatoland*, which brought the harsh reality of Florida's tomato fields to my attention (and many others') back in 2009. Eric Schlosser's revolutionary *Fast Food Nation* hit hard in 2001, taking a no-holds-barred look at the rise and perils of fast food in the United States. That book continues to be a benchmark for those who care about food policy and the sources of our food. Schlosser caused readers to think about the food we eat and the effects of our consumption, not only on our health but also on agriculture, the environment, but particularly the people who grow, harvest, process, and serve what we eat. Schlosser extended this story in *Reefer Madness: Sex, Drugs, and Cheap Labor in America*, taking on the issue of worker exploitation and the determined turning away by people to avoid looking at these undersides of the American economy. On a personal level, Eric was strongly supportive of my writing about the CIW. It is true that in February 2015, Eric asked, "So, does RAND know you've become a communist?" While in jest, Eric was not the first to respond with some surprise when he discovered the topic of my book, given my substantial career in "guns and bombs." We first met when I hosted a discussion of nuclear security with Eric and RAND researcher Lynn Davis, in conjunction with Eric's recent book *Command and Control*. But Eric was intrigued that I was seriously researching the Coalition and tomato workers in Florida. He understood from the beginning that I was approaching the Coalition's work from a very different perspective from those in the field of agricultural labor and labor rights. I had long been a fan of Eric's work and an admirer of his breadth of knowledge and interest. His support gave strength to my belief that I was on the right path.

Essential to my being able to write this book has been my professional home, the RAND Corporation and the Pardee RAND Graduate School. Now more than ever, the world needs RAND's commitment to objective, nonpartisan policy analysis and the talent of graduates of Pardee RAND. Michael Rich, president of the RAND Corporation, made it possible for me to gain some distance and time to pull my thoughts and research together while in residence for two months at the RAND Europe office in Cambridge, England. Anita Szafran provided early guidance and troubleshooting on citations. Jane Ryan helped me find my way through book publishing while at RAND. Christopher Dirks has been invaluable in making my manuscript ready for publication. Pardee RAND Graduate School students Sara Kups and Ben Colaiaco helped me in 2013 with background research on American agricultural labor and corporate social responsibility programs. And Rachel Swanger and Jennifer Prim have been patient and encouraging when I've wandered into their offices needing to share my latest thought about why the Fair Food Program has worked.

Fran Benson and the Cornell University Press have provided a literary home for *I Am Not a Tractor!* It was exactly a year ago from the time I am writing these words that Fran responded quickly and enthusiastically when I sent her an e-mail asking if she would be interested in publishing my book on the Coalition of Immokalee Workers. Since that time, some of my most enjoyable discussions about this book, long-standing issues in labor rights, and the state of the world have been in conversation with Fran. She has shepherded this project through with kindness and commitment. I found my way to Fran through the advice of Bob Lockhart of the University of Pennsylvania Press. Bob and my RAND colleague and author Shelly Culbertson read my proposal and provided guidance and spirit lifting as I discovered the world of agents and publishers. Jim Brudney and Lance Compa offered highly helpful external reviews and comments.

John DiIulio has once again been generous in his intellectual and personal support of my endeavors. John was my dissertation advisor back in the day. We have become both friends and colleagues over the many years since then, and it is to John that I first turned when deciding to write *I Am Not a Tractor!* John read early, laborious outlines and papers as I wrestled with the purpose of the book and the value I might bring to the topic. He was the first outside reader of my proposal, sample chapter, and the full draft manuscript. John also funded three University of Pennsylvania Fox Leadership Fellows, Nicolas Garcia, Aaron Wolf, and Harrison Pharamond, to track down background information on international labor reports and social responsibility auditing firms. John is a wise man and a dear friend.

Most important, I thank my husband Chris Thompson. Chris is not necessarily known as a patient man but his patience was without measure as I devoted every weekend to writing. We developed a new approach to vacations where I wrote during the day and Chris explored lovely places on his own. More importantly, Chris was my first reader and my first editor. He was more than willing to let me know when something I had written was "like reading a PowerPoint presentation," but he was also sincere when he thought I had hit just the right note. Chris has spent much of the past several years discussing my ideas, listening to tales from the tomato fields, and giving me the time and space to write. Thank you.

GETTING TO IMMOKALEE

Late spring 2009 and I've been carrying the March issue of *Gourmet* in my bag for a couple of months. "Mind, Body, and Seoul. Korean food is America's next new cuisine." "Easy Does It. Sometimes all it takes is a simple roast chicken . . ." One of the values of yet another flight across the country is the chance to catch up. "A World Away. Stretching west from Castile toward the Portuguese border . . ." Truth be told, I'm a good cook. I'd broadened my food magazine selection to include more "sophisticated" journals such as *The Art of Eating*, but *Gourmet* had been there the longest, an old friend for stolen moments on the road or after a busy day . . . letting the image of "communal tables filled with soul-satisfying food and new-found friends" fill my head.

Somewhere over Oklahoma and flipping to page 40. "The Price of Tomatoes. If you have eaten a tomato this winter, it might well have been picked by a person who lives in virtual slavery." I knew Barry Estabrook had long been a contributing editor at *Gourmet* with his *Politics of the Plate* features, but this article was different. Estabrook opens with what I have since learned is a signature of writing about Immokalee, Florida, and the migrant workers there. He describes the jarring transition when driving from Naples to Immokalee. In thirty-five miles or so you travel from multimillion-dollar homes, Saks Fifth Avenue, and luxury golf course after luxury golf course through the Corkscrew swamp at the north end of the Everglades, past tomato fields and orange groves partially hidden behind scrub oak, palmetto, and sand berms, into the trailers, low-rise apartments, small single-family homes with more than a few cars up on blocks, and the bars and bodegas that make up most of Immokalee. The scruffiness and poverty are worse than most, but the cars up on blocks, drainage ditches, and burned-out grass look a lot like much of rural southwest Florida. But it was not the scenery that caught my attention in Estabrook's article. It was the story of unrelenting abuse of farmworkers, of modern-day slavery, complete with beatings, wage theft, and workers locked in the back of a box truck that served as their "home." These workers were not in Thailand or Mexico or Kenya. They worked on tomato farms in Florida. And the setting was not the pre–Civil War or Jim Crow South; it was 2009.

Tucking the copy of *Gourmet* into my bag, I was thinking through what I had read, but I needed to turn to other matters. As it turned out, I was headed to Naples to touch base with one of the board members of the graduate school where I'd recently been appointed dean. After fifteen years with the Department of Defense leading warfare and operational analysis organizations and a half dozen years running a defense, healthcare, and analysis group in a Washington, DC, nonprofit, I had been ready to try something new. The stars aligned, and in late 2008 I had joined the RAND Corporation, not as a national security expert but as the dean of the Pardee RAND Graduate School, the oldest and largest public policy PhD program in the United States. David Wang was on the school's Board of Governors, and he was ready to step down with the arrival of a new dean.

I soon found myself in an elevator headed to David Wang's penthouse apartment. Once inside, looking across the vast expanse of his living room, with its sharp-edged formal furniture, I had a hard time making out his features. He sat in shadows that contrasted with the glare of Naples sunshine flooding through the floor-to-ceiling glass windows that looked out onto the Gulf of Mexico. David Wang had immigrated to the United States at the close of World War II, joining his father, a pioneer in nuclear physics in China, who had served as an envoy to President Roosevelt at the behest of the Chiang Kai-shek government. An engineer by training, with a long and successful career at Union Carbide and International Paper, David is a formal, somewhat impatient man. He gave little indication that he looked forward to our meeting. Struggling to find a connection, I made uncomfortable small talk mixed with his brusque interrogation about the Pardee RAND Graduate School. As the minutes crept by, he made a reference to work he was doing with an agricultural workers group. "The tomato pickers in Immokalee?" I asked (mispronouncing the name as "Immikley"). Intrigued, David responded, "Yes, yes, in Immokalee [rhymes with "broccoli," it turned out]. I've been working with the Coalition of Immokalee Workers for years." My old friend *Gourmet* saved the day and set me on the journey that yielded this book.

Where does our food come from? Like many others, I've become more thoughtful over time about the food I eat. At some point I moved beyond aspirations to dine in high-end restaurants or track down unusual ingredients. I try to keep it local and seasonal and have learned to get to know the farmers at the markets. And professionally, I knew that large-scale industrial agriculture can feed the world with "cheap food" but has hidden costs that any good economist will tell you must be taken into account: costs to the environment and in community health. This is the agricultural system version of the total cost accounting I had worked on when looking at major weapon systems in the Pentagon. But as I learned to take into account the costs to the soil, costs to the air, pesticides, antibiotics, obesity, food security, and the treatment of animals, the piece that was missing was the farmworkers. The people who put the food on our tables. For "foodies" and those who just care about what they serve their families, journalist and author Eric Schlosser was one of the first to raise his voice and point out this blind spot. Schlosser stood up and said, "I'd rather eat a tomato picked by fairly treated labor than an organic tomato picked by a slave."

In the months that followed my trip to Florida, I began to read more about the Coalition of Immokalee Workers and their Campaign for Fair Food. What was this farmworker organization fighting for and how did it ever cross their mind to take on fast-food chains like Taco Bell, Burger King, and McDonald's? Why did the CIW think these corporate giants were key to increasing farmworker pay or eliminating the violence and abuse in the fields that Barry Estabrook, Eric Schlosser, Kevin Bales, and Ron Soodalter wrote about? And where was the government in all of this? As I came to understand, the problem of agricultural labor, particularly fair and humane pay and working conditions for the farmworkers in the fields, had been with us since our nation's founding. Slavery, immigrant workers, African American workers in the Jim Crow South; the source and color of the workers changed over time but in many ways conditions in the fields were nearly as brutal in twentieth-century America as they had been at the time of the Civil War. They were just less visible as Americans became increasingly removed from the source of the food on their tables, selecting fruits and vegetables from brightly lit produce displays in grocery stores. Did the CIW really have a solution that would make a difference in workers' lives? Was it really possible that farmworkers themselves, as a community, could successfully take on agricultural labor problems that have existed throughout the history of United States? As I came to learn, the answer is yes. There is a reason to tell and to read this story. At a time when there is great frustration that we seem to be making no progress in solving most of the persistent and complex problems facing our world, the Fair Food Program works. The Coalition of Immokalee Workers has transformed the tomato fields from the worst agricultural labor situation in the United States to the best. There is victory in this. There is also the promise of expanding what the CIW has done far beyond the tomato fields to other agricultural workers and even to industrial and low-wage labor more broadly. To achieve the potential of the Fair Food Program, we need to know how we got here and why this has worked when so many other efforts have not. This is what *I Am Not a Tractor!* is about.

As David Wang and I connected on these issues and possibilities, he introduced me to Greg Asbed, Lucas Benitez, and Laura Germino, three of the principal cofounders of the Coalition of Immokalee Workers. I visited Immokalee for the first time, making that drive from Naples to the CIW's offices on Second Street. I saw the chickens in the yards, workers lined up to get food from a local charity, and the black mold on the walls of the one-room apartments with six mattresses stacked waiting for the workers to return from the fields. I also saw the banner that had first announced the Coalition, "¡Una Sola Fuerza! [loosely translated as Strength in Unity!] The Coalition of Immokalee Workers."

I also read more about agricultural working conditions not only in Florida but across the United States. For most of our nation's history, we've struggled with the role and place of agricultural labor in our democracy, and in particular the treatment of the men and women who grow and harvest the food we eat. Our history is a troubled one that didn't end with the Thirteenth Amendment and the conclusion of the Civil War. The more than four million slaves that worked the sugar cane, tobacco, rice, corn, and particularly cotton fields of the South became the sharecroppers and agricultural workers who worked the land and never seemed to earn enough to cover their debt to the landowners.

In the West, a different story unfolded, or at least a new variation on the story of American agriculture. Open spaces and fertile land offered the possibilities of large-scale farming. Western farmers, particularly those in California, quickly saw the advantage of an immigrant workforce that would provide temporary and seasonal labor. Mexican immigrants came first, after the end of the Mexican-American War in 1848. Chinese immigrants soon followed when the demand for Western produce grew in the East with the opening of the transcontinental railroad in 1869. By 1882, Chinese immigrants provided more than 50 percent of the agricultural workforce in California. This situation changed at the turn of the century, when the US Congress passed exclusionary legislation limiting both Chinese immigration and the ability of existing Chinese immigrants to work in the United States. The loss of Chinese workers did little, however, to slow the development of large-scale commercial agriculture in California. The need for labor was massive, and new sources of immigrant labor from the Philippines and Japan, as well as a resurgence of Mexican workers, picked up the slack. Each new wave of immigrants was willing to accept lower wages and accept worse living conditions than those who came before. This pattern of immigrants providing cheap agricultural labor, US citizens feeling the work was beneath them, and xenophobia pushing out one immigrant group to be replaced by the next was repeated time and again.

By 1930, Mexican seasonal workers and Mexican Americans made up 80 percent of the harvest labor in California, following the harvest and then returning to their homes in the Southwest or in Mexico. The Great Depression saw new restrictions on immigrants and an attempt to attract American workers, but the legendary "Okies" who traveled to California looking for work couldn't meet the labor demand and the wages promised were often not realized. With the Second World War, domestic farm labor was again in short supply and Mexican immigration increased once again, encouraged by the Bracero Program, which facilitated a steady supply of Mexican farmworkers until the Kennedy Administration ended it in 1964. The ending of the program did little to change the makeup of the western workforce, particularly in California. To this day, the great majority of California produce is harvested by Mexican immigrants.

If western farming, particularly in California, drew on a vast pool of poorly paid immigrant labor, the southern and southeastern states continued to leverage the legacy of slavery, adding a particularly grim twist as Reconstruction came to an end. Formerly enslaved African Americans and their descendants provided most of the labor on larger farms and plantations. Southern farmers preferred to hire black agricultural laborers who were willing to work for lower wages, and southern whites considered farm labor beneath them and were unwilling to work alongside freed slaves. Unlike the migrant workers in California, farmworkers in the South were less mobile, tied to the land through sharecropping and debt peonage. It was not uncommon for African Americans to be tricked or coerced into signing contracts as field workers or sharecroppers. Farm owners held the workers' pay and took out money for expenses from the company store, for seed and supplies, and other debts. Workers were often not paid for the work they were doing. When their contracts concluded at the end of the year, sharecroppers and farm workers still owed money. The penalty for nonpayment was jail, so they kept working in the hope of paying off what they were told they owed.

Farmers and other employers worked with county sheriffs and state prison officials to develop the southern innovation of convict labor and debt bondage. Local authorities were allowed to "bind out" to local farmers anyone convicted of a crime, felonies and misdemeanors alike, and unable to pay off their fines. Courts would even skip the intermediate step of a fine and impose penalties of fixed terms of labor, particularly during the harvest season. Convict leasing began in Mississippi just after the Civil War ended and quickly spread across the southern states, establishing strong roots in Florida and Alabama. Historian

David Oshinsky points out that as Florida's agricultural industry took off in the late 1800s and early 1900s, first with turpentine and then citrus, and Florida's interior developed the infrastructure needed to support the new industries, the southern practice of convict leasing "turned a serious problem (the punishment of troublesome ex-slaves) into a remarkable gain." The economic benefits went to the growers and other employers, to brokers between the prisons and the producers, and to the state and local governments that benefited from this new source of revenue. Convict leasing provided a functional replacement for slavery that was, if anything, even more brutal without the brake of ownership investment. Oshinsky quotes one southern employer of convict labor: "Before the war we owned the negroes. If a man had a good nigger, he could afford to take care of him; if he was sick get a doctor. He might even put gold plugs in his teeth. But these convicts: we don't own 'em. One dies, get another."

Florida and Alabama were the last two states to allow the leasing of state convicts. But when Florida ended the leasing of state prisoners in 1919, the county jails were quick to help with a steady supply of cheap labor, rounding up African American men for petty or nonexistent crimes when it was time for the harvest. When the leasing of even county prisoners was outlawed in 1923, enterprising sheriffs used a version of debt peonage to provide growers with an able-bodied and cheap workforce. Once arrested, men were assessed exorbitant fines that they worked off in the groves or work camps.

Convict leasing and debt peonage from courthouse fines were not the only ways to maintain cheap labor in the southern states. Tenant farming and sharecropping had their own variation of debt peonage and wage theft. Wages were low. Workers were at the mercy of farm and packing house owners in terms of what they were paid and what they might owe. By the early 1960s, little had changed in the southeastern states. Workers were black and poor and it was often a buyer's market, with more people who wanted to work than the fields and groves required.

The opportunity for change had come during the Great Depression. Concerned for the state of workers in the United States, Congress passed two foundational pieces of labor legislation: the National Labor Relations Act of 1935 and the Fair Labor Standards Act of 1938. The first gave workers the right to organize, join unions, and engage in collective bargaining. The second piece of legislation set basic standards for the fair treatment of workers that are still followed to this day: minimum wage, overtime compensation, the maintenance of timekeeping and other records, and significant limits on child labor. The American public, perhaps spurred on by early investigative journalists like Upton Sinclair or later by the documentary photographs of the Depression by Walker Evans and Dorothea Lange, had focused on the abuses found in poor working conditions and pay for factory and processing plant workers in an increasingly industrialized economy. Congress's passage of these landmark labor laws was a transformational moment in US labor relations and working conditions.

True enough. But two groups had been deliberately excluded from the new legislation: domestic workers and agricultural workers. They were excluded because of negotiations between the authors of the legislation and southern congressmen needed for passage of the bills. Blacks were the South's farmworkers and domestic servants. The congressmen were adamant that black farmworkers or "field hands" and domestic servants be excluded from any guarantee of labor rights, and this exclusion and separation from a broad category of labor laws and regulations has largely continued to this day. The National Labor Relations Act excluded agricultural laborers through its definition of an employee: "shall not include any individual employed as an agricultural laborer." The Fair Labor Standards Act extended this exclusion, defining agriculture broadly to include cultivation, harvesting, dairying, raising of livestock or any animals, and forestry, and anything related to those, such as delivery or storage for markets. In 1966, the Fair Labor Standards Act was amended to prohibit children under sixteen from "hazardous" agricultural work and to require minimum wage for farm work, although the minimum wage was lower for agricultural workers until 1977. The requirements for minimum wage for farm work are not as strict as for factories or other employment and do not require overtime pay. And minimum wage is difficult to track without timekeeping systems and when farmworkers are hired through contract labor agents and work in fields far from the eyes of farm managers. To make it even more difficult to track down violations of farmworkers' legal rights, there are still but a handful of inspectors from the Wage and Hour Division in the individual states, most speak only English, and, although there have been some improvements, many spend most of their time with the growers rather than in the fields.

Farmworkers lack the common benefits of health insurance, disability insurance, paid time off, or any sort of retirement benefits. Most have no access to social safety net programs such as SNAP/food stamps, workers' compensation, Social Security, or Medicaid, even though if they are on the payroll they are paying taxes into these systems. And agricultural work is one of the most dangerous occupations in the United States, with an exceptionally high death rate and exposure to pesticides and chemical poisoning.

In 1960, Edward R. Murrow introduced *Harvest of Shame*, his devastating documentary exposé of agricultural labor in the southeastern states. The setting was Immokalee: "This is not South Africa, or the Congo. This is a scene from America, home to the best fed people in the world." As he speaks, we see a crowd of African American workers bidding to work in response to the call of crew leaders, and then crammed into the backs of trucks to head into the fields outside of Immokalee. An Immokalee grower comments on the scene, observing, in an echo of Oshinsky's employer of convict labor in 1883, "We used to own our slaves. Now, we just rent them."

Into the 1970s, Immokalee's and Florida's farmworkers were largely African American, in direct contrast to farmworkers in the western states who were primarily from Mexico. Not until the late 1970s, as African Americans left agriculture for other industries, did the demographics change and the number of immigrant workers increase. Haitians, later followed by Mexicans, as well as others from Central America, particularly Guatemala, largely replaced the African American workforce. By the 1990s, farmworkers in Florida were mostly young immigrant men.

Lucas Benitez was one of those young men. Seventeen years old, he had family in Immokalee and the pay sounded good. "They told me how it was difficult in Immokalee, but they didn't tell me the whole story. I had been working the fields [in Mexico] since I was six years old . . . [and] I was ready to work hard." It had been dark when Lucas first showed up in the Pantry Shelf parking lot, joining the crowd of mostly men looking for work. Lots of Haitians plus others from Mexico and Guatemala. Parking lot lights cut through the predawn gloom as the men gathered around the crew leaders looking for the strongest and youngest for their harvesting crews.

He was in. Onto the bus and out to Immokalee's tomato fields. Lucas knew what hard work was. He also understood the dignity in it. "My dad worked very long days but every night he sat with us kids, five boys and a girl. We talked and he told stories. My dad said, 'remember, we are poor but we have something very important. We have our labor. The rich people of the world have storehouses of money. If you don't go to work, this money doesn't work. You need to ask a reasonable price for your labor. You do not give it for free.'"

Lucas's dad taught his children well, but his message hadn't quite made it to Immokalee. "When I came to Immokalee, I saw the cheap price for labor, verbal abuse, physical abuse, and sexual abuse." But at seventeen there wasn't much Lucas could do about it. First, he needed a job and he needed money. So into the fields he went, where he was fast and could keep going forever.

It's November now, and the first planting of tomato plants was growing fast in the heat. Lucas remembers: "I was staking tomatoes. You did this by the hour, not a piece rate. I saw that my coworkers were slow and I was going fast. I finished a row and waited ten minutes for the other workers. A big truck arrived. 'Hey,' [the crew leader yelled], 'what are you doing?'"

Lucas replied, "Waiting for the crew."

"Go back!" the crew leader shouted. His whole life, Lucas had never liked if a boss yelled at him, particularly when he wasn't doing anything wrong. He had his dignity.

"No." Lucas wasn't moving.

"I said go back, motherfucker!"

"No, motherfucker."

Looking back, Lucas still can't quite believe the scene in that tomato field. "I think it was the first time any worker said 'motherfucker' to him. I was about 120 pounds then. This guy was about 300 pounds and six feet tall. He was called 'El Picudo' after the bird that bites at you and that you should be afraid of."

The crew leader climbed from the truck, furious at the upstart kid. "What did you say?!"

Lucas didn't budge. "What you heard."

Lucas continues: "The guy went to hit me and then saw I had a [tomato] stake in my hands. I said, 'Hit me! If you hit me, you will definitely get one of my hits back.'"

Welcome to Immokalee.

TO BEAT ONE OF US IS TO BEAT US ALL!

God, it was frustrating, but the two knew they were in the right place. When Greg Asbed and Laura Germino looked out the window of the small storefront office, they faced the cracked asphalt, broken concrete dividers, and courageous weeds that made up the Pantry Shelf parking lot. Throughout the day, the occasional beat-up Ford or rusted Chevy would pull in, seeking the shade of the grocery store wall. But most were walking. Women, arms loaded with bags, walked out the market's doors and down streets patterned by the shade of trees loaded with Spanish moss and the glaring sun of southwest Florida. Some carried fruit that reminded them of home in Haiti, but most were carrying the soda, chips, and other junk food that was cheapest in the overpriced market.

The two paralegals, who made up two-thirds of Florida Rural Legal Services' Immokalee operations, had to arrive early if they wanted to witness the reason for this unincorporated town's existence. Immokalee was effectively a labor reserve for the big citrus, pepper, tomato, and other produce farms that filled the interior of the state. In the dark of predawn, a hundred or more (mostly) men shifted from one group to the next, clumped around the late-model pickups, the harshness of the headlights emphasizing the exhaustion on their faces. Men stood in the beds of the trucks or on the concrete dividers, shouting in Spanish and English, and indicating with a jerk of the head, a wave of a thumb, that the lucky souls could board the worn-out buses waiting there. If you didn't get on the bus, you weren't working that day.

Greg Asbed and Laura Germino were here because of this flood of farmworkers. If you were going to work with farmworkers, if you believed it was possible to take on one of the most intractable labor issues in the United States, Immokalee was the place to be. Laura had seen the opportunity first. Over and over again she heard the name: Immokalee. Working intake for the farmworkers picking apples in the mountainside orchards outside of Gettysburg, Pennsylvania, she kept writing it down as the migrant workers gave Immokalee, Florida, as their permanent address. Laura had just returned to the United States after serving with the Peace Corps. And what she saw was troubling. First with the workers in Pennsylvania's apple orchards and later with the migrant workers arriving in Maryland, Laura learned more about the working and living conditions of those who moved up and down the East Coast, following the seasons and the crops. "Poor" was the kinder term. "Beaten down" seemed like a better fit. Three things became increasingly clear: outside of the workers, few seemed to care about their plight; conditions were bad everywhere; and Florida in particular was an arena of untrammeled abuse. Even as she worked for the advocacy nonprofit Friends of Farmworkers, it wasn't clear that her work—or the work of similar activist groups—was doing much to improve the lives of farmworkers.

While Laura was in Burkina Faso, Greg had been in Haiti. He was now in graduate school. When Greg and Laura found time together, their conversation returned time and again to two subjects: the seemingly insurmountable challenges facing farmworkers and the profound lessons Greg had learned during three years in Haiti. Stepping off the plane in Port au Prince, Greg had been reasonably sure this was not what the other neuroscience majors from Brown University had been preparing for. Haiti was in the turmoil of the last six months of the twenty-eight-year Duvalier family dictatorship. That was followed by Duvalier's overthrow and two-and-a-half years of military junta, when the real violence and instability broke out. Undaunted, Greg joined in, becoming part of the grassroots movements building in protest across the island. The protests weren't the blindness of angry mobs, but Greg realized instead that communities were organizing themselves. Most importantly, the organization was done from the inside; it was community-led action, declaring the right to jobs and housing and their right to elect the nation's president. When Jean-Bertrand Aristide reclaimed the presidency from the military junta, these community groups cheered the victory they helped make possible.

Now, back in the United States, Greg asked, "What if?" The conversations he and Laura were having converged. What if instead of concerned outsiders advocating for workers, the workers themselves came together as a community? What if instead of legal aid groups fighting individual legal battles, playing whack-a-mole with those caught violating the law, the workers' community fought for their human rights? What if the lessons of Haiti were applied in the farm fields and communities of the United States? What would change then? And could it be done?

It was increasingly apparent that Immokalee was the key. It was the hub of the East Coast farmworker community, the source of the river of migrant workers that flowed from Florida to Maine. And while issues of wage theft, dilapidated housing, and poor working conditions existed in all of the eastern farming communities, the abuse was greatest, the conditions harshest, in Florida. If anyone was going to shed light on the treatment of farmworkers, Greg and Laura knew it had to be there. So, like the immigrants who flooded into Immokalee each season, the two Brown graduates looked for a way to get there.

"Community specialist paralegals," that's what the Florida Rural Legal Services advertisement said. Florida Rural Legal Services, FRLS (sometimes jokingly referred to by themselves as "Frills"), was one of those organizations, like Friends of Farmworkers, inspired by *Harvest of Shame*. The legal advocacy group had been founded as a branch of the Legal Services Corporation in 1966. The often Ivy League–trained lawyers who moved to Florida or other rural areas believed in the power of the courts and in attacking farmworker abuse and exploitation as a series of legal violations. FRLS worked through "impact litigation," social change through the law. FRLS took on cases of migrant worker abuse, usually representing a single worker or small group working for the same employer. The most frequent violation was wage theft, but they also went after cases of unsafe working conditions and overcrowded and filthy housing. At the time, FRLS also helped workers get their immigration documentation. Three lawyers and six paralegals made up the FRLS troops representing a half-million Florida farmworkers. In the early 1990s, one of these lawyers and two paralegals ran the "Immokalee district," which covered about half the state. For FRLS, success was winning reparations for their worker clients related to specific legal violations. Success required workers willing to come forward to file the case and then all the complications and delays of working through the court system.

Let's be clear up front: Laura and Greg weren't heading to Florida to join in the FRLS program of addressing specific violations of laws rarely enforced when the victims were migrant workers. Not at all. Whether it was vision or cluelessness, they were headed to Immokalee in hope of effecting cultural change in the direction of human rights and dignity, and not for a single victim at a time but for the entire community of workers. The two did not hide their purpose: "We gave FRLS fair warning. We were coming down [to Florida] to work with the community on self-directed change." Despite this warning, or perhaps recognizing that there weren't that many people with Greg and Laura's experience and training willing to settle into Immokalee, Florida Rural Legal Services hired them. It quickly became apparent that FRLS hadn't realized what they had signed up for.

Laura, of course, knew Florida. Though she grew up in Virginia, Laura is a fourth-generation Floridian and spent her summers as a child there. She knew the light and beauty of the Atlantic beaches not far from Deland. She knew warm nights with grown-ups on the porch while she raced around barefoot with her cousins during summers spent with Granny. She knew also the darkness of Florida, hidden from beachgoing winter visitors: early childhood memories as segregation ended, kicking and screaming, and unsettling stories Granny told about Florida's not-too-distant past. Pulling into the parking space next to the FRLS office, Greg and Laura were greeted by the same Immokalee that greeted the flood of new and old immigrants completing their long and crowded van rides from Arizona and Texas at the start of the season in late September. Like the rest of Florida, Immokalee offered the workers, Greg, and Laura both light and dark. The promise of work and the possibility of effecting real change mixed with the reality of abusive working conditions and growers who had been running their farms the same way for a long time and had little interest in doing things differently.

Arriving in Immokalee, Greg and Laura showed up with the commitment you'd expect from all who worked for Florida Rural Legal Services, people who picked up their lives to fight for migrant farmworkers. But Greg and Laura brought something else, something new to the equation. Experience working in struggling "Third World" communities was a plus. After all, as one observer noted, up through 1969 "the Peace Corps used Immokalee as a training area for people who were going to the Third World [and] it seemed like the Caribbean coast of Costa Rica even in the early 1990s." Immokalee's newer immigrants were from Mexico and Guatemala, joining the Haitians who had begun to arrive over the previous decade. English was rare. Spanish was often a second language at best. Greg's and Laura's ability to speak Haitian Creole and Spanish was invaluable. Along with suitcases and duffel bags, they brought to Florida their experience and the intelligence to apply what they had learned in new ways in a new world.

Many days at FRLS, the incessant demands of trying to right the often routine, and too frequently gross, abuse of Immokalee's farmworkers threatened to overwhelm the small staff. The lawyer and the two paralegals pushed against a tide that had rolled in a hundred years before and always seemed to be flowing in one direction. There was a never-ending stream of workers coming to the office to report not being paid, crew leaders who subtracted "taxes" or "Social Security" from workers' pay and pocketed the money, crummy housing, and the risk of being beaten if you dared complain.

It could have played out in two ways. Helping this steady stream of clients could take over all available intellectual and emotional energy. Recovering a few hundred dollars in back pay or assisting a Guatemalan worker in getting his work permit and legal documentation were victories. But these small, albeit real, victories were not why Greg and Laura had moved to Immokalee and not why they stayed. Small victories were not why Greg and Laura were patiently taking the time to become part of the community, talking and listening with workers not only in the FRLS office but also in the housing areas, on the steps leading to overcrowded trailers, and on the corners near convenience stores. They learned about price gouging in Immokalee's stores, exorbitant rents, and little to do when there was no work. At some level, to understand what is to come, it might be helpful to understand Greg Asbed and Laura Germino. There's an intensity there, grounded in deep belief. This belief was in the need to take a different approach if farmworkers were ever going to be able to positively change their lives, and a belief that focusing on the community was the first step in attaining this objective. The strength of Greg and Laura's belief resulted in an unswerving commitment to fighting this fight. Come to think of it, this same determination and persistence in commitment is the characteristic that ties them all together: Greg, Laura, Lucas, Gerardo, Steve. But first things first. Let's start with Greg and get to know each in turn.

Settling in at the table at the shop in Ave Maria, the closest "real" coffee shop to Immokalee, it doesn't take long to see that Greg Asbed is one tightly wound, highly physical man. Spend some time talking with him and you'll see that all that barely controlled energy is linked to a tremendous analytic intellect. This is not the scattered energy of hyperactivity. This is the tightly focused energy of someone who is confident he knows where true north lies. Leaning forward, hands tight on his knees, there are things to be said, things to be explained. There's a lot going on: Walmart, Pacific Growers, training, audits. So much finally happening that it all comes out in rapid fire. Look, he says, here's what you need to understand.

Greg reads everything and is an accomplished writer, having published academic book chapters, commentaries in traditional newspapers such as the *Los Angeles Times,* and online in blogs including the *Huffington Post.* Greg is an avid basketball player and a fanatical Dallas Cowboys fan. Both are essential to keeping Greg sane in the midst of twenty-five years fighting this battle and figuring out how to make it work. With some pride in his willingness and ability to do hard physical labor, Greg waxes rhapsodic when telling of the skill and talent of the CIW's much-sought-after watermelon harvesting crew that he worked on for years. It is not hard to imagine what he dreams of when tossing or catching a melon.

Born in Baltimore and raised in Washington, DC's suburbs, Greg attended the prestigious Landon School before heading to Brown. But, like many Americans,

Greg traces his family history to immigrants arriving in Baltimore in search of a better life. Greg's history is just a bit more recent than some. After seeing all but her older sister killed in their village of Izmit by Turkish gendarmes during the Armenian genocide in 1917, Greg's grandmother Hripsimee survived a five-hundred-mile forced march and was then sold by Turks to itinerant Kurds, who in turn sold her to another Armenian family fleeing Turkey into Syria. The two goats and a single coin paid for her as a child bride also likely saved her life and resulted in the son who became Greg's father, Norig Asbed. Settling in what is now Kobane, Syria, Norig revealed himself to be a brilliant student. Upon his completing the village's parochial school, the village supported Norig's enrollment at age eleven at the Melkonian Institute in Cyprus, a school for Armenian children. Norig was unable to return to Kobane and his family for six years. When he did, he taught at the local school and elsewhere in the Middle East, eventually becoming a student of nuclear physics with Nobel laureate Niels Bohr and then taking on doctoral studies and completing his master's degree at the University of Maryland and Johns Hopkins University. Norig fell in love with Ruth-Alice Davis, a noted pediatrician and early woman graduate of Columbia University's medical school, who was chief of the maternal and child health clinic at Johns Hopkins Hospital while Norig was in graduate school.

When Greg talks about his grandmother's strength as a young girl in the face of so much violence and fear, his pride in his father's overcoming poverty, and his admiration for his mother's work in the Philippines and in public health in Maryland, it is evident that this history is still very much alive and running through his veins. Out of his family's history grows a strong sense of the risk of the vulnerability of immigrants, anger at injustice, and a belief in the strength of community. Greg's anger combines with respect for the courage and hard work of the farmworkers, a respect born of eighteen years harvesting watermelons side-by-side with other CIW members from Florida to Missouri.

It's worth talking for a moment about those watermelons. Harvesting watermelons is hard. Unbelievably hard. You may remember Edgerrin James, an all-pro running back who played for the University of Miami and then for the Indianapolis Colts. James was raised in Immokalee and harvesting watermelons was, as he lets us know, "the highest-paying job I had before my $49 million one with the Colts." The point here is that when James showed up at "the U," his coaches were in awe of his strength and endurance. Summers harvesting watermelons built James. "It helped shape me so much that I was all muscular when I got to Miami even though I never lifted a weight in my life. I was hardened in every way." Florida watermelon crews—known as "gators" when they were largely African American and then "sandillero" when the demographic shifted to Latinos—were known for their skill and strength. The CIW watermelon co-op was no different.

Members of the co-op proudly declared, "Yo soy sandillero" as they headed north with each season's harvest. Harvesting watermelons is another one of those jobs, like picking tomatoes, that you might take for granted. But this is a skilled trade. Greg gives us a feel for the work:

> Workers must learn the complex interplay of five or six different signs that indicate when a melon is ripe and ready for harvest—or else get fired without recourse for cutting green melons. They must learn to throw and catch twenty- to thirty-pound oblong fruits with just the right arc, often keeping pace on foot with the moving field truck. Thousands of times a day they must pitch melons to another worker up to ten feet away. . . . They must also accurately estimate the weight of melons flying by at a rate of two or three per second on a fast-moving conveyor belt or risk having a load rejected for mis-sized melons—another fireable offense. But perhaps the most important skill watermelon workers must develop is an almost Herculean endurance . . . sixteen hours a day under a hot summer sun, in temperatures that often climb well over 100 degrees.

Hripsimee's strength? Greg called on that strength when he first started with the others picking watermelons. "[I] wanted to pass out in the 100-degree temperatures and endless heavy-ass work and I wouldn't let myself because I knew she suffered far worse on her forced march across that desert. Knowing that I came from that strength—forged and tested in the most intense crucible of survival. . . . Sounds dramatic, but it's real."

That physicality and stubborn strength that wouldn't let Greg give in to the heat combines with an exceptional ability to analyze and see the big picture. Impatience with those who don't understand how the pieces fit together combines with patience and persistence to do what must be done to win the fight he and Laura have taken on.

Patience was essential as the two of them took time to learn the details of the lives and work of Immokalee's farmworkers. On the other hand, impatience was a daily factor in their work with Florida Rural Legal Services. The lawyer and paralegals in Immokalee and other Florida offices were dedicated. They often won the cases they took on. But victories in court only served to reinforce the paralegals' conviction that real and enduring change would not come from "helping" workers with a legalistic approach that "atomizes the process and then monetizes it." Greg and Laura argued that the traditional approach to advocacy did not take on the agricultural labor situation as a whole and therefore could not transform the system. This is where the most powerful element the two brought to Immokalee comes in. The changing of just a few words, from "for" to "with" and from "individual" to "community," belied what was in fact a radical change in perspective: instead of advocating *for* individual migrant workers, FRLS and other legal and social advocacy groups needed to be working *with* the worker community as a whole, "finding a way for the [worker] community to analyze and understand its own situation so that it could bring its voice to the table with the growers."

There's something to good timing. In the early 1990s, what Greg and Laura recognized as they listened was that Immokalee was changing. The difference was in the people streaming into town. What was to become the Coalition of Immokalee Workers had a critical asset from the beginning: recent immigrants from those nations where there was a long history of political organizing. The Haitians were particularly important. Fleeing the violence and retribution that followed the military's overthrow of President Jean-Bertrand Aristide (who himself had come to the presidency after a popular coup against Jean Claude Duvalier in 1986), Haitians from the second boatlift joined a Haitian community established in Immokalee in the early 1980s. These new arrivals were political, not economic, refugees, and many had been involved in political activism in Haiti, the same activism that Greg had become a part of. At the same time, there was an increasing number of immigrants from Guatemala, El Salvador, and Chiapas and Oaxaca in Mexico. Like the Haitians, they were also fleeing violence and desperate economies. Although the new immigrants had come to Immokalee to work, what Greg and Laura soon understood was that many of the new immigrants had a hidden experience and skill, distinct from those who had come before, that offered new tools for change. Guatemala, El Salvador, Chiapas, and particularly Haiti, all had extensive grassroots popular organizations that had achieved some success.

"All of these people were trying to survive in farm work, but [they] had experience from home. Deep, smart, organizing experience . . . not like anything in the United States." Remembering their early years in Immokalee, Greg and Laura realized that the lessons Greg had learned in Haiti and the idea that had brought them both to Immokalee could resonate with these newest immigrants. There was a real possibility of "bringing together the community to ask 'why they were poor' and what they could do to change their lives."

Cristal Pierre was one of the new immigrants arriving in Immokalee. Pierre had long been an "animator" (i.e., a trained organizer and educator) in Haiti. Like Greg, Pierre had been trained in the Mouvman Peyizan Papay (Peasant Movement of Papay, or MPP). The MPP had built on the popular education ideas of Paulo Freire and variants of liberation theology, joining other Haitian-born organizations including the Association of Peasant Animation, as part of the island-wide congress of community activists and animators. Reconnecting with Greg in Immokalee, Pierre understood the promise of his and Laura's ideas.

Jean-Claude Jean, likewise trained in Haiti as an animator, also found his way to Immokalee, as did Pedro Lopez and Felipe Miguel. And so it began. Knocking on doors, through FRLS, on the work crews, quietly making connections, finding those who had the organizing and education skills but "weren't using [them] in Immokalee because of the daily struggle to survive," Greg and Laura began reaching out. Cristal, Jean-Claude, Pero Pilen, Pedro . . . finding each other and starting to build a community. By 1993, old friends and new connections had formed something novel and unlike any other organization seen in Immokalee: the Proyecto de Trabajadores Agrícolas del Suroeste de la Florida, or Southwest Florida Farmworker Project. It's possible they knew where this might lead. It was no doubt an ambitious vision for the future of the community. But it is certain that the rest of Immokalee's agricultural community had no idea where this would go.

"Don't come back tomorrow!" Lucas Benitez stood his ground as he faced off with the furious crew leader in the tomato field. Lucas shouted back at the crew leader. "I'll come back and if you don't hire me, it is revenge and illegal!" Here's what the crew leader didn't know about this young guy, new to Immokalee: "I had read the booklet. I came back the next day and worked." The "booklet" was "The Green Book" Greg Asbed and Laura Germino had put together in their first steps toward informing the Immokalee worker community of their legal rights. The Farmworker Project was just beginning and its "media plan" was to tack up flyers on telephone poles and around Immokalee in the workers' housing areas. "Come see a movie!" Nobody had TV, and a movie at the church sounded better than hanging out on the steps of a trailer. When Lucas and his brother Ramiro saw a flier, they looked at each other. "Let's go!"

Wednesday evening, the brothers found themselves in Sanders Hall, a common room at Our Lady of Guadalupe Catholic Church. The church, one of a few small social service providers for farmworkers in Immokalee, had made its spaces available to the small farmworkers group for their movie nights. The movies were popular and had the advantage of seeming innocuous if noticed by the crew leaders and supervisors in town. That Wednesday night, as the movie ended, "a guy from El Salvador said 'let's discuss other issues.'" The film that evening was *El Norte*, and the connections were real between the brother and sister in the film, who had suffered crossing the border into the United States, and the immigrants and workers in the room. Lucas and Ramiro stayed, and by the end of the night the Salvadoran had invited the pair to attend the Farmworker Project's regular Sunday evening meetings.

Meeting in Sanders Hall or under the trees on the church lawn, there were just a handful of people. Greg, Laura, Lucas and Ramiro, the worker from El Salvador,

Cristal Pierre, Felipe Miguel (known as "Pilin"), Jean-Claude Jean, Andres Lopez, and a few others from Haiti and Guatemala. The central idea Greg brought to Immokalee—an idea that resonated with familiarity to many of these workers from Haiti, Mexico, and Central America—was Consciousness + Commitment = Change. "Consciousness" meant understanding and diagnosing the situation they were in. Lucas explains, "We had to understand what we saw when we arrived in Immokalee . . . the cheap price for labor, verbal abuse, physical abuse, sexual abuse." Consciousness also required addressing the fundamental question of "why are farm workers poor?"

After a couple of the Sunday meetings, Lucas and Ramiro began animating the Wednesday movie nights and the conversations that followed. In no time the brothers were actively involved, working with the other cofounders to let new workers know about the Project, plan the movie nights, and bring the community together.

Talking with Lucas, you have to ask why; why did he and his brother get involved? There were tens of thousands of workers flooding into Immokalee each season. Some of them would join the movie nights, but most workers were keeping their heads down. Earning enough money for food and shelter was tough enough; making enough money to send home was even harder. And those who joined the Southwest Florida Farmworker Project ran a real risk of being blacklisted for work or being beaten up for their impudence. So why join?

"Why?" says Lucas. "It was our history. From our mother and father, standing up for yourself. Mexican culture is matriarchal; the real decisions are from the mother. 'Macho' is just a figure, a pose. My grandmother is my hero. She was a widow when my dad was two or three years old. At that time, being a single mother was very hard. She was a midwife and never married again. . . . My grandmother taught my dad from 'the school of life.'" Lessons Lucas's dad passed onto his kids, telling stories each night about possibilities for the future and the dignity of work.

The Green Book, flyers, movies, these were all first steps in connecting the community. Of great value was the "participatory community survey" the Project held in 1993. The survey was essentially "a month-long 'listening' exercise . . . to learn what people in the community felt needed to be changed." The survey, knocking on doors and quietly talking to workers as they sat exhausted outside their cramped trailers, let more people know about the new organization but established from the beginning the principle of "worker-driven change." The workers themselves made clear the problems they were facing: low wages, violence in the fields, a lack of respect from their bosses, and wretched and expensive housing. They also identified an immediate need: affordable food. The markets in Immokalee were notorious for their exorbitant prices. Their owners, like the landlords who could charge Naples-luxury-level prices for broken-down trailers, had a captive market. On the workers' hierarchy of needs, cars fell well behind food, rent, and money to send home. Vans brought them to Immokalee and the buses took them to the fields. Market owners could charge two to three times the retail prices found in other southwestern Florida towns. The intent from even these first years was for farmworkers to organize to improve their own lives—distinct from the charity of others—and this first step of surveying the workers had a real effect. Farmworker Project members soon pooled their resources to buy food staples, and Greg and Lucas could be found driving a rented U-Haul truck to Miami to buy rice, beans, and tortilla flour in bulk from the Latino warehouses on the western outskirts of the city. Project members sold the supplies, at first from a stand on the street as an informal co-op. Co-op participants received a dividend based on how much time they spent working in the co-op and on their initial financial investment. Even better, as the co-op expanded, prices dropped at the other markets and grocery stores in Immokalee.

Consciousness + Commitment = Change. A lesson taught and lived in Haiti, Chiapas, and Guatemala. And a lesson well-learned by Greg Asbed. Greg Asbed described what occurred in the early years of the farmworkers group as a "reverse technology transfer." The new immigrants brought knowledge and skills of community building to the other workers in Immokalee. As Greg and Laura came to know workers through their work with FRLS, Cristal Pierre, Lucas, Ramiro, Pedro Lopez, Felipe Miguel, and others connected through work crews. The new Southwest Florida Farmworker Project began to tap into the experience new immigrants had with "sophisticated organizing skills with a culture of 'consciousness precedes change.'"

Connecting with members of the community, the cofounders focused first on the "Consciousness" piece of the equation, or "*concientizacion.*" In the early meetings beginning in 1992 and 1993, perhaps talking late into the night in the church yard, the workers moved from talking about their own experiences in the fields to recognizing a long pattern of abuse shared by all the workers. With many of the workers having been active in, or at least familiar with, popular movements in their home country, they soon came to recognize that they were facing in Florida a "systemic denial of . . . their fundamental equality and dignity as human beings." This recognition seemed to call for a substantial break with the traditional advocacy approach of fighting legal violations piecemeal. Still working for Florida Rural Legal Services, Greg and Laura argued that there was little hope for real change in the lives of farmworkers if advocacy organizations continued to battle a series of legal violations. Success required a change of perspective, moving to the argument that farmworkers, instead of facing occasional and specific violations, were up against a "denial of human rights." It was not simply a matter of violating minimum wage laws, but of denying workers their right to a living wage. Or, in a second example of violation versus denial, not an issue of violating laws on the use of pesticides, but a denial of the workers' right to safe working conditions. In contrast to the approach of their colleagues at FRLS and other legal aid organizations, Greg and Laura decided to take a systemic approach to the working and living conditions of migrant farmworkers in Florida. It was a perspective, with its human rights framework, that resonated with the new immigrants when they had the opportunity to look up from the imperative of survival and connect their individual experiences with those of the other workers that attended the early meetings and to their lives as citizens in their home countries.

A radical change in perspective was needed, but from that recognition to actual transformation of workers' lives was more than a leap. The early members of the Coalition of Immokalee Workers recognized that the first step was to raise the farmworkers' awareness and understanding of their situation, to see themselves as part of a community that could stand together rather than as individuals who had to bear the burdens alone. Commitment to take action would follow. Drawing lessons from experience in Haiti, Mexico, and Guatemala, Greg, Pilin, Lucas, Laura, Pedro Lopez, Cristal Pierre, and the other cofounders identified three tools to bring the community together and develop the commitment to fight for change. The first of these, "popular education," drew from ideas originated with Brazilian Paulo Freire in the late 1960s and 1970s. Freire's ideas moved to Haiti, where they took root and developed throughout the Caribbean and Latin America. Popular education provides a framework for viewing the situation in which the farmworkers live and determining why the problems exist. It emphasizes understanding the problems they face both in concept and in concrete terms directly tied to their daily lives. Freire wrote about popular education as a method for providing those who have been marginalized socially and politically with an understanding of where they are on the "social and economic continuum." In Immokalee, beginning in the early 1990s, workers discussed their daily experiences and soon recognized that others had the same experiences of stolen wages, substandard housing with exorbitant rents, and working under a real threat of violence. Workers who took part in the Farmworker Project discussions and meetings began to see themselves as no longer alone but part of a community with shared interests. Together they took the next step of analyzing where their community fit into broader society and then identifying potential solutions for the problems they faced.

Greg Asbed makes the case that popular education really is a sophisticated methodology using deliberately simple tools to facilitate communication with a community that, like Immokalee, is made up of people who are putting most of their energy into survival and who likely have limited formal education. The tools, referred to as "codes," include drawings and flyers, skits or "teatro," stories, and songs, all designed to present and explain information without requiring formal education or even literacy. Importantly, popular education is done in groups. Unlike traditional education, popular education moves quickly from "telling" or lecturing to mutual learning. Essential to its effectiveness is that it is participatory, designed for workers to share their own experience and together develop insight and understanding that moves beyond recognizing their common situation to identifying actions they can take to affect their situation. Popular education is "education for action, and as such its effectiveness must ultimately be measured by the degree to which it moves the community to take action, fight for change, and win a degree of control over its collective destiny."

Drawings and flyers were particularly effective in the early years of what became the Coalition of Immokalee Workers (although they have become less so in recent years as workers increasingly have gotten cell phones and smartphones). With a half dozen or more languages spoken, low literacy levels, and a wide range of cultural and ethnic backgrounds, communication across these divides was a challenge, and it was difficult to foster a sense of a "worker community." Drawings cut across these divides. Cartoons showing crew leaders sitting on the backs of the workers and the growers sitting on the backs of the crew leaders connected with the situation all workers faced each day, regardless of where they came from. As more workers attended the weekly meetings, skits and songs provoked discussion. The earliest Southwest Florida Farmworker Project members focused their analysis on the situation workers faced in the fields, or what they came to regard as "inside the farm gate." Coming together in the weekly meetings, the workers came to recognize that the community was divided by language, culture, country, and region of origin and was an ever-changing, transient population. Separation and loneliness increased the fear of individual farmworkers who trusted no one and had to fight their own individual fights against the crew leaders and growers. Standing alone, they always lost. The effectiveness of the Farmworker Project's original approach to popular education continues to this day; it remains at the center of the weekly meetings of what is now the Coalition of Immokalee Workers. As new workers come to Immokalee and find their way to the Coalition's offices, the skits and discussions push past the fear and the separation between workers and begins to bring them together as a community with a changed perspective on their common situation. Reflecting on the process, one worker explained, "At the beginning, you unlearn what you know about the world and start seeing it from a different perspective. You start examining the system."

"*Todos somos lideres.*" (We are all leaders.) Leadership development, with the broadest possible scope, was the second tool adopted in the early 1990s by the CIW's precursor Southwest Florida Farmworker Project. From the first meetings in Our Lady of Guadalupe's church hall, the founders emphasized wide participation in determining the group's activities and tactics. Again drawing on the lessons learned from the Caribbean and Latin American popular movements, Greg and Laura, Lucas, Ramiro, Cristal, Jean-Claude, Pedro, Pilin, and the others believed that everyone has the potential to lead in some manner, whether through organization building, leading meetings or training sessions, reaching out to community members, leading protests or other actions, in the fields, or simply by example. To this day, "*todos somos lideres*" is featured in Coalition literature, is on their website, and is painted on the front of their office. The declaration comes naturally out of the idea of workers coming together to pursue change from within, rather than outside activists leading the fight. As Lucas Benitez reflected on these early years, he wondered, "At seventeen, when would I ever have time to be 'an activist'? It was the commitment that grew here and the consciousness that grew here. Some call me an 'activist' but I'm a worker looking for change. We're not 'activists' because we are not from outside."

It is also true that this early emphasis on leadership, and of always developing new leaders, turned a difficulty in organizing a migrant worker community into a strength. A decade later, a CIW member working on a watermelon crew talked about the migrant nature of the community, with its pluses and minuses. "That's one of the main challenges of our organization. Every season our members come and go. New workers come to town. That's the nature of the agricultural industry. But we know that without an informed and conscious group of workers and members our struggle won't progress. We must always work to build consciousness in the whole worker population in Immokalee. We use popular education to grow new leaders every year . . . and never stop coming up with new ideas."

Workers who attended the weekly meetings and indicated they were interested in doing more were included in strategy and planning discussions, taking on responsibilities as Lucas and Ramiro did when they first planned and led the movie nights. The Farmworker Project's initial emphasis on "consciousness" gradually expanded to explicitly strengthening commitment and broadbased leadership, providing leadership workshops for any who were interested. Workshops emphasized sharing and building leadership skills like planning and running meetings and communication. Early workshops were run by founding members who had trained in their home countries, as well as by trainers experienced in popular education who traveled to Immokalee from Haiti and Mexico, expanding the pool of those who could train others. Those leading these sessions were referred to by the Haitian title "animators." They inspired others to come together to understand their situation and take responsibility for developing actions in response.

At the most practical level, a collective approach to planning and decision making plus deliberate leadership training available to all addressed the reality of a migrant workforce that arrived in Immokalee and then moved on, following the season and the crops. Some workers returned to Immokalee each October, but there was no denying that the workforce was always in a state of churn. Additionally, those who committed to bringing the community together to fight for the human rights of farmworkers were strengthened in that commitment by taking on leadership responsibilities. As they learned the techniques of popular education, learned meeting planning and facilitation skills, and strengthened their communication skills, workers themselves took on the responsibility to improve their lives. And an emphasis on consensus and an active role for all Coalition members avoided the distance that is common in organizations with a traditionally hierarchical relationship between leaders and members.

"It was around Christmas, and all these Christmas lights were everywhere, and we're out there with this bloody shirt and there were twenty-eight patrol cars around the house and cops with camouflage on from Collier County." Greg Asbed and Lucas Benitez describe the surreal scene. Four hundred or more farmworkers surrounded the house, just a block or so away from Our Lady of Guadalupe church in Immokalee. Between the workers and house was a line of police and between the police and the house was a cluster of Campbell family members. For men that usually ruled by fear, notorious for their abusive treatment of their crews, the Campbells' shouts were thin and hard to hear over the energy of the gathering crowd. Even as they swore at the farmworkers, you have to imagine the men's confusion, and even a bit of fear. What the hell was going on? It wasn't the first time some punk field hand got what was coming to him. How could it be that there were hundreds of workers protesting in their front yard? How could it be that the Campbells had to be protected by the police?

Before we can answer the Campbells' questions, we need to go back in time a year or more to the fall of 1995. Standing in the parking lot of what was then the Pantry Shelf, Lucas Benitez described the first signal that something had changed in Immokalee. Then, as now, the parking lot was where the workers gathered in the predawn dark, hoping to be selected by the crew leaders to join a work crew. For three years, the Southwest Florida Farmworker Project had been building a foundation, defining itself, and connecting with the worker community. Membership in the Project was growing, and in this third season, people were not only attending the weekly meetings but also taking part in the leadership workshops. Through popular education and leadership training, "consciousness" was spreading among the migrant workers, and commitment was deepening in those who had returned to Immokalee each season.

In the fall of 1995, it was time for the third tool of the workers' group to kick in: action. For decades, farmworkers picking tomatoes had been paid a straight piece rate for their work, which in the mid-1990s was forty cents per thirty-two-pound bucket of tomatoes. The average worker, on a good day, could pick two and a half tons (5,000 pounds), or about 156 buckets of tomatoes, earning just over $62 for the day. A particularly fast worker might pick as many as 200 buckets of tomatoes (6,400 pounds) in a day, earning $80.

Leading up to the start of the tomato-harvesting season in 1995, many of the largest growers had shifted from this traditional piece-rate system to a combination of hourly pay and piece work. Workers were paid minimum wage for eight hours plus 10 cents for each bucket picked. The new system was known as a "day and a dime" and was intended to further reduce workers' pay, in full recognition that the full piece rate was about the same as workers had been paid in the 1970s. The two workers described above, who earned $62 and $80 respectively under the traditional piece rate, would earn $49 and $54 under the new "day and a dime" system. That November, Pacific Land Co., one of the largest growers, further cut wages. Rather than paying $4.25 an hour plus a dime per bucket, workers already living in poverty were told by the company to make do with $3.85. Take it or leave it.

Wages were going down, but rents and the prices in Immokalee's few stores surely weren't following. And there seemed to be no way to fight back except to seize the first opportunity to leave Immokalee or try and find other work. But— quietly, quietly—by the fall of 1995 the Southwest Florida Farmworker Project had been gaining members and a shared understanding of where they fit in within Immokalee's agricultural industry. The revelation for the migrant workers was that the community held a power that no individual could claim. And when Pacific Land announced the wage cut, the community decided to test that power. Soon, members of the group were knocking on doors and passing out flyers calling for a general strike against the growers. The morning of November 13, 1995, the crew leaders arrived at the Pantry Shelf parking lot and found a thousand or so workers waiting for them. Only this morning, the workers were not getting on the buses. The tomato workers, joined by citrus workers, refused to go to the fields until the rate was changed. By standing together in the parking lot, "the workers made it clear that the agricultural machinery would not turn without their participation."

This first-ever general strike by Immokalee's farmworkers lasted for five days. The *Fort Myers News-Press* reported that as many as three thousand workers had participated in the strike, occupying the Pantry Shelf parking lot all through the days and nights. When they showed up at the parking lot that November morning, the crew leaders couldn't believe what they were seeing. The crowd of workers carried signs and banners, calling for a reversal of the pay cut. Work stopped on the farms. Pacific Land Co. reversed their wage cut and the workers returned to the fields. To be fair, even with a couple of the growers increasing their hourly rate to $4.50, the financial effect on either workers or growers was minimal. Workers still made less than they did with the straight piece rate of forty cents per bucket and, like those paid at the old piece rate, were still living in deep poverty. What had changed that November morning was something the crew leaders and the growers didn't yet fully understand. But the workers got it. As individuals, they would have had to accept the reduced wage or leave town. As a community, they had fought the cut. And they had won.

Not long after the 1995 strike, if you had walked into what had become the farmworkers group's office, you could not have missed a large banner hung on one wall. One of the striking workers arrested during the protest was a Haitian artist named Joseph. When he got out of jail, he painted the banner in tribute. The painting shows a group of workers—Haitian, Mexican, Guatemalan, Salvadoran, men, and women—standing together with their arms in the air and combining into one large fist. They are shouting "Yon Sèl Fos!" and "¡Una Sola Fuerza!" (effectively "Strength in Unity") and at the top of the banner, in English and Spanish and at the bottom of the banner in Creole, is written "The Coalition of Immokalee Workers." What had been the Southwest Florida Farmworker Project became in November 1995 the Coalition of Immokalee Workers. No longer would there be the structure that developed over the first few years of committees and activities organized by nationalities. Instead, there was a single Coalition that included all members of the worker community.

A lot had changed by Christmas 1996, a year after the first strike and the declaration of the Coalition. And a lot had not. Workers were still poor. Wage theft and physical abuse were far too common. But what was now called the Coalition of Immokalee Workers was getting some traction in Immokalee and attracting attention beyond the fields. The churchyard where the group held nighttime meetings became known as "strike central" after the 1995 strike. The church's large donors, supporting Guadalupe Social Services and other church activities, were from Naples. When church leaders learned that "Naples doesn't like strikes," Our Lady of Guadalupe had little choice but to kick the Coalition out of church spaces. After using Our Lady of Guadalupe's 501(c)(3) for early funding from the Kellogg Foundation, in 1996 the Coalition legally established itself as a stand-alone nonprofit under its new name. Elected by the strike leadership council of thirty-five or so key early CIW members, Lucas Benitez, Cristal Pierre,

Greg Asbed (who then left Florida Rural Legal Services), Pedro Lopez, and Jean-Claude Jean formed CIW's first full-time staff. They received a salary, also set by the strike's leadership council, of roughly $10,000 a year. The salary was tied to average farmworker wages, a policy that still holds today. The new staff members were also required to maintain contact with work in the fields, leading to the establishment later that year of CIW's watermelon labor co-op. Wages tied to farmworker wages and continuing to work in the fields were another reflection of the CIW's organizing roots in the peasant movement of Latin America and the Caribbean.

So, in 1996, squeezed into a small storefront next to a popular center where workers could call home from private telephone booths before the advent of cell phones, the Coalition of Immokalee Workers settled into their new home. The single room included a couple of desks and a corner for the co-op store, and it served as the site of weekly meetings. The banner that had debuted at the November 1995 strike covered one wall.

One December afternoon with the season in full swing and the office quiet, a young man stumbled through the door, his face savaged and his shirt covered in blood. Lucas Benitez tells the story. Edgar, a boy of sixteen, was picking tomatoes in the high heat, working on the Campbell crew. He asked if he could get a drink of water. No, replied the farm boss. Get back to work. Again, the boy asked. Can I get some water? No! Dehydrated and about to pass out, Edgar walked from his row to get some water. Enraged, the crew leader pounced on the boy, savagely beating him and screaming, "You are paid to pick tomatoes, not drink water!"

As crew buses arrived from the fields, farmworkers soon heard what had happened and word spread through the trailers and worker housing camps. A crowd gathered at the Coalition's office and all agreed the first step was to confront the Campbell crew leader. Surprisingly, the crew leader and his unofficial bodyguards showed up at the office on Third Street. Smirks on their faces made it clear that they thought this was a joke. They sure as hell didn't care what happened with the boy, and what could the CIW do about it anyway? File a complaint with the Department of Labor? There was one DoL representative for all of southwestern Florida agricultural labor issues. And he didn't speak Spanish. Not much to fear on that one.

But the Coalition had no intention of turning to the Department of Labor or any other authorities. They'd exercised their vocal cords in last year's protest and they were ready to take the stage once again. Taking the time to analyze the situation and consider their alternatives, a pattern that was becoming characteristic of the Coalition's actions, the workers met over the next several days. A plan took shape and the next morning the workers gathered at the Pantry Shelf parking lot as usual. The show was just getting started. It was getting dark early as the shortest day of the year crept up. Getting off the buses in the early evening darkness, the workers headed over to the CIW's office. As the crowd grew, the march began, heading past the Pantry Shelf, a couple of hundred strong. Edgar's bloody shirt was the marchers' banner. The crowd made a right and turned toward the Campbells' house, more and more workers and families joining the parade. The CIW and others in town had let the Collier County sheriffs know about the attack on Edgar and the increasing tension. The sheriffs followed the workers in their patrol cars, lights flashing and mixing with the multicolored Christmas lights strung on many of the houses.

The Campbells' house was like the others in this part of Immokalee. A modest house, perhaps, but a mansion compared to the workers' six-to-a-room apartments. On the lawn were decorations and a collection of vehicles, including their red bus. Perhaps appropriately, the house sits just down the street from Our Lady of Guadalupe, and the church's priest watched the gathering crowd from the same church grounds that had hosted so many of the early meetings. Lit by the stars and Christmas lights, the protesting crowd, now numbering four to five hundred workers and their families, made their way to the house chanting, "*¡Golpear a uno es golpear a todos!*" ("To beat one of us is to beat us all!"). Awaiting them was a wall of police officers ringing the Campbells' yard. Crew leaders and assorted family members stood behind the blue wall, shouting insults at the protesting workers. On closer inspection, Lucas realized that rather than threatening the workers, the police seemed to perhaps be on their side. The police officers were lined up, with their backs toward the Campbell house, facing the protest. They were, in fact, standing at ease, each clasping their hands at about waist high. More than a few of the officers were discreetly giving the protesting workers a "thumbs up." "The police were tired of the abuse by the crew leaders and supervisors. In the 1990s, [the police] didn't care about papers or immigration status. Every week there were many complaints against the crew leaders and supervisors." The police responded to the call for support in response to the march. They formed a human fence around the Campbells' home and would, of course, protect the family and their house. But they also made it clear that the workers could protest Edgar's beating.

For the second time, the Immokalee workers had come together, giving voice not only in protest but in declaration of their newfound strength as a community. With the 1996 protest, the "March against Violence," the relationship between crew leaders and workers shifted slightly, just as the relationship between growers and workers did following the 1995 strike. It was weeks before the Campbell crew leader could find enough workers to field a full crew. Crew leaders saw the possibility of consequences, losing their work crews as a result of indiscriminate beatings and violence in the fields. The greatest shift, however, was once again a change in how the workers in Immokalee viewed themselves. The CIW had focused initially on "consciousness," but the leaders knew that understanding alone would not change their situation nor develop the commitment necessary to force change. Both commitment and change would only come through action. Change would take time but the commitment of the workers to working for that change strengthened with these first two actions and the many that would follow. As described in one foundation's later evaluation of the Coalition of Immokalee Workers' effectiveness, "Human rights education alone is insufficient to mobilize farmworkers. It is through the process of growing participation in CIW's campaigns that farmworkers' confidence and determination grows." With the 1995 strike and 1996 protest, the CIW took their first steps in the direction of systemic change rather than righting individual wrongs. These actions also served to demonstrate to early and potential members that workers coming together had strength, the strength to reverse a wage cut and to eliminate (or at least reduce) the frequent beatings faced by tomato workers in the fields.

With these first victories, the Coalition shifted their attention beyond standing up to an individual crew leader or even a single grower. They set as their target the Florida tomato industry as a whole, launching what would be called the Campaign for Dignity, Dialogue, and a Fair Wage, defining their strategy for the rest of the decade. In the brochure they gave not only to workers but to others who were beginning to pay attention to this Immokalee workers group, they declared:

"Together we fight for a fair wage for the work we do, more respect on the part of our bosses and a more powerful voice in the industries where we work, the right to organize without fear of retaliation, better and cheaper housing, and stronger laws and stronger enforcement against those who violate workers' rights, with a particular focus on those employers who continue today to hold immigrant workers in debt bondage."

"BANG YOUR HEAD AGAINST THE WALL LONG ENOUGH . . ."

Immokalee? Immokalee was the place you wanted to leave as soon as you arrived. It was a place notorious for abusing workers, not for making them rich. Gerardo Reyes was little more than a kid when he followed the siren's call to Florida. Tall and thin with a small gap between his front teeth that shows up when he smiles, Gerardo was wiry and strong when he showed up in Florida in 1999. Gerardo backtracks to fill in the details over lunch in a Cuban restaurant a few blocks from the Coalition of Immokalee Workers' offices. His family needed money and he and his friends knew they would be the ones who worked hardest and could make a lot more. What they hadn't understood before they came north was that there is a common characteristic to the stories told by those who went before. "People who immigrate—really it is humanity in general—don't want to talk about when you lose, or something [that] went wrong, or it wasn't what you expected. They don't want to look like fools. These stories don't make it back when people return to their home country. They'll talk about the one moment when it was incredible." The recruiters play to that legend. Let your sons come with us to work in the United States, they say to the fearful moms and dads. Dignified wages. Fair treatment. "It's a mirage that serves as a façade for a painful reality."

The pain of that reality had become fully evident to the three young men. They'd started out near Winter Haven, further north in Central Florida, picking oranges. But Gerardo and a few of the others had heard the legend in Mexico. "People who pick tomatoes make a minimum of $70 a day; those who worked hard could make a lot more." Immokalee was where they needed to go. They did find work, on a pinhooker crew. Pinhooking is, according to one story, a word derived from the Spanish verb "pintar," meaning "to paint" or "to ripen." Pinhookers can pick and sell any produce, but are most common in tomatoes. Most workers harvesting Florida tomatoes are picking the hard, round green tomatoes later sprayed with ethylene gas to get that orange-red color of out-of-season supermarket tomatoes. In the fields, color on a tomato means it must be left behind to prevent the risk of being damaged in shipping. Pinhookers come behind these workers, glean the tomatoes that have begun to ripen and any others not picked, and sell them locally.

A dollar a bucket of tomatoes sounded good, but it was the end of the season. You could pick thirty-five or forty buckets a day, fifty if you were really expert. For forty dollars a day, Gerardo and his friends met the crew leader at 3:30 or 4:00 in the morning for transportation to the fields in Palmetto, shut into the box of the truck along with the stacks of tomato crates. Once it got dark, after a full day in the fields, the crew leader and his crew went to the packing house to drop off the tomatoes. Dropped off in Immokalee at close to midnight, the guys would fall asleep on mattresses on the floor of a trailer where they were staying, and get up a few hours later to start all over again.

The work was hard. The truck box baked in the sun. But what was worse was that it had been two weeks and the three had run out of money and hadn't been paid, and debt was building fast. The crew leader had paid the deposit for the trailer but was paying himself back before he paid Gerardo and his friends a dime for their labor. And they still had to pay rent and buy food. Two weeks without a paycheck meant the three couldn't buy cooking utensils or basic supplies and so couldn't cook their own food. They were surviving with the help of a relative who had a *lunchero*, or food truck, that came by the fields each day. They could get one meal a day from the *lunchero* on credit. It was food and kept them going, but the debt just kept growing.

Finally, a couple of days before they expected to actually get paid, the young men had to do something. Gerardo asked the crew leader for an "advanced payment" so that the friends could buy cooking utensils and food to cook in the trailer. The crew leader said no. "I have no obligation to pay you in advance." "We said we understood but. . . . Because we insisted, [the crew leader] got annoyed with us. We said that where we grew up [in Mexico], denying a basic request like this was a big insult. We were not going to work for someone who was unwilling to give us $20 so we could cook our own food." And so Gerardo and his friends left the crew leader and the job.

Having stood on principle, they were now standing in the dark on Immokalee street corners. "We were jobless, homeless, and penniless, all in the same week!" The pinhooker crew leader had told the trailer's owner that his workers no longer needed it. When the young men showed up after leaving the crew, the trailer was locked. Fortunately, the guy who maintained the trailers took pity on them and said they could sleep in the trailer for a couple more nights, if they stayed hidden. But they still had no money and now couldn't even get something to eat from the *lunchero* in the fields.

The optimism of youth, or ingenuity that comes from desperation, led to a plan. Waking up at 4:00 in the morning and sneaking out of the trailer, the three men stationed themselves at corners along the main street in Immokalee, where the crew leaders and their buses or trucks drove each morning. The first person to see a crew leader would ask for work. When Gerardo saw headlights heading his way he followed the bus to where it stopped to load farmworkers. Waiting for the other workers who were already on the crew to board, Gerardo could hear the men talking to each other. Orange groves. Gerardo would tell the *chivero*, the name used for citrus crew leaders because of the mechanical arm on a citrus truck that was known as a goat or *chiva*, that he and his friends were experienced workers.

Gerardo stood on the steps of the bus. "We're looking for work. Will you hire us?"

Having learned the ways of Immokalee, "I negotiated the money up front" and then continued. "We don't have a place to stay and we haven't eaten very well lately and have no money. So could you give us money in advance if we work with you?"

"Wow! You're really screwed! Get on the bus and we'll figure it out."

The *chivero*'s laughing acknowledgment of the possibility of work was the first ray of light to cut through the grim circumstances in which the three workers found themselves. What they didn't yet know was that fate had put them on a bus driven by a longtime CIW member, Silverio. The door closed and they were on their way again.

After a brief stay in a trailer that had too many people doing too much drinking, Gerardo and his friends were sleeping on the *chivero*'s bus. It was quieter than the trailer but clearly not a long-term solution. "Los Tigres" were coming back to Immokalee. The *chivero* made this announcement to the three bus dwellers. Antonio Martinez and his nephew Francisco, known as Los Tigres for reasons not yet apparent to Gerardo, were heading back from Chicago and needed roommates. They'd be joining the *chivero*'s work crew. The *chivero* knew a guy with a trailer so the deal was done and the five moved in together.

Fast friendships were often unwise in Immokalee. Too much change. Too much suspicion. So the men kept their distance at first. Answering a knock at the trailer's door, Gerardo opened it to find Laura Germino and Lucas Benitez. They had heard Los Tigres were back and asked for the men. Afterwards, the puzzled roommates began talking and Gerardo and his friends heard a story that was shocking but, after what they had seen over a couple of months, not surprising. Los Tigres were so named because they had survived and escaped from a group of about thirty farmworkers bought and held as slaves in two rundown trailers in the swampland west of Immokalee. The Coalition of Immokalee Workers, particularly Laura and Lucas, had helped them after they'd escaped and then developed the evidence that helped with the eventual prosecution of their bosses, the Cuello brothers, for slavery. Lucas and Laura could be trusted, Antonio and his nephew told Gerardo. And the workers of the Coalition were fighting to change the ways of Immokalee's fields.

Invited to attend a Wednesday meeting by Lucas, Gerardo found that by 1999 the Coalition of Immokalee Workers, and what was going on in Florida's fields, were starting to gain attention well beyond Immokalee. Following the Christmas 1996 March against Violence in protest of Edgar's beating, the workers had achieved notable success. General strikes against the growers, as part of the declared Campaign for Dignity, Dialogue, and a Fair Wage, continued to push for an increase in wages for tomato workers as well as "a seat at the table," the right to be part of the decisions that affected their lives and their livelihoods. But change was slow in coming. They increasingly felt like they were hitting a wall.

The strike for the 1997–1998 tomato season had kicked off with a letter to the ten largest Florida growers, signed by more than two thousand workers. Pacific, Gargiulo, Six L's, and the other growers received the letter and the CIW's demands and, perhaps not surprisingly, responded with silence. The growers didn't even say "no." They didn't bother to respond at all. The Coalition then declared their second general strike on December 1, 1997. Immokalee's workers supported the protest, but they knew they couldn't stay out of work for long. Agricultural workers can't afford to miss many days of work, and the CIW could only provide the most modest of assistance to those who protested. The December 1997 general strike did, however, last long enough to get the attention of Gargiulo, at that time the largest tomato grower in the United States.

Two days into the general strike, Gargiulo's rep called and said okay, we'll meet. This was the first time a grower had negotiated with the Coalition acting as representatives of the worker community. Over the course of two meetings at Our Lady of Guadalupe, the Catholic church that had provided the original meeting place for the farmworkers, Gargiulo and the CIW agreed to a 25 percent rate increase from forty cents per thirty-two-pound bucket to fifty cents. Gargiulo would not publicly announce this agreement, but they stayed with this rate for the decade that followed. This negotiation with a single grower did not change the tide in the Florida tomato industry. It did, however, provide an early example of how the CIW was different from traditional unions. In these early years, the CIW used the tools of labor unions like the groundbreaking United Farm Workers, which included strikes and protests, but it was representing workers across the Florida tomato industry, whether they were members or not. Additionally, CIW argued for changes across an industry, not in workplace-specific situations, particularly important since Immokalee's individual workers harvested and prepared fields on multiple farms owned by different companies.

As the year and general strike came to a close, CIW was looking for a new approach to turn attention to the other growers and the workers' plight. The Coalition then drew on an old tactic used by Gandhi, Cesar Chavez, and religious groups. On December 20, 1997, CIW members Domingo Jacinto, Pedro Lopez, Antonio Ramos, Abundio Rios, Roberto Acevedo, and Hector Vasquez launched a hunger strike to represent the suffering of Florida's agricultural workers. They set up camp in the Coalition's office, next to the Pantry Shelf parking lot where the buses met the farmworkers each morning. The hunger strike was a protest over low wages, but, unlike the strikes, it was not directed solely at the growers. Recognizing that the growers could largely ignore their workers, the more important audience was the public and press outside of Immokalee. Declaring, "This is just a faster death" than that experienced by other farmworkers due to subpoverty wages and dangerous working conditions in the fields, the hunger strikers caught the attention of the press on Florida's Gulf Coast, including the *Naples Daily News* and the *Fort Myers News-Press*.

The men's suffering continued for weeks. Domingo Jacinto collapsed and was rushed to the hospital. The drama gained more coverage and the tomato growers and the industry's Florida Fruit and Vegetable Association took increasing heat. The growers protested that they were facing stiff competition from Mexican tomatoes; costs had increased for petroleum-based inputs; and, oh by the way, they had proof that Florida tomato pickers could make up to $8.50 an hour. Jay Taylor, president of Taylor and Fulton growers, tried out a new explanation for the strife. Taylor pointed out that growers in other parts of Florida provided housing for their workers, and part of the problem in Immokalee was that the growers didn't control the housing, which resulted in greater strife and less stability in the growers' workforce. In Immokalee, "[e]very day, pickers mill about town seeking the highest daily wage, secure in their housing no matter whom they work for," he said. "What they are literally doing is going to the highest bidder." This was an interesting perspective on the early morning gatherings in the Pantry Shelf parking lot, but the very idea of workers negotiating within the limited range of piece rates was viewed by the growers' association as a direct challenge to an industry that had historically had access to a large, fungible pool of labor, contracted through crew leaders. As the hunger strike succeeded in focusing new attention on the workers' fight, the growers' exasperation was summed up when one of them was asked yet again why the growers would not just meet with the CIW. When the interviewer simply didn't seem to get it, the grower fumed and spouted a telling analogy: "The tractor doesn't tell the farmer how to run his farm!"

1997 rolled into 1998 and the hunger strike neared the thirty-day mark. The sight of men starving for their principles reached beyond Florida and drew the attention of national media, including the *Washington Post*, the *New York Times*, and *USA Today*, along with faith-based groups across the country. In the end, former president Jimmy Carter called on the men to stop their strike on humanitarian grounds, offering to personally reach out to the tomato growers. With the drama and poignancy that would continue to be hallmarks of future CIW actions, the three remaining workers ended their strike at a Catholic mass in Naples, one of the wealthiest cities in the nation and just forty minutes from Immokalee, on January 18, 1998.

Two years later was the start of a new century. Gerardo Reyes spoke his first words in English. "Single file!" He was working security for a Coalition-led march from Fort Myers to Orlando. The hunger strike had marked a shift in the Coalition's tactics. The visual sacrifice of the CIW members showed the value of bold statements and a touch of drama. The Coalition of Immokalee Workers began to build a statewide and national profile. Taking this lesson to heart, following what had become a traditional general strike at the start of the tomato season, the Coalition brought farmworkers and some of their new external supporters together in February 2000 for a fifteen-day, 243-mile march, culminating in a rally at the Florida Fruit and Vegetable Association's headquarters in Orlando. History marched alongside, as it was not hard to hear echoes from the National Farm Workers Association's 1966 *"perigrinación"* from Delano, California, to Sacramento. The "March for Dignity, Dialogue, and a Fair Wage" combined the drama of personal sacrifice and striking visuals that have become the signature of CIW actions. Walking hundreds of miles, marchers carried signs, banners, and the American flag. A white pickup truck led them all, ferrying in its bed a large Statue of Liberty made from papier-mâché and duct tape. Liberty cradled in her left arm a tomato bucket with the words "I, too, am America" inscribed on its side and offered a single tomato in her raised right hand. Today that statue is part of the permanent collection of US protest artifacts housed at the Smithsonian Museum of American History in Washington, D.C.

The tomato workers and the Coalition were being both heard and seen, at least by a growing external audience. This audience was beyond the growers and the crew leaders, who continued to dismiss these presumptuous "tractors," and even beyond Florida. The march to Orlando and a protest at the governor's mansion in Tallahassee built on the statewide and national attention that had come the Coalition's way with the hunger strike. Even Bruce Springsteen knew of the tomato workers. Not long after the march, Springsteen gave concert tickets to the Coalition, and Gerardo Reyes was invited to join the group who attended the concert. "We met with Bruce Springsteen, gave him a T-shirt of the march, a painting of the Statue of Liberty with a tomato bucket, and a booklet of [worker] rights. Bruce dedicated a song to the Coalition." It all seemed a bit hard to believe but it was inspirational for these workers to know that the wider world was learning of their fight. Although they didn't have the star power of Bruce, the faith-based groups, first in southeast Florida and then nationally, also began to rally behind the Coalition. These critical new allies provided true grassroots support as church members housed marchers, invited Coalition members to give talks to their parishioners, and provided increasing support and charity to the workers in Immokalee.

But Immokalee's workers and their Coalition were not looking for charity. Some years later, walking back to the Coalition's office, Lucas Benitez and I walked past a van with a line of people, mostly Haitian women, waiting their turn to receive a bag of groceries. I commented on the good being done for the community. Lucas stopped, turned, and looked me in the eye. "Every time I pass by this truck, I get angry." Such good intentions were, in fact, subsidizing the growers who were not paying the workers enough to live on. As faith-based groups moved to the side of the workers at the turn of the century, the workers had similarly "gently but firmly challenged" their new allies. The workers pointed out what was obvious only in hindsight to the church and other charities. "We work six days a week. Why can't we feed our families?!?" It wasn't bags of food and second-hand clothes that the workers wanted. They were marching and protesting for reasonable pay for their labor and for safe working conditions.

In 1999 and 2000, seven years after the Coalition first came together, the members had taken stock of the situation. Analysis was an essential element of the CIW's work, even in its earliest days as the Southwest Florida Farmworker Project. This analytical approach reflected and benefited from Greg Asbed's nature and training, and reflection was a component of Caribbean and South American "popular education." In the Wednesday night meetings, at multiday retreats, the Coalition members were questioning: What is the situation in which we find ourselves as a worker community? Who are the major players affecting our work and lives? What are our alternatives for changing our situation? As the century turned, the group went back to the fundamental question: Why are farmworkers poor?

In this analysis the Coalition asked: What have we changed? We've held general strikes, protested violence, written letters laying out our case, gone hungry, and marched. Our objectives have been to create and claim our human rights to a living wage, freedom from violence, and a seat at the table in partnership with the growers. How have we done?

This questioning and evaluation yielded frustrating results. The Coalition members felt they were at a stalemate. Yes, the farmworker community had come together in Immokalee. Yes, wages were up. Strikes had initially gained some attention from the growers, but they had almost become routine, were difficult to sustain, and were having little effect. Lucas Benitez recounts the difficulty of strikes for farmworkers as compared to traditional labor unions. "[From] 1995 through 1999, every year we had a work stoppage for 3–5 days. Realistically, it is impossible to stop the whole town [of Immokalee] for a long time. In 1997, there was a big UPS strike. We saw that these people, [even though] they received a full check from the union . . . didn't get 100% of the drivers to participate. It was impossible for the CIW, without being able to pay the workers, to get all the workers [participating]." The personal sacrifice of the workers who had taken part in the hunger strike had brought national attention to the workers' situation and the Coalition, but it had not resulted in transformational change.

Farmworkers in Immokalee did now have a "voice" that had captured the attention of faith-based groups, national newspapers, and even former president Jimmy Carter. And coming together as a community and exercising this new-found voice had the real effect of reducing direct violence in the fields in 2000 compared to 1996. But the power of the workers' voice to effect greater change seemed to have stalled out. In December 1999, the CIW had tried going Florida-wide with their movement with a three-day march to the governor's mansion. But even with Gerardo on the megaphone, wages were still below poverty level; they had "increased" in real terms only to the level they were in the late 1970s and early 1980s. And workers weren't close to getting a seat at the table to work with the growers.

It was worse than that. When Greg Asbed, Lucas Benitez, Laura Germino, Cristal Pierre, and the other early members were forming the Coalition's precursor in the early 1990s, they discovered that the continuum of violence and abuse against farmworkers extended beyond what they had imagined. Call it forced labor or debt peonage, modern-day slavery was alive and well in Florida's fields. And by the time the CIW was evaluating their progress in 2000, it was clear that what they had discovered were not isolated incidents.

When you meet Laura Germino, the first thing that comes to your mind is not "internationally recognized human trafficking expert." Laura is tall and thin, far more comfortable in jeans than in the trappings of the White House recognition ceremonies at which she and the Coalition have been honored. With a wicked sense of humor and a remarkable commitment to holiday decorating, she is perhaps more self-effacing than her husband Greg, but no less impatient with those who don't get it. Laura's demeanor conceals an intensity every bit as fierce and, if possible, an even greater determination to pursue the sources of injustice in often forgotten lands, agricultural or otherwise.

Running errands in LaBelle, with a stop at Winn-Dixie after dropping her son off for a piano lesson, Laura remembers summers in Deland, Florida, and the stories her Granny would tell. Laura comes by her fearlessness honestly. Granny told of the KKK, rampant in Florida—it included sheriffs, judges, lawyers, and governors—in the 20s and 30s and well into the 40s. They were still around during Laura's childhood in the 60s and 70s. It had a long history of operating outside the law and of informal justice in Florida. The neighbor's kids, for example, ran up to the porch of Granny's house one day, before Laura was born, to announce that "the KKK had a made a man of daddy," castrating him for philandering. And the story of Laura's great uncle who saved a man from a lynching; and another of Granny resisting when the KKK offered to pay her poll tax during the Great Depression. Granny was shunned by some after that.

This was about the time of the Groveland case, four teenage African American boys charged with gang rape of another teenager, a white woman newly married. There was never any evidence connecting the boys to the alleged rape; in fact, two of them were probably not even in town when it was said to have happened. But this was Lake County, Florida, in 1949, and Sheriff Willis McCall was one of those Klan members who ran county and local governments. McCall took pride in using a heavy hand in keeping "lawanorder" among the blacks who lived there and worked in the citrus groves that filled the county. Granny talked about Sheriff McCall, pulling kids out of class in the school where another of Laura's great-uncles was principal. Principal Daniel Douglas Roseborough, lacking the courage to stand up to racism, gave in to McCall when the sheriff determined that new students at the all-white high school in Mount Dora had too much "Nigra" blood to attend.

And so what the cofounders of the CIW discovered just as they were organizing in the early 1990s echoed the stories Laura had heard growing up. In the early years of what became the Coalition, Greg, Laura, and Pilin Miguel reached out not only to workers in Immokalee but to workers who were moving through the southeastern states, following the crops and seasons. Finding the workers and talking with them without putting them at risk of reprisals from crew leaders wasn't easy.

It's July 1992 and Julia Gabriel, Didier Velasquez, and a couple of other workers approached Laura, Pilin, and Greg. They hadn't been paid all their wages at their last labor camp. The CIW team asked, "Why didn't you get paid?"

The reply: "Because we had to leave the camp in the middle of the night."

"Why did you have to leave the camp in the middle of the night?"

And this is where the situation turns. Laura recounts the reply: "Because the boss shot a worker who still owed him a debt and who wanted to work elsewhere."

The CIW had to put the pieces together. All the workers in Beaufort knew was that the camp was about three hours away, in Manning, South Carolina. The crew leader's name was Miguel Flores. But there were other pieces to this puzzle. Just a month before, in Immokalee, Pilin had reported a rumor. Another crew leader, Sebastian Gomez, had reportedly killed a worker at a camp up in South Carolina. The CIW knew that Gomez and Flores worked together; they brought farmworker crews to Florida and Immokalee. Word also had it that when crews climbed out of the vans in Immokalee, Gomez would warn, "If you go to the law, I'll cut your tongues out." As Julia and the others told their story, these pieces started to fit together.

"Red Camp?" The CIW would later learn that "Red Camp" was the largest of the many labor camps Flores maintained: wooden barracks down unlit dirt roads, remote even from the small town of Manning, South Carolina. For now, without another concrete lead to go on, Laura, Pilin, and Greg headed to Manning to find Flores' workers. It was Sunday and they figured correctly that farmworkers would be at the laundromat. As the workers looked over their shoulders and spoke in hurried whispers, Laura and the CIW noticed a henchman watching the workers in the laundromat and as they got on and off the bus that had driven them there. Wage theft and appalling working conditions were par for the course in agricultural labor, but this was something different. As Laura explains, we asked "'Where can we find Miguel Flores?' and the man answered (less than brilliantly) 'Who wants to know?'" The story became more bizarre as the Immokalee group found themselves talking with Flores' wife Cruz Cortez about the workers not being paid. She agreed to pay the six workers to avoid a scene, but in the course of the conversation, Cortez blurted out that Sebastian Gomez had been arrested on a firearms charge but had then been let out on bail.

Shocked by what they had learned, Laura and the others realized they couldn't reveal what they had heard from Julia and the other workers. The back pay was the issue. Thanks a lot. . . . The CIW team got out of Manning and returned to Immokalee to start figuring things out. As they fit the first pieces together, CIW contacted the Department of Justice. Look, this guy is holding people as *slaves*. They can't leave. They're not being paid. And they are afraid for their lives. But when Laura called, the Department of Justice's prosecutors and the FBI's investigators didn't jump to investigate. To be fair, the government had not prosecuted slavery cases in years and years. It wasn't clear even how to approach such a case. Who had jurisdiction? How do you investigate and what do you look for? What does "modern-day slavery" look like? The feds, like most Americans, found it hard to believe that agricultural slavery really existed at the turn of the twenty-first century.

In the early 1990s, no one was paying attention to human trafficking and "modern-day slavery." By the late 1990s and early 2000s, attention began to turn in the United States, but the focus was largely on the sex trade, whether runaway girls in the United States or Asian or Eastern European young women being unwittingly enticed into sex slavery or forced prostitution. Agricultural slavery was largely unknown to most Americans, including members of the justice and law-enforcement agencies. Everyone knew that slavery had been abolished more than 130 years before. In 1992 and 1993, Laura had initially had a hard time figuring out what was going on. When she, Pilin, and Greg uncovered the Flores case, they thought it was an anomaly, an exceptional extreme. But as they looked further into it, they soon learned that farmworker slavery was pervasive, to some extent the natural result of the conditions in the fields. In fact, farmworker slavery was particularly common in the southeastern United States well into the 2000s, to the extent that chief assistant US attorney Douglas Molloy declared Immokalee and the surrounding farm region "ground zero for modern-day slavery."

Whether described as debt peonage or human trafficking, there is both evidence and acknowledgment that the word "slavery" is neither a metaphor nor an exaggeration. In this case, the Reverend Noelle Damico, the Presbyterian Church USA's lead for work with the CIW, explained, "Rather it is a new form of slavery in which people are held against their will and forced to labor through force, fraud, or coercion." Importantly, human trafficking is not human smuggling. "Human trafficking involves coercion. [And] you do not have to cross a border to be trafficked: people can be and have been trafficked within their own country and state." Lucas Benitez explained in his 2008 Senate testimony that the Coalition of Immokalee Workers does not use the term "slavery" lightly. "[M]odern-day slavery, in the form of debt bondage, is different of course from the legally sanctioned chattel slavery of the plantation era. . . . [But] when we use the term slavery we confine it to operations that have met the high standard of proof necessary to prosecute under Federal law." Collier County, Florida, detective Charlie Frost expands on Lucas's definition, "Human trafficking is nothing less than modern-day slavery. It is the recruitment, harboring, transporting, and obtaining of a person for labor or services through force, fraud, or coercion, involuntary servitude, peonage, and debt bondage." Frost continues, tying modern-day slavery to Florida's growers. "[T]raffickers who have forced their victims to work in the agricultural fields of Florida . . . [a]common denominator . . . is that traffickers are usually subcontractors of large corporations, larger businesses.

The system allows the larger corporation to remain willfully blind of [*sic*] any abuses occurring and minimizes any liability."

Florida's farmworkers are particularly vulnerable because of the social isolation that comes from being in a foreign country, likely not speaking English and possibly not Spanish, with little money and less understanding of the culture and laws. Traffickers build upon this isolation by preying upon undocumented immigrants as well as homeless Americans. To further isolate the worker, the crew leader who is using trafficked labor typically keeps the workers far removed from the larger worker community and frequently uses armed guards and threats of violence. Also at play is a cultural factor. In many of the communities that are home to the trafficked workers, keeping one's word is of the highest value. Workers believe they have a debt to pay, regardless of the debt being built up through exorbitant charges for food, showers, or simple wage theft. They feel morally obligated to pay off their "debt" even in the face of abuse.

Crew leaders Miguel Flores and Sebastian Gomez were good at what they did, taking advantage of all the tools of modern-day slavery. In the year that followed the chance encounter in the Manning laundromat, and unable to get local law enforcement or the Department of Justice to take the case seriously, Laura Germino and the CIW persisted, interviewing witnesses and collecting evidence. It turned out that Flores had a thriving contract labor business, profitable in part because his workers were legally enslaved. He had established labor camps in Florida and Georgia in addition to South Carolina and had built a captive workforce of four to five hundred. The hub of Flores's operation was in Hendry County, Florida, just north of Immokalee. One of the first signs of Flores's enterprise there was when sheriff's deputies came to Laura and the CIW. Laura describes the pieces coming together. "We were investigating in SC [South Carolina] and trying to figure things out, when we came back home and some deputies we were friends with approached us in LaBelle and asked if we knew of a crew leader named Miguel Flores, because [they believed] he was behind the bodies showing up in the river in our town." Bodies of Hispanic men kept showing up in the Caloosahatchee River. The deputies couldn't definitively connect the bodies and Flores, but they had noticed that the bodies stopped showing up when Flores was in jail.

As described by Julia Gabriel and the other workers, life behind the barbed wire of Flores's and Gomez's camps began each morning with the firing of pistols to wake the workers. Whether in the fields or at the laundromat, the workers were watched by armed guards and spied upon by informants. Flores and Gomez chased away any vendors or visitors in the fields or at the unmarked camps with gunshots. As one might expect, shooting those who tried to escape was effective in shutting down the other workers. Over the years, Flores or his employees were occasionally arrested on firearm or abuse charges, but jail time was usually short, and bail was sometimes provided by the growers who used Flores's work crews. The more Laura learned, the more it sounded like the stories she had heard during those Deland summers with Granny. Like the citrus growers in the 1940s and 1950s, Florida's produce growers were turning a blind eye while the crew leaders kept up a steady supply of cheap labor and getting away with, literally, murder.

By 1993 and 1994, when the CIW had put together enough evidence that the Department of Justice could no longer deny the Flores case, the case was assigned to one FBI agent and then another, and to several different federal prosecutors. There were, of course, language barriers when interviewing workers, but the biggest barrier was that neither the Department of Justice nor the FBI recognized at first that since these were *migrant farmworkers*, you couldn't schedule interviews midday, whenever it fit your schedule. Farmworkers are in the fields during the day and had to follow the crops over the season, so they weren't permanently located anywhere. In any event, the Department of Justice and the federal prosecutors were ready to pursue the case well before the FBI. From the FBI's perspective, investigating slavery cases just wasn't what they did. It wasn't a bank robbery or even a drug case. A slavery case required working with other agencies, perhaps including US Border Patrol or even the Department of Labor. If an FBI agent expressed a willingness to work on the case, it was quickly quashed by supervisors who reminded the agent that it wasn't exactly career enhancing. In a classic case of "selective attention" and the difficulty government agencies have in taking on new tasks, one willing FBI agent commented to Laura Germino, "Gee this is hard. I can't wait to get back to my bank robberies and drugs!"

At the start of 1996, four years after the CIW team spoke with Julia Gabriel, the federal government hadn't fully decided to pursue the Flores case, but they were getting better at the investigations. Playing a critical role was Border Patrol agent Mike Baron. Baron was bilingual and had picked crops as a teenager. He got it. Seeing the success of his work, the Border Patrol gave Baron a budget and free rein to work with the CIW, find the workers, and track down the evidence. He did his interviews in the evenings and on the weekends, and he gained the trust of those he spoke with. Not long after, a young federal prosecutor, Luis "Lou" C.deBaca, began to understand that "slavery" really had returned to Florida's fields. Soon he too was meeting with Laura Germino and Greg Asbed in Immokalee, going through the evidence CIW had painstakingly collected and building the Department of Justice's case against Flores and the others.

Even as the CIW worked to gather evidence and push for prosecution, the case was almost blown with the airing of a CBS news documentary marking the thirty-fifth anniversary of Edward Murrow's groundbreaking *Harvest of Shame*. Journalist Randall Pinkston confronts Flores first in a field and then at his home in LaBelle, Florida. Pinkston is told by Flores's lawyer to "kiss my ass," and there is dramatic footage, but it does little to help the case. At one point, the CBS crew identifies Sebastian Gomez on the screen but it is an entirely different person.

The case gained traction, and in October 1996 the US District Court in South Carolina indicted Miguel Flores, Sebastian Gomez, and two of their recruiters. The men were charged with conspiracy, involuntary servitude, extortion, and transporting and harboring aliens, among other charges. With their guilty plea in May 1997, Flores and Gomez were each sentenced to fifteen years in federal prison.

The successful prosecution of the case against Flores and Gomez was the first such contemporary case to gain national attention and marked a turning point for federal and local authorities. Laura and the Coalition soon realized, however, that the Flores case was not an anomaly. Slavery was turning out to be pervasive in the Florida fields and up through the southeastern states, and the CIW quietly gained a reputation for helping those workers who were trapped.

One of the cases that followed not long after the Flores conviction picks up on the story Gerardo Reyes heard in 1999 from his new roommates, Los Tigres. "We were being sold like animals." Antonio Martinez and seventeen other workers had been stuffed into the van that had just driven from Arizona to southwest Florida. Antonio Martinez and his nephew Francisco Martinez, Los Tigres, had crossed the Mexican border and were sold by the van driver, or *raitero*, who picked them up from the coyote in Arizona. Told they would be paid $150 a day picking tomatoes, Antonio and his nephew crowded into the van driven by El Chacal. Surviving on a couple of bags of potato chips, the men relieved themselves into plastic jugs while the sole woman in the group held on for two days until the van had to stop to change a flat tire. Arriving in Florida not far from Immokalee, the workers heard the driver negotiating with crew leaders Abel and Bacilio Cuello at the labor camp they owned. "$500," El Chacal demanded. "$350," the brothers insisted. The deal was done, the price paid in cash, and the men were now owned by the Cuellos.

Antonio and the others were locked in with what grew to thirty or so workers, living in two broken-down, fetid trailers at 1369 Sanctuary Road, deep in the Corkscrew Swamp outside of Immokalee. "You were locked up . . . you couldn't stick your head out," Francisco said. The floor of the trailer had holes through which they saw snakes, their mattresses were on the floor, and scorpions were frequent visitors. They were locked in at night and by day worked in the Bonita Springs fields of Manley Farms North. The $150 per day promised in Arizona quickly disappeared as the Cuello brothers charged for food, water, rent, and transportation to the fields, plus the $700 smuggling fee. Beatings and death were promised to those who considered escape. "I thought I was going to die there . . . and I knew that if I escaped, he [Cuello] would beat me," recounted Antonio. One afternoon, desperation and courage beat out fear when Antonio, his nephew, and a couple of other workers noticed that Abel Cuello had fallen asleep while standing guard outside a small market where the workers were buying toiletries. Slipping out the door and racing to the nearby highway, the men escaped. Soon after, Antonio ran into Abel Cuello. Screaming obscenities, Cuello chased Antonio in his Chevy Suburban, demanding his coyote fee back. The newly free men found their way to Lucas Benitez and Laura Germino. CIW began their investigation and notified the now receptive Department of Justice. Following the Flores conviction, the federal government had established the National Worker Exploitation Task Force. The assistant attorney general for civil rights, then Bill Lann Lee, cochaired the task force, which included members from the Border Patrol, INS, the Department of Labor, and the US Attorney's office in Fort Myers. The CIW notified the Department of Justice in April 1999. That May, Abel Cuello pled guilty to "smuggling individuals from Mexico, holding them against their will, and forcing them to work in Immokalee's tomato fields." In September 1999, Cuello was sentenced to thirty-three months and ordered to pay $29,000 in restitution. Bacilio Cuello was sentenced to two years.

In these and other cases, Laura Germino, Lucas Benitez, and other members of the Coalition had brought to light the shocking reality of men and women held captive through debt peonage, threats of violence against them or their families, and fear of the authorities. In a collaboration that none of the cofounders might have imagined when it all started, by the late 1990s, the CIW had become an essential partner with the Department of Justice, the FBI, the Border Patrol, and other federal agencies in successfully prosecuting human trafficking, leading the effort in US agricultural labor. Laura Germino was soon developing training programs for law enforcement in the United States and then internationally. The work of the CIW had led to the creation of the Collier County, Florida, Antislavery Task Force, and the Flores case had been a primary driver of the Victims of Trafficking and Violence Protection Act, passed by Congress in 2000. Border Patrol agent Mike Baron praised the CIW's antislavery work for not only influencing the federal legislation but increasing attention paid to human trafficking beginning in the 2000s. "If law enforcement had the same dedication and tenacity as the CIW, and weren't bound by our restrictions, there wouldn't be a place for criminals to hide. They maintained contact with the workers and tracked the movements of the crew leaders. Without the CIW, we wouldn't have had any witnesses; we never would have found the victims." In 2010, for the first time, the United States was included in the Department of State's annual Trafficking in Persons Report.

The successful prosecutions of these contemporary slavery cases were remarkable. It had become clear to the CIW members that slavery in the fields in Florida and up the southeastern coast was real and pervasive. "Liberation of the enslaved" was an explicit goal in the Coalition's fight for fair pay and human rights for farm workers. But they realized that human trafficking and forced labor was just one end of the spectrum. As with issues of wage theft and violence in the fields, the CIW believed that it was not enough to prosecute violations of the law. Instead, they were fighting to end the conditions in the fields that made it possible for these violations to occur. Laura Germino described how eliminating slavery should be the result of CIW's overall success. "[W]e came to ask ourselves a very important question: Is it truly 'success' to have brought those already-existing operations to justice? We helped pioneer the worker-based, victim-centered, multi-sector approaches to investigations, collaborating with law enforcement. We know the work is urgent and essential. Actual success, however, is getting to the point where the "Slavery in Fields" is history, not 21st century headline news."

It may have been at one of the Wednesday CIW meetings in 2000 when a farmworker asked, "So, if Taco Bell can drive the price of tomatoes down, can't they also drive them up?" Now, there's an idea. Why can't the huge retail buyers drive prices up, not just down? As Laura was asking questions about the meaning of "success" in antislavery work, Lucas, Greg, Gerardo, and the other members of the Coalition were questioning the future direction of the Coalition of Immokalee Workers as 1999 turned into 2000.

"You bang your head against the wall long enough and you decide that it hurts. And you want to find another way to get around the wall. And if there is a way to get around it, you do." Greg laughs as he gives the assessment of what drove the CIW's change in strategy, but there's a lot of truth to what he says. The strategy of using traditional tools of labor protest just wasn't going to get the workers to the transformational change that was their true north. They had to do something different.

And that's where the CIW member's question came in. "If Taco Bell can drive the price of tomatoes down, can't they also drive them up?" Recognition that the strategy wasn't working was a critical first step. Where it got interesting was trying to figure out *why* it wasn't working. Over the course of months—in the Wednesday meetings during the season, in longer discussions with the group's Central Comité, and in multiday retreats—the Coalition did the analysis and considered alternatives. Why are farmworkers poor?

The obvious first-order answer was because they were paid so little. The more complicated questions came when the CIW determined why farmworkers wages were so low and why the growers refused to budge on even the smallest of raises.

Answers organized themselves into two threads. The first was the limited power of the farmworkers themselves, at least as manifest in their attempts to change their situation using traditional tactics of strikes and protests. Further, and crucial, was that farmworkers were excluded from the National Labor Relations Act and so were not able to use traditional organizing mechanisms such as unions and the National Labor Relations Board. The migrant nature of the workforce exacerbated these limitations. The same could be said for language and cultural differences that split the community. These were challenges the CIW had taken on from the beginning. But perhaps more important was the second thread, the growers themselves. First, Florida's tomato growers have little or no "public face." They don't sell directly to consumers. Florida's tomatoes are commodity produce that the growers sell wholesale to grocery and fast-food chains. Consumers had never heard of Gargiulo, Six L's, or Pacific Tomato Growers. Calls for fair treatment of tomato pickers by the Presbyterian Church or even former president Jimmy Carter got some press coverage but had little effect on the growers. Largely immune from the effects of bad publicity, it was easy for the growers to stay united in their refusal to raise workers' pay or even talk with the Coalition.

The CIW was just beginning to understand an additional strand in this thread. Even if they could force the growers to join them at the table, the Coalition was beginning to suspect that the growers might not be in a position to pay much more, and certainly not the "living wage" that workers were demanding. This realization came about as the CIW rethought their approach to increasing workers' wages. The debate with the growers over the piece rate or price per bucket had lost track of the objective. It wasn't a matter of simply increasing wages to the minimum wage. The Coalition's argument was a claim for human rights, and the right of all workers to a "living wage." A nickel or dime increase for a thirty-two-pound bucket wasn't going to do that. It had to be something bigger. CIW members did the calculations. What did it cost to live in Immokalee? To buy food? To pay rent? To work and earn enough that there was no need for charity or the need to live with ten other men in a small trailer?

The math arrived at the fact that the minimum wage of $5.15 an hour in no way equaled a living wage, even in Immokalee. In 2000, if a tomato worker could pick 2.2 tons in a ten-hour day, that worker would earn about $62, picking 137 buckets of tomatoes. (Using thirty-two-pound buckets with about a hundred tomatoes in each bucket, that's just over 13,700 tomatoes.) At peak harvest time, that number might go as high as 156 buckets (2.5 tons) in ten hours for just over $70. This is more than minimum wage, but these scenarios are close to perfect days. Weather, time of the season, and other factors beyond the workers' control mean that some days there is no work and some days, as when Gerardo worked for the pinhooker, a lot of work results in less than minimum wage for those hours.

Most tomato workers made about $8,000 to $9,000 a year as they worked through a season in Florida and then followed crops up the coast. These workers needed to make something closer to $16,000 to $17,000 a year to live, and that would take a rate of something close to 75¢ per bucket. It was hard to imagine how the workers could win a 70 percent increase in the bucket rate. But what if the CIW changed the way they presented the increase? As it turned out, the rate they wanted figured to be about a penny per pound more than what tomato pickers were being paid. Framing the demand differently, getting away from incremental changes in the per-bucket rate, could make a difference in the case they made to the growers. This industry-wide increase could be analogous to the surcharge the growers were now charging buyers to cover the cost of phasing out methyl bromide, a highly toxic pesticide. For just a penny more per pound, a farmworker picking tomatoes at peak season for ten hours a day would make $96 to $120.

This was a simpler argument. A penny per pound was easier to understand and would likely sound reasonable to the public. If all the growers paid it, no one grower was at a disadvantage. But there were new signals coming from overheard conversations in the fields and in articles showing up in industry publications like the *Packer*. What if it was not just stubbornness in the face of the tractor telling the growers how to run their farms? What if the growers couldn't actually afford to pay workers more?

Tomato growing in Florida is petroleum-intensive. Fuel for farm machinery, plastic coverings for the fields, and plastic bins and buckets for the tomatoes are obvious petroleum inputs, but there are also the petroleum-based chemicals that were essential to large-scale tomato farming. Some years later, I was driving through acres of tomato fields with Miguel Tavaras, a long-time farm manager. (The other two passengers were two women rabbis.) In between entertaining the rabbis with stories of cougars and wild pigs in the scrub and pointing out alligators in the irrigation ditches, Miguel explained Florida farming. "You have to use lots of fertilizer and pesticides. Florida 'soil' is not really soil. It is sand and effectively a neutral medium. Think of it as large-scale hydroponic farming. The good news is that you don't have to balance out the additives to account for nutrients and characteristics of the soil because there are none!"

By 2000, petroleum prices had been going up for years, increasing cost pressures on the growers. At the same time, the buyers of Florida tomatoes, the large grocery chains, fast-food chains, and increasingly the big box stores like Walmart were consolidating and using their increased size and market power to push *down* the price of tomatoes and other produce. "Everyday low prices" for consumers meant everyday low prices for the growers. The growers may be large, wealthy agribusinesses, but they were also largely family-owned businesses, easily outmuscled by the oil companies, Monsanto, and the large retail buyers.

It was time to gather data. Greg Asbed and other Coalition members started doing some investigating. "[We] talked to some growers outside of tomatoes who supported [us] and it became clear that growers had no money to cover a pay raise." Help in tracking down hard information came from another outside source.

After retiring as executive vice president and director with International Paper, David Wang split his time between Maine and Naples, Florida. He was the operating partner of a private equity firm while also devoting substantial time and resources to philanthropic efforts. His manner is formal, with little interest in small talk. Lunch with David means diving into the substance, skipping the preamble. What are you doing? What effect are you having? And what's your evidence?

David remembers how he came to know of the CIW: "I went to Immokalee to visit a guy who had a very novel idea about how to develop low-cost housing. It was a step up from Habitat [for Humanity] with the intent [of providing] housing for the entry-level professional person who could not otherwise afford to buy a house." The plan never got off the ground in Immokalee but the entrepreneur did introduce David Wang to Laura Germino, Greg Asbed, and the Coalition of Immokalee Workers. Several years later, in 1999 and 2000, CIW was deep in its rethinking of its strategy. In a conversation with David, Greg and Laura were filling him in on how the group's thinking on how to push for a wage increase was starting to change as they assessed the effect of their efforts.

At the time, Gargiulo, one of the largest of the tomato growers along with Pacific Tomato Growers and Six L's, had recently been bought by Procacci Bros. David knew the new CEO, and it did not make sense to him that the company would not now raise the workers' wages the small amount needed to have a real and positive effect on their ability to support themselves. He looked into it with characteristic tenacity, and, as David recounts the story, the grower finally said, "Look, I'll show you why we can't do this." David continues: "[Gargiulo's] new owners offered to open their books to me, in full confidentiality at the time. It was clear in five minutes that their margins were pretty squeezed, and, furthermore, their business was quite volatile with the swings from bad weather and good weather and therefore high prices/low volume and low prices/high volume." At the time, Gargiulo was only getting two cents per pound in pretax cash flow. "So a pay raise of one cent per pound would have been devastating to the grower. And Gargiulo was the largest of the growers, bigger even than Six L's!"

David went back to Greg. "You were talking about getting a penny per pound from the buyers. I now have proof that the growers cannot pay this premium. If Gargiulo cannot, no grower can." When combined with what CIW had learned from growers of other produce, the intuition of Lucas, Greg, Laura, and the other members of the Coalition that the buyers actually couldn't pay the penny-per-pound increase was no longer just intuitive. It was empirically based.

So there they were. As the Coalition held many discussions with the farmworker community and gathered data that supported their intuition, they had come to some key realizations. First, what they had been doing the past eight years was revolutionary in the context of Florida farmworkers, but it was never going to lead to the transformational change that was the Coalition's objective. Second, it was less and less clear that the growers were where they needed to focus.

It was an article in the *Packer* in 2000 that provided the key that unlocked the door and led to an epiphany for the Coalition. At the weekly meeting, Coalition members were discussing the article in which, with pride, Taco Bell announced that it had negotiated a new agreement for buying Florida tomatoes. The fast food chain "had successfully reduced prices by forcing/negotiating lower prices with their suppliers." The suppliers were the Immokalee growers.

"If they can drive down the price, why can't we force them to drive up the price?" Lucas Benitez considers what the worker asked. "A good question!" Thinking through what this meant, Coalition members agreed that Taco Bell and the other corporate buyers should take some responsibility for the conditions in the Florida fields. Going back to the foundational question—why are farmworkers poor?—the CIW began to realize that they needed to look beyond the growers. CIW's counsel Steve Hitov looked back at this period of questioning and evaluation and concluded that "the first phase was when we were thinking like everyone else: the people right above me are my enemy. The [traditional] organizing perspective is that [the growers] are my problem. As it turns out, that's not true. They were not THE problem. [The growers] were part of the problem but not the main problem." The answer and the solution would come through the farmworkers lifting their gaze to look beyond the vast rows of tomatoes, outside of the farm gate and up the food chain, looking at the food system as a whole. Greg explained that "the logic of the realization was that Taco Bell set prices and set the parameters of our poverty. They also had the power to alleviate our poverty." Or, in the characteristically simple but evocative terms that have become a trademark of the CIW's communication style, "Taco Bell makes farmworkers poor."

Lucas, Greg, Laura, Gerardo, and the other Coalition members began to discuss, as Greg recounts: "what is the power these companies have and can we use that power to change our lives?" Coalition members saw that "Taco Bell's [market] power of their purchases also gave them . . . power over [wages] and conditions." Companies like Taco Bell could pay the penny-per-pound premium and put market pressure on the growers to cooperate. As the farmworker at the

Wednesday meeting had understood, Taco Bell could force prices up as well as down. This was the shift. The top of the food chain was as responsible for the farmworkers' pay and treatment as the growers who employed them. Soon, this conclusion was seen in the cartoons or codes used in education at CIW's weekly meetings. The iconic drawing used for much of the CIW's first decade pictured a farmworker laboring in the field. On his back was the crew leader and on the crew leader's back was the grower. As the century turned, CIW's artist added a new character. Sitting on the shoulders of the grower was a larger man holding a fistful of dollars: the corporate buyers.

Lucas Benitez describes what happened next as the CIW began to leverage its new insight. "We started to think what we could do with this information." The workers held weekly meetings and longer retreats considering and debating options for convincing corporate buyers who took pride in driving prices down to force prices up enough to cover a living wage. As they considered alternative strategies and tactics, Coalition members test-drove some of their ideas with their growing number of allies, asking, for example, what the Presbyterian Church's response might be to a particular tactic. As an opening shot, the CIW sent a letter to the fast-food corporation mentioned in the *Packer* article. "[We] sent a letter to Taco Bell, asking for their help with working conditions and pay," Lucas recalls. "They don't respond. We send a second letter. They don't respond." Okay, Taco Bell was no different from the growers in ignoring the workers.

But Taco Bell was unlike the growers in two important ways. The first was, of course, its sheer size. But it was the second that provided the key for CIW's new strategy. Greg Asbed walks us through the logic: Unlike the growers, fast-food chains and other major corporate buyers had a brand to protect. McDonald's, Taco Bell, Burger King, and the like were known throughout the country, and their brands were their strongest marketing tools, their greatest strengths. Brands were also where retail food corporations were most vulnerable. Threatening the brand by tying it to the poverty and abuse of farmworkers could provide the leverage for the CIW. In 2001, not long after the Coalition came to this realization, Eric Schlosser published *Fast Food Nation*. In that book, Schlosser uses the most well-known brand in the world, McDonald's, to demonstrate the power of a brand to drive sales with brand loyalty that may last a lifetime. "Ray Kroc and Walt Disney realized long ago—a person's 'brand loyalty' may begin as early as age two." Greg describes the moment. "I was reading *Fast Food Nation* and finished . . . it in the van going to Tampa [for a march]." Then he "realized at the end that Eric was making the point that you can't make change through the government, you have to go to the brands. CIW was at the same place but had reached it from a different starting point." Greg and the members of the CIW, in their weekly discussions and strategy retreats, had come to the same conclusion. Taco Bell, McDonald's, Burger King, and the other fast-food giants controlled the market. They could move prices up as well as down and could force the growers who supplied their tomatoes to increase farmworker wages. The corporate buyers' vulnerability was in their brands. To go after brands, the Coalition had to connect with consumers. If they brought consumers to their cause, the corporate buyers would have to listen.

3

CAMPAIGNING FOR FAIR FOOD

All right, it's a plan. Or at least a plan was starting to come together. Once CIW members stepped back and started to both see and understand the system as a whole—that the food chain led from workers to growers to the large corporate buyers—the necessary strategy became apparent. They stopped banging their heads against the wall the growers represented, looked outside the farm gate, and reset their target to the top of the chain.

The CIW's objectives hadn't changed: increase farm workers' wages to a living wage; turn farm fields ridden with the dangers of violence, sexual harassment, and chemical poisoning into safe workplaces; and ensure that the workers "had a place at the table" when making decisions that affected their pay and safety. What was different was a profound change in perspective and strategy. The CIW's target was now the major corporate buyers of tomatoes, the national fast-food chains and, eventually, grocery stores.

The CIW's logic went something like this. The large corporate buyers—fast-food and grocery store chains—had the power and the money. Tomatoes were a small part of the chains' costs. The growers had little leverage against McDonald's, Taco Bell, Kroger, Giant, Walmart, and the like. The chains' purchasing power, as workers saw in the article in the *Packer*, enabled them to push down the prices they paid the tomato growers. Lower prices for commodity tomatoes increased a profit margin that already dwarfed the margin the growers could ever hope to achieve. The Coalition's logic said that the same power that made it possible to force the price of tomatoes down could also pull prices up to cover the cost of a wage increase for tomato pickers.

It was one thing to consider the possibility of using the buyers' market power to bring prices up and another to know how to do it. Unions and advocacy groups have used consumer pressure before, a notable example being the United Farm Workers' grape boycott of the 1960s and early 1970s. If the CIW could successfully pressure buyers to move prices up, what mechanism could they use to ensure the increase went to increasing workers' wages, not just to the growers' bottom lines?

Answering the first question required locating the CIW's particular leverage point against these goliaths. What Greg Asbed realized was that the buyers' strength, the power of their brands, was also their vulnerability. The large buyers' brands, their reputation, was what brought customers to their stores. Customers went to a McDonald's in Poughkeepsie not because they had read all the reviews and knew that was the best hamburger in town. They went to the McDonald's store simply because it was McDonald's. They knew the brand, knew what it promised, and knew it would deliver. Put the brand at risk, link it to a danger or unacceptable behavior, and the company and its shareholders were at risk. Food poisoning examples abound, but in the 1990s there were also examples related to labor concerns, most notably Nike's use of cheap labor and sweatshops. The corporate buyers' vulnerability could be exploited through consumers. The people who bought McDonald's fries or Burger King's Whopper were the force the CIW could use to counter the power of the corporations. If tomato growers were anonymous to consumers, and thus largely impervious to bad publicity, the opposite was true of the major buyers and their brands. Link that tomato on that Whopper to the abuse and poverty of farm workers, and consumers might join the Coalition's fight.

Answering the second question, the mechanism for getting any price increase to go to workers' wages went back to the conversations Greg Asbed and Laura Germino had with David Wang. To get to a living wage, tomato workers needed to be paid about 70¢ a bucket of tomatoes. Fighting for a nickel-per-bucket increase was not going to get the workers where they needed to be. In another *Packer* article, the CIW learned that the Florida Tomato Exchange, the industry group representing the tomato growers, assessed an industry-wide surcharge to cover, for example, the cost of switching from one pesticide to another that was less toxic. Why couldn't the CIW take the same targeted approach? This time, the "premium" would be for the workers. The CIW would hold the major buyers accountable for the low pay for farm workers and call for the chains to pay a premium of a "penny-per-pound" of tomatoes targeted to the workers. If they did so, worker wages could as much as double.

After months of discussions in the CIW's weekly meetings, General Assembly meetings for all members, full-day strategy sessions with the newly established Central Comité, and investigations and reality checks with friends and allies, the major elements of the Coalition's strategy fell into place. The buyers' power could be leveraged to change the system. Their purchasing power could be used to compel compliance with farmworkers' human rights, and their resources could be used to increase worker pay. The mechanism for increasing workers' pay would be the surcharge or "premium" of a penny-per-pound increase in the price the buyers would pay for their tomatoes. Consumers could provide the power to force the change.

The new strategy was certainly creative and innovative. If successful, it could force a systemic change across the fresh tomato industry. Of course, there were a few things to be done to get from here to there. What, for example, would the first step be for the workers of Immokalee to take on America's corporations?

"[I]f we'd done a marketing study before deciding to go out on the edge of US 41 in Fort Myers with a big papier-mâché tomato and announce a national boycott of Taco Bell, I believe the consultant would have advised against doing it." Looking back, Greg had to admit that no matter how thoughtful the process, regardless of the elegance of the strategy, there was something crazy about the whole idea. In 2001, the CIW thus declared its "Campaign for Fair Food" with a few dozen people marching in protest of Taco Bell.

A dozen years later, Lucas laughed as he leaned back in the booth in the Mexican restaurant and looked back to the start of the campaign. Mr. Taco is Lucas's wife's restaurant, on Main Street in Immokalee. There are Mexican favorites and killer molé. (It's actually Lucas's molé recipe; he used to do most of the cooking for the family. Now, however, Lucas proudly declares that his wife cooks better than he does.) After diving into *carnitas* and chorizo tacos, Mr. Taco's "*un bocado de satisfaccion*" slogan seems about right. Lucas's sons play nearby after finishing their homework. The youngest checks on Daddy from time to time, getting a hug or sitting on his dad's lap. Yes, Lucas confirms, the *Packer* article on Taco Bell was a turning point. Taco Bell became CIW's first target corporation in part because of the article, but they were also first because Taco Bell played on Mexican culture with their brand and slogan "*¡Yo Quiero Taco Bell!*" spoken by a Chihuahua that had become a pop culture icon in the late 1990s.

How to address the target was yet one more question. Not long after the article in the *Packer*, the CIW decided to send a letter to Taco Bell asking for their help with working conditions and pay. First one letter and no response, and then a second letter and continuing silence. Frustrated with the silence, Lucas remembers, "a worker from Oaxaca, in Mexico, said, 'I remember when one of the businesses, they didn't want to do the right thing. The people [did] something called "boycott." What is this?' [Some of the members] explained and [we agreed] it was a good idea. Okay, we're going to discuss the idea of a boycott at the next meeting. We became more familiar with boycotts in this country. . . . After many, many meetings, we talked with the other Alliance members. What [resulted] was a national boycott of Taco Bell."

True to form, by taking the time to analyze where they and other players fit in the food chain as a system, the members of the CIW came up with a plan. It's not always the speediest of processes but the result is often richer than any one individual might develop, and taking the time to think questions through as a community ensures broad understanding of, and commitment to, the path forward. A critical idea that came out of the consideration of the first actions for executing the new strategy was that boycotts could hold out for the long term in a way that workers on strike cannot. Work stoppages and strikes might succeed in getting some attention from the growers and even the broader public, but the workers could not afford to be out of work for long. A boycott by customers would take the burden of striking off the workers and would extend the reach of the CIW far beyond Immokalee. Of course, a boycott would only work if the Coalition could connect with customers by linking Taco Bell to the poverty and abuse of farm workers.

If you pulled up to the drive-thru of the Taco Bell on Highway 41 in Fort Myers on Florida's Gulf Coast on Martin Luther King Day in January 2001, you might have caught the small press conference held by a couple of dozen CIW members and wondered what was going on. And you might have laughed with your buddies to hear that this was the start of a "national" boycott of Taco Bell. But if you looked a bit more closely you would have seen that the handful of CIW members in front of the restaurant already had key elements in place to launch the Campaign for Fair Food. In particular, you might have noticed that there were people who had never worked in the fields standing shoulder to shoulder with the workers. These were members of CIW's nascent but growing network of allied groups. To be fair, on that day in Fort Myers you would not have seen that CIW also had nearly two years of experience using the Internet, a virtual network just coming into its own. The organizational and virtual networks made it possible for farmworkers in Immokalee to connect with the fast-food chains' customers and the media in a way they could not have just a few years before.

Alliances and supporters were important from the earliest days of the Coalition, when the priest at Our Lady of Guadalupe Church let the workers use the church's meeting rooms. David Wang connected with Greg and Laura a few years later. And even Florida Rural Legal Services was an ally of sorts. Greg's tenure lasted until 1996 and Laura's until 2000. Steve Hitov also worked for FRLS and initially provided legal counsel to the CIW through the legal aid group until about the same time Laura left. But the Coalition's outside support really picked up speed in the late 1990s. Marches on the Florida governor's mansion and press coverage of the Christmas hunger strike in 1997 may not have measurably changed the workers' conditions but they were essential to attracting the attention of potential allies. The first were church groups that had been providing charitable services to Immokalee's workers. They were soon followed by college students and eventually the "food community."

The development of allies was already under way by 2001. By the time the workers went on the Christmas 1997 hunger strike, the Presbyterian Church USA had been supporting the Immokalee House charity for several years. Talking about the movement of the Presbyterian Church from supporting a charitable organization to becoming the staunchest organizational ally of the CIW, Reverend Noelle Damico remembers the vital role of Laura Germino and CIW's anti-slavery efforts. "[W]e became aware of [agricultural labor] trafficking and were astounded and appalled. The church had never understood the consequences of living in this situation." The CIW welcomed the support but from the beginning challenged the church's assumptions and perspectives. Education was vital to establishing the Coalition and in building alliances. Coalition members invested time and energy educating potential supporters and established ground rules for those who joined their network. As they declared the Campaign for Fair Food, Coalition members met with countless congregations and parishes and traveled to college and university campuses, teaching their audiences about the food system as a whole, the workers' place within it, and the costs to consumers of being part of the industrial food chain.

This schooling was needed in the earliest days of the campaign, and it continues to be important to this day. Lucas's anger at seeing a church group hand out bags of food to workers while we were walking back from lunch got across the same message that he, Greg, and Gerardo were teaching the Presbyterian clergy in the late 1990s. Coalition members were not looking for charity. Instead, the workers of the CIW asked, "We work six days a week. Why can't we feed our families?!" Despite the good intentions of the church and its congregations, charity through food and clothing banks was really a subsidy to the growers and the whole food system and made it possible for workers to survive on below-poverty wages. It was an entirely new perspective for the church groups who had been working in the Immokalee community or in similar communities across the United States.

The CIW made it clear to all their supporters that it was the workers who were leading this campaign. As a few church groups grew into a national network of alliances, the CIW emphasized that allies did not speak *for* the workers. Allies worked with, not for, the Coalition and from the beginning of the campaign "the very workers whose labor conditions were the subject of the boycott were the unquestioned and ever-present leaders of the campaign." This was not an accident. Coalition members had raised concerns about leadership and the risk of their being overwhelmed when they were developing their new strategy. They had seen other protests against abusive labor practices and working conditions, such as the protests against Nike, where members of church groups, students, and others concerned about these conditions were the face of the protests, with not a worker to be seen. While the absence of workers at antisweatshop protests was unavoidable because most apparel workers were located overseas, that was not the case with the US tomato industry. Workers in Immokalee were determined to be not only present at protests in their support, but front and center. Just as farmworkers of the CIW called for a seat at the table with their employers, they expected to lead their fight. CIW's insistence on worker leadership and coordination of the alliance network also came from their analysis of what would sustain interest and participation of their new allies, which would reduce the probability of losing ground should those allies turn their attention to the next cause. Allies could initially be motivated by the workers' struggle but they would sustain the effort if they recognized a "common interest in a more just, more transparent, food industry." As the campaign matured, the Presbyterian Church and other faith-based groups "question[ed] their participation as consumers in an industry so dependent on exploitation," while students were made aware that they were specifically targeted by the very fast-food chains that were exploiting cheap labor. Members of the alliance were to take part in defense of their own interests, as the workers were fighting for their rights.

Lucas touches on a sensitivity of longtime CIW members that as the CIW developed the campaign strategy, "The allies did not create or lead the ideas . . . a few allies attended strategy sessions but we asked them, 'if we did this, how do you think the people of the church would take it?'" Gerardo Reyes bristles at the idea that anyone from outside the Immokalee community told the workers what to do. "People have a tendency to see [CIW's] allies as saviors of what we are trying to do. That's wrong and this is important. For example, embracing the students as 'experts' when the expertise is from the workers." In conversations with CIW founders Greg Asbed, Lucas Benitez, and Laura Germino, CIW members such as Gerardo Reyes or Silvia Perez, as well as early allies including Reverend Noelle Damico and Sean Sellers, the source of the ideas behind the campaign is without question. The new understanding of the food system—the relationship between workers, growers, corporate retailers, and consumers—came from the founders and early members of the CIW and the many workers who were part of the two years of consideration and deliberation. The idea of targeting the fast-food chains came out of the weekly meetings and retreats held in the CIW's offices. As Greg wrote after the boycott, "The Taco Bell boycott was rooted in years of hard-fought organizing in Immokalee, spearheaded by workers whose leadership and vision was forged in those battles on the streets of Immokalee, and given life by the participation of thousands of workers over the four-year campaign . . . [they] filled the campaign from the beginning to the end with their presence, spirit, and consciousness."

But these concerns are about more than ensuring that history has this right. Understanding the leadership of the workers in the Campaign for Fair Food and what followed is to recognize that the CIW's approach is distinct from most social-responsibility efforts spearheaded by ad hoc coalitions or nonprofits advocating for oppressed workers, much as they do for the environment in industrial farming or the treatment of cattle or chicken. As Gerardo put it, "We [the workers] can be portrayed in two lights. One is as 'victims' and our stories can be compelling. People then act because they pity us. Or, we can be portrayed as architects of the future we want. Then the work we do is the work to protect our dignity as workers. It is difficult to *inspire* others if you are put in the box of 'victim.'"

Inspiration was key if the CIW was to develop new alliances and convince consumers to take up the cause and boycott Taco Bell. Inspiration could be taken from the actions of the workers, but people had to know about the fight if they were to become a part of it. "Strategic communication" was essential to the CIW's fight even before the Campaign for Fair Food. At first, strategic communication meant painting colorful signs that caught the eye and were instantly recognizable, like the full tomato bucket or the papier-mâché Statue of Liberty. But the timing was right to reach beyond bold imagery that grabbed a couple of minutes of attention on the local news. In the late 1990s the Internet was just coming into its own and Greg figured it out early on. Referencing Chris Anderson's book *The Long Tail*, Greg talks about the Internet's "democratization of information" that made it possible for many more voices to get their message out to a wide audience.

By 1999, six years before the founding of YouTube, CIW's iconic images of workers' dirt-stained hands or a tomato bucket carried on a shoulder were combined with videos and reporting from marches and protests. With the launch of the campaign, images of workers and allied marchers waving banners and papier-mâché tomatoes, Chihuahuas, and kings (as in Burger) on the Internet made it possible to reach students and faith communities as well as journalists and the targets of the Campaign for Fair Food. Those who scrolled through the site saw announcements of upcoming marches and the latest abuse or victory combined with an analysis of the current event and how it fit into the campaign.

The Internet made it possible for students in Texas and church leaders in Kentucky to follow the lead of farmworkers in Immokalee.

Unlike labor movements that had come before, CIW's Campaign for Fair Food and antislavery efforts had the ability to connect directly to allies and consumers, and Greg and the CIW had the vision to leverage that power from the beginning. Arms crossed, leaning back on Lucas's desk in the CIW office, Greg was unequivocal in his assessment:

> CIW could not have succeeded without the Internet. [With the Internet] workers could talk to consumers about the conditions behind the food they ate, providing a market analysis of [who was] responsible for the conditions and [who] was capable of forcing change. Ninety-five percent of consumers are unaware of what's behind their food. Instead of brand communications being the only communication with consumers, the Internet made it possible for those producing to connect with those consuming. . . . If producers reach consumers, consumers become the top of the food/supply chain. . . . Without the Internet, we would have depended on the media. If workers protest at corporations, the corporations don't care. If workers and consumers protest together, the corporations had to care! Without our own form of communication, we couldn't have done this.

The Reverend Noelle Damico was one of those church leaders who supported and followed the lead of the CIW from its early days. She saw the critical role the Internet and the CIW's strategic use of images played in building a remarkably large and diverse alliance network, ranging from "anarchists to archbishops." Ordained in the United Church of Christ, Noelle joined the national staff of the Presbyterian Church to coordinate the church's involvement with the CIW and the Campaign for Fair Food. She recalls that "clergy got involved first, then led the parishioners." Leadership came through small group meetings at individual churches, with clergy and students joining workers, and where education often combined with action through protests at the local Taco Bell. The Presbyterian Church, led by the Tampa Bay Presbytery, was part of the Interfaith Action of Southwest Florida in the late 1990s, and perhaps the earliest strategic ally. Asking "how the Campaign for Fair Food 'lives and grows' within the culture of religious institutions, such as the PC (USA)," Rev. Damico responds to her own question. "One way it does is through preaching. [The sermons'] focus is on modern-day slavery and the fair food [sic] agreements but . . . comes at this topic through a biblical lens and uses deep, church-y language to relate biblical narrative to our contemporary narrative." Whether in Presbyterian churches or in

Jewish community centers, clergy might draw on Isaiah's vision of the wolf and lamb feeding side by side or on Jonah's gaining understanding and a conscience while in the belly of a whale to encourage their flocks to open their eyes and then take action alongside the tomato workers.

The Presbyterian Church (USA) as an institution was joined over time by other national churches, the National Council of Churches, and "Rabbis for Human Rights" (now known as T'ruah). As the CIW considered its new strategy, David Wang believes "what sustained the organization was the tremendous moral and financial support from major faith organizations." Early allies provided a national network, a moral foundation for the Coalition's cause, and critical financial support, enough that the CIW was able to not only sustain but build. The financial support of the faith organizations was particularly valuable because it meant that the CIW did not have to spend its time and energy raising money, a skill that its members had not yet developed and an effort that would have distracted from the campaign itself. Demonstrating once again that the best laid plans sometimes cannot beat good luck, it turned out that the Presbyterian Church (USA)'s headquarters was in Louisville, Kentucky, just a few miles from the headquarters of Yum! Brands, the corporate owner of Taco Bell. The boycott of Taco Bell became not only a corporate issue but a personal issue for Yum's executives. "Yum leadership could ignore the Episcopal Church headquartered in New York, or the Catholic Church. But they went to church and [their kids went to] school with the Presbyterian leadership. Yum could not ignore the church's calling attention to the situation of the tomato farmworkers!" As the campaign raised its profile, safe space was getting tighter for the executives.

So . . . "excitement" was not how Sean Sellers described his parents' reaction when he announced his new job in 2004. Just graduating from the University of Texas, Austin, Sean tried to explain that this was a "leadership opportunity." He was going to be in charge, the coordinator for the Student/Farmworker Alliance (SFA), working out of the CIW's office in Immokalee. Okay, the pay wasn't perhaps what his parents' had imagined for their new college graduate, "room and board and a few hundred dollars a month." Yes, he'd be working with migrant farm workers. No, he "didn't even really speak Spanish." Well, it was true that "funding for the group was uncertain and so they were not exactly flooded with applicants." But this was a chance to *do something*, something that mattered. Sean would be organizing a student alliance with the Coalition of Immokalee Workers.

Although Sean's parents "didn't think this looked like a career path," there was saving grace in that the CIW was starting to get some national attention. Over the prior year or so, John Bowe had published an article on human trafficking and modern-day slavery in the *New Yorker*; *National Geographic* had featured the CIW; and Lucas Benitez, Romeo Ramirez, and Julia Gabriel had been the first US recipients of the Robert F. Kennedy Human Rights Award. By the time Sean connected with the CIW, the Student/Farmworker Alliance was starting to gain some traction, particularly on college campuses. The alliance with students was a natural. Students ate fast food and, as noted, were the prime audience of fast-food marketing. Taco Bell in particular was commonly found at college and university food courts. Drawing students into the boycott was critical.

The first connection between farmworkers and students had come through colleges and universities in Florida. Brian Payne was in the first small group of students that began meeting during the last throes of the CIW's more traditional, Florida-centric protests and strikes in the late 1990s. Brian and other students read about the hunger strike and CIW's protests at the governor's office. Moved by the workers' cause, they wanted to get involved. By 2000, their early meetings became the Student/Farmworker Alliance, joining with the faith-based allies to march with the workers and to volunteer at the CIW's offices. When the CIW announced the Campaign for Fair Food and the national Taco Bell boycott, the SFA had contacts in every major Florida university and had begun to reach out nationally. At Notre Dame, Melody Gonzalez, herself the daughter of a farmworker, organized an SFA chapter with an innovative and increasingly high-profile effort that became a model for other campus organizations. Melody and the other Notre Dame SFA members created an "alternative spring break" program where students would join the workers for marches or volunteer with the CIW.

Around the same time Melody was organizing at Notre Dame, Sean had been getting settled at the University of Texas, Austin after transferring from Baylor. True to the school's reputation, Sean soon found kindred spirits and joined a "renegade" branch of the Campus Greens. Jumping right into the fray, Sean was part of a protest of the US School of the Americas in November 2002 when he first heard about the Coalition of Immokalee Workers and the Taco Bell boycott. Not long after, he got involved. Julia Perkins, who had joined with Brian Payne in building the Student/Farmworker Alliance, and Lucas Benitez were doing the type of grassroots outreach that had become a signature of the CIW. What had started as meetings in church halls was now extending to college campuses across the United States. The UT (Austin) Campus Greens invited Lucas and Julia to their campus in August. They responded, "We'll come, but only if you host us once again in November when the CIW's 2003 'Truth Tour' was kicking off." Lucas and Julia rallied support not only for the Taco Bell boycott but for the protest of the Free Trade Area of the Americas meeting soon to be held in Miami.

"The Taco Bell campaign was in full swing and Taco Bell was the target of the campus boycott effort" when Sean and Melody joined up with other students across the United States. When the CIW began to reach out to the campuses and students like Brian, Melody, and Sean, student interest in the protests was not a given. David Wang laughed when he thought about the early days of the CIW's building an alliance with college students. "I thought it was a crazy idea at the time. I thought today's students were too self-centered, uncaring about the world, and lacking idealism. I did not see any way the students could be motivated to pull off a boycott." Looking back, David said, the Campaign for Fair Food changed dramatically when the students joined in.

In fact, the students did rise to the occasion and to the cause, even beyond their campuses. The Student/Farmworker Alliance joined religious groups, took part in marches, held meetings on college campuses, and traveled with CIW members to churches and synagogues as part of the Truth Tours central to the Campaign for Fair Food. Students worked, and still work, as volunteers and paid SFA staff in the CIW's offices, supported by funding from other alliance members. Guided by the CIW, the SFA built a national student network that included high school and college campuses demanding that schools "Boot the Bell" until Taco Bell signed on in support of the workers. The broad awareness of the Taco Bell boycott in the early 2000s is remarkable. It was likely helped by increased campus attention to globalization and the use of overseas sweatshops, issues that gained much attention beginning in the 1990s and included high-profile protests against Nike. Even today, when talking with those who have not heard of the CIW but were in school during this period, the words "Taco Bell boycott" often bring recognition and memories.

The SFA message then was the message their members still receive: "Our struggles are not identical, but they converge. Farmworkers and young people are objectified by the corporate food industry: farmworkers are seen as tractors that harvest raw materials cheaply while youth are seen as mouths that obediently consume branded products." As was true with the religious organizations, the CIW invested in the education of their new student allies, appreciating their commitment but needing to adjust perceptions and encourage the students to develop their own motivation for protesting the behavior of the corporations at the top of the food chain. The first step was highlighting the strategy of Taco Bell and other fast-food chains to focus and build their brands on youth culture. But the important second step was managing student perceptions to ensure they understood that the workers were leading this fight and even to protect the workers from the enthusiastic, if ill-advised, good intentions and self-righteousness of students. These concerns are still seen today.

Emanuel Martinez looks every bit the student activist with his red, black, and white dashiki and close-cropped beard. He also displays the intelligence and thoughtfulness that is a common denominator in the leaders and student volunteers of the SFA. Growing up in Passaic, New Jersey, Emanuel saw the life his parents led as factory workers and became increasingly interested in immigrant and labor rights. Community college in Newark led to a generous scholarship to the University of Pennsylvania. Still reeling a bit from the culture shock that came with his trip across the Delaware River, Emanuel met two students who invited him to join the SFA's fall action in Ohio at Wendy's headquarters.

Student interactions with farmworkers are carefully managed by CIW to provide much-needed experience and education to those new to the SFA. Each year, the SFA has a fall and spring "action" to which all interested students are invited. These actions are usually marches or protests against corporate buyers such as Publix or Wendy's that are not yet part of the Fair Food Program (or "future partners" as CIW likes to call them). During summer, SFA holds an *encuentro*, or workshop, for a few days at CIW's offices in Immokalee.

Numerous actions and two *encuentros* later, Emanuel explained what he has found distinctive about the approach of the CIW and its alliance with the students. "The CIW thinks deliberately on how to curate the spaces and the process itself as to who is included in the conversation, who leads the conversation, etc." The SFA's Steering Committee "has a sense of where they are in the structure, and they recognize the workers lead. This idea is deeply embedded and they are guided by the will of the worker." Students are separated from the workers at these actions. You might ask why? Think about it, Emanuel gently prods. Think about students on college campuses. They care deeply but they also think they have it right. "College students come from all over the world and they have different levels of politicization and understanding. They don't have sophisticated sensitivity yet . . . you [can] have students who think they should lead, not the workers, because of who they are." CIW organizes *encuentros* as an "encounter" between students and workers, to educate and energize the students with contact and familiarity with the workers who they are fighting with when they return to their campuses.

Once students get some experience and recognize that perhaps the workers will be the ones doing the teaching, they may apply to attend the annual *encuentro*. Three days of workshops bring together popular education, discussion, and preparation for the next action, the techniques used by the CIW since its founding. The workshops are intended to inform and animate student leaders, teaching about the workers' lives and planting "seeds of consciousness and commitment." Women farmworkers, many with their kids playing in the room, opened a recent *encuentro* weekend. They spoke about working in the fields and life in Immokalee. Over the course of three days there were shared meals and "Café Cultura" where students and workers exchanged poetry, songs, and dancing. If you looked in the door of the CIW offices that Saturday, you would have seen eighty students, many wearing "Justice for Farmworkers" T-shirts, sitting in groups on the floor intently working on strategies for this year's actions and coming up with ideas for the multiyear campaign against the Publix supermarket chain. Capping off the weekend, two buses of students and workers headed to Naples to protest at Wendy's and Publix. When one sees students and workers chanting and brandishing signs with tomato buckets labeled "justice" and "dignity" or "Students Boycott Wendy's" it is difficult not to reflect on how the CIW's emphasis on popular education, leadership development, and action continues to resonate nearly twenty-five years later.

It was late February and the 2005 Taco Bell Truth Tour was getting underway. What had begun as a couple of dozen people waving signs on Route 41 in Fort Myers now included the actors Jeff Bridges and Martin Sheen, activist Dolores Huerta (cofounder of the National Farmworkers Association that later became the United Farmworkers), and a broad national alliance of supporting groups. The 2005 tour included a series of educational meetings, marches, and protests that started on Route 41, extended across Florida, and then moved cross-country. Busloads of workers traveled from Immokalee and met up with allies including religious groups, students, community groups, and labor organizations. Taco Bell was starting to feel pressure unimaginable four years before. Not long before the tour began, Lucas Benitez, Julia Gabriel, and Romeo Ramirez and the work of the Coalition of Immokalee Workers had been recognized with the Robert F. Kennedy Human Rights Award. University boycotts had removed or blocked Taco Bell restaurants from twenty-three campuses and raised the profile of the boycott with a protest of Boise State University selling the naming rights of its basketball stadium to Taco Bell. In two different votes, approximately 40 percent of Yum! Brands shareholders voted in support of resolutions supporting the CIW.

With stops in Atlanta, Nashville, Cleveland, and Chicago, the Campaign for Fair Food was "Bringing it to Yum's backyard!" in Louisville. Five days in Louisville would culminate in the Our World, Our Rights: Conference on Global Justice. Recognizing what was now inevitable, Yum! and the CIW were in intense negotiations even as the Truth Tour got underway. And then it happened. On March 8, Yum! Brands and the CIW held a joint press conference. The corporate giant had signed an agreement to "work with the CIW to improve working and pay conditions for farmworkers in the Florida tomato fields." Taco Bell and Yum! declared they would "take a leadership role within our industry . . . and work with the CIW for social responsibility."

It was stunning. The roadside protest four years before had become a truly national campaign. By 2006, the network that began with the Presbyterian

Church (USA) and the Student/Farmworker Alliance was formally named the Alliance for Fair Food, with nearly two hundred participating organizations ranging from the AFL-CIO to to Moviemiento Estudieantil Chicano/a de Atzlán (MEChA), and including the Episcopal Church USA, the National Family Farm Coalition, and the Miami Workers Center. As the alliance grew, protests had become increasingly creative and colorful, with sometimes thousands of people carrying papier-mâché tomatoes, Chihuahuas, and many signs with the imperative "Boot the Bell!" Taco Bell had, not unreasonably, ignored the workers at first, then dismissed the idea that they were responsible for the entirety of their supply chain. When revelations came to light of slavery operations affecting hundreds of people, Taco Bell and its parent Yum! had no answer to CIW's question, "Can Taco Bell guarantee its customers that the tomatoes in its tacos weren't picked by slaves?" That question, combined with increasing pressure not only from customers but also from shareholders and fellow parishioners, caused Taco Bell's management, led by Jonathan Blum, to step back and consider CIW's demands. By 2005, a combination of pressure and reconsideration had done its work. "When we decided to announce the national boycott of Taco Bell, it was crazy! . . . It was like confronting the monster without knowing if we could defeat it. What we did know was that we were not going to let it go." As buses of workers and people from the churches and synagogues, the labor unions, the students, and the writers and Hollywood stars headed to Louisville, the "monster" blinked and joined hands with Immokalee's tomato pickers.

It's about a decade after Taco Bell signed that agreement. Steve Hitov walks into Ted's Bulletin, a long-time Capitol Hill hangout; his khakis and worn polo shirt are DC's casual uniform for the summer heat still hanging on in mid-September. You can pick him out because he's the one wearing a CIW baseball cap. "Bad knees," he explains when it takes him a bit to get to the booth. Black coffee and then the conversation gets started. We're talking about what has become the Fair Food Program and its future. Doesn't the CIW hope that the standards, monitoring, and enforcement are picked up by the federal government? "So, when people ask me, where do you see this going? Do you expect it to become law? I hope not! I've worked on the Hill. It would be watered down and compromised . . . diluted to pass. Even if the idea is good to start, what will come out will be the minimum of what they [the corporations and the growers] have to do."

We really should go back and get closer to the beginning of Steve's story. Steve's been around from the earliest years, hired by Florida Rural Legal Services in 1993 when he and his wife returned to her home state. He'd taught at Harvard Law School and been at Boston Legal Services. His job? That's simple. "I represent poor people." Steve soon found out that there was a growing dispute between FRLS and two of the paralegals working in Immokalee. Steve had actually met Laura and Greg at an earlier conference in Dallas, so he was not surprised that they were in the center of the conflict. "The paralegals had an idea and the lawyers thought it was ridiculous, so they hired me to see who was right." The debate was between FRLS's approach to migrant worker advocacy through "impact litigation" versus Greg and Laura's idea of the community organizing "to analyze and understand its own situation so that it could bring its voice to the table with the growers." When Steve announced that "the paralegals are right and have an idea that might work," the FRLS attorneys threw up their hands and said, fine, you work with them.

Ever since, Steve has been CIW's counsel, first through FRLS, then providing free representation during the early years of the Campaign for Fair Food, and finally working directly for CIW from 2007 to the present day. Those earliest years included getting Greg out of jail, but as the Coalition's strategy became increasingly sophisticated, so did the legal and representation strategy. There's that energy again, that intensity that you see in Greg, in Gerardo and the others. Steve's hands cut through the air. "It's a balancing act being a lawyer for an organization that by definition is radical, not in a sense of politics but in a sense of 'radical change,' balancing while protecting them within this conservative system in which they are operating." As a good trial lawyer does, Steve switches to an analogy. "Do you know what a left tackle does? Protecting the quarterback from blind-side hits on pass plays. But also, busting through the defensive line so that the running back or QB can gain yardage on a running play."

The Campaign for Fair Food needed these balancing skills. In contrast to the strikes and protests of the late 1990s—traditional tools of labor—the CIW's tactics increased in sophistication with the campaign. Signs and banners, the iconic papier-mâché figures, songs, and even puppeteers "get people's attention, but don't get people arrested. And we don't get arrested!" Adding interest and complications to the job of legal advice and representation was the effectiveness of the campaign. As CIW won battles with Taco Bell and other fast-food chains, Steve and Greg in particular began negotiating with billion-dollar corporations.

It took four years for Taco Bell to agree to CIW's demands, with the drumbeat of pressure getting louder each year. By the time Yum! vice president Jonathan Blum announced the groundbreaking partnership with the CIW, Steve and Greg could tell that they had his respect for holding the line and staying true to CIW's principles. The negotiations also required CIW to add detail to their demands and start considering what it would take to implement the agreement. They'd won the battle and now needed to move from a symbolic victory to something that would begin to actually change workers' lives.

When they had first announced the campaign, CIW had called for Taco Bell to pay a "penny per pound" more for tomatoes, passed down the supply chain to the workers; for the involvement of CIW and the workers in modifying, implementing, and monitoring Taco Bell's supplier standards of conduct; and for the corporation to use its market power to bring in the Florida growers and influence other fast-food corporations. The agreement CIW and Taco Bell announced on March 8, 2005, included provisions in two categories: (1) an increase in farmworker wages and (2) farmworkers' rights.

The first category was simple in concept and less certain in implementation. Farmworker wages would increase through Taco Bell's paying the penny-per-pound premium. How to do so would need to be worked out between CIW and the company. Less easy to understand but just as important, and certainly unprecedented, was the section on farmworker rights. Yum! Brands, as was becoming increasingly common for major, consumer-facing corporations, had its own "General Supplier Code of Conduct" that applied to Taco Bell and all of its fast-food chains. Jonathan Blum acknowledged at the March 2005 press conference "We recognize these workers do not enjoy the same rights and conditions as employees in other industries, and there is a need for reform." Blum and Yum! Brands agreed to modify their code of conduct specifically for Florida's tomato growers. Taco Bell's suppliers, the tomato growers, were required to abide by all local, state, or federal laws and regulations "regarding wages and benefits, working hours, equal opportunity, and worker and product safety." Yum! also "strongly encourage[d]" Florida tomato growers to "provide working terms and conditions similar to those provided by suppliers outside of the agricultural industry." Again, how to enforce this standard and ensure growers met its requirements remained to be worked out. Yum! and the CIW agreed to work together to investigate "a credible complaint" of a violation of applicable laws, codes, or regulations. If Yum! and CIW "determine that the violation was serious or systemic, Yum! would stop buying from that grower/supplier until it remedied the situation. Finally, Yum! strengthened the prohibition against indentured servitude (first added in 2003 in response to CIW's discovery of new slavery cases) and maintained a right to unannounced inspections and enforcement of violations of the firm's code of conduct.

Implementation was the hard part, both for getting the penny per pound to the workers and to ensure compliance with the code of conduct. For this first agreement, CIW called for modifying the Yum! standards to explicitly guarantee workers' rights. Taco Bell would work with the CIW to figure out how to track and pay the premium and to monitor and enforce grower compliance. Looking forward, CIW understood that if "we won against Taco Bell, we'd need some sort of code for the agreement. We always knew that the complaint system would be the critical element. Looking at other social responsibility programs, the only ones with any effect had complaint systems. The Workers Rights Consortium had a complaint system for sweatshops, [and] for workers to have a real, meaningful role in the program, there had to be a complaint system."

What is a "complaint system" and why is it so difficult to put in place? Aren't we just talking about a hotline of some sort? In fact, no. A complaint system begins well before a hotline and ends far beyond. Before workers can file a complaint they must know what the rules and standards are that might have been violated. Workers and other employees then need to know how to file the complaint and be protected from retribution. Once someone has filed a complaint, there needs to be a process for investigating the accusation and then sanctions if the complaint is found to be valid. To say that setting up a complaint system that included response and sanction mechanisms was new ground to break in agriculture is certainly an understatement. For that matter, such systems would be groundbreaking in most other industries, clothing manufacturing for example. Getting past the simplistic idea of setting standards and establishing a hotline was a real step forward. Figuring out how to do this and then making it happen would take much longer.

Figuring out how to track and pay the penny-per-pound premium to workers wasn't a whole lot easier. The initial mechanism for doing so was rudimentary at best. As Steve Hitov describes it, "Yum! was essentially writing individual checks to workers, and it was a disaster. The checks were too small to cash. Tracking was a mess." Greg Asbed laughs as he refers to this effort as the "Wright Brothers program." Two Florida tomato growers, East Coast and Six L's, were participating in the program and "they didn't care. They just thought it was cute. 'Look what CIW did with one small buyer.'" Learning comes through doing and failure teaches most of all. This first agreement and the attempts to implement it provided many learning opportunities.

No rest for the weary. Even as the Taco Bell victory was announced, CIW turned its sights on the other major fast-food chains. McDonald's was next. CIW's strategy had matured after four years of fighting. Keeping the campaign's profile high, leveraging the power of its allies, and bringing on new partners, CIW knew it had to keep the pressure on. In March 2006, the McDonald's Real Rights Truth Tour kicked off in Florida, continued through the South, Midwest, and East with stops that included Atlanta, Madison, St. Louis, Ann Arbor, and South Bend and ended at McDonald's corporate headquarters in Chicago. Students, church groups, and labor groups joined with workers carrying signs declaring "I'm Leaving It," "Wanted: Ronald McDonald. For Exploiting Farmworkers," and "McXploitation." The Presbyterian Church urged parishioners to pray for McDonald's and farmworkers, and a dramatic flourish was added when the protesters delivered to McDonald's doorstep "3,500 signed cards by Immokalee workers demanding human rights in the field!" In a particularly pointed jab, paradegoers at the 2006 McDonald's Thanksgiving Day Parade in Chicago were visited by "Rolando," Ronald's "long-lost half-brother," who shared stories of how McDonald's thanks (not) the workers who provide the food it sold.

April 7, 2007, marked the beginning of the next McDonald's Truth Tour, and the publicity and pressure grew to be unbearable for the corporation. Using a technique common in camp ghost stories to build tension, CIW announced the tour well in advance and kept up a steady rhythm of Internet updates and press releases that made it painfully clear to McDonald's executives and public relations staff that the show would be arriving soon. Similar to the 2006 tour, the plan was to once again start in Immokalee and head north, ending up at McDonald's headquarters in Chicago and then holding a combination rally, protest, and concert at the House of Blues.

Steve Hitov remembers that "by the time the tour reached the Carter Center in Atlanta, McDonald's began negotiating." The intensity and speed of the negotiations between CIW and McDonald's was remarkable, with fourteen-hour days over the weekend before the Truth Tour arrived in Chicago. Just days later, on April 9, 2007, senior officials from McDonald's joined Lucas Benitez and a number of CIW members on stage at the Carter Center to announce their agreement and the ending of the boycott. McDonald's agreed to the penny-per-pound premium, to work with the CIW to develop a mutually agreeable code of conduct, and to investigate a possible third-party monitor for a new complaint system. Former president Jimmy Carter again voiced his support for the CIW, stating, "I welcome McDonald's commitment to work with the [CIW] to improve the lives of the workers who supply their 13,000 US restaurants with tomatoes. This is a clear and welcome example of positive industry partnership. . . . I encourage others to now follow the lead of McDonald's and Taco Bell to achieve the much needed change throughout the entire Florida-based tomato industry." The signing was covered by major news outlets including the *Chicago Tribune*, CNN, *Business Week*, and a number of Florida papers.

Agreements came fast and furious after the McDonald's signing. Yum! Brands extended their agreement to cover all their fast-food chains, including Pizza Hut and Kentucky Fried Chicken. Just a year later, Burger King came to agreement, joining CIW and members of Congress for a signing ceremony on the steps of the US Capitol in May of 2008. The pageantry was significantly in response to revelations that the company had hired a private detective to spy on the Student/Farmworker Alliance and one of the corporation's vice presidents had used his daughter's bedroom computer to make anonymous Internet attacks criticizing the Coalition. Adding to Burger King's humiliation was Eric Schlosser's withering commentary published in the *New York Times*.

With each of these agreements, Steve Hitov and Greg Asbed negotiated with the corporations to modify the companies' existing standards and codes of conduct. Questions about how to effectively implement the codes of conduct and the penny-per-pound premium remained. More frustrating was each corporation's attempt to negotiate the least demanding standards possible. When the McDonald's negotiation over implementation of the original agreement stretched across a year, CIW considered developing its own code of conduct that would then be included in future corporate buyer agreements and set the standards for the growers. Early on, Workers Rights Consortium attorney Mark Barenberg met with CIW staff in the old office to help think through what agriculture would look like in the frame of a code of conduct. Barenberg also joined in some of the thinking that went into a very early prototype of the CIW's code of conduct that they called "The Real Rights Code." Ultimately, meeting the workers' objective of safe and humane working conditions required the CIW to write its own code of conduct. "The original DNA of the code of conduct," Greg Asbed explained, "came from the workers and their concerns: the right to leave the field when there is lightning; no 'cupping' of tomato buckets; the right to shade and water." The CIW's code of conduct continued to evolve, independent of buyer negotiations, but was first incorporated into a buyer agreement with Subway in 2008.

Steve explains the evolution. In the agreements that followed over the next several years, the CIW code of conduct remained a constant while the Fair Food agreements that included the code were "tweak[ed] for each buyer to accommodate their legitimate needs and harmless idiosyncrasies, while maintaining the core requirements of the agreement." The specifics of what workers care about and their detailed knowledge was ultimately codified in what is known as the "Guidance Manual," forty pages of detail that make it possible to fully implement and monitor the code of conduct. All versions of the code required growers to "abide by all applicable laws, codes and regulations, including but not limited to this Code, and any local, state, or federal laws regarding wages and benefits, working hours, equal opportunity, and employee safety." All versions required buyers and growers to participate in, and comply with, the "penny-per-pound" premium. And all included zero tolerance of forced labor, illegal child labor, and use or threat of physical violence against an employee.

Todos somos lideres. It's written on the wall off to the left as you walk into the CIW's pink stucco offices on Second Street in Immokalee. If the sun's high in the sky, the light is blinding and the heat more than oppressive as you duck into the air conditioned space and are grateful for the relief. Across the room the banner from the protest, the first public declaration of the Coalition of Immokalee Workers, still hangs on the wall. And to the left you can see that Radio Conciencia 107.9, known as La Tuya ("yours"), is broadcasting, reaching into the camps and farmworker housing areas that are spread throughout Immokalee. The quarters are tight but there's a window into the studio and you can find a marimba stashed in the narrow hallway. We've looked at the CIW's allies, but what about the farmworkers who make up the staff and membership of the Coalition? "We are all leaders" is apparent as the farmworkers of Immokalee reach out to each other, to allies, and across the country through media and actions. La Tuya is often the first connection between farmworkers and the CIW, connecting them to their home and to the workers' group. The station is also one of the first venues for public leadership by CIW members. Cruz Salucio remembers arriving in Immokalee and discovering the radio station. "After a while in Immokalee. . . . I bought a small radio. At first, I was just flipping through the stations and I found some commercial stations and then I found Radio Conciencia. On a Sunday. I encountered a radio show in Kanjobal, a language spoken in Huehuetenango where I'm from. . . . So the *campanero* on the radio was speaking my language! It was strange to hear someone speaking in your language and also playing the music of the marimba. Listening to that made me feel closer to where I came from as a Guatemalan. Then, I heard them talking about my rights as an agricultural worker."

Like Cruz Salucio, you'll likely hear music from Mexico, Guatemala, or Haiti if you tune in to La Tuya. That and announcements of the CIW's Wednesday meetings or Saturday movie nights during the season, or the Sunday meetings of the womens' group. The station brings live coverage of Truth Tours and other actions back to the Immokalee workers. Each offering is a connection bringing together the community and inviting workers to the Coalition. La Tuya announcers extend the popular education of CIW's weekly meetings into the camps and fields. CIW staff member Nely Rodriguez sums up the effectiveness of the station: "[T]he radio . . . is how we are able to tell about what we are doing and the struggle that we are part of. Most importantly, so that people understand what we are asking of the corporations and why we are fighting against these corporations." Silvia Perez has been in Immokalee since 1993. Picking jalapenos, cucumber, and tomatoes, Silvia was one of the few women working in the fields back then. "I heard about the Coalition in 1994 when Greg, Laura, and Lucas were doing door-to-door knocking, inviting people to go to the Wednesday meetings. Soon we came a lot to the Coalition offices because of the co-op and its lower prices than the other Mexican stores." Silvia was one of the earliest members of the CIW womens' group, Grupo de Mujeres, and was invited to join CIW's staff in 2007. Tune into La Tuya and most days you'll hear her radio show with its call-in requests for music from Mexico or Guatemala, and messages to loved ones. After he joined CIW's staff, five in the morning was Cruz Salucio's slot, timed to energize workers as they headed to the fields, but also reminding them of their rights as farmworkers. Cruz goes old school, playing *rancheros* to help "animate people who are going to work and working in the fields."

Cruz and Silvia are two of the many workers who are the voices of the Coalition. In declaring popular education, leadership development, and action its cornerstones, the cofounders were both sincere and prescient. The firm belief that "we are all leaders," the intellectual foundation provided to all engaged members through education, and insistence that the workers would lead the early protests and then the Campaign for Fair Food has helped ensure the long-term sustainability and growth of the CIW despite its being a migrant workers' group. A small staff with an even tighter budget means leadership is shared by staff and CIW members. It is a notable experience to read interviews and presentations by CIW members and staff and even more so to spend time with them. Visiting Immokalee, I often spoke with whoever was available, rode along with the education team that happened to be scheduled for that day, or met with workers on farms who were on that day's work crews. The consistency of message, the depth of understanding of the food supply chain and the workers' place within it, knowledge of the specifics of the Coalition's demands, and an ability to explain the intricacies of the workers' rights and the code of conduct that supports these would be rare in the most high-profile corporation or government organization.

From the earliest days, many voices joined those of Greg Asbed, Laura Germino, Lucas Benitez, and the other founders in talking about the Coalition's objectives of fair pay, safe working conditions, and a place at the table alongside the other players in the food chain. Antonio Ramos spoke out as part of the hunger strike in 1998. Romeo Ramirez not only went undercover to gather evidence that led to the conviction of Ramiro Ramos and his bosses for slavery but became a frequent speaker in actions from Fort Myers to Chicago, and he even addressed the UN Human Rights Council in Geneva, Switzerland. Gerardo Reyes found himself introduced to the world of public speaking not long after his first encounter with the CIW. It turned out he had a real talent for not only speaking but leading. "I became part of the Coalition and went to different actions. And I began to meet with groups that visited to talk about my experience. I had never before that moment talked to a group. [In fact] I was very timid to people who didn't know me. . . . The first time I held a megaphone was at a protest trying to get the attention of the governor. I was effective with the megaphone." Like many members of the CIW, whether or not they were staff members, Gerardo was soon traveling the country as part of the Truth Tours and smaller actions. As the CIW's media presence grew, Gerardo found himself appearing on television and even giving a powerful TEDx talk on the importance of corporations recognizing their responsibilities to all levels of the food chains that supported them.

Women have long been important voices for the CIW. The courage Julia Gabriel had when she reached out to Laura Germino and the CIW to report on Miguel Flores's labor camps continued when she testified at Flores's trial. A different type of bravery was required when Julia went from a victim of modern-day slavery to speaking out against slavery with CIW. Guadalupe "Lupe" Gonzalo brings to life the situation faced by women farmworkers when she speaks at CIW actions or in interviews. "Women often felt there wasn't any recourse. They felt there weren't any protections from that kind of abuse. Scared. Scared to say anything." Lupe has been featured in videos on women farmworkers, in the press release announcing the Fresh Market agreement, and as a spokesperson in the ongoing boycott against Wendy's fast-food chain.

"In another world, another environment, these women would be real leaders, recognized leaders . . . but they work in the fields that are dominated by men." Steve Hitov speaks with something close to awe of the particular strength and courage of the women who work in the fields, the nature of the work and the roughness of the environment. Sexual harassment, and sometimes sexual assault, by the women's supervisors was common. Nely Rodriguez and the other women on CIW's staff often work with women who have suffered such abuse in their work and might also be dealing with domestic abuse at home. These women tend to carry more responsibility for maintaining the household, providing healthcare and child care, and finding and preparing food for their families, even while working ten hours a day. They are also at particular risk from exposure to toxins in pesticides and herbicides.

Raised in a small town in northern Mexico with eight brothers and sisters, Nely first came to the United States to work Michigan's fields but then moved to Immokalee in 2000. Within a few years, she was attending CIW's Wednesday meetings and taking part in actions just as Burger King was signing the Fair Food agreement. With three children of her own, Nely often speaks for the women farmworkers where the ritual of daily life can be overwhelming. "Wake up very early, drop off your child under someone else's care, then you are working for about ten hours, picking tomatoes. Come back, pick up your child, go back home and cook dinner because it is already very late. Prepare everything you need that night for the next working day. That's a typical day, every day, for a woman who works in the fields." Steve believes the particular story of women farmworkers has not yet been recognized. Nely echoed this missing piece: "This is a history that is not written in any book and I don't think there would be enough paper to do justice to the daily life of a strong woman, fighting to provide for her family. And what we want as women is to continue this struggle so that our children . . . will not have to continue to suffer."

The philosophical importance of "we are all leaders" to the Coalition's work was evident from its founding, but the practical need for many leaders and many voices accelerated with the declaration of the Campaign for Fair Food and as victories mounted. The persistence of the Coalition's efforts has been possible in part because of the breadth of their leadership base. As each corporation signed Fair Food agreements, the CIW launched its next campaign against the next corporate target. Campaigns included marches and Truth Tours, protests and educational sessions at fast-food and grocery stores, college campuses, and church meetings all across the country. Each tour, event, and visit required workers like Cruz, Nely, and Romeo to lead. *Todos somos lideres.*

The demands don't only come from outside of Immokalee. Immokalee has become a social responsibility destination, with a trickle of visitors sometimes becoming a river after a flood. Early on, visitors like David Wang were few. But by the late 1990s, church groups began visiting Immokalee to understand what farmworkers were facing. The Student/Farmworker Alliance became increasingly sophisticated in training and educating students, but this further ramped up the visitors. As the Alliance for Fair Food grew, coordination and education workshops in Immokalee were vital to ensure all were in sync in their understanding of the problem. After the hunger strike and declaration of the Campaign for Fair Food, high-profile visitors such as Jimmy Carter and Ethel and Kerry Kennedy met with the CIW, soon joined by more than one United States senator. Journalists came next. The *New York Times'* Steven Greenhouse first mentioned Immokalee's workers in a 1998 article on migrant worker housing. John Bowe wrote about "Nobodies" and modern-day slavery first in an article in the *New Yorker* and then in a 2007 book by the same name. Major series on working conditions and human trafficking appeared in newspapers such as the *Miami Herald* and the *Christian Science Monitor*. Vital support and intellectual influence has come from Eric Schlosser. Schlosser's seminal book, *Fast Food Nation*, confirmed the Coalition's strategy of targeting fast-food and grocery brands, as he had come to the same conclusion for fighting fast-food chains over the treatment of animals. In *Reefer Madness*, Schlosser wrote about the CIW's worker-led, industry-wide approach, distinctive from traditional union organizing, and he wrote a scathing commentary criticizing Burger King as a series of embarrassing revelations came out leading to the chain's capitulation. Schlosser was also an executive producer of *Food Chains*, a James Beard award–winning documentary largely focused on the CIW and their fight against the supermarket chains. Each of these visitors was welcomed, offered a presentation, a tour to see what $1,000 a month or more bought in run-down trailers, a walk through the Pantry Shelf/Fiesta parking lot and along the path of the 1996 protest of Edgar's beating. Some took the time for longer conversations with Lucas, Greg, Laura, Gerardo, or other members of the CIW staff, and were perhaps able to get a glimpse into fields or the sites of prosecuted modern-day slavery cases. Taking time with visitors puts a heavy burden on the small staff, but it also demonstrates the long game the CIW has played all along: developing leaders, building alliances, and gaining the attention of consumers, supporters, and policy makers.

Senator Ted Kennedy's introduction, not to mention that his Senate committee was investigating working conditions for farmworkers, indicated how far the Coalition of Immokalee Workers had come in their fight as the first decade of the twenty-first century headed to a close. "[I]t's a special pleasure to have Mr. Benitez here. He was an award recipient of the Robert Kennedy Human Rights Award in 2003, as well as many national and other international awards. We have a very distinguished panel, but we have a very courageous spokesman for workers as well on this panel. We thank him." Kennedy was the chairman of the Senate Committee on Health, Education, Labor, and Pensions, and the hearing the committee held on April 15, 2008, raised the profile of the CIW and offered an analysis of the state of agricultural labor in 2008.

Look around the Senate hearing room. Joining Lucas was Eric Schlosser, as was the first head of Collier County's new antitrafficking unit, detective Charlie Frost. Mary Bauer from the Southern Poverty Law Center would be testifying. And, receiving more attention than he likely wanted, was Reggie Brown from the Florida Tomato Growers Exchange (FTGE), the industry group. The four senators looking magisterially down on the speakers from their large wooden desks at the front of the room were chairman Ted Kennedy, Bernie Sanders, Sherrod Brown, and Dick Durbin. Senator Sanders and Eric Schlosser had been two of the many visitors to Immokalee, visiting together in January 2008. Senator Sanders worked with Senator Kennedy to call the hearing on "Ending Abuses and Improving Working Conditions for Tomato Workers."

Clearly, national attention was not the issue for the CIW. They were getting a lot of it. The frustration came with the realization of how little had changed in farmworkers' lives. The Coalition was slaying giants one after another. What took four years with Taco Bell took two with McDonald's, then Yum! extended the Fair Food agreement to all of its chains. Burger King came to agreement not long after the Senate hearing, embarrassed by the series of amateur-hour scandals. By the end of the decade, Subway, Whole Foods, and corporate food providers Bon Appétit Management Company, Compass Group, Aramark, and Sodexo had all signed on.

But a critical piece was still missing. Turning the demands of the campaign into real changes in workers' lives required the workers, the corporate buyers, *and the growers*. The farms were, of course, where the tomato pickers worked. Although Reggie Brown argued otherwise, passing on the penny per pound had to be done through the growers who paid the workers. Perhaps more importantly, improving working conditions and eliminating the conditions that allowed slavery to fester required the cooperation of the growers and their employees. As the tide shifted and more corporate buyers signed on, Florida's tomato growers dug their heels in deeper. Two growers had originally worked with Taco Bell to pass the penny-per-pound premium to their workers. When McDonald's and Yum! signed on, the members of the FTGE said "enough!" Not only did the FTGE oppose participation, but its members, who represented 90 percent of Florida's tomato production, agreed to a $100,000 fine for every instance of any member grower cooperating with the CIW and the Fair Food Program.

The growers' logic was difficult to follow. The first attempt at paying the premium may have been clunky, but it did demonstrate that doing so wasn't an impossible burden to bear. What was most frustrating to the senators that day in April was the refusal of the tomato growers' representative to acknowledge any sort of problem. Reading his testimony, as Reggie Brown spoke at the hearing, it was hard not to imagine him with his fingers in his ears, eyes closed, and repeating "naaah, naaaah, naaah, I can't hear you!"

Photos show Brown leaning in to speak into the hearing room microphone. He focused his objections on the penny-per-pound payments to workers. "First, let me state unequivocally that Florida's tomato growers abhor and condemn slavery. . . . It is outrageous to have slavery happening in Florida or any other State. . . . The reality, however, is that there are, indeed cases of slavery and human trafficking occurring in many States today, and that is a tragedy." But, he said, the growers were neither aware of, nor responsible for, trafficking of their workers. "Broad charges have been made that workers are being exploited and that Florida growers are not following labor standards. We firmly deny those allegations." The real disagreement, Brown explains, was over the penny-per-pound charge. "Two fast-food companies, Yum! Brands and McDonald's, agreed to the deal and, in turn, have pressured Florida's tomato growers to take on the role of passing the extra payments onto their workers. For a number of sound business reasons and legal reasons, the producers have declined to participate."

In his testimony and subsequent questioning by Senator Sanders, Brown argued that the penny-per-pound charge violates antitrust legislation, raises concern about fraud and "RICO" violations, puts the Florida tomato farmers at a "competitive disadvantage," and puts unwanted liability on the growers related to joint employment with the corporate buyers. Brown faced withering questioning from Sanders and had to field question from the other senators and panelists about the veracity of his claims. The senators asked about one letter of support for the Fair Food agreements from McDonald's and another letter submitted into the record by twenty-five law school professors of labor and antitrust law calling the Tomato Exchange's legal arguments "mystifying."

To his credit, Reggie Brown did his job, taking the heat for growers. Brown stood firm that the FTGE and its members would not cooperate with the CIW, despite its growing number of corporate partners. Instead, Brown suggested, "We call upon CIW to take on the task of providing a way for Yum! Brands and McDonald's to distribute monies to its members and workers without involving the growers. CIW, as a representative of its members and workers, should gladly accept the challenge of getting this job done. . . . Alternatively, like our growers do, McDonald's could contribute to charities that are helpful to CIW's members and workers, and their communities such as Catholic Charities, the University of South Florida Migrant Scholarships, the Redlands Christian Migrant Association and others."

As the testimony of Lucas Benitez, Mary Bauer of the Southern Poverty Law Center, and Eric Schlosser made clear, without the growers' participation, the farmworkers' effective wages continued to decline and working conditions had yet to improve. By 2008, there had been seven confirmed slavery cases affecting a thousand or more workers, immigrants and US citizens alike. The CIW's anti-slavery work and success in bringing on many of the largest corporate buyers to the Campaign for Fair Food had received deserved recognition. But, as Senator Kennedy summed up, where the workers found themselves without the growers' participation:

> Farmworkers in Immokalee and nationwide have some of the hardest jobs in America. Yet they often toil for the lowest wages and under the most dangerous conditions. For the tomato workers in Immokalee, the pay they receive hasn't changed in a decade. They head off into the fields before the sun rises, and they are still working hard when the sun sets. During the harvest, they work ten- to twelve-hour days, seven days a week with no overtime pay. They each pick as many as two tons of tomatoes per day, and they earn only $40 to $50 for this hard day's work. Their work can disappear for weeks or months, leaving them without the means to support their families. Their working conditions are deplorable. But most of them are afraid to demand fair treatment because they know they will be fired, blacklisted, or turned over to immigration officials. These conditions are not limited to Immokalee. They are widespread and getting worse.

Tomato harvest

Chavannes Jean Baptiste (center, holding pad) conducts a leadership development workshop with Greg Asbed (seated, first from left) for early CIW members in Our Lady of Guadalupe Church. Chavannes was a cofounder of Haiti's Mouvman Peyizan Papay (MPP), Haiti's largest peasant organization, and a leader in the country's democratization movement of the 1980s in which many of the CIW's early leaders also participated. Also pictured is Cristal Pierre (standing), another early CIW leader and former peasant leader from Haiti.

1995 strike for better wages

In 1996, CIW protested the beating of a young farmworker by a Campbell Bros. field boss.

Popular education "teatro"; photo is from a 2012 CIW weekly membership meeting.

March for Dignity, Dialogue, and a Fair Wage (February 2000). The papier mâché Statue of Liberty is now housed at the Smithsonian Museum of American History as part of its permanent collection of American protest art.

Pyramid of buckets in front of YUM! Brands headquarters in Louisville, KY, during the Taco Bell boycott (2004). The pyramid represented the number of buckets each worker needed to pick to earn minimum wage for an eight-hour day at the going rate of $0.40 per bucket.

Alliance for Fair Food members march with CIW's farmworkers in Mississippi (2016)

CIW watermelon cooperative loading melons in the field. Gerardo Reyes is center, tossing a watermelon into the converted bus. Greg Asbed is second from the right (2007).

CIW offices in Immokalee. Lucas Benitez is to the right.

HAS ANYONE TALKED WITH THESE GUYS?

"Test driving a shopping cart." That's how Jon Esformes describes what he was doing in 2002. This was clearly going to be a different sort of "personal journey" story. As you stop fumbling for the appropriately concerned response (shock, pity, awkward laughter) and begin to listen to Jon's dizzying tale, you realize that the extremes of Jon's life are essential to what came next for the Coalition of Immokalee Workers. Jon's moving between the extremes of business success, suicidal addiction, and back again made it possible for him to find the middle path of humanity and the courage to claim it.

When you first meet Jon Esformes, you will likely underestimate him and you will certainly not understand him. Jon is a farmer. Jon grew up in Beverly Hills. Jon is a high school dropout, and one of the smarter people you'll meet. Jon is an alcoholic who has been sober for more than a decade. Jon is an instinctive and savvy businessman who believes deeply in the humanity and dignity of every person. When you meet Jon, he's likely to be in jeans and an untucked white button-down, hands in his pockets and itching to get outside and grab a cigarette. Roughly handsome, with eyes that welcome you with some skepticism, he's got a face that indicates a life lived hard. He's disarmingly open and brutally frank about himself and others.

About the same time the Coalition was struggling to find a new approach to getting workers paid more and to end the abuse in Florida, Jon was fighting his own battles with addiction. Those battles—or really Jon's many losses in those battles—had recently led him from being drunk and living in hotels to being drunk and living on the street. There was of course much more to this, depending on how far back you want to take the tale. You could start a couple of years back with Jon being kicked out of the family business, now known as Pacific Tomato Growers, or even further when Jon was eight and began working, making box tops and crates for the company. But if you really want to understand what follows, you should probably start in New York's Lower East Side in the early 1900s. There you'd find Jon's great-grandfather, a Sephardic Jewish immigrant from what is now Greece, selling watermelons from a pushcart after working in a glue factory destroyed his lungs. By the 1940s, the Esformes family had joined other families who emigrated once again, this time from the northeast to Florida, to grow the produce they had been selling. Italians, Greeks, and Germans took advantage of refrigeration, trains, and Florida's weather to start growing citrus, tomatoes, and other fresh produce craved in their home cities of Philadelphia, New York, and Boston. By the end of the twentieth century, these family histories were shared, torn apart, and intertwined again many times over. Some combination of escaping and being rejected by these connections played a part in Jon's finding himself on the streets of Los Angeles. And these same relationships help explain why the Florida tomato growers stood together in united and obstinate opposition to the Coalition of Immokalee Workers and the major corporations that had signed up for the Campaign for Fair Food.

From early in his life, Jon moved back and forth between Florida and Los Angeles, pulled in both directions by the family business. Jon discovered his taste for drugs and alcohol at an early age, but he was a straight-A student and worked hard. "I had aspirations and dreamed of being a senator, even while I was getting stoned." Grades got him into Andover but he was lonely and unhappy there and wanted to go back to high school in LA. "That's when I got really deep into dope, at Beverly Hills High." It didn't take long for Jon to find himself on the road again, dropping out at sixteen, and heading to northern California, where the Esformes had operations. When the Esformes and Heller families came together to form Pacific Tomato Growers, he headed back to Florida. At Pacific, Jon's intelligence and innate business sense served him well when he was not thrown off track by his addictions. For a while, countervailing forces did just that: Jon's increasing involvement in running Pacific's operations, particularly in Mexico and California, fought with the claim alcohol and drugs were making on him. Making a long story short, Jon was fired in 1995 and by the late 1990s he was back in LA, trying to hold his life together while tightening his grip on the bottle.

No longer capable of holding a job, Jon "stayed drunk for a couple of years" and by May of 2000 was drinking himself to death. "I was at a hotel down by the [Los Angeles] airport and my genius plan was that I was gonna hop a plane back to Florida. . . . I was gonna rent a boat and I was gonna go out into the Gulf [of Mexico] and end my life." Fearing for her son, Jon's mother reached out for help to a woman associated with the residential substance abuse center called Beit T'Shuvah. Could the center's leaders Harriet Rossetto and Rabbi Mark Borovitz find Jon and take him in?

Beit T'Shuvah has now been around for more than thirty years. The center provides a religion-based, twelve-step program with an emphasis on rebuilding fragile and broken relationships and centered on the deeply held belief of Harriet and Rabbi Mark of the value and dignity of every human being. A self-described "wild child," Harriet rejected married life in Minneapolis, went home to New York City, and then headed to California to start over. Her significantly oppositional perspective, or at least a stubbornness that refused to give in to common wisdom or the counsel of her betters, gets much of the credit for why Beit T'Shuvah not only exists but now thrives.

The origins of Beit T'Shuvah are found in the prison ministry Harriet Rossetto took on in the 1980s that evolved into a halfway house for prisoners to transition back into society. Naive is one way to describe Harriet's early attempts. The first group of prisoners she housed stole her jewelry and "helped" her look for it. It was in one of California's prisons that Harriet met Mark, where he was once again serving time. The idea that the two of them might become husband and wife was only slightly less far-fetched than that this check-kiting con would become a rabbi. The seeds for their partnership were sowed when Mark criticized Harriet's approach to helping prisoners' transition. "If you're so smart, then when you get out of here, you can stop talking and help me do it better." Needless to say, Harriet was astonished when Mark's first stop out of prison was onto her doorstep.

Twenty years later, when Jon's mother called for help, Harriet and now-Rabbi Mark Borovitz had pulled thousands of people back from the edge. When Rabbi Mark called Jon, it took only a few words for Rabbi Mark to know Jon was drunk. Yes, I'll come to the center, Jon assured the rabbi. Let me clean some things up and I'll be there tomorrow. Not surprisingly, Jon didn't show up. Breaking his word yet again, Jon was about to discover that these two were not your usual social workers. Rabbi Mark called again and told Jon he was sending someone to pick him up and get his ass to Beit T'Shuvah. Jon was not going be allowed to drift into death. Soon after, knocking at Jon's door was "the type of person [Jon] absolutely couldn't say no to." Wearing a cowboy hat and blocking the light from the doorway, "he picked me up . . . threw my clothes into a bag and we snuck out of the hotel because I had a bill pending."

Reeking of alcohol, Esformes arrived at Beit T'Shuvah disoriented and heading into a brutal detox. "I walked into the room, as best as I could walk at the time, and lying on the other bed was a guy with a purple Mohawk and tattoos all over his body. He was reading the Torah. I thought to myself, 'where am I? What am I doing here? And how the hell do I get out of here????'"

Jon began his time at Beit T'Shuvah in the fetal position, fighting through detox. As he came out of those grueling first weeks, he took tentative first steps but then threw himself into the Beit T'Shuvah program, working in the facility and spending each morning in Torah study. This study was "a gateway for me . . . discovering my own soul and making a connection between my head and heart." It was also through these morning sessions that Jon developed his deep friendship with Rabbi Mark. Of particular delight was playing "stump the rabbi" as Jon dove deeper into the scriptures. Jon, recounts the rabbi, "fell in love with, and I fell in love with learning with him, [learning] about truth, about decency, about really what we're here for as human beings." Together the two men examined Maimonides and the idea, as Jon describes it, that "when you're at one end of the spectrum, you have to go all the way to the other end in order to find the middle path. The middle path isn't just the straight and narrow, it is this continuum, and everybody's got a different place on it."

A lifetime of addiction and self-medication was not easily overcome, even with the support of Mark Borovitz and Harriet Rossetto. Jon left Beit T'Shuvah and relapsed twice. The last time nearly killed him. Drunk and suffering from severe pancreatitis, Jon was homeless and "test driving a shopping cart" on the streets in Culver City. Getting sicker by the minute, within a few days Jon realized he couldn't survive on the streets by holding onto his "shopping cart and a bottle of booze," Jon called Jeff Rubenstein, a friend from Beit T'Shuvah, and asked for help. Jeff called Harriet and Rabbi Mark. Rushed to the hospital and near death, Jon eventually returned to Beit T'Shuvah for his third and last residency.

In wide-ranging conversations that included describing Jon's collapsing on the floor of Beit T'Shuvah to Mark and Harriet's (very opposite) Myers-Briggs scores to their approach of "being transparent as healers," Rabbi Mark and Harriet reflected on why Jon was eventually able to achieve sobriety in August 2002. Jon "kept coming back and he kept coming back because he knew what he wanted and he . . . believed it was attainable . . . [Jon] was wrestling over those first two years about that connection . . . where he didn't let his soul override his mind and his emotions. In 2002 he really got to 51 percent, where his soul was going to run him. The soul became the arbiter of his life. His mind and his emotions certainly have votes and information, yet he goes with what he knows to be right deep inside of him." Central to Jon's sobriety was a belief that the needs of others had to be his concern, that there was value in every human life, and that he was called to a life of service.

Turning into the driveway of a mansion in Beverly Hills, Jon readied himself for the first day of his first job sober, working for a catering company. Pulling the van around to the back, Jon noticed the house looked familiar and then recognized some of the cars parked in the driveway. Walking into the house and looking in from the kitchen, Jon saw his classmates from Beverly Hills High School. Fighting back the fear and shame, Jon took strength from Rabbi Abraham Joshua Heschel's idea, much discussed in the study sessions with Rabbi Mark, that "something sacred is at stake in every event." At this defining moment, Jon decided that if "[I] was going to serve canapés, I would do it better than anyone else."

That first step turned into a path that brings to mind Victor Kiam's catch phrase about the Remington electric razor: "I liked the shaver so much I bought the company." Although he struggled with the fear of leaving Beit T'Shuvah and living on his own, Jon's intellect and business instincts kicked in full force once sober. Jon bought the catering company that had provided his first job and then established a successful residential addiction treatment center, Authentic Recovery, in Los Angeles.

The relationship that took longer to rebuild was with Jon and his family. The catering business and recovery center were important not only for Jon's financial recovery but for establishing himself apart from the family business. He had once been a shareholder but had lost even that connection when he was fired in 1995 and then disappeared into the bottle in 1998. After he left Beit T'Shuvah, the Esformes and Heller families who owned Pacific Tomato Growers asked Jon to come back. Not ready to get caught back up in the family dynamics, Jon kept them at arm's length. Convinced in 2005 to at least return to the board meetings, Jon discovered all that had occurred over the past decade. What he learned was shocking. The battle between the Coalition of Immokalee Workers and the Florida tomato growers was in full force. The accusations of worker abuse and the attempt to distance the company from those who worked in their fields didn't reflect the company in which he had grown up. After one board meeting where Jon declared, "I don't know who you guys have become," his generational counterpart in the Heller family pulled him aside. "If you don't like where we are, you need to get involved and do something, not just complain."

But Jon wasn't there yet. He was running his new businesses, and the family's tomato and citrus farms had been one of the complications in his life of addiction. Eventually, the pull of family and concerns about the direction of the company drew Jon back. Joe Esformes, Jon's father, removed the final obstacle when he sold Jon half his interest in the company. Still running his other businesses, Jon returned part time as chief marketing officer, running sales and marketing, and building Pacific's Mexican operations. In the mid-2000s, the company was one of the largest growers in Florida and a leader in the produce industry. It was also closely tied to the other old-line Florida growers like Six L's and Gargiulo and run by a CEO with deep roots in the grower community.

Billy Heller, no relation to the Heller family, partnered with the Esformes, was that CEO. "Billy and I, we liked each other. We made a deal to form an alliance." They eliminated the CEO position and created a joint leadership model, with Jon and Billy working side by side. Jon returned to the Esformes family and Pacific Tomato Growers full-time on June 1, 2008. Ironically, or perhaps appropriately, June 1 was also the day the US government announced a salmonella outbreak, declaring (mistakenly) that the illness had come from fresh Florida tomatoes. As a result, Pacific lost $15 million the first six months of Jon's return. Ultimately the federal government's announcement and misdiagnosis cost the Florida tomato industry $100 million. During Jon's first two years leading Pacific, the company faced the salmonella crisis, the economic meltdown of 2008, and two devastating freezes. In addition, Jon had a major health crisis when he caught dengue fever while in Mexico. But despite all these obstacles, under Jon and Billy's leadership Pacific reorganized, jettisoned nonproductive business units, and focused its attention on the company's core business, what Jon called "Tomatoes 101."

Where Jon could not lead the others during those first two years was in addressing the increasing success, and genuine concerns, of the Coalition of Immokalee Workers and the Campaign for Fair Food. Pacific had stuck with the other members of the Florida Tomato Growers Exchange in staunch opposition to the Coalition. In 2005, the campaign had its first major victory when the four-year boycott against Taco Bell resulted in the fast-food chain's signing the campaign's Fair Food agreement. Taco Bell's parent company Yum! Brands soon followed and by 2008 Burger King, McDonald's, and Subway had joined. With each signing, the Florida tomato growers' opposition only grew, taking heart in the belief that if they stuck together, the corporate buyers had no option but to buy from the suppliers of virtually all the United States' winter tomatoes.

If the Esformes family hadn't actively worked against the CIW, Jon reflects, the family's long-standing relationships with the other growers resulted in Pacific "abdicating individual responsibility to a grower organization [the Florida Tomato Growers Exchange] that had to reflect the lowest common denominator [among Florida growers]." Returning full-time in 2008, "I had the luxury of absence and the resources of profound experience." He brought a new set of eyes and a new understanding of "true north" to the problem in which Pacific had long been entrenched. What the other growers didn't realize was that refusing to talk with the tomato workers and ignoring their calls for basic human rights flew in the face of Jon's new commitment to a life of service. It violated the covenant that was at the core of Jon's sobriety and beliefs: "the covenant that says we're human." Jon's beliefs may have empowered him but his gradual education in 2008–2009 on the conditions in the fields moved him to apply his core beliefs to the idea of farmworker rights. Only then could he begin to move the members of the Esformes and Heller families away from the other growers. What eventually forced a change was a linking of the unthinkable and the banal.

"Family accused of enslaving workers at Immokalee camp" was the headline greeting readers of the *Naples Daily News* on December 7, 2007. Over their first cup of coffee, citizens of Florida's wealthy Gulf Coast learned that the Navarrete family had kept tomato workers locked in panel trucks and trailers in the yard of their Immokalee home. Cesar and Geovanni Navarrete, along with their half-brother Ismael and mother Vihinna, had been charged on November 20 with enslaving twelve men who worked on their tomato crews. Three of the men broke through the roof of the box truck where they had been imprisoned, rescued the other workers, and reported the crime to the Coalition of Immokalee Workers and the Collier County sheriff. The men had been kept in the windowless box truck without air conditioning, forced to relieve themselves in its corners and chained to a pole and beaten for punishment. They were released only to work in the fields, where they were threatened with death if they tried to escape.

If the news of modern-day slavery only forty miles from Naples was shocking to most readers of the *Daily News* and the *Fort Myers News-Press*, it was significantly less surprising for those in the Florida agricultural community. The Navarrete case became the seventh slavery case in which the Coalition actively assisted (or led) the investigation and worked with federal and state prosecutors. And as then chief assistant US attorney Douglas Molloy made clear, this was only one of several such ongoing investigations at the time.

Florida's produce growers, particularly the tomato growers, were well aware of the abuses and of the half-dozen successful slavery prosecutions in the United States since 1997, most tied to Florida's fields. Even before the national Campaign for Fair Food, the Coalition had attracted outside attention to the abysmal working conditions and below-poverty pay through the Christmas-time hunger strike in 1997. As the campaign picked up speed and got one fast-food chain after another to commit to better wages and refuse to buy tomatoes picked by "the hands of a slave," the growers took protective action. After Taco Bell and Yum! Brands signed the Fair Food agreement in the spring of 2005, the other fast-food chains and the National Restaurant Association asked what the growers were going to do about this, since the other chains could hear the bell tolling for them. Slavery was not good for business. The urgency was real when members of the Florida Fruit and Vegetable Association, including the tomato growers, met in a Palmetto tomato packing house that fall. They came up with the perfect counter to the Coalition's demands for reasonable pay and safe working conditions. If you can't beat them, imitate them. With great fanfare the growers announced in early January 2006 that they were partnering with the nonprofit Redlands Christian Migrant Association in establishing the Socially Accountable Farm Employers, SAFE, program.

SAFE listed standards for farmworker treatment, including prohibition of forced or child labor, the payment of full wages and benefits, a "healthy and safe work environment," and adequate housing. The growers contracted with the international firm Intertek to provide auditing of member farm operations to verify compliance with the standards. McDonald's was early out of the blocks in declaring that compliance with SAFE's standards would be mandatory for all their Florida produce suppliers. This may have been because the industry giant now found itself, as did Burger King, in the sights of the Coalition of Immokalee Workers.

There were real differences between the demands of the mid-2000s Campaign for Fair Food and SAFE's declared standards. To begin with, SAFE was a collaboration between the growers and a charity group, with significant support from the restaurant industry. Farmworkers were not included in the organization, in the setting of the standards, or in the monitoring effort. Additionally, there was no provision for increasing the pay for farm work, the most visible element of the CIW campaign and its call for "a-penny-per-pound" more for tomato workers. The growers made no secret of their intention for SAFE to counter the Coalition's efforts. As one farmer explained to a local reporter, "We need to have some kind of mechanism in place to assure our customer base that they are not going to be a target of an outfit like the CIW."

"No slave labor" and the fields were safe for workers. So announced Andrew Raghu, Intertek's global managing director as he declared that Florida's tomato growers had earned a clean bill of health. This was just what the growers and their restaurant chain buyers had been waiting for. Raghu's announcement came at a major promotional event sponsored by the Florida Tomato Growers Exchange and Burger King on November 20, 2007, attended by a reporter from the *Miami Herald* and other press. In recounting the day's events, Greg Asbed cannot but quote the *Matrix*'s Morpheus: "Fate, it seems, is not without a sense of irony." November 20, as it turned out, was also the day that the three tomato workers first met with Collier County sheriff deputies to recount their two years of captivity, and abuse and charges were filed against the Navarrete family members who held them in Immokalee.

Jon Esformes was not yet back as operating partner at Pacific Tomato Growers when SAFE was established in 2005 or when the Navarrete slavery case first hit the headlines at the close of 2007. But he was in charge when the Navarrete case came to its conclusion a year later, with all four members of the family convicted and Cesar and Geovanni sentenced to twelve years in prison. The conviction was another victory for Laura Germino and the Coalition's antislavery efforts, but what was unprecedented was what happened in the coverage of the sentencing. Amy Bennett Williams was a reporter for the *Fort Myers News-Press* and had long written about Florida agriculture and the Coalition of Immokalee Workers. In her December 20, 2008, article, Williams included the following:

> The Navarretes took their crews to work on farms owned by some of the state's major tomato producers: Immokalee-based Six L's and Pacific Tomato Growers in Palmetto. Both tomato growers are part of the Socially Accountable Farm Employers program, designed to prevent labor abuses.

With this paragraph, Williams not only put a stake in the heart of the SAFE program but also did what had never been done before: directly connect tomato growers with slavery. By naming names, Williams' article changed the game, amping up the pressure on the growers even as their opposition to the Coalition hardened even further.

Tension between growers and the Coalition was reaching a combustion point. The Florida Tomato Growers Exchange had banned its members from working with the Coalition and had imposed a $100,000 fine for those who did so. The blowback from the Navarrete conviction hadn't let up, particularly for Pacific Tomato Growers and Six L's. As more buyers—including Subway, Aramark, and Whole Foods—signed the Fair Food agreement, the market pressure designed into the Fair Food Program was building.

The battle between the Coalition and the Florida growers had long since gone beyond a matter of worker pay and treatment. It was a conflict tied to the pride of families who had been in Florida for generations, built their businesses through hard work, sometimes lost them, and then built them again. They had become the elite of rural Florida, worlds apart from the coastal elite of snowbirds and retirees. Although these families had decreasing power in the face of pressure from the major retail corporations to keep prices down, they were used to having absolute power over their farms. Farmworkers were yet one more input into operations and had always been so, whether they were Jim Crow–era African Americans or the ever-shifting tide of immigrants. Who was the tractor to tell the farmer how to run his business?

If pride made it difficult for the tomato growers to sign on to the Fair Food Program, family and community ties made it nearly impossible. Nonetheless, at the end of the first decade of the twenty-first century, there were tentative steps forward, even if they were sometimes followed by a quick return to the security of established positions. In 2009, East Coast Growers, in an attempt to rescue their overextended and floundering business, left the Florida Tomato Growers Exchange in the hope of capturing the market from the buyers who had signed Fair Food agreements. With the signal of East Coast's leaving the growers group, the FTGE rescinded its fine for cooperating with the Coalition but continued to refuse to sign on to the program. In February 2010, the tomato growers announced that they had established their own social responsibility program, similar in standards and methods to the wider SAFE program, but the growers also said they would pass on to the workers the penny-per-pound premium paid by the buyers who had signed Fair Food agreements. As had been true for SAFE, the new program mimicked the surface of the Coalition's Fair Food Program but refused to include the workers in enacting or enforcing the new standards and payments. Even more problematic for the growers, buyers, including McDonald's, said they would stick with the Fair Food agreement they had signed with the Coalition.

He was now in charge, but Jon Esformes understood that Pacific Tomato Growers was run by the Esformes and Heller families and that change could be slow. He had the responsibility but didn't yet have the authority to make the sweeping changes needed to treat farmworkers with the respect Jon believed they deserved. Battle lines had been drawn and were not easily crossed, particularly when the grower families had linked arms. It would not be easy for one company to break away.

In the fall of 2009, perhaps because of the pressure from the Navarrete case, both growers and workers seemed to consider taking a tentative step toward each other. The One Stop unemployment center in Immokalee provided a neutral site for Florida Tomato Growers Exchange members and Coalition of Immokalee Workers members to meet. Whatever hope either side had for some sort of agreement was abandoned as the two sides talked past each other. The CIW presented a vision of collaboration that included a prototype label design "Fair and Fresh from Florida." The growers made it clear they had no interest in working together. In Lucas Benitez's recounting, the Tomato Exchange's Reggie Brown made it clear that "we're here to tell you we will not work with you! We have SAFE. They can certify the tomatoes. We don't need you." As the two sides preached to their choirs, the Procacci owners somehow brought in a comparison with Philly sausages, and Lucas gave rapid-fire speeches in Spanish that required Julia Perkins to translate. The conversation, as Greg Asbed remembers, "pretty much died by itself for lack of oxygen."

After the meeting was over, a grower they had never met walked over to the CIW delegation as they got ready to leave. It was Jon Esformes. Handing Greg and Lucas his card, Jon caught them by surprise when he mysteriously said, "We should talk." The discussion ended there. The room cleared out and Lucas, Laura, Greg, and Julia headed back to their cars. Gathering back at the CIW office, the group reported back to some of the other CIW staff and members. Okay. The growers weren't interested in listening. But, we were "in the same room with them, at the same table, after years of their refusing to even recognize us. That was drama enough."

A business card wasn't enough to break from more than two decades of opposition and confrontation, but Jon was troubled by his company's, his family's, part in the battle. Practically, there was continuing market pressure as more commercial buyers signed on to the campaign. As important, the Campaign for Fair Food's code of conduct stood in real contrast to the standards declared by the SAFE program and the Florida Tomato Growers Exchange's next offering in April of 2010. The CIW's code of conduct had been developed by the workers and required their involvement in the monitoring and enforcement of its requirements. Jon knew that under Billy's leadership, Pacific had already made notable steps in improving working conditions on their farms, establishing a human resources department and reducing the independence of crew leaders. But how could he refuse to even *talk* with the Immokalee workers?

By the summer of 2010, Pacific Tomato Growers was reputationally and financially feeling the effects of the relentless hammering of new articles about slavery and abuse in the fields. Surprisingly, one of the retailers that staunchly refused (and still staunchly refuses) to work with the Coalition was the first to apply the market sanctions called for in the Campaign for Fair Food. Florida's largest grocery chain, the family-led Publix, had stopped purchasing tomatoes from Pacific and Six L's because of the earlier slavery connection.

As the furor increased, Pacific's board, composed entirely of Esformes and Heller family members, met in Florida. Harvey Heller, president of Heller Bros. Packing Company and managing partner of Pacific, reported with frustration that a family member had been accused by a business associate of being a slaveholder! With rising intensity, the board members complained bitterly about the Coalition and declared that they needed to be dealt with and pushed back. Pacific should sue the CIW for libel. As the furor increased, Jon Esformes jumped in and asked, "Have any of us ever met [the Coalition]?"

The answer was no.

Jon then asked, "And you trust the Tomato Exchange???"

The overwhelming response from around the table was, "But, they are *our people!*"

"No!" replied Jon. "They are our *competition!*"

Jon continued, making the case that the company needed to talk to the CIW to get their message directly, rather than through the Tomato Exchange. The board could then decide if they could work with the Coalition. The current situation was untenable. Murmurs around the room. Then someone suggested Pacific go with a couple of other growers. "No," Jon replied, referring to the meeting in Immokalee that had gone nowhere. "I'm interested in my perception of CIW, not theirs."

Deciding to take the next step is not the same as knowing how to do it. And perhaps, in retrospect, Billy Heller is not who Jon Esformes should have asked to have Pacific's first one-on-one discussion with the Coalition of Immokalee Workers. Old patterns are hard to break, and Pacific's first attempt had the positive of reaching out to the Coalition and the decidedly negative of bringing decades-old patterns and perspectives about power and who ran the farm. But Billy Heller did make that first visit to the Coalition's offices in Immokalee. Immokalee was not new to Billy. Pacific has a farm just down the road. What was new was walking into the CIW offices on Second Street, greeted by the banners from countless campaign actions declaring "Boot the Bell" and "Exploitation King!"

Billy Heller, despite not actually being a member of the co-owning Heller family, had been CEO of Pacific when Jon Esformes returned full-time to the company and took over as the operating partner. Billy then became the chief operating officer. Billy had been with the Pacific Tomato Growers companies since 2003 but in the produce industry for more than twenty years. Billy was held in high regard by the other tomato growers; he was vice president of the Florida Tomato Growers Exchange. These credentials are impressive evidence of Billy's accomplishments within the grower community, but they also made it less likely that Billy Heller would be able to step outside his usual role and be a disruptive force. You could use the phrase "old guard," but "good ol' boy" doesn't get it right. Billy grew up in a military family and had lived around the world. He'd fight for his position, but once a decision had been made, he was going to carry it out.

"Cease and desist" was the primary message Billy Heller brought from Pacific's board to the Coalition in the summer of 2010. Get Pacific Tomato Growers' name off your website, where it was linked to the Navarrete slavery case, or we're taking you to court. Both sides were still on a wartime footing and the Coalition responded in kind. Greg Asbed, Lucas Benitez, and CIW counsel Steve Hitov dismissed the threat. Pacific's name along with Six L's had been published in the press. There are no grounds for a suit, so waste your money if you will. The meeting quickly came to a close with the Coalition members saying, "If you're here to talk about the future of the industry, okay. If not, then the lawyers can talk."

"The first meeting with Billy is a bad memory," recounts Lucas Benitez. The Coalition was not truly surprised, even if they had allowed themselves the slightest hope that something would change. What the Coalition had missed, however, was that Billy Heller had a two-part message. Take Pacific's name off your website and we'll talk. In retrospect, the second part of the message was not simply a negotiating ploy. Then the phone in the Coalition's offices rang. It was Jon Esformes. Let's talk. Forget the lawsuit. I want to talk with you about the future of the industry. When the Coalition agreed to another meeting, Jon and Pacific kept this conversation quiet, even from their own corporate counsel.

This time, it was Jon's turn to walk across the gravel parking lot, past the chickens looking for bugs in the tired grass, and through the Coalition's front door on Second Street. Lucas was there, with Greg, Julia Perkins, and Gerardo Reyes. Billy had arrived with Jon. Steve Hitov joined by phone. Skepticism would be the polite term for what awaited Jon. The gathered group expected the same message Billy Heller had delivered at the last encounter, the same attitude the growers had offered for two decades. And, truth be told, the Coalition's own approach was still more confrontation than collaboration. Expressing the tension of the moment, Lucas explained, "The very first meeting with Jon was interesting. . . . First, we came from a rugged terrain with plenty of miscommunication in the industry [and] between Pacific and the Coalition. . . . We didn't know, from either party, how this conversation was going to go." What Lucas, Greg, and the others sitting around the table did not know was what drove Jon. As good a businessman as they come, determined to strengthen the business the Esformes and Heller families had built across generations, Jon was also committed to stay true to the values brought to life by Rabbi Mark and Harriet: "Seeing each person as an individual, as a human being with infinite value." Jon came into this first conversation with confidence in his own intelligence and instincts, but even stronger was the confidence that came from the foundation built at Beit T'Shuvah.

In fact, this meeting was the first time a tomato grower and the Immokalee workers "came to the table" figuratively as well as literally. Sitting at the long, beat-up conference table off to the side of the main meeting room, perhaps over a cup of coffee, Jon was characteristically direct. Looking at Greg, Jon said he was there to see if Greg, Lucas, and the other members of the Coalition were people he could work with. "I don't do business with people I don't like. If we don't like each other, we will not continue this conversation." Even this opening was different from any other interaction between the workers and the growers. In his directness was sincerity. It was, as Lucas describes, "an opportunity to sit down and see each other as we are, first as human beings and second as partners within the same industry." The systemic problems of a deeply troubled industry were not by any means solved in this first hour, but the anger and frustration were not there. Jon was genuine and honest, and the group connected as people who shared concerns for the future of the industry. The Coalition described their vision and argued that treating farmworkers with respect could differentiate Florida tomatoes in a commodity market. Even if unprecedented in agriculture, the logic was there and Jon saw the potential for shaping his company consistent with what he had learned at Beit T'Shuvah, with the possibility of its eventually being good for business.

The September meeting in Immokalee didn't last long, but it was a first step that required a leap. What mattered most, explained Lucas, was the taking of "that first step. We were standing on common ground at last, looking for a solution to everything that had happened over the course of many years." Discovering common ground provided the basis for Pacific and the Coalition to start to develop the understanding and mutual trust needed before any agreement could be signed. "We started from there. Open minds. Open hearts. On both sides, we put the past behind us and saw the future."

Greg Asbed talks about the remarkable and rapid evolution of this relationship. "For years we have been adversaries. We had been two groups that believed their interests were . . . forever . . . against each other. And yet, once we got the chance to sit down as people and talk . . . [we made] that human connection that just never existed before for us as an organization with anybody on the other side of the battle lines." Taking the analogy further, Greg compared these first conversations between a grower and the workers to the stories from World War I, "where people on Christmas Day came out of the trenches and spent the day playing soccer together and exchanging gifts, seeing [the other soldiers for] who they were. And we never went back to the trenches."

Negotiations went on for a couple of months, with Pacific's lawyer and the Coalition's counsel Steve Hitov working through the details. At least once, the connection established between Jon and Greg in that first meeting was critical. The lawyers were at an impasse, and so Jon and Greg got on the phone. Perhaps five to ten minutes of a two-hour call were spent on the details of the negotiation. Most of the conversation was about "who we are and what we think and what we believe. And we found we had a lot more in common than we ever knew." The connection between Greg and Jon moved beyond a shared vision for the future of the tomato industry. It went through their souls to reach back to their ancestors who had traveled through Turkey, Greece, Kurdistan, and Armenia as dispossessed and persecuted immigrants and refugees, eventually making their way to America and the promise it had long offered to those who had the courage and drive to start their lives over again. From such histories came an understanding of each other and of the farmworkers who asked to be respected in their labor.

"In a free society, few are guilty, but all are responsible." So spoke Jon Esformes on October 13, 2010, as he and Lucas Benitez announced Pacific Tomato Growers' agreement with the Coalition of Immokalee Workers. In signing the Fair Food agreement, Jon Esformes smashed through the decades-long, linked-arm resistance of the Florida tomato growers, providing the opening that brought down the dam and unleashed a transformation of Florida's tomato fields.

The actual agreement had come into place at the end of September, with Jon in the Coalition's offices signing with Lucas Benitez and the rest of the Coalition staff standing behind them. The press conference and announcement was held at Pacific. The day before the announcement, Jon "made a couple of phone calls" to growers he was close to, particularly Six L's and Gargiulo. Toby Purse at Six L's said, "Why didn't you come to me? We would have gone along." Agreeing this was likely true, Jon made it clear he was done with "groups." After the agreement, Pacific quit the Tomato Exchange and all other industry organizations that were voluntary. The other growers were "furious and pissed off," but Jon was fine with the disruption of the community, saying, "I don't want to be invited to their barbecues!"

The press conference for the announcement was a remarkable event. Rabbi Mark Borovitz was there, along with Coalition allies such as the leaders of the Interfaith Coalition, and Billy Heller was in the audience. Jon stood off to one side, listening as Lucas Benitez spoke for the Coalition and thanked Pacific, the Esformes and Heller families, and particularly Billy Heller and Jon Esformes. Both hands tucked into the pockets of his jeans, yellow plaid shirt untucked, and head cocked to one side as he listened, Jon didn't look like someone fearlessly disrupting an entire industry. Observed Rabbi Mark Borovitz, "Jon was alone" as he made the announcement of the new agreement without any of the other growers. The rabbi watched with pride as Jon declared, "For us, you wake up and you realize that maybe this is something we could have done yesterday, but I am certainly not going to wait until tomorrow." Pride joined with amusement for Rabbi Mark when one of the Interfaith clergy "turned white and then red with excitement" as he heard Jon Esformes quote Rabbi Heschel. "I never expected to hear Rabbi Heschel quoted by a farmer!"

This was not the last time the Coalition and its supporters would hear Jon Esformes quote rabbis or reflect on the importance of moving now. With the support of Pacific Tomato Growers' board and the company's partners, Jon continued to speak out publicly on the need for the industry to change and "the urgency of the situation." Mistreatment of workers and below-poverty wages were not only immoral; these abuses were undermining the industry as a whole. Talking much later about the requirements of the Fair Food Program, Jon made it clear where he stood. "What we're talking about here . . . are basic fundamental human rights and human dignities. We're talking about obeying the law. If you need to break the law to make your business model work—first of all, I hope you get caught. And, if you don't get caught, I hope you make the decision to get out of the business."

The Coalition of Immokalee Workers is unreserved in declaring that Jon Esformes was essential to the breakthrough with the growers, without which there might not be a Fair Food Program, and the growers certainly would not have signed at the end of 2010. The Coalition had unimaginable success ratcheting up the pressure on the growers with each new signing of a major corporation and continuing publicity about abuses in the fields and enslaved farmworkers. But as long as the growers, particularly large growers, presented a united front, there were no alternatives for those buyers who needed to buy American winter tomatoes. CIW's Steve Hitov draws a mental picture of a dam: "Pressure behind a dam. . . . I always thought of it as a beaver dam. As you remove sticks, it makes no difference but then you remove the key stick and the dam breaks and the water bursts through." Jon Esformes kicked out that key stick.

"We needed someone to think differently on the side of the growers. We needed a unique person. We needed someone who was not afraid to be different. And that was Jon." Greg Asbed continued,

> [Jon took] the lead that broke the resistance of the industry as a block. It allowed [the workers] to be part of the industry . . . and it recognized in us the humanity of the workers who have always been part of the industry but were not allowed at the table . . . to have a voice in decisions [about] their lives. . . . Without Jon doing that, I don't know who that person would have been. I don't know if it would have happened. In breaking with the other growers, Jon argued that the industry had to see this as a turning of the page, a new chapter, not just a marriage of convenience. For fifteen years, the growers declared that there was absolutely no abuse in the industry. Any discoveries of abuse or slavery were labeled "anomalies." Jon broke through that wall and paid a price for this break. Once he broke through, the others could not stop it. The denial was broken.

Within a week of Pacific Tomato Growers' announcing their agreement with the Coalition of Immokalee Workers, Larry Lipman was true to his word and led Six L's (now Lipman Produce) to sign the Fair Food agreement. Six L's was Florida's largest tomato grower. The two major growers, joined with the Coalition, could provide nearly all the tomatoes needed by the corporations that had signed Fair Food agreements over the previous decade, and if Gargiulo signed, they could cover the market. Now the Florida Tomato Growers Exchange realized they had no choice. The group's executive director Reggie Brown called the Coalition's offices. "We're interested in an agreement." On November 15, 2010—just over a year since the confrontation in the Immokalee unemployment center and a few months after Brown told author Barry Estabrook that the FTGE had no contact with the CIW—an unprecedented group gathered. In the sunny yard of the Coalition's offices, a yard often used by the children of tomato workers to play during the Coalition's meetings, the signing ceremony was about to take place. In the audience, sitting on folding chairs or standing on the edges with arms folded were Coalition members, including Greg Asbed and Laura Germino. The Reverend Noelle Damico was joined by members of the Interfaith Alliance and other clergy. At a table in front of the group were Lucas Benitez, Nely Rodriguez, and Geraldo Reyes from the Coalition, and Reggie Brown. The Tomato Exchange included 90 percent of Florida's tomato growers, and this industry-wide agreement between workers and employers was unprecedented. Growers were committing to following the Fair Food Program's code of conduct, to passing on the penny-per-pound premium paid by the participating corporations, and to acknowledging the workers as full partners. In fact, the tractor was going to join with the farmer in running the farm.

As always, Benitez looked somber and contained as he opened the proceedings. "With this agreement, the Florida tomato industry—workers and growers alike—is coming together in partnership to turn the page on the conflict and stagnation of the past and instead forge a new and stronger industry." Benitez then cautioned, a point later echoed in the Florida Tomato Growers Exchange statement, "This is the beginning, not the end, of a very long journey. But with this agreement, the pieces are now in place for us to get to work on making the Florida tomato industry a model of social accountability for the 21st century."

EYES WIDE OPEN

"What were you doing in the wee hours of this very day in 2007?" So opened the Reverend Noelle Damico in her sermon at Peace River Presbytery just a few days after Reggie Brown and the Florida Tomato Growers Exchange signed the Fair Food agreement with the Coalition of Immokalee Workers. Noelle spoke with a mixture of awe and pragmatism, reminding her audience of the recent Navarrete slavery case. "[A]s most of us were dreaming, Mariano Lucas hung from the ceiling inside the cargo hold of a box truck a few blocks off Main St. in Immokalee, punching his way through the ventilation hatch. . . . Mariano Lucas and other workers were chained, beaten, and locked in trucks at night, in order to deliver cheap produce, not simply to grocery stores and restaurants, but to you and me."

With that harsh reality now in our heads, Noelle turns to the scripture lesson for the day, Isaiah 65:17–25, using the "very church-y language" appropriate for this small congregation just about an hour and a half away from Immokalee. "When we hear stories of human anguish like that of Mariano Lucas and we consider the complexity and scope of the phenomenon of human trafficking, the prophet Isaiah's jubilant proclamation of well-being can feel hopelessly idealistic. He announces on behalf of God: There will be no more weeping or distress . . . [and then his] phrases crescendo to a climax: 'The wolf and the lamb shall feed together, the lion shall eat straw like the ox. . . . They shall not hurt or destroy on all my holy mountain.'" Noelle asks, "Is there some way to put Isaiah's vision into practice, given the real-world reality that predators always eat their prey? How might a wolf and a lamb be able to live together without the lamb becoming lunch?"

With her mind on the nine human trafficking cases that had been prosecuted since CIW began their antislavery work, Noelle expresses the likely frustration of any practical application of Isaiah's vision. "Case after case. Horror after horror. We imprison the wolf. We assist the lamb. But the cycle of predator and prey continues. So much for a realist application of Isaiah's prophecy." But then she brings us to what had just occurred that fall of 2010.

"This poetic vision from the prophet is not blind. It does not ignore the fact that there are wolves or lions in our world that devour lambs and oxen. The very power of this passage depends on the assumption that there are real predators and real prey. This poetic vision is honest. It demands that we keep our eyes wide open by naming the predators. There are real stakes. This poetic vision is surprising, though, because it gives us a glimpse of predator and prey reconciled."

Turning to the Coalition of Immokalee Workers and the major corporations, from Taco Bell to Burger King to Subway, that have signed Fair Food agreements, Noelle explains that "growers who turn a blind eye to slavery in their fields . . . now fac[e] market consequences as giant retailers are cutting their contracts with those who have been found to have used slave labor." And then she moves to the possibility of Isaiah's vision coming to life. "Three years ago this very day, Mariano Lucas punched his way out of the ventilation hatch of a cargo box truck. In 2010, the growers in whose fields he and his coworkers were forced to labor, Pacific and Six L's, have together with the FTGE forged a partnership with the CIW to address abuses together so that they can be eradicated once and for all."

"So when we hear the prophetic poetic words of Isaiah and think 'there's just no way,' I want you to think about the fact that the corporations that benefited from millions of cheap tomatoes and the growers who benefited by squeezing the cost of labor to the point of turning a blind eye to slavery in their fields, are now sitting at the table with the farmworkers that they used to devour."

"Wolves and lambs are being reconciled and are dedicating themselves to creating an industry where there are no more predators and prey, but people having faith in each other, respecting human rights, and working to hasten the day when the tomatoes that you and I eat were not produced through exploitation or slavery."

Noelle ends with realism drawn from a decade of leading Presbyterian Church USA's alliance with the CIW. "Is everything better? Not yet. Things don't change overnight, but change is under way right now as farmworkers, growers, corporations and consumers keep their 'eyes wide open' and work together with mutual respect and determination to create a food system that ensures the well-being of all."

Rev. Damico's sermon gives us a glimpse of the power of CIW's faith-based allies to motivate congregations to support the farmworkers. Wolves and lambs, predators and prey, these were just a few of the images crossing the minds of CIW's members and their allies that fall of 2010. The awe, the joy CIW members and their allies felt when nearly all of Florida's tomato growers signed the agreement with CIW was profound for those standing in the small yard behind the Coalition's offices. Nearly twenty years of work had paid off to a degree unimaginable to most outsiders and maybe even to those who had been doing the fighting.

But there are victories and there are victories. A dog with his teeth locked onto the bumper of a speeding car has caught his prey, but . . . what next? What's next is that this analogy didn't hold. Even before 2010, as Jon Esformes was considering reaching out to the Coalition, Greg Asbed, Lucas Benitez, Steve Hitov, and other members of the group had recognized that before there could be extraordinary change, the Campaign for Fair Food had to be more than an idea. It had to become an effective and enforceable Fair Food Program. Winning the battles against the fast-food chains and the growers were steps forward, but not enough. The CIW's goal was not signatures on agreements but real and measurable change in the lives of farmworkers. Paying attention to the end-game details, continuously learning and recalibrating, are essential if an idea is to result in actual change. This is where many ideas, public policies, and programs fail. A critical characteristic of the CIW is that unlike many other movements or causes, it paid at least as much attention to making the program real as it did to orchestrating the campaign that got the program on the table.

The roots of the Coalition's implementation planning can be traced back to those first meetings in the churchyard of Our Lady of Guadalupe, when the group's founders had focused on the worker community and its rights, rather than on legal battles for individual wrongs. By the late 1990s, the CIW's strikes and protests called on the Florida tomato industry as a whole to improve farmworker pay and end abuse in the fields, rather than attempting change through specific workplace-focused actions. Launching the Campaign for Fair Food, the CIW had taken a systemic perspective, linking together all elements of the food chain, from farmworkers to the major retail food corporations. Now each element of the food chain had to play its role in the new Fair Food Program: worker-driven rights and standards, a monitoring and complaint system that included investigation and resolution, and enforcement of workers' rights through market consequences.

First things first. If the CIW and corporate buyers were going to hold the growers accountable for the farmworkers' rights to safe working conditions and fair pay, workers and growers had to know what this meant. What were the standards and how would compliance be measured? This is where the wolves and lambs came in, although you have to think that there were days when it wasn't clear to those at the table who was playing which role. Eyes wide open, indeed.

It's a bit beat up, the long wooden conference table in an open room between Lucas's desk and the radio station. Now there are computers along one wall for farmworkers to check their latest Facebook posts from home, and some of the numerous awards and recognition for the CIW are on the walls. But there were fewer awards back when Jon Esformes of the Pacific Tomato Growers and Toby Purse of Six L's (soon to become Lipman) sat at the table with Greg, Lucas, Gerardo, and other CIW members. Steve Hitov was usually there at the beginning, later on calling in from Washington, DC. They had come to this table because at the press conference for the signing of the agreement between the Florida Tomato Growers Exchange and the CIW, Lucas and Reggie Brown had announced that the next step would be for Pacific Tomato Growers and Six L's to join with the CIW in a working group to turn the CIW's code of conduct into something that could be executed.

It turns out that moving from a statement of rights and standards to guidance and policies clear enough to be easily understood and carried out by growers, farmworkers, the growers' managers, and crew leaders would be a lot of work. The Coalition's code of conduct was just a few pages long. It was a bold declaration of farmworkers' rights and standards, including any and all legal requirements but then going far beyond. What the working group needed to figure out were the details needed to follow the code and evaluate compliance.

The code was divided into two sections. The first was "Employment Practices and Minimum Requirements for Participating Growers" and included participation in the "penny-per-pound premium pass-through Program," recording of all "compensable hours," direct hiring of farmworkers as employees by growers, health and safety requirements, transparency of all grower practices, and education of farmworkers on their legal rights and those contained in the code. The second section, "Violations," included a list of violations and their consequences, beginning with the most severe. The most severe violations—use of forced labor or illegal child labor—resulted in suspension of the grower from the program and a prohibition on buyers from purchasing tomatoes from the offending grower. Use or threat of physical violence by a supervisor or crew leader, use or display of weapons of any kind, and sexual harassment involving physical contact resulted in suspension if the grower did not immediately terminate the violator. The less severe violations—including sexual harassment not involving violence or physical contact, negligent endangerment, wage violations, retribution against a worker who filed a complaint—required a quick turnaround on mitigation and elimination of the offense. If a grower failed to take the corrective action, suspension would follow.

The agreement between the growers and the CIW was a significant accomplishment but the transition from confrontation to collaboration is rarely an easy one. The conflict between the CIW and the Florida Tomato Growers Exchange had been long, and postconflict negotiations are always tricky. Greg was fascinated by watching the changing dynamic between the workers and grower members of the working group. "[We] had been two groups that believed their interests were, or forever want to be, against each other, and yet, once we got the chance to sit down as people and talk," Greg concludes, "[w]e became a force that has changed the industry."

Billy Heller from Pacific occasionally joined Jon and Toby in the working group meetings. A bit later, the two growers were joined by Mike Sullivan from Gargiulo, Inc. and then, as Steve Hitov recalls, independent grower Jimmy Grainger. CIW's team was led by Greg and Steve and often included Lucas and Gerardo. Nely Rodriguez and Julia Perkins participated from time to time. Working group membership has remained essentially the same in the more than five years since it was established, with the exception of Jimmy Grainger, who later stepped down. A "guest grower" might join for a meeting or two when the group was working through a specific issue and, similarly, other CIW staff members might join a meeting to provide expertise.

Officially, the working group in 2011 (and still as of 2017) met quarterly in person and monthly over the phone, but the frequency then and now varies depending on the demands of the issues at hand. The dynamics of the initial group had to have been interesting and certainly complicated. It wasn't just a matter of having the CIW and the workers on one side and the growers on the other. Jon Esformes had ripped apart grower solidarity when he pulled out of the Florida Tomato Growers Exchange and signed the agreement with CIW in October 2010. But Gargiulo and Six L's were still in the Tomato Exchange and had to balance between the FTGE position and where Pacific was leading the growers. Jimmy Grainger was an independent grower and had been hard in opposition to the CIW and could not have been further away from Jon in his view of the new world. Jon was all-in but, as Steve Hitov points out, he was still a grower and a businessman. He was willing to make changes, even if they cost money, but he wasn't going to lose the family's business. Although he had embraced the concepts of the code and the CIW's human rights argument, Jon wasn't going to accept the requirements until he understood how they'd need to be implemented and enforced. Details matter. Jon looked back in 2014 and described the lineup of the growers during that first year and as the working group evolved with time: "Pacific is on the 'left' in terms of accountability. Lipman and Gargiulo are pragmatic; if Pacific does it, they have to or they look bad. Jimmy is a reaction-ary." Toward the end of 2011, Kent Shoemaker became CEO of Six L's/Lipman. Kent moved the company even further in its support of the Fair Food Program and later wrote about the program's benefits. Kent could do this because, as Jon explains, he had joined Lipman from the food distribution company Sysco. With his long experience with unions, Kent "knew [the Fair Food Program] was some-thing they had to get behind" and saw the benefits of getting in front of these issues.

The dynamic in the working group was sometimes stormy, but there were good reasons to include the growers in these efforts to translate the code of con-duct into operational guidance. The first was what Greg Asbed described as the "business case for the program"; real change could only come through what actu-ally happened in the growers' fields. The second was the CIW's recognition that the new Fair Food Program would not work unless the growers and workers could move from confrontation to collaboration. The CIW and the farmworkers had to "encourage them [the growers] to philosophically buy into the program" by making the specific changes in practice relatively easy to put in place.

It's one thing to state this transition in the abstract—sure, we all need to get along—but it is another to see it in action. Implementing the code of conduct meant paying attention to the small things, the details of running and working on a large-scale farm. Working through these details brought the farmworkers and growers closer. This was their business; it was how both sides earned a living and they all brought professional experience to the table. As it turned out, they each brought different, and usually complementary, expertise to the discussion. "The early days of the working group . . . the bland way of putting it was that it was a 'trust-building process.'" Steve continues thinking this through: "The par-ticulars of that is that we [CIW] had to establish our bona fides about knowledge in the field. Even though the CIW was workers, the growers didn't think we knew anything. The growers have their perception of what is going on in the fields and they sometimes don't have a clue. And the workers have their perceptions of what is going on the fields and sometimes they don't have a clue." CIW staff members who were regularly working in the tomato fields played a particularly active role in these early discussions since they had often been in the fields the week or even the day before.

Perhaps the turning point in these early days of figuring each other out was over a basic issue, the filling of tomato buckets. "Basic" it may be but working through what it meant to "fill" a bucket addressed one of the most significant trig-gers of violence in the tomato fields. Tomato pickers put the green field tomatoes into large buckets. Hoisting the buckets onto their shoulders, the workers run to the flatbed trucks parked in the rows, and toss the buckets up to the "dumpers" who empty the tomatoes into large bins and put a chit or ticket into the empty bucket and toss it back to the picker. A bucket filled to the rim weighs about thirty-two pounds and tomato workers are usually paid a piece rate, or price per bucket. The flash point was that crew leaders insisted that tomato workers pick more than a "full" bucket, mounding the tomatoes on top. This "*copete*" or the "cupping" of a tomato bucket can add as much as 10 percent more tomatoes by weight. Crew leaders are paid by weight, not by buckets. The *copete* was an easy way for crew leaders to make extra money, effectively one free bucket of tomatoes for every ten picked. If a farmworker tossed a bucket of tomatoes up to the "dumper" on the truck without the *copete*, he was likely to have it thrown back at his face or simply dumped on the ground. Frustration and disagreements over how tomato buckets were filled frequently resulted in threats of violence, fights, or beatings.

Not surprisingly, given its worker-driven origin, prohibition of cupping was in the earliest versions of the CIW's code of conduct. "Growers will regularly reconcile wages paid, including buckets picked, to pounds harvested, and if that reconciliation indicates uncompensated pounds harvested, using a 32-pound bucket for calculation for round 'gas green' tomatoes . . . the Grower shall adjust the amount paid to Workers in the next payroll so that they are fully paid for the uncompensated pounds." The language of the code was clear, a bucket of picked tomatoes weighed thirty-two pounds. But this is where the working group was needed. A bucket of tomatoes is a bucket of tomatoes, but how do you actually fulfill this requirement? Given the speed and rhythm of the work, you couldn't weigh each bucket in the field.

This then is where the magic began, or at least where the working group figured out how to solve problems together. After a lot of back and forth, they came up with the idea of a "visual standard" for what it meant to have a "full" bucket of tomatoes. Greg describes the scene as the group worked through this fundamental issue. "The discussion was open and it didn't matter who offered the ideas . . . with the growers and all of the [CIW] staff members pulling out buckets and working on how to implement [the code]. All of us realized that you could not make the [code's] standard weight-based since you cannot be weighing the buckets in the field. The group also realized that you couldn't allow any [tomato] above the rim of the bucket because this loophole would be exploited and the requirement [for pickers would] mushroom. So, it was a big deal for all of us to say, 'a bucket is a bucket and no more.' This simple standard, 'no single tomato can be above the rim,' avoids all disputes."

Methodically moving through the code, opponents who had only disdain for each other "got to a place where both sides felt they were doing business with someone they could work with." Their expertise established, Greg and Steve became the primary CIW working group representatives, calling in the other members for specific issues. The working group sessions were not just all kum-baya. They had a lot of work to do and needed concrete results. The code of conduct that existed when the growers signed their agreement with the CIW was, as Steve describes it, "accurate in reflecting what workers care about in concept" but it was intentionally kept short. The code of conduct was about six pages long with thirty-two requirements or standards. The working group had to make their way through each of these, providing the detail needed to enact and measure each. The product was the "Guidance for Implementation of the Fair Food Code of Conduct," usually referred to, poetically, as the "Guidance Manual."

Forty-three pages long, the Guidance Manual is of note for its clarity and use-fulness, and it could well serve as an example for government and private-sector organizations moving from "policy" to implementation. For each element of the code, the Guidance Manual states the original language from the code and then more detailed "policies," which apply to the farmworkers as well as the growers. In the case of the definition of a full tomato bucket, Policy 3.1 explains, "Cupping of buckets is not permitted under the Code, nor is fluffing of buckets by [farm] Workers. A bucket is cupped if any tomato in the bucket is fully above the rim of the bucket. Fluffing is shaking a bucket to make it appear fuller than it actually is. In addition, no bucket shall weigh more than 34 pounds gross. A properly filled bucket is pictured immediately below." And then there is a photo of two buckets: "*Con copete*" with a red X over the bucket and "*Nuevo Estandar sin copete*" with a check mark on the bucket.

Another requirement of the code has to do with accurate recording of all hours worked. The requirement itself seems fairly simple: "All compensa-ble hours shall be recorded, and Growers will keep accurate hours through a system . . . in which employees control their time cards." For those working in an office or factory, it might not take much explanation to understand the require-ment. For agricultural labor, however, this requirement was exceptional, and how to implement was not at all clear. Farmworkers are often paid through piecework if they are harvesting, not through time on a clock. For those activities paid for at an hourly rate, perhaps staking tomatoes, the crew leaders often reported the time worked. For those paid for hourly work or to determine whether workers made at least minimum wage, the question on the table was always when "time worked" actually began. It was standard practice for buses to arrive early to the fields and the farmworkers to sit on the bus until the dew dried and they could pick the tomatoes. At the end of the day, workers often had to wait while the crew leader counted bucket tickets for each worker. Waiting time was not included when the crew leaders figured out time worked.

And so, once again, the working group had to think through the detail needed to implement and confirm this requirement. In this case, the resulting section in the Guidance Manual includes three policies further explaining the code's requirement: workers should clock in as soon as they arrive and just as they leave the grower's property; those workers who arrive on their own should clock in at the directed arrival time, whether or not work begins then; and, most importantly, workers themselves control their time cards and clock themselves in. This section of the Guidance Manual also includes five detailed examples of how to implement this requirement. If a worker drives to the farm and arrives an hour earlier than his or her starting time, the worker does not get paid for that hour. If the grower provides transportation for the workers and they arrive an hour before they can begin work, the workers must be paid for that hour. And the Guidance Manual prohibits crew leaders or bus drivers from picking up workers very early and then parking at the convenience store near the farm for an hour before driving onto the farm at the appointed time, while also allowing for the traditional gas station or convenience store stop so that workers could pick up food and drinks.

What is notable about the combination of the code of conduct and the Guidance Manual is the focus on what it would take to make the requirements and standards "implementable" and therefore real in terms of changing the practices of the farms and the working lives of the workers. The US government routinely uses detailed regulatory guidance to provide further explanation of congressional legislation, but anyone who has worked in government knows that it is all too rare that that the regulations make the law easy to understand for those who have to carry it out. The Guidance Manual, however, explains the code's standards in clear language with practical examples that come directly from working on tomato farms. As a result, the Guidance Manual strengthens the code by providing specifics that can be both implemented and measured.

Stepping back and looking at the combination of the code and the Guidance Manual, CIW's attorney Steve Hitov makes the case that they are the foundation of a "privately negotiated 'legal system.'" In establishing this legal system, the first requirement ensures that "no worker gives up any legal right, or cause of action, that he or she now has or in the future may acquire." Beyond these individual, government-originated legal rights, the code and its guidance "emphasizes community as opposed to individual rights and justice." The strength of a community-based, rather than individual-centered, approach to rights goes back to the argument Greg and Laura made when they went to work at Florida Rural Legal Services in the early 1990s. Steve extends the argument, explaining that "focus on the community as opposed to individuals makes it possible for the CIW to ensure the protection of the rights of all covered farmworkers, "whatever their legal status" and even if they have "been excluded from large swaths of the formal legal system." And, one should note, this applies whether or not the workers are formal members of the Coalition of Immokalee Workers. At least as interesting is the Fair Food Program's move beyond the traditional union approach, centered on employer agreements with grievance and arbitration processes, to the full worker community within an industry. Steve argues that "the communal nature of the approach . . . [has the] potential to improve the industry as a whole, and therefore the working and living conditions of all workers, as opposed to . . . making 'whole' individual workers who have been harmed in some way."

It is one thing to have a set of standards and requirements and quite another to ensure those standards are carried out. Many corporate social responsibility programs have established standards for their suppliers. As we learn time and again, "compliance" is where many, often well-intentioned, social responsibility codes and standards fall down. The social responsibility monitoring and audit organizations are for-profit and nonprofit companies whose services are paid for by major corporate buyers. Audits are often tied to corporate standards and codes of conduct for the buyer's supply chain. These codes may focus more narrowly on workplace safety or more broadly to include worker pay and working conditions. And, as James Brudney writes, "the regulatory landscape in which voluntary compliance programmes typically operate is a far cry from the U.S. or European settings." The buyers, usually major retail chains, have set the standards for reasons of good intentions and to protect their brands. In the global supply chain, workers may be afraid of speaking out and consumers may have little knowledge about pay or working conditions in other countries or in long-ignored sectors such as agriculture or low-wage production. Unfortunately, there's a high likelihood of conflicts of interest with such arrangements as buyers trade off between costs and the rigor of inspections while also worrying about their relationships with preferred suppliers. At least as prevalent a problem are the workarounds made by factory owners who use unauthorized subcontractors or deliberate deception to fool inspectors. We don't have to look far to find recent, high-profile examples of the difficulty of getting standards to have meaning. On April 23, 2013, in Bangladesh, the Rana Plaza clothing manufacturing factory that supplied Walmart, among other major US companies, collapsed, killing 1,129 workers and injuring about 2,500 more. Like another Bangladesh factory that had suffered a major fire just a few months before, the problem was not that the Rana Plaza factory complex didn't have safety standards. Nor was the issue that no one had set up a monitoring program for these standards. In fact, as reported in a *New York Times* article published a few months after the Rana Plaza disaster, Bangladesh factories had been monitored for safety and working conditions for at least twenty years and the number of audits had increased as the country became one of the world's largest garment exporters. Why weren't the factory standards and audits sufficient? The experience of the Fair Food Program argues that corporations cannot establish relevant and useful standards without the on-the-ground knowledge of the workers. And external audits alone cannot provide the depth of inspection or persistence of monitoring needed to ensure workplace safety and are vulnerable to being gamed by owners and managers.

Safety and working condition audits through corporate-driven social responsibility programs had become big business by the time the CIW was establishing the Fair Food Program in early 2011. Auditors and monitoring organizations have largely focused on factories. Going back to the concern in the mid-1990s with Nike using "sweatshops" to manufacture workout gear and shoes, consumers and advocacy groups frequently criticized major retailers for the unsafe working conditions and poor pay at their suppliers. Protecting corporate brands demanded responding to these charges. In the 1990s and 2000s, Nike, Walmart, the Gap, and other major retailers established standards and codes for their overseas suppliers and hired social responsibility monitoring or audit companies to monitor compliance. Corporate responsibility business soared in the early 2010s, with 50 percent growth in the largest of the monitoring companies over just a few years.

Companies in the "corporate social responsibility" or "social auditing" field include Verité, SGS Group, AccountAbility, Social Accountability International, Fair Labor Association, and Intertek, whom we met earlier in the Navarrete case. They are essentially consulting firms that conduct audits of manufacturing, electronic, energy, food and beverage, and (more recently) agricultural sectors; provide certification of social responsibility programs; advise companies on establishing corporate social responsibility standards; and provide research support. It would not be unfair to label the track record of this growing sector as mixed. Audits may be thorough or surprisingly brief, depending on the quality of the auditor and the preferences of the company paying for the service. Across the board, auditors were unable to uncover violations of social responsibility standards. For example, in August 2012, Social Accountability International's inspectors gave SA8000 certification, meaning it met nine international standards, to the Ali Enterprises factory in Karachi, Pakistan. Just weeks later, in September 2012, the factory burned to the ground, killing more than 260 people. Similarly, also in 2012, the Fair Labor Association declared after inspecting Foxconn, a supplier of Apple products, that working conditions were improving and a "genuine transformation is underway." Soon after, the Economic Policy Institute (a nonprofit think tank focused on low- to middle-income labor) found to the contrary; working condition improvements were "modest, fleeting, or purely symbolic." EPI also found violations in record keeping of hours and pay that FLA had missed.

The challenge faced by even well-intentioned corporate buyers and social audit organizations is the limitations of an audit-centric approach to monitoring compliance with standards. "Check the box" and cookie-cutter approaches to audits will likely miss the particulars for a specific industry or workplace. Workers can easily be coached by supervisors to deceive auditors. Factory owners and supervisors can prepare for an audit when they know the inspectors are coming. Heather White, founder of Verité, sums up the risk in a 2013 *New York Times* article: "It starts a dream, then it becomes an organization, and it finally ends up a racket."

The Bangladesh factory tragedies were still a few years away when the Coalition of Immokalee Workers began to take concrete steps toward making the Campaign for Fair Food's aspirations real through establishing and implementing the Fair Food Program. CIW members knew they needed some sort of third-party organization to monitor the growers' compliance with the code of conduct. Steve Hitov recalls that "Greg and I reached out to four or five commercial auditing companies." They also "read something like fifteen sets of standards" to understand what others were doing in social responsibility. CIW members were aware of the weaknesses of the social auditing industry. Many of the buyers who had signed Fair Food agreements had standards and conducted audits. "But, we knew that it wasn't what you said, it was what you did." Audits weren't the purpose; they should be one of the means to enforce standards. Even before Jon and the other growers signed on, Greg, Steve, and the CIW imagined a new approach to compliance, linking together standards, monitoring, and resolution. Effective monitoring required audits that went into far greater depth than standard factory audits plus a complaint line so that workers could report concerns. Finally, the CIW wanted a process that would resolve problems and improve the system, not simply report violations.

The Coalition of Immokalee Workers had been getting great press as one fast-food giant after another signed on in the late 2000s. So when they initially called, the auditing companies were eager to get involved; this was an opportunity to move into the agricultural industry. Enthusiasm declined when Greg and Steve explained what they believed needed to be done. "Just not what we do." Several of the companies simply stopped returning the CIW's phone calls, believing the task impossible (and certainly not one where they could make some money). In the end, CIW went with Verité, one of the most well-known of the social responsibility monitoring organizations. A nonprofit corporation, by 2009 Verité had been working with Patagonia and building a good reputation. When CIW, Pacific Tomato Growers, and Six L's (Lipman) launched the pilot, Verité appeared to be the professional organization that could teach the CIW how to do this work and carry it off with credibility.

Few things are easy when breaking new ground, a truism verified in CIW's experience with Verité. Verité, perhaps not surprisingly, had little knowledge of the agricultural industry, not to mention the specifics of operating and working on Florida's large tomato farms. This was a new area for most, if not all, of the commercial audit firms. In early 2011, Sean Sellers moved from the Student/ Farmworker Alliance office at CIW in Immokalee to Sarasota, Florida, and "embedded" with Verité. "I did a whole season of shadow monitoring, learning what was and was not adaptive to this environment." What he, Greg, and Steve learned was that where CIW wanted to go really was virgin territory. Typical of the social auditing industry, Verité used a model similar to a large consulting firm: templates and checklists combined with standardized and replicable processes to minimize the amount of time spent in the audit or reporting. Auditors used standardized questions often augmented with questions provided by the companies being audited. Although they were most likely to know where problems of abuse, safety, or wage theft occurred, workers were not involved in developing questions. Consistent with factory and other workplace audits, Verité usually interviewed about 5 percent of the workers on a farm and viewed interviewing 10 to 15 percent of the workers as exceptional. The percentage didn't change regardless of the farm's having 30 or 600 farmworkers. Sean Sellers recalls with amazement that "one early Fair Food Program auditor trained by Verité described a visit to an organization with thirty workers and explained they had interviewed six. Why wouldn't they just interview all of the workers? Samples are for large populations, not small ones where you can talk to everyone." Additionally, workers wouldn't risk talking to the outside audit teams because they didn't know them and weren't sure they could be trusted to maintain confidentiality, and history justified the fear of being fired if they spoke up. Perhaps the greatest frustration was with the Verité audit teams' lack of knowledge of the industry. The combination of the code of conduct and the Guidance Manual developed by the working group had resulted in more than four hundred standards and requirements for the teams to monitor. The brief, standardized audits weren't getting into the details and and it was easy to fool the outside teams.

As the pilot season came to an end, the CIW staff realized that the problem was not just Verité. It was unlikely that any existing social auditing organization would be effective. Sean points out that there was value from the CIW's experience. "Verité served as a bridge at the moment. They provided some training and some credibility for the monitoring effort," but auditors "parachuting in" wasn't going to work. CIW needed indigenous expertise and to have monitoring embedded in the farms, not just showing up for audits. "Look," says Steve Hitov, "we knew we wanted audits. We knew we wanted a complaint line. We knew we wanted worker education. We knew this before we learned there were no commercial firms that could do all of this." The CIW and the Fair Food Program were, as later described by Judge Laura Safer Espinoza, "blaz[ing] new ground. There were no roadmaps, or 'experts' with truly relevant experience to consult."

The clock was ticking. The pilot season was coming to a close in the spring of 2011. In the fall, the first full season of the Fair Food Program would begin, with the program expanding across Florida and including about thirty growers. Greg, Lucas, Steve, Laura, and the other leaders of the CIW believed "none of the gains recently won through twenty years of commitment and sacrifice would become real, unless the monitoring and enforcement . . . made them so." Weak, inept, easily gamed monitoring and enforcement would lose the respect of the growers and risk losing the opportunity to change the conditions in the fields. The appearance of monitoring wasn't enough. The Fair Food Program needed much more.

If the big-name commercial social auditing companies couldn't do the job, how then could the CIW get the needed expertise and "embedded" monitoring they believed was necessary for the success of the Fair Food Program? The CIW concluded they would have to do it themselves. A decade before, CIW founders and members completely changed the way farmworkers thought about the food chain and how to change it. Now, to ensure that the worker-centered code of conduct was more than an idea, they would just have to create an entirely new approach to compliance monitoring and enforcement. They'd build their own, a third-party agency focused solely on the tomato industry, at least for now. The new organization would be responsible for monitoring and enforcing the standards and requirements of the code of conduct and the Guidance Manual for not only the growers but for the buyers and the workers as well.

They needed to move quickly. Steve got to work writing bylaws and incorporating the new organization. Meanwhile, Greg, Laura, and the rest of the CIW staff worked on position descriptions and recruiting the people they'd need. It wasn't that clear how to staff the new organization. The first challenge, of course, was that a compliance monitoring organization like the CIW imagined didn't exist. The new Fair Food Program system needed compliance monitoring that could not easily be gamed, a process for responding to violations, and effective sanctions for violations that were not corrected. The second challenge was also nontrivial: How could the CIW, working with a shoestring budget, afford to establish this new enterprise? And the third? Finding the right people to build the Fair Food Standards Council at the same time they were conducting audits and investigations for the first full season of the program. Truth be told, this was a bit like building an airplane while flying it.

FORGING THE PATH BY WALKING IT

About the same time the working group began their deliberations, Laura Safer Espinoza moved with her husband to Florida's west coast. After a career as a Legal Services attorney and then a New York State Supreme Court justice, she now found herself in retirement, supporting her husband's dream of leaving New York's winters for life in sunny Florida. When she first ran for office at thirty-eight, Laura had been one of the youngest civil court judges elected to the bench in New York State. Her philosophy on the bench emphasized problem solving rather than only punishment. Mental health or addiction problems were common in the courtroom. The judge believed that when the only option was locking them up, the court was failing, feeding the cycle of incarceration, release, and a quick return to jail. Likely true, but the limits of the court system didn't give the judge and her judicial colleagues a lot of options. It was time to try something new, and that something was the Bronx Treatment Court, which she led the way in helping to create and then becoming its first presiding judge. Treatment Court offered a nonadversarial alternative to incarceration, as those who pled guilty were sentenced to drug and alcohol or mental health treatment. The alternative court was in stark contrast to the harsher, three-strikes approach prevalent then, but as the new court succeeded in reducing recidivism, it became a model for similar courts established in New York and across the country.

But that was then and this was now, a new phase of life for the judge. Retirement had its pluses. Florida's Fort Myers was lovely, of course. Restless in her new retirement, Judge Laura was able leverage her experience into setting up part-time consulting work, directing judicial training programs in Latin America. As she recalled her first years in Florida, "I had a great gig . . . leading State Department–funded workshops with a couple of trainings a month. We [Laura and her husband] would both go and stay in Mexico for a bit as I ran these in Latin America, training judges, prosecutors, and defense attorneys as they moved into oral, adversarial trial systems from written, inquisitorial systems. . . . It was a great life!"

But while interesting and enjoyable, the training program was just a few days each month. Playing neither golf nor tennis, Laura had discovered not long after arriving in Fort Myers that she was nowhere near ready for a life of country clubs and ladies who lunch. And the State Department work didn't take advantage of her real skill in solving problems. Listening to the radio one day, she "heard a . . . program describing parts of southwest Florida as 'ground zero for modern day slavery.' Federal prosecutors of human trafficking cases had given it this label that was so incongruous with the beautiful surroundings of our home." Newspaper coverage that followed the Florida Tomato Growers Exchange's signing of the Fair Food agreements with the CIW further caught her attention. She headed online to learn more.

The CIW was on to something with the Fair Food Program. And that something resonated with Laura's experience in the Bronx. "I saw another groundbreaking effort to move beyond adversarial relationships to put an end to deep-rooted problems." She realized that "I could be part of this." Laura wasn't sure how she could fit in with the Immokalee effort. Perhaps the CIW would set up some sort of board for compliance hearings and could use her help? Surely there was something she could do. And so in the summer of 2011, the judge e-mailed Laura Germino, offering to help in any way, stuffing envelopes or whatever might be useful.

Establishing a wholly new type of institution takes time, just what the CIW didn't have. Sean Sellers remembers, "Days and months were ticking by and we were getting more nervous." After deciding they had enough funding to hire six people for the Fair Food Standards Council, Greg Asbed and Steve Hitov finalized the position descriptions. They'd need several investigators, including one with expertise in financial audits. An experienced attorney was essential for staying current on applicable laws and regulations as well as working with Steve on the agreements with growers and buyers. And then there was the executive director. They weren't asking for much, really. The job announcement called for "Experience in human rights, workers' rights or some other field of social change. . . . Experience working with immigrant populations. . . . Familiarity with negotiating and enforcing contracts. . . . Fundraising experience [and] significant public speaking experience." Plus, a proficient Spanish speaker with a master's degree or equivalent with excellent management skills and the ability to work across "a broad array of constituencies, including immigrant workers, growers, [and] Fortune 500 companies." And, oh by the way, the new executive director would also need to lead and build an organization that had never before existed. Easy!

As Laura Germino, Greg, Steve, and the CIW's network of allies worked their networks and advertised the new positions, they received applications from enthusiastic potential investigators. They were about to entrust the gains from twenty years of work to this new organization, and so they had to have someone from the CIW become part of the new staff. Putting together a short list of current CIW staff members, Sean Sellers ended up at the top. Looking back, Laura Safer Espinoza made the case. "[Sean] had dedicated much of his life to this program. Sean was that guy who had the trust and the knowledge. . . . Sean is a great communicator." Sean had never picked tomatoes, but he had joined the CIW's watermelon crew, learning from the CIW members he worked with in Florida and Georgia. "I had experience working with the growers and supervisors [and it] helped provide a reality check" on life in the fields, learning from, and working with CIW members. Added to his experience shadowing the Verité auditors, Sean was an essential hire.

But the CIW still needed the new executive director. With the announcement of the position in July 2011, they got plenty of applications ranging from good people without the needed experience to the truly "batshit crazy." Laura Safer Espinoza's e-mail to Laura Germino arrived not long after. "I shared my background and offered . . . to do anything needed. I wasn't looking for a job—I didn't even have a resume." Looking for a job or not, it was difficult for Laura, Greg, and Steve not to consider the possibility of divine intervention.

Laura let the judge know the CIW greatly appreciated her interest in volunteering. Why don't we meet for lunch at the coffee shop in Ava Maria? Greg Asbed and Steve Hitov would be there too. Sensing she may be getting into more than she intended with this volunteer opportunity, Laura Safer Espinoza invited her husband to come along. She found herself "across the table from the founders of CIW who listened respectfully" to her offers to help out with hearings or other legal work. After being atypically patient, Steve then said, "You didn't realize that the entire thirty years of your career was destined for this one moment." When her husband exclaimed, "But she was only going to volunteer one to two days a week," Greg, Laura Germino, and Steve declared that Laura (now referred to as "Judge Laura" to avoid the obvious confusion) had to become the founding director of the Fair Food Standards Council. They were right. And she said yes.

Judge Laura was the last hired of that initial Fair Food Standards Council, officially taking on the role of executive director when the organization opened for business on November 1, 2011. She quickly discovered that the argument the CIW had made was true: the skills she had gained from years on the bench and in her earlier years as a Legal Services lawyer were not a bad match at all for the new FFSC. "Interpreting the Code of Conduct, drafting findings, negotiating corrective actions, and communicating with participating growers were tasks for which my experience had prepared me well." Her title of "Judge" turned out to be invaluable for gravitas and credibility in dealing with buyers and growers. Whatever they think of this vertically challenged woman from New York City, the growers always come back to "but she's a judge." The title had value but the reality was that the executive director had to do the grinding grunt work that faced all the new staff members. But the early days of the Bronx Treatment Court, working with "one assistant, a cramped courtroom, and a shoestring budget," offered up yet one more experience for the judge to draw upon. The office for the new FFSC was better, but the skeleton team and little money were familiar.

There were more than two of them on November 1, but not much more as the team of six took on the first full-fledged execution of the Fair Food Program with all the elements in place. Working over the summer, Greg and Steve had identified and developed a first-order design for the major elements of the FFSC. The CIW was the parent organization; it was responsible for negotiating agreements with the corporate buyers and it had developed the code of conduct and the Guidance Manual. The FFSC would enforce these agreements and the code. Their tools would be operational and financial audits, a complaint system, investigations, complaint resolution or "corrective action plans," and sanctions for those growers that did not come into compliance. The CIW's worker education program would ensure workers knew their rights.

It was critical that the Fair Food Standards Council operate independent of the Coalition staff. Although there was day-to-day overlap, it was more a matter of complementary responsibilities than integration. Lindsay Adams, a monitor/investigator for the FFSC, explains how it worked out: "It's a Venn diagram in some situations but they are our parent organization . . . the CIW does worker education while we do monitoring of code compliance. . . . The CIW chose to establish the FFSC to do third-party monitoring." The Campaign for Fair Food continued, encouraging and pressuring major corporate buyers, fast-food chains, and grocery chains to sign Fair Food agreements. The more buyers in the program, the greater the leverage the CIW had to enforce the code with growers, the greater the benefit to participating growers, and the more buyers contributing the penny-per-pound premium. Much of what the CIW does is intended to get people to care, and even be excited, about agricultural labor rights and working conditions. This is not the role of the FFSC. Judge Laura points out that "the campaign is a lot more fun than FFSC work . . . documentation and databases are a whole nother skill set. . . . It is very important to understand that the FFSC and its staff are not flag-waving campaigners [and] the FFSC does not participate in actions." She picks up on these thoughts in a later conversation. "Governance is different from a campaign. [As with the CIW] people sign up to work with the FFSC because of their passion, and we have to transform them into professional-acting, objective fact finders, respectful in collaboration and in the relationship with the growers."

The differences in culture of the two organizations today can be seen immediately. Walking into the CIW offices in Immokalee, you'll see walls covered with campaign and other protest banners. Staff members are likely wearing CIW T-shirts, perhaps asking "Is your food fair?" calling for "Justice for Farmworkers," or announcing the Coalition. The campaign is a movement, with hard-fought and hard-won victories. A sense of "the struggle" is often palpable in the CIW's offices, particularly when allies are in Immokalee for popular education and to prepare for the next action.

The principles established by the strike leadership in 1995 are still to be found in the CIW's offices. The majority of CIW's staff members are current or former farmworkers. Staff members are paid the same salary—whether they started work with CIW last week or twenty years ago—a salary commensurate with wages earned by workers in the fields today. Most live in and around Immokalee. CIW staff members only recently began to receive health insurance, but they earn no other benefits, again because benefits are not common in the fields. CIW's staff is supplemented by volunteers or interns paid for by alliance members, particularly the Student/Farmworker Alliance and faith-based groups. Many work for housing and a small stipend. In addition to their commitment to the CIW's work, CIW members are smart, on-message, and excellent communicators.

The FFSC office is not in Immokalee, the agricultural labor hub, but in Sarasota, on Florida's Gulf Coast and home to the Ringling Brothers Circus museum. Judge Laura explains the separate locations are in part because "it helps with recruiting and is centrally located for Florida farms. [But] the optics are also important. The FFSC is a separate organization from the CIW [and] it provides professional office space to meet with growers, crew leaders, and buyers." When the team is out in the fields monitoring or conducting investigations, they look different from the farmworkers and the CIW staff. The choice is deliberate. You won't see a CIW T-shirt or hat. The FFSC is a third-party monitor. The sartorial choice is along the lines of REI hiking wear, or the Target equivalent. Hiking pants and long-sleeved button shirts with generic baseball caps are the typical uniform of audit teams. None of the FFSC members so far have been farmworkers, but many are second-generation, Spanish-speaking Americans. Most of the investigators are between twenty-five and thirty-five years old, mature enough to handle difficult situations in the field and young enough to deal with the working conditions, hours, and travel. You will probably not, however, hear any complaints about the physical demands from the successful investigators, since they all know that the workers have even greater physical stress. It was 96° F with 95 percent humidity and a heat index well above 100° F when one of the crew leaders asked an investigator if she'd like to get out of the sun. While an observer took advantage of the shade from a crew bus, the FFSC investigator responded, "Nope. I don't mind the sun. If the farmworkers can handle it, then I can as well."

Like the CIW staff, Fair Food Standards Council's investigators and monitors tend to be smart. Good communication skills are a must. The FFSC's work combines formal auditing with detective work, counseling, and arbitration. Speaking at the beginning of the second full season of the Fair Food Program, Greg Asbed got a bit giddy talking about what was going on. "FFSC is like the Mod Squad, young people taking an alternate approach to law enforcement for labor rights." Although CIW had known they needed legal and financial auditing skills when building the initial staff, they did not yet fully understand the difference between the CIW's needs and those of the new FFSC. Judge Laura explains where they started and how the requirements have evolved: "We didn't understand the needed skill sets for the FFSC work; they were not as sharply understood. . . . We thought that if a person said 'human rights are good' and spoke Spanish that was great. But this is not enough and those with only these basic attributes don't necessarily do well." Like the requirements for the executive director, the requirements for "investigators," the primary positions, are demanding. "Passion for the cause" of protecting human rights is a starting point, but it needs to be coupled with a wealth of specific skills. Successful investigators have "analytical minds" and the "ability to think not anecdotally but systematically." They must write well and have good quantitative skills. The work is physically demanding, with day after day spent traveling to farms and interviewing workers in the fields. Investigators "need stamina and wisdom, stamina and professionalism . . . the maturity and sophistication to develop a rapport with [farm] management and workers."

So, where does the FFSC find its staff? Most have master's degrees or law degrees, and the Latin American Studies program at UT–Austin, the program Sean Sellers attended, has been a good source. The need for fluent bilingualism, with language that allows them to deal with workers and management, would tend to select for those whose families recently immigrated to the United States, but first-generation college-goers often have college debt and less flexibility to pursue jobs that don't pay particularly well. As a result, few of the FFSC are first-generation immigrants, even if their families have recent immigrant roots. Talking with some of the FFSC investigators highlights the characteristics they share.

Veronica Musa graduated from the University of Florida, where she had taken part in the Taco Bell boycott. Veronica received her law degree and then joined the FFSC. Matt Wooten is a Fulbright Scholar and a friend of Sean's from the UT program, with a specific interest in farmworker issues in the American South. Mike Towler was the only full-time financial investigator in the first year or two of the FFSC. He has the lead on payroll audits and tracking and reconciling the Fair Food premium. Graduating with an accounting degree from Georgetown University, Mike initially followed the expected path to the consulting firm KPMG. "I worked for KPMG for about a year and a half and then started thinking there has to be something more!" Mike is starting to get at the deep sense of commitment to supporting the CIW that motivates the FFSC crew. The FFSC staff members who thrive in the work have a profound respect for the farmworkers, the fights they've won, and the program the CIW has designed. Lindsay Adams is another UT–Austin alumna who "moved halfway across the country with two kids to take this job." Asked about how she manages the fifteen-hour days and travel as part of the monitoring or audit teams, she is quick to reply. "Farmworkers manage this kind of schedule with kids so I have no complaints about the juggling." Like Lindsay and Sean Sellers, most of the FFSC staff got to know of the Campaign for Fair Food in college. Some were members of the Student/Farmworker Alliance. Victor Yengle connected with the campaign in 2009 and became part of the FFSC staff in 2013. His Peruvian parents and grandparents moved to the United States as political refugees. There's pride when Victor describes the willingness of his engineer father to work in a car wash to support his family. Eventually invited to join the FFSC staff, Victor remembers, "I have to admit I was thrilled when I began working with Lucas and Gerardo." Others have joined the FFSC staff after working for unions or NGOs, but those who make it have strong analytical skills, often honed with an advanced degree.

When the FFSC officially came to life in November 2011, Greg and Steve had already identified the major elements of the Fair Food Program. Greg and Sean had used their CIW experience to build on Verité's approach in designing the initial grower questionnaires. That first year, the FFSC continued this work and developed the protocols and detailed compliance monitoring system. They were also out on the farms conducting the baseline audits for the thirty growers officially participating in the Fair Food Program.

This was where the dance was the trickiest, the "postconflict period" where, as Judge Laura describes, "the partnerships [between growers and the CIW] were new and had to be cultivated and nurtured. You didn't go out there [into the fields] with the intention of blowing things up but people (crew leaders and field supervisors) were exploding in our faces, unprovoked." This transition from confrontation to collaboration had begun with the working group, but now, as with the code itself, it had to get into the details, into every aspect of the farms and the work, into the same rows of tomatoes that had often been the site of abuse and violence.

The FFSC's early audits were fraught with danger. The danger was in the teams' taking the "gotcha" approach of military IGs and auditors and losing the trust of the growers. The danger was also in the teams not being thorough enough, being fooled by the crew leaders and supervisors, and seen as just as ineffective as other audits. There was danger of crew leaders and supervisors punishing workers who spoke with the teams, in investigators not being grounded enough to talk as peers, rather than saviors, with the workers in the field, and in falling on the wrong side of the line of showing respect for the growers and their managers but not backing down when threatened. And the danger was in something going terribly wrong with consequences for the entire program.

These dangers were and are among the reasons that selecting the right people for the FFSC investigator roles is difficult. Analytical skills, writing skills, quantitative skills are necessary, but the investigators also do much of their work in the farm fields. Judge Laura explains that the audit teams "are dealing with grizzled and often crude farm managers and crew leaders who will roll over you if given the opportunity. You need to be able to stand your ground but in a manner that is constructive." Sean Sellers led the initial teams so that the FFSC would come across as experienced, and Judge Laura was involved in many of the early audits as well, particularly during the first year as the FFSC worked to establish baselines for each farm. Although the title "Judge" got the growers' attention, it didn't always carry a lot of weight in the fields. She gives us an example. "At one of the farms, Sean tried to do a management interview and the farm manager wouldn't get out of his truck."

"How long will this take?" he growled.

Sean replied, "Forty-five minutes."

The manager yelled, "I don't have the time. Fuck you and fuck your program."

A little edgy, but scenes like this actually helped to establish the program, making clear that this was no joke and that the FFSC would not be blown off. Judge Laura went to the grower who owned the farm and said, "The atmosphere is poisoned, the workers won't talk, and we can't do the interviews. You have an obligation to be cooperative in the audit process and if not, you'll be put on probation." Soon after, the grower, who had not been present on the day of the audit, publicly apologized to the FFSC and the company's farmworkers at the field in front of all the workers and the farm's staff.

Earlier we talked about the importance of paying attention to the details of implementation. It's the details that make the difference in moving from an idea or cause to a real program and then to success. Thinking through the details and what it would take to turn the Campaign for Fair Food into the Fair Food Program is one reason the CIW's work stands apart from other social responsibility programs. Even as Gerardo Reyes, Lucas Benitez, Leonel Ramirez, Silvia Rodriguez, and the others were continuing to lead the campaign, Greg Asbed was shifting some of his attention to working with Steve Hitov on how to make the code of conduct real. Before the growers signed with the CIW in 2010, Greg, Steve, and others in the CIW were thinking about how the code could be implemented. Even as the working group was diving into the details of the code and its implications, the CIW, with help from Sean, were designing a comprehensive system of monitoring, reporting, investigating, correcting, and imposing sanctions. Once Judge Laura and the early FFSC investigators were on board, they worked out the details and developed the supporting systems for bringing the design to life.

Given the amount of time the CIW and FFSC have spent thinking this through, we ought to take the time to understand the major components of what the FFSC does and how it fits into the overall Fair Food Program. There are a lot of moving pieces here, and each is necessary if the Fair Food Program is to be effective.

The foundation of the Fair Food Program is the *code of conduct* and the supporting Guidance Manual. The code, of course, was developed by the CIW, and the policy of the Guidance Manual comes out of the working group. The next component is *monitoring* the growers' compliance with the code. This is where the Fair Food Standards Council comes in. In addition to the formal monitoring of the FFSC, the farmworkers themselves play a critical role through a 24/7 *complaint line.* (Think about it. Potentially more than thirty thousand people monitoring every minute of every day!) The CIW's *worker education* program ensures that farmworkers know their rights and responsibilities so that they can serve as front-line monitors in the fields. The FFSC *investigates* potential violations of the code and, if they've confirmed violations, develops *corrective actions* the grower must take to return to compliance. Finally, if a grower does not take the required actions and fix the problem, the FFSC, supported by the CIW, invokes *market sanctions*, suspending the grower from the Fair Food Program and alerting buyers (e.g. McDonald's, Taco Bell, Whole Foods, Fresh Market, or Compass), who then cannot purchase tomatoes from the grower. The CIW leads the Campaign for Fair Food, establishes the standards found in the code of conduct, oversees the Fair Food Program, and provides farmworker education. "The Fair Food Standards Council," as Judge Laura describes it, "monitors and enforces legally binding [Fair Food] agreements won by the Coalition of Immokalee Workers with major corporate buyers and growers."

The FFSC's monitoring and auditing responsibilities may not sound that exciting from afar. But, as touched on above, the work requires intelligence and physical stamina and, particularly in the early years in Florida and now as the program moves into new regions and crops, has some risk of physical danger from angry crew leaders. There are two aspects worth considering: what the FFSC monitors and how it does so. Let's go back to our example of the code's requirement that "All compensable hours shall be recorded, and Growers will keep accurate hours through a system . . . in which employees control their time cards." In addition to three more detailed policies and five specific examples of how this requirement should be implemented, the Guidance Manual provides several specific "Audit Measures." The audit measures include what information worker pay slips must include (e.g. the pay period, hours worked, wages and itemized deductions but also the Fair Food premium and the telephone number of the complaint hotline) and the grower's ability to demonstrate that the time cards record all hours at the job site.

To evaluate a grower's compliance with the code, the FFSC's investigator/ monitors conduct three broad types of audits. Farmworker/fieldwork audits include extensive time in the field and in worker housing areas. By the conclusion of each farm audit, the FFSC team will have spoken to a minimum of 50 percent of the farm's field workers, even for operations having as many as a thousand workers. For smaller operations, it is not uncommon for the auditors to talk with 75 percent or more of the workers. The teams spend time in worker housing areas to check the quality and safety of the housing and because the workers can be more willing to talk as they relax after their day in the fields, out of the eyes of supervisors. System audits are the second type of audit. Here the focus is on the farm and grower management and the systems they have in place to comply with the code, including timekeeping and payroll as well as health and safety standards and processes. FFSC teams question farm and grower management, from field-level supervisors and crew leaders, to farm managers, and up through and including corporate officers. Taking the information gleaned from supervisors and managers, the FFSC staff members cross-check it with what they learned from the fieldworkers. Judge Laura gives us an example of how this works. "A particularly effective cross-check or feedback loop regarding compensable hours is to compare the dates when workers received their required education with the grower's payroll information. We know when the education sessions took place; was the time recorded and were the workers compensated for it?" The code is the guide here. Sean Sellers explains that "lines of questioning for management interviews follow the requirements of the code of conduct. 'How are you implementing this aspect of the code? What happens in this scenario? And in this other scenario?' The questions and their answers reveal fairly quickly those who believe in the value of the code and those who cram for the test but [where] nothing ever changes."

Financial audits are the last category. (Stick with us! There really is a lot going on here!) FFSC monitors Mike Towler and Matt Wooten are more than willing to dive deep into all that is required to effectively monitor compensation and payroll within an industry with a long tradition of wage theft and debt peonage. The FFSC monitors review the growers' payroll records and time registration or timekeeping system. They conduct a minimum-wage analysis for each and every worker (excluding the penny-per-pound or Fair Food premium) and audit the grower's own system for identifying minimum-wage shortfalls, adjusting or rectifying accordingly. The grower's Fair Food premium process, including its receipt of the appropriate premium from the buyers and its distribution to the workers as a line-item bonus on their payroll stubs, is thoroughly reviewed. In recognition of a legacy of wage theft by crew leaders, the FFSC reviews signature sheets for payroll checks and ensures there is a reasonable process for forwarding paychecks to workers who leave the farm before harvest ends. And underlying all this is the effort to determine whether all compensable hours (work time, waiting time, education and training time, lunch breaks not taken) have been accounted for and compensated with at least minimum wage. Mike points out that there is more to this than reviewing worker attendance logs and timekeeping records. It's often a matter of detective work with "formal investigation methods supplemented by intuition and experience. For example, we have rules of thumb about the standard ranges of what is possible for workers to pick including benchmarks for young workers, older workers, pregnant workers, or first-harvest versus third-harvest. We also compare the formal information with observations from the FFSC team members who follow workers throughout the audit days." The team members, for example, take note of how long workers are waiting to clock in and if they control their time cards.

Were you to follow one of the audit teams out to the field, you might be led by Matt Wooten. Tall and thin, hair cut short, he's likely wearing the requisite REI hiking pants and shirt plus a dark ball cap. His dark-rimmed glasses don't quite hide the fatigue in his eyes that comes from a week-long audit trip and a 4:30 wake-up time to be at the farm by 5:30 a.m., waiting for the buses to arrive and the farmworkers to start clocking in. Matt joined the FFSC staff that first season and he's one of its unquestioned leaders. Laughing, Judge Laura fills us in on how well-matched Matt is for this work. "He's one of a kind, a workaholic and great at figuring out systems and how they work. He's leading the newer staff, guiding them, and helping them to learn how to do the work in the field." Matt understands that for the Fair Food Program to succeed, the FFSC and its monitoring and enforcement capabilities have to be able to expand its capacity. The CIW recognized from the beginning that it needed "We are all leaders" to be more than a tagline, and the same is true for the FFSC. Although necessarily more hierarchical than the community-oriented CIW, the FFSC requires, for its own logistical needs, that each of the FFSC's investigator/monitors reach a point where he or she can lead an audit/investigation team. In its first season, beginning in the fall of 2011, the FFSC had statewide jurisdiction for the Florida tomato industry. Florida is an enormous state. It takes about six hours to drive from the northernmost Fair Food Program tomato farm in Jennings, Florida (right up against the Georgia border) to the southernmost farm in Homestead, between Miami and the Florida Keys. FFSC's home in Sarasota is about equidistant from farms at both ends of the state, approximately 250 miles in either direction and, according to Google maps, an estimated driving time of four hours. With the program's expansion up the East Coast in 2015, distances to be traveled now cover Georgia, South Carolina, North Carolina, Virginia, Maryland, and New Jersey. This is with an FFSC staff of about thirteen people.

So, maybe it was more than the early hour after a late night of report writing that was showing in Matt's eyes. But he took note of the beauty of the first signs of dawn coming through the mist rising up from the vast acres of tomato fields. A quick huddle forms as the FFSC team organizes. A few break off to quietly chat with a regional operations manager for the large grower, a man many of the FFSC have known a long time. The first crew bus arrives, headlights still needed. The other buses, painted green or blue or red with white stripes, crew leader names on their sides, are soon rumbling across the dirt and gravel road. The workers climb off the buses carrying bags of food and cups of coffee and wearing early-morning faces. They're from Mexico, Guatemala, and Honduras, with a significant minority of Haitian workers, wearing T-shirts over long sleeves, baseball caps, and the occasional straw cowboy hat. The Haitian workers have a distinctive sartorial style, with several choosing to wear bolder straw hats with enormous brims. Lining up to clock in, the farmworkers soon head back to the buses to get out to fields ready for harvest. A couple of white pickup trucks show up, carrying field supervisors or crew leaders who join the line and then the caravan to the fields. Large flatbed trucks trundle on by, carrying bins for the tomatoes and providing a platform for the dumpers.

Although the shorthand is "farms," the units the FFSC teams audit are better described as "regional operations." For each grower, there are sets of fields, each set with a farm office. Near Naples, Florida, the growers have been able to buy land so they can have many contiguous fields. Around Miami, that's less true, and operations similarly vary as you move up the East Coast. On this day, a couple of the FFSC investigator/monitors head over to the farm offices to talk with the farm manager and the grower's human resources managers. The rest head to a field where a couple of the crews are picking cherry and grape tomatoes. Moving fast, the workers take advantage of the relative cool as the sun is just coming up.

The humidity is at 96 percent and a mist still hangs over the field, not yet burned off by a sun that will soon turn up the heat to close to 100 degrees. Grape and cherry tomatoes don't make the distinctive and rhythmic thumping you hear in Florida when the workers are picking the large green "rounds" or slicing tomatoes. Grape and cherry tomatoes are much smaller and are picked ripe and so lack the baseball hardness of their cousins. It's more like the patter of rain on a front porch as workers quickly search through the thick web of tomato plant stems and leaves to find handfuls of red and drop them in their buckets.

It's a bit tricky talking to the workers in the fields. Most importantly, they're working to earn a living, and the FFSC monitors need to respect their time. It's here in the field that you see the hard-to-find combination of skills and personality needed for the FFSC team to be successful. Victor Yengle explains, "You can be a good analyst and write long reports but you need the human factor. You need to encourage workers with eye contact and body language to help them feel comfortable. You have to appear open and trustworthy." Walking into one of the rows, Victor begins talking softly to an older man. The worker wears a white T-shirt over another long-sleeved shirt, arms stained green and brown from the tomato plants, and a baseball cap tied to his head with another T-shirt to protect him from the sun and foliage. The farmworker is focused on his work and doesn't seem eager to talk. Victor keeps speaking softly and respectfully, leaning over, hands clasped behind his back to stay out of the man's space. Victor's got an ear for languages, speaking not only English and his family's native Spanish but Portuguese and a smattering of some of the indigenous languages of Central America. He tries to quickly pick up where the farmworker is from. Guatemala is this man's home and he speaks Mam, a Mayan language. A smile in his voice, Victor begins to break through, keeping it relaxed. As the farmworker begins to talk, Victor "walks through the code," crouching down when asking about more sensitive topics, using the tomato vines to block the sound of his voice from other workers or supervisors. Victor thanks the man as the first conversation concludes, handing him a card, Spanish on one side, Haitian Creole on the other. "Consejo Por Comida Justa," is the title; Fair Food Standards Council. "*Asegurando sus derechos bajo el Programa por Comida Justa*"; Ensuring your rights under the Fair Food Program. The card has on it the number of the "*gratuito y confidencial*" complaint line and a summarized list of violations of the code that should be reported. Failure to pay the Fair Food premium or bonus. Not recording all hours. Not paying minimum wage. Cupping. Worker health and safety issues. Sexual harassment. Verbal abuse. Slave labor. Victor reminds the man, if you think the supervisor or grower is violating your rights, report it. Confidentially and without fear of retribution.

Handing the card to the Guatemalan farmworker and then to every other worker he speaks with this day, Victor, like every one of the FFSC monitors, is giving the worker access to the real power behind the Fair Food Program's monitoring system. Steve Hitov stresses this point. "Audits are just point-in-time snapshots, especially when auditing labor. How a worker is treated on a Monday doesn't mean they won't be mistreated on Tuesday. So, it is not just the quality of the audit, it's the complaint line behind it."

Complaint lines aren't new to Florida; the Department of Labor has had one for years. Miguel "Mike" Rios has run the Tampa office of the US Department of Labor and is now the regional enforcement coordinator for the Southeast Region of the department's Wage and Hour Division. Mike has spent about twenty years addressing violations of federal labor laws that apply to agricultural workers. He's lived in Tampa, Florida, for nearly forty years and admits with a laugh that working on labor issues for the DoL was his dream job. Mike has no illusions about the DoL's ineffective record in addressing the long history of farmworker abuse in Florida and elsewhere in the Southeast, but he's proud of the work he and his coworkers have been able to accomplish, particularly in recent years, despite the severe limits of federal law covering the sector. When he later got the chance, he became a senior investigator advisor and then the enforcement coordinator for the DoL's Southeast Region so he could specialize in agriculture. "I started leaning toward agriculture because it is clear; it is the chance to help the most vulnerable workers on the planet. That was the appeal for me."

Asked about the oft-repeated story that the DoL's hotline for farmworker complaints had live support only between 8 a.m. and 5 p.m. Monday through Friday and otherwise relied on a voice messaging system in English, Mike was chagrined but also pushed back. It wasn't that the Department of Labor didn't take complaints over the phone. "Over the years, there have been different attempts made for a hotline. There has always been the opportunity to call an office and speak with a human being. And there has always been an attempt to have people who are bilingual." But execution has been spotty, success varies by office, the volume of calls is enormous, and like the Department of Justice investigators' initial approach to slavery investigations, the DoL is a government office that has traditional hours. The Tampa District office is head of the pack, receiving close to two hundred phone calls a day from workers in all sectors, and quickly responding to most of them. In Tampa, there is now always a bilingual, Spanish-English person to handle calls. But not every DoL office in Florida can make that claim, and the only office with Haitian speakers is in Miami. The DoL's website is in English, with options to get "How to File a Complaint" cards in about ten languages. The website seems to be designed for employers to get the information they need to provide to their employees. The Wage and Hour Division's national phone number is automated and asks callers to type the ZIP code of their employer and then directs them to the appropriate district office. The good news is that the voice messages for the national and the local numbers provide the option of Spanish language. The challenge continues to be that whether you call in through the national or the local line, the DoL office is only open 8:15 a.m. until 4:45 p.m. Monday through Friday, except for federal holidays when they are closed.

The Wage and Hour Division has made improvements over the years, but an 8 to 5, Monday-through-Friday office phone is still unlikely to help a migrant farmworker with possibly only limited Spanish and no English and whose phone card has run out of money. There's some evidence that this might be true in the relatively few calls related to agriculture, even in the Tampa office. The CIW knew that farmworkers needed an always available, more flexible complaint line. The code of conduct requires that "Growers will work with the CIW to: . . . Establish, implement, and enforce a process acceptable to the CIW for complaints to be filed by, and credible complaints to be investigated on behalf of, employees without fear of retribution." The working group's clarification states, "The grower must maintain an independent, toll-free complaint call-in service, and provide the number for the service to . . . Workers." Importantly, "the complaint call-in service must be able to handle calls competently in at least Spanish, Haitian Creole, and English." Growers then have options. They may maintain the line themselves; contract the service out; or, as of the 2011/12 season, use the complaint line run by the Fair Food Standards Council.

A handful of the growers, particularly those like Pacific Tomato Growers with strong human resources staffs, now have effective complaint lines. In the first years of the Fair Food Program, those growers who chose to contract out the complaint line found them both expensive and not particularly effective. The contracted service is usually an HR call center that services complaints from many industries. Like the auditing companies, these services don't have the expertise to decipher what Sean Sellers describes as sometimes "rambling calls and tomato field jargon." And they're expensive. As a result, "the growers have increasingly gone with the FFSC line." In addition to the cards provided by the FFSC teams, the code requires that the hotline number is included on the workers' pay stubs and is posted in work areas and in any grower-provided housing.

The FFSC staff members cover the line on a rotating basis, and Lindsay Adams has complaint-line duty this particular week. She is part of the team traveling for midsummer audits, but any calls that come in are automatically redirected to her cellphone. Whether a call comes into Lindsay, to one of the grower's complaint lines, into CIW's offices, or is picked up in the course of an audit or education system, the process is the same. Most calls come in the evenings and on weekends. Judge Laura reminds us that "it takes particular skills to talk to a worker who is often upset or frightened" and that for many Spanish is their second language, adding to the challenge of reassuring the caller and also getting the information needed to begin an investigation. "You need staff who are really invested in what they are doing, with strong knowledge of the industry and field conditions."

There's a perhaps unexpected secret weapon behind what happens next. The power of the complaint line is supported by the institutional memory, a database that may be unique in the agricultural industry or even within social responsibility programs in general. Database discussions may not be your idea of excitement, but the database is in fact the "secret sauce" of the FFSC, underlying the Fair Food Program's monitoring and reporting. It's an example of the systemic perspective, the analytic nature, the distinct combination of advocacy and geekiness that is characteristic of the CIW and the Fair Food Program. There's true delight in Greg Asbed's eyes as he exclaims, "The database the FFSC has is incredible! No one else has this!" Judge Laura picks up on Greg's excitement. "The database is essential and amazing. . . . Not only are all the crew leaders and assistant crew leaders listed, but the nicknames of everyone in the growers' and crew leaders' supervisory structure are included as well as their contact information." The database includes reports from every audit and investigation, as well as every complaint called into the FFSC, growers, or the CIW. It is a comprehensive knowledge base for not only the tomato industry covered by the Fair Food Program but for any complaints made by farmworkers who have moved to other crops and growers outside the program. When a worker calls with a complaint but isn't sure of the name of the farm where he or she is working, the FFSC staff member asks for the name or nickname of the crew leader and can cross-check with the database. The effectiveness of this institutional memory was demonstrated by a case during the Fair Food Program's second full season. An Immokalee crew leader had already been noted in the database as a "bad actor," responsible for forced labor and threatening workers' families in Mexico. A farmworker called the FFSC complaint line with a new incident that had echoes of the bad old days. Judge Laura went to the grower's management with evidence from the original case and the initial investigation of the new incident. The grower quickly fired the crew leader.

Let's go back to Lindsay and her week of monitoring the complaint line. She may get a call about a crew leader who is cashing workers' checks and keeping the money. Or a complaint about a younger worker who abused an older worker, throwing him down into a truck. Or a woman who was sexually harassed by a supervisor who made raunchy comments. Lindsay is going to keep the caller on the phone, calming him or her down if necessary, asking a series of questions to figure out where the worker is working, whom the worker is making the complaint against, whether or not the potential violation affects other workers, and getting the caller's contact information while assuring the worker of confidentiality. Once off the phone, Lindsay immediately enters all the information into the database. Lindsay's completion of this initial contact report triggers an auto-mated e-mail to the entire FFSC staff, the CIW, and CIW's counsel Steve Hitov. Matt Wooten explains, "From this moment on, every step taken in the complaint investigation and resolution will be entered into the database and any member of the FFSC staff can look up subsequent information. The culture of the FFSC, supported by practice, is that a particular complaint is not 'your case' with 'your files' in 'your desk.' Anyone can pick up a case at any time."

Whether the complaint comes in through the FFSC hotline, a grower-run complaint line, or through the CIW, the FFSC has the power to determine how complaints will be investigated and is the ultimate finder of fact. Whoever inves-tigates the complaint—the grower, the FFSC, or the CIW—they must notify the others within two working days. As Lindsay prepared to report a serious case of abuse of a farmworker harvesting in a crop outside of the Fair Food Program, she explained, "[The FFSC and the CIW] communicate with each other about cases and complaints. If the CIW receives a complaint from a Fair Food Program farm, they do the initial intake and then hand off to the FFSC." Usually, the FFSC will conduct investigations of potential code violations on the farms of Fair Food Program–participating growers and the CIW will investigate complaints coming from outside the program. But "the CIW accesses the FFSC database to inform investigations even if they are not on Fair Food farms."

In stark contrast to more traditional legal processes, the complaint investiga-tion and resolution process for the Fair Food Program moves quickly. According to Judge Laura, "we try for a speedy resolution due to the dynamic nature of the [migrant] workforce with high turnover. Simple cases are resolved in a few days and it takes one to two weeks if they are more complicated." Even with the most serious and complicated cases, notifications must go out to growers within two days and any worker who makes a complaint gets follow-up from the FFSC or CIW, whether the investigation revealed a code violation or not.

If the investigation reveals a violation of the code's requirements, whether by the grower's management or supervisors or a crew leader, the FFSC works with the grower to develop a corrective action plan and then continues to monitor to ensure that the grower carries out the plan. Sanctions vary with the severity of the violation, intention, and grower involvement. Growers are held accountable, but as the program has matured, the complaint-resolution process begins with the assumption that the growers want to improve the operations of their farms. "The assumption is that the growers want a healthy and safe environment for their workers, want to pay their workers fairly, and want to resolve any problems that the FFSC identifies. It is often true that the Fair Food Program growers appreciate finding out about a problem. They view it as risk prevention." Similarly, Judge Laura and the FFSC staff knew they, the CIW, and the growers had to successfully transition from confrontation to collaboration. "Communication with the growers had to be careful, measured, and respectful. We were moving into a postconflict period. . . . I wrote to them not like a court, but respectfully. There had to be a measure of formality, but I also left the door open for communication."

Looking at some of the cases that came up during the first few years of the Fair Food Program, it's hard not to notice the combination of practicality and creativity in the sanctions and corrective action plans. In some of the simplest cases, the grower may write up a crew leader, issue a warning, or discipline the crew leader. Since this process is outside the judicial system, the offender is not incarcerated or fined but may be docked wages or terminated. In cases where there are systemic failures, the FFSC may work with the grower to identify best practices and guide them into professionalizing their payroll or accounting systems. Complaints related to wage-and-hour issues are by far the most common. Historically, growers gave a check or cash to the crew leaders, who then paid the workers, facilitating the common problem of wage theft. Now, individual farmworker checks may be given to the crew leaders, who distribute them to the workers, or the workers may get their checks directly from the grower's management. If there is an incident of wage theft, FFSC corrective action plans focus on minimizing the time the crew leaders have the checks. If there is a second instance, the crew leaders are stopped from distributing checks. And nearly all corrective action plans require workers to sign for their checks and all require the crew leaders or, if necessary, the grower, to pay the workers their lost wages.

The "communitarian" nature of the code comes through in the corrective action plans. Early on, the FFSC realized that in the case where a worker was humiliated or abused, the acts occurred in public in front of coworkers, and therefore the corrective action needed to have a public component. The intent is, according to Judge Laura, "to move the growers further toward being part of the solution, not simply implementing required sanctions." When the farm manager refused to talk to Sean Sellers and yelled "Fuck you and fuck your program" to the audit team, the FFSC required a public apology by the owner to the workers. As Sean Sellers described the scene, "It was a turning moment, to see the workers' faces light up as the owner said he was sorry for the incident. He told the workers you can talk to the FFSC and that we want you to do so. These moments are unprecedented in agriculture, and that farm manager is now a perfect gentleman." The code prohibits any retribution by crew leaders or farm management against a worker who files a complaint. In the case of a grower whose supervisors abused a worker after a complaint, the grower made a public apology to him and to all the workers present and affirmed the company's support of the code of conduct. In these cases, "the company's owner or representative must clearly state that the specific behavior by the crew leader, supervisor, or manager is wrong and that they will not tolerate this behavior." There is no requirement for the victim of the violation to come forward or confront the violator in public.

There have been cases where the growers were not as quick to accept responsibility, and it is then that the power of the market backs up the FFSC. The Fair Food Program's enforcement of the code of conduct is given its clout because of the agreements with Taco Bell, McDonald's, Compass, Whole Foods, and the other participating buyers. The code includes a set of "Article 1" violations, often referred to as "zero tolerance" violations. These are the extremes: sexual assault, gun violence, physical violence, or forced labor. Crew leaders guilty of these violations are immediately fired and may be banned from working at Fair Food Program–participating growers for several years, or permanently. If the grower himself commits one of these violations, the grower will be suspended for a fixed period of time. Buyers may not purchase tomatoes from that grower during the suspension and until the FFSC confirms the grower is in compliance with the code. But growers may also be suspended for lesser violations of the code—such as sexual harassment, discrimination, wage violations, retribution against a worker, or using farmworkers who are not direct hires of the company—if they do not quickly implement the FFSC corrective action plans and come back into compliance with the code. If suspended from the program, they can immediately lose the significant market of most of the major fast-food companies and an increasing number of food service companies and grocery chains. Nearly every year, a grower has been suspended, most recently DiMare Homestead, based just outside of Miami. Just reminding a grower of the possibility of suspension can quickly change their willingness to cooperate. In the first years of the full program, FFSC's investigator/monitors realized that one of the farmworkers had not been registered as an employee of the company. When the FFSC asked questions, the grower's management denied the worker even existed. Making no headway, the FFSC went to the grower's primary buyer to report the situation and then, as described by Judge Laura, "explained that this sort of behavior is what facilitates slavery cases." Immediately after the call, the buyer called the grower and said, "What are you doing??? For $300 [in wages] you've put your market share at risk?" The result, continued the judge, "was that the worker walked through the front door of the grower's office, continued to the payroll office, and received a check in his name." It seems likely that it could have taken years to resolve this case in court.

We've discussed the power of giving workers 24/7 access to a confidential complaint line, but it may not be clear how the workers are aware of their rights and of the code that protects them. Things will become clearer if we join Cruz Salucio, Silvia Perez, Brian Kundinger, and Wilson Perez in a van for an early morning drive. Waiting next to the CIW office, you can look across the street at the La Fiesta parking lot, what used to be known as the Pantry Shelf. As has been true for decades, the workers begin to arrive. This dark, early November morning some walk down Immokalee's quiet streets, saluted by the occasional rooster as the chickens join the workers in getting the day started. The time just changed and it didn't rain the night before, so the crews can start picking earlier than usual. A few of the workers show up slow-pedaling their bikes. Long-sleeve Ts, baseball caps, small backpacks with lunch supplies are standard as the workers converge on the parking lot. Buses are waiting. Hands in their pockets, the workers cluster under the pink glow of La Fiesta's parking lot lights, waiting to board. Brian is driving the CIW van this morning, making stops to pick up Wilson, Cruz, and Silvia. The team is heading to a farm near Bradenton to conduct a worker education session as the tomato harvest season gets started. The team settles in and quickly falls asleep as Brian heads to highway 75 and north, face lit by the dashboard lights. Brian has recently joined the CIW staff after working as a volunteer with the Student/Farmworker Alliance. When he graduated from Brown, he had joined a Legal Services office in Miami. His colleagues were dedicated to helping immigrants, but he couldn't find anyone interested in the bigger picture, using data and understanding the context. CIW's Marley Moynahan called Brian and said, "We've got a position and you can't say no." Brian didn't pause before passing "Go," and he has loved the work. He gets a small stipend and housing. CIW loans him a bike. You can hear an echo of Sean Sellers' story as Brian continues. "The lifestyle is very different than Miami but it is very accessible. I was hired at CIW because I had proven myself, not because of my degree, and that is dignifying."

The code requires growers to hold an information session for each and every worker at the point of hire. The growers' sessions usually include company policies and practices but must include all applicable laws, codes, and regulations, particularly the code of conduct. "Conoce Tus Derechos y Responsabilidades" (Know Your Rights and Responsibilities) declares the cover of the booklet each worker receives. Perhaps even more helpful is the CIW-produced training video, opening with scenes of workers harvesting tomatoes and starring CIW staff members and other workers playing out scenarios and talking about the workers' rights. Right up front the workers talk about "Un Centavo Mas," covering the penny-per-pound premium and making clear the importance of clocking in at the beginning and end of each day to ensure being paid for every hour on the grower's property, and "El Copete," the prohibition of "cupping" of tomato buckets via the Fair Food visual standard. "Los Derechos de los Trabajadores" opens with a sexual harassment scenario. A crew leader is coming on to a woman farmworker. Quickly, the other workers emphasize the right to work without sexual harassment or assault. The farmworkers explain that workers have "El Derecho de Quejarse Sin Miedo," the right to complain without fear of retribution. Both the video and the booklet also explain the worker's responsibility not to abuse the complaint system or the health and safety program and to be conscientious in filling the tomato buckets to the top. The booklet and the video give every worker the context for these rights, including the buyers' commitment to the Fair Food Program and the strength of workers coming together in the Coalition. The training material ends on a note that emphasizes the collaboration needed for success. "If all of us—workers, owners, and the CIW, work together, we can achieve a great deal in the Fair Food Program."

It's one thing for a worker to get the booklet and see the video. These are the first steps in educating workers about the Fair Food Program and their rights. In-person worker education sessions are a linchpin in the effectiveness of the Fair Food Program. CIW teams hold sessions at every farm toward the beginning of each season (November and March in Florida). Leonel Perez is a long-time CIW staff member and, like most, has worked on the education teams since they began with the growers' signing. The worker education sessions inform the workers of their rights but, as Leonel explains, they do much more than that. "The education sessions are really important especially for the workers because they can have conversations with other workers, crew leaders, supervisors, and even sometimes growers. It is really important because the workers then see that this program is real and taking place.... The workers on their own then start defending their own human rights . . . and start spreading the word."

Leonel's comments get us back to the van, where the crew is waking up as Brian pulls into the parking lot of McDonald's. Coffee and breakfast bring focus as the team spends the last half-hour in the van preparing for this morning's session. Pulling onto the dirt road leading to the farm, the van stops in an open field, acres of tomatoes on one side, stacks of tomato crates and a few flatbed trucks on the other. These education sessions are required by the code, on the clock and with farmworkers paid minimum wage. Buses pull up. This is a crew from Palmetto. As Brian explains, it's not the first time the CIW team has been to this farm. "This is the fourth visit . . . so the expectation is that there will be few if any problems raised. You can view these repeat education visits as the vaccination to reduce the likelihood of problems.... Once workers know their rights and understand they can voice their concerns, the complaints decrease over time."

A bit of an awkward start for today's session. The sessions work better in the shade and in an enclosed area to reduce distractions. But not today. It's getting hotter by the moment and Cruz and the others will be talking to the workers in the open field. The workers are slow to get off the bus, and the farm manager, dressed in jeans with a camo long-sleeve T-shirt, aviator sunglasses under a trucker cap, is trying to get things organized. Turning to the CIW team, he opens with an attempt at a joke. "I can't even yell at people and cuss at them because you guys here. This is hard!" Silence from the team and a dead look from Brian results in a mumbled "just kidding" and then moving on to tell the workers to be sure to sign the rosters.

If you were expecting something along the lines of a Sunday school class with eager workers attentive and jumping in with thoughtful questions about their rights and responsibilities, this isn't quite that. Most of the workers form a loose semicircle around Cruz, Wilson, and Silvia. There are few, if any, Haitians in this group and the uniform is mostly T-shirts and baseball caps, with quite a few of the workers wearing separate pull-on sleeves that run from their wrists to above their elbows. As Cruz starts talking, a guy is cutting stakes with a machete, the rhythmic chopping creating background music that's not quite disruptive. A man in a sleeveless shirt and aviator sunglasses is watching from behind a white pickup, choosing not to engage but still there and listening. The crowd is all men except for a woman who is hanging out with the guy behind the truck. The scene has a sense of suspicion and restlessness that's reminiscent of a high school assembly with the possibility of something important coming up. That sense gains traction when some of the younger workers start cutting up and an older man shushes them.

The CIW team keeps their cool and their dignity. They've done this many times before and they know that despite the distractions, most of the workers are thinking about what the team is saying and will take these rights into the field. The crowd pays attention when a worker in an enormous white T-shirt, camo pants, baseball hat, and bandanna walks up to Cruz. He's asking a question and keeps pressing. There are a few smiles as the worker keeps talking. Cruz responds and then ignores him to continue with the presentation. As Cruz later described the situation, "In every group, there is someone a little different. He had a good question. He just asked it in a disruptive way. Now at the education sessions, the workers are listening. Even the crew leaders are listening. Before, the crew leaders tried to interrupt, particularly when discussing the *copete*."

There's a crew leader here this morning on the edge of the circle, close to the CIW team. Arms folded across his chest, he's wearing jeans and a short-sleeve gray polo shirt, bareheaded but wearing the aviator sunglasses that are the fashion on this farm. He'd been quieting the workers acting up but now is engaged with Cruz. The crew leader turns to confront Cruz directly. Soon his hands are out of his pockets and the intensity is picking up. Cruz keeps talking to the crew leader in a steady voice. Silvia is next to him, listening even as she shades herself from the sun with the *Know Your Rights* booklet. Wilson, baseball cap on backward, stands by, listening, hands in his pockets. Crouching down, the crew leader draws circles in the dirt with a piece of straw. A worker joins in, more soft-spoken, and the whole group, even the two workers crouching in the shade of the white pickup truck, is watching and listening.

Reflecting later that afternoon on his exchange with the crew leader, Cruz notes the dramatic change in the tenor of the education systems from when they began five years before. "It was interesting [early on] because for the first time we were entering the farms. This was a historic moment for us because before we, the CIW, couldn't even be at the door or talk to crew leaders or the growers as an organization. We would take journalists to see the fields from afar and very quickly trucks would come and tell us to get out of here. . . . At the beginning, we would start presenting these education sessions to workers. Crew leaders and growers would be present and that made us a little nervous. Now, seeing the reality that the growers are participating and big buyers of tomatoes are on board, that gives more power to what we are doing. That first season, we would talk about all of the rights in general but season after season, we now see what isn't going right at a particular company and we make sure to reinforce that. Each season, we tighten our rights."

The crew leader had jumped in when the CIW team told the group that the *copete* was prohibited by the code. As Cruz and the others understood, "The *copete* is how crew leaders made money [and] it was how they held themselves above the other workers. If a worker brought a flat bucket, the supervisor or crew leader gave it back to humiliate the worker. Now the workers can file a complaint without fear." The disruptive worker and the intensity of the crew leader were actually signs of progress. Cruz continues, "Before, on some of the farms, people would sit there listening but they were still afraid to make complaints. But at this farm, they weren't afraid. They asked questions in front of the crew leader. And the crew leader is one who before made a lot of disruptions. But this time, he was more respectful in his comments. What came out today, the people were not afraid. They have the trust and they know when they speak, solutions will be found."

Cruz wraps the worker education session up. "That's all? It's all okay?" Wilson and Silvia join him in handing out the *Know Your Rights* booklets and answering questions. The workers get back on the buses. They'll be staking and harvesting today. Brian and the farm manager are talking. The company's compliance manager and a farm supervisor join them, soon followed by Silvia, Wilson, and Cruz. The farm manager had been complaining about competition from Mexican tomatoes and the burden of the Fair Food Program. Brian explained that the CIW is working with the growers, helping them to differentiate Florida "Fair Food tomatoes" from what's coming in from Mexico. Relaxing, the farm manager nods. "That's good to know. I didn't realize that. It makes it easier for us." The

CIW team and the company managers review issues that came up during the session: providing disposable gloves, disgruntled workers complaining about the mix of harvesting and staking, and what's covered in the company's employee handbook. The farm manager notes the workers getting a bit rowdy and the crew leader jumping in. "I will deal with the crew leader and I apologize for his disrespect." Handshakes all around and it's back in the van.

Stopping for a real breakfast on the way back to Immokalee, the team goes through what had happened in the morning's session. Cruz points out, "It's important to realize that it is not 'now that the Coalition is here, everything is rosy.' There is nothing that can't be solved. The farms all have some workers who have been there and some who are new. . . . The goal is always, of course, that everyone pay attention. . . . This session could have been a little better [the one the next day went much better] so we'll get back to the company on how to improve the session."

Cruz later steps back to look at the big picture. "It was beautiful and interesting because not only can we go into these farms, what was most interesting is we'd be talking face-to-face with a grower about our rights as workers. For the first time, we could shake hands as equals and the growers would be present for these education conversations. For years, the first thing a worker would see when they arrived at a farm, you would see a food safety video. How to pick clean tomatoes, wearing gloves, and how the tomatoes would be safe for consumers. . . . But today, the first thing you see is about the rights we've been able to win as workers."

As they did in this session, the CIW worker education teams, like the FFSC's audit teams, often learn of problems or potential problems. Sometimes it is from the questions the workers ask. Sometimes it is an issue raised by the grower's managers. And sometimes it is from calls that come into the CIW once the teams leave the farm. After an early December session in the third full season of the program, Lucas Benitez, Oscar, and Santiago walked into the CIW offices after a training session for one of the largest growers. Sitting in the rocking chairs in the main room of the CIW's offices, they talked through a sexual harassment case they discovered during the education session. The grower hadn't reported it and CIW would be following up. Leonel recalls another incident when a woman called right after the CIW left the farm. "She called because the crew leader was demanding the workers have a *copete*. The woman told them they couldn't demand that and the *copete* was no longer allowed. She then called us while the education team was still on the road, heading to Immokalee. She called and said, 'who's right here? The crew leader or you?'" The CIW immediately called the company and "very quickly, one of the company employees went out into the fields and told the crew leader that it is true: they are no longer allowed to demand a *copete* from the workers. The following morning, the company had to get together all of the workers and apologize and the crew leader also had to apologize to all of the workers because he had threatened to fire this woman." The problem was solved and the CIW closed the complaint.

The real strength of the worker education program is not from the complaints that the CIW teams receive. As Cruz says, "we go to education sessions and we talk with the workers about problems and how to fix them. That is better than saying everything is okay. Before, when the investigators from the government showed up at farms, the growers would say that everything was okay and the workers didn't have the space or the ability to speak up about conditions. But today, they can voice all of this and the growers have to do something about it and enforce the workers' rights." The workers receive the education booklet and take part in the education session and then take this knowledge into the tomato fields or when they move to other crops like strawberries or peppers or potatoes. The combination of worker education and the complaint line that Lindsay was manning means that monitoring of the Fair Food Program and compliance with the code is not limited to the reach and staffing of the FFSC. Instead, there are thirty thousand or more monitors, watching over every field and every row where you might find a farmworker, every minute of every day.

7

"VALUE" CAN HAVE
A DIFFERENT MEANING

Miguel Talavera is driving the large white SUV on the dirt roads running between
tomato fields and irrigation ditches. He's taking some pleasure in talking about
the gators in the ditches and the Florida panthers that have eaten all the deer and
are now going after cattle. The women in the back seat of the truck are looking
a bit nervous, checking out the ditches with some concern. They're rabbis from
the social justice group T'ruah. They might be missing some of the detail Miguel
is providing: Pacific Tomato Growers has about eleven thousand acres across
Florida, and the fields up the East Coast in Georgia and Virginia add another
three thousand acres available for tomatoes. Pacific plants tomatoes in Florida
every week beginning September 1 and continuing into January. A hundred days
to ripen means picking Florida tomatoes into May.

Miguel is a big man, with a clean-shaven head that only adds to his imposing presence. Jon Esformes doesn't disagree. "He's a real tough guy . . . the real
deal, like Honduran special forces." Miguel has settled into life in Florida after
more than twenty years with Pacific. Power boats and hunting take up his time
outside of work, although there's less of that now that he's director of East Coast
farming operations and Pacific continues to expand. There's a lot of experience in Miguel's past, all of which has helped Pacific but some of which made
it challenging to get on board after Jon Esformes signed with the Coalition of
Immokalee Workers. Miguel has been raised in the agricultural business and
combines hands-on experience with extensive education. His father, a farmer in
Honduras, attended the Zamorano Pan-American Agricultural School. Samuel

Zemurray, head of United Fruit Company and known as the "Banana King," founded El Zamorano in the early 1940s and it is now a university known for strong programs in agribusiness management and agricultural sciences. Miguel's degrees are also from El Zamorano. He has taught at the school and has owned and managed citrus and poultry farms in Honduras. When Pacific first approached him about joining the company, Miguel was working on his master's degree in Florida in an exchange program. Although he turned down that first offer, Pacific didn't give up on him. He was finally convinced, joined the company, and has since worked his way up to one of the most senior operational management positions.

There have been a lot of changes over twenty years. The first step, as Miguel recalls, was getting used to a family-owned company with a strong sense of its own immigrant history. "There was a cultural issue. I'm from Latin America where we had strong differences between classes. But in the US, people at Pacific saw [me] as part of the family, part of the team. I [began to feel] a sense of ownership." That sense of family is something Pacific Tomato Growers takes pride in. Liz Esformes is Jon Esformes' cousin, and she is frank about the ups and downs over five generations: "My brother and I are half Esformes and half Heller. The marriage didn't work but the business relationship has been good!" Dad was Nate Esformes, described by Reggie Brown as "one of the old-line heroes" of the tomato industry. He and his brother Joseph, Jon's father, founded what is now Pacific Tomato Growers with the Heller family in Palmetto, Florida, more than sixty years ago. Liz explains, "Pacific is a family business and the family extends to the employees. Many, many of our people are twenty-, twenty-five-, thirty-five-year employees, their entire lives spent working in the company."

Sarah Goldberger and Liz Esformes met in Miami when Sarah was a secretary for Liz and Jon's grandfather and where "we got into some trouble," Sarah remembers with a laugh. They've both worked for Pacific ever since. Sarah is now the director of human resources and Liz is a vice president working in HR and community outreach. Jon Esformes, Liz, and Sarah will tell you that Pacific Tomato Growers was already ahead of most of the Florida tomato industry in treatment of their workers even before the Fair Food Program. Jon points out that while he was still fighting addiction in Los Angeles, "We already had developed a full-fledged HR department in [the early 2000s], the only one in the industry. . . . Everyone on the farms was already an employee. Pacific was already putting shade in the fields." In another conversation, Sarah makes these same points: "We decided over ten years ago to make all workers 'employees' and pay them with a company check. Then, after realizing that wasn't enough, we stopped providing checks through crew bosses and handed them directly to the workers. . . . Why did we do this? It was a good business practice." Liz joins in, "[We] started making small changes to improve the situation. . . . These were small steps but the wider industry still has people with bags of cash who pay the workers." Both agree that "HR departments in agriculture were unknown. Nobody was doing this. But Pacific decided to set up an HR department before ever working with the Coalition." Having taken those first small steps, Sarah, Liz, and Pacific made what turned out be a leap. Pacific realized they needed a professional HR manager and convinced Angel Garcia, who was working HR for the Wyndham hotels in the Caribbean, to join them in 2007. Jessica Abrigo, born and raised in Immokalee, rounded out the HR team.

Although they didn't yet know where it would lead, the new HR team gave Pacific the foundation to make Jon's agreement with CIW come to life. Even before the agreement, Jon had come to believe that "the most effective tool for the CEO and the board is the HR department. . . . Food safety and HR touch every part of our business. . . . HR is how to drill into my company." Supporting Liz and Sarah by adding Angel and Jessica was revolutionary in the agricultural business, but changing Pacific's HR perspective wasn't easy, even as the company took the first steps toward professionalizing its approach to managing a workforce. Angel pushed the hardest to change age-old practices and relationships. Sarah describes what Angel brought to Pacific: "Angel Garcia is a warrior. [He's] earned his stripes in more ways than one, leading HR changes, bringing discipline to the program, and coaching us all." Jessica points out that even the HR staff pushed back. "I thought Angel's ideas had no place here!"

And then everything changed. Jon had told Liz what happened at Pacific's board meeting after the company's name showed up in the Navarrete slavery case. The company had to do something, and the board's resistance to the CIW had become counterproductive. Liz remembers, "Jon talked to the Coalition and realized that they wanted the same things we did." He was going to move forward. When Jon signed the agreement in September of 2010, there was disbelief and shock after so many years of unquestioning opposition. "When we decided to make the agreement with the Coalition, I was completely against it," Miguel Talavera remembers. He was out in the fields and in the thick of the fight, mentored by one of the growers' most vocal opponents in the late 1990s. "We weren't doing anything wrong and we didn't need to change!" Even Angel was "resistant to the Coalition at first" since Pacific was already leading HR in Florida agriculture.

But Jon wasn't kidding. He had signed the agreement with the CIW, and Pacific was now going to work with them to bring the code of conduct to life in their fields. Jon and Billy Heller met first with Greg Asbed, Steve Hitov, Lucas Benitez, and the others, eventually setting up the working group. Jessica, Angel, and Sarah followed, making their first trip to the Coalition's offices. Liz remembers these earliest discussions. "The two sides started to get to know each other.

What we wanted. Where we each were. Our different visions [and perspectives]. It was a three-hour sit down. We came as individuals and left as collaborators."

Talking and listening caused Pacific's HR department and the CIW to realize they already had many of the same goals. Unexpectedly, working with the CIW made it possible for Pacific to articulate where they were trying to go and to move in that direction. Sarah, Miguel, and Liz feed off each other's enthusiasm as they recall the excitement that began to build in the group once they began to move from confrontation to collaboration with the CIW. "What we've all seen, and continue to see, is that you set up what you think are 'best practices' and [think] that you've eliminated the problem. But you are really in a vacuum in management. So we thought we [Pacific] were doing the right things . . . different from the rest of the industry . . . and we didn't see beyond the condition we knew." Liz picks up from Sarah. "The code of conduct and the collaboration with the Coalition have helped us to get better." And then Miguel steps in, "Yes! They've helped us get better at what we were trying to do." Finally, Jessica can't help but jump in. "Angel and I were trying to develop a sense of trust on the farm . . . but you max out on your own plateau. The Coalition really opened doors for us, for things we couldn't imagine."

It turned out that the CIW and the requirements of the code of conduct gave Pacific the leverage they needed to change the relationship between agricultural workers and the companies who employed them. Angel had already been pushing Pacific to lead the industry, but all of Pacific quickly realized that collaboration with the CIW would lead to radical change and transformation of the fields. The transformation was grounded in what the CIW had been calling for since the mid-1980s: workers having "a place at the table." Angel gives an example. "I was very involved with improving safety [on the farms] prior to the Coalition. When the code required a Health and Safety Committee, I thought, 'this will be very easy for me! We already have it.' But the Coalition said no, we want you to include workers from the field on the committee." Angel pauses, laughing a bit himself. "I had never thought of this. I had no agricultural experience (except picking mangoes in Puerto Rico by throwing stones at them) and yet I thought I could effectively manage safety at the farm."

It's important to remember that Jon's signing with the CIW didn't eliminate the problems that had existed for generations not only at Pacific or in Florida agriculture or even across the United States. By 2010, Pacific didn't have quite as far to go as some of the other Florida growers, but it was going to take some time for any grower to change the perspective and behavior of every crew leader, every field supervisor, and every farm manager. And for that matter, it would take time to convince the workers, many of whom had been working in the fields for years, that these changes were real. What *did* change quickly for the Fair

Food–participating growers was the ability to identify problems through worker education, audits, and the complaint line. First with Pacific, Lipman, and Gargiulo in the 2010–2011 season, then spreading the next season to the other members of the Florida Tomato Growers Exchange, the ability to identify problems was followed by a surprisingly rapid, albeit uneven, changed attitude within the tomato growers. Problems continued but they were now something the growers could work on with CIW and the Fair Food Standards Council to fix. Also during the first season, growers distributed to their workers the penny-per-pound premium paid by the buyers into an escrow account.

True to form, Jon was going hard after this new world. Once they had decided to sign, Jon and Pacific made the decision that "everything for us would be under the Fair Food Program. . . . When we signed we never intended to isolate the program to Florida, and it was immediately spread up the Eastern seaboard." That conviction was tested soon when "a week after we signed the [Fair Food] agreement, there was an incident and an investigation [at our farm] in Georgia that needed to be done. We invited the CIW to join us."

The same full-speed-ahead approach was not necessarily true for the other growers, particularly in the first full season of the Fair Food Program in 2011–2012, when the Fair Food Standards Council (FFSC) was just getting its feet on the ground and the growers tested it. Sean Sellers remembers that "crew leaders in Florida would sometimes tell workers that 'we're in Florida now but just wait until we get over the Georgia border,'" not really believing the growers would stand for new regime. To be fair, it wasn't unwise of the growers to keep their powder dry, holding back to see what would happen and whether this thing would really stick. The "pilot season" (really just half a season) for the Fair Food Program was spent with the working group figuring out the details of the code of conduct. The first full season of the program was 2011–2012, and even then the new Fair Food Standards Council wasn't in place until more than a month after the season began. Laura Germino looks back with some awe. "The leap we made was incredible. We went from a couple of farms and growers in the pilot to more than thirty farms all at once. . . . Market incentives really forced the fast scale-up. Once the first two growers signed up, the others had to as well."

Judge Laura Safer Espinoza, Sean Sellers, and the new Fair Food Standards Council team went from zero to sixty in the first full season of the program. The first task was conducting baseline audits to collect information about where each of the more than thirty participating growers was, relative to the code of conduct. These were thirty-seven farm locations ranging from Homestead to just south of the Georgia border, and at each farm the newly formed teams, often led by Sean or Judge Laura, interviewed grower management and supervisors, crew leaders, and at least half of the workers. During this first season, the FFSC's new staff of about a half-dozen interviewed nearly 1,200 workers, as well as something approaching three hundred managers, supervisors, and crew leaders. The FFSC also conducted their first extensive financial and payroll audits, looking at compensated time and payment of the Fair Food premium. They reviewed operations, including existing health and safety practices. And they worked through each element of the code and the new details on policy and standards from the Guidance Manual.

Even while getting the baseline data in place, the FFSC and the CIW were handling complaints from the hotline (now in place across the entire state) or from calls to the CIW. More than a hundred complaints came in this first full season, many requiring visits to the growers to investigate. Even in this first year it became clear that the Fair Food Program was having an effect outside of the participating growers and locations. About a quarter of the calls that came in were from workers on farms that were outside of the program: different crops, out of state, or nonparticipating growers. In nearly all cases, whether the farm involved was in the program or out, the FFSC or the CIW (for non-FFP farms) and the grower successfully reached a resolution. Judge Laura and the FFSC were building a reputation for working with the growers to find a resolution. If a complaint could be resolved, often to include a public apology to the farmworkers, without a formal investigation and FFSC finding, this was viewed as a success by both sides. In those cases requiring more formal action, or in response to the baseline audits, the FFSC developed the first corrective action plans to get the growers into compliance with the code of conduct.

In the seasons that have followed, the Fair Food Program and its monitoring agency, the FFSC, gained additional traction. With time, the FFSC conducted more audits, more workers were interviewed, and the audits and corrective action plans became more nuanced and tailored to operations of individual growers. By the third full season, Sean Sellers, Matt Wooten, and Victor Yengle and their FFSC investigator colleagues were interviewing more than three thousand workers a year. Since they saw the operations of nearly all the Florida tomato growers, the FFSC could now bring unprecedented expertise that benefited the participating growers, letting them know about best practices in the industry. As Judge Laura explains, "We [now] have intimate knowledge of each grower's systems. The FFSC now behaves almost as a very knowledgeable consultant to their operations." Giving an example, she continues, "Corrective action plans are detailed and written with deep knowledge. It is not 'strengthen your timekeeping system.' Instead the plans say 'take specific steps A, B, C, and D to make the [timekeeping] system work as it should to be in compliance.'" As the FFSC's approach matured, "the level of sophistication dramatically increased.... If the growers make a good faith effort, the FFSC will provide a great deal of help to enable them to comply with the code of conduct." This help includes draft model policies the growers can use for providing training for supervisors. The result, according to the judge, is that "trust continues to grow as the growers see the FFSC is not coming and running roughshod over their staff and operations when the growers show good faith."

Farmworkers learned more about their rights and began to trust that the FFSC and CIW would take action, resulting in more calls to the hotline or the CIW each new season of the Fair Food Program. An increasing percentage of complaints came through the FFSC complaint line, since it was included in the cards handed out by the investigator/monitor teams and was most often the number on each worker's paystub. By the third season the FFSC and the CIW received 274 calls, nearly all of which were investigated. More than a third of the calls were reporting an incident or situation that was not a violation of the code of conduct, but half of these were valid concerns and the FFSC and the growers were able to find resolution. The complaints from farms outside the Fair Food Program were consistently the result of workers moving from participating growers to other crops, recognizing their basic rights and reporting violations.

What became quite clear in the first couple of years of the program was that the CIW and the FFSC not only had information; the Fair Food Program also had teeth. The fast-food and institutional food service buyers who had signed Fair Food agreements in the 2000s now got a chance to put their market power into play. The code of conduct was quite clear. If a grower committed an Article I violation—such as use of forced labor, threat of violence, or sexual harassment with physical contact—the grower would be suspended from the program and Fair Food Program buyers would not buy the grower's tomatoes. Consequences for other violations of the code could be probation and quick execution of the agreed-upon corrective action plan. The FFSC expected "continuous improvement and eventual full compliance" often within just a few weeks. Market consequences behind the Fair Food Program were real. In the first full season the CIW suspended two growers, in the second suspended one, and the third full season suspended three. Nine growers were put on probation during the same period.

By the end of the fourth season (2014–2015), the structure of the FFSC's work was firmly in place: audits, complaints, investigations, and corrective action plans, and the growers understood what was required. Asked about the probation and suspension numbers, Laura Safer Espinoza observed, "There is now [2015] not a huge amount of churn. . . . The numbers have gone down significantly in this fourth season. Three out of four growers have had their probationary status lifted. Two out of three [growers] that were suspended will be restored in good standing." Even as the number of complaints continued to increase, their nature had changed. Judge Laura laughed when she talked about the change in just three years. "The fourth season has been wonderful in that the level of compliance continues to increase. It has reached a point where our auditors go out to the farms and are 'shocked' that not everyone understands the pregnancy nondiscrimination requirement. One investigator who handles the complaint line jokes that she is now the 'last check' lead as in 'I didn't receive my last check.'"

The auditors and investigators still found problems on the Fair Food Program farms, but they were only rarely issues of deep concern. Judge Laura compared what the teams found in the first full season of 2011–2012 and what they were finding in the fourth season that began in 2014. "Even when an issue of deep concern does arise, it is not at the level of abuse that the FFSC originally found. An example is the [recent] issue of subcontractors. There were 'overtones' of forced labor but they did not meet the legal definition. . . . The biggest difference was that when they were told of the issue, there was immediate cooperation from the grower. The rapidity was breathtaking and the collaboration was complete." She concludes by noting that "we are happy to get boring phone calls!"

Why the nature of the problems and the complaints changed over these first few years deserves more attention, but for now we'll go back to the original point made by Greg Asbed when he was thinking through how to make the code of conduct real. Put most simply, Greg's point was that the mainstays of most corporate social responsibility programs, standards and audits, weren't enough. As the major social responsibility auditing programs have demonstrated, the traditional approach of corporations like McDonald's or Walmart or the Ahold grocery chain was rarely effective in discovering, much less preventing, the type of worker abuse found in American agriculture or in Bangladesh garment factories. This is in part a problem of persistence, or a lack thereof.

After signing the Fair Food agreements, most of the growers adopted a bit of "wait and see" in how they approached the code and the new Fair Food Standards Council. By the end of the third season, the growers had realized, as characterized by Judge Laura, "We are the houseguests who stay. You can stuff things in the closet but eventually it will all begin to fall out." One FFSC investigator picked up on the judge's annoyance theory of success: "Because the FFSC is persistent, we've become effective. The FFSC doesn't go away, it develops relationships. It is far easier to avoid change with a short annual audit. The issue is not how many audits overall in the industry. The need is for multiple and repeated audits and investigations for each grower, to ensure compliance and demonstrate change, or not. Has there been follow through on the corrective action plan, or not? Complaints must be followed up within forty-eight hours and the FFSC works with growers to resolve issues whenever possible. There is individual investigator knowledge but also institutional knowledge, the . . . database." Matt Wooten summarizes the difference in approach. "It is a collaborative program. The conversation never ends. The relationship continues on."

As Lucas, Cruz, Silvia, and Leonel could tell you, the Coalition of Immokalee Workers wasn't resting on its laurels now that the Fair Food Standards Council was in full swing. First of all, they were already leading worker education sessions when the FFSC was a gleam in the CIW's eyes and Laura Safer Espinoza was still thinking she'd make a go of retired life in Fort Myers. As Cruz Salucio noted, each step onto a new farm was "historic," particularly during the pilot season immediately after the tomato growers signed with the CIW. Instead of being threatened and chased away by the farm managers, the education teams now arrived in the fields wearing T-shirts announcing the Coalition of Immokalee Workers and asking "Is Your Food Fair?" and were greeted with a handshake. The worker education sessions, in a room in a packing plant or under newly provided shade between fields or in a semicircle formed by crew buses and pickup trucks, were the first visible sign that something was changing. Cruz was deeply moved by these early visits. "When we would go, we would also see workers who have been participating [with the Coalition] for years—protests, coming to meetings—coming to these education sessions. They would say, 'At last the CIW is among us.'"

The CIW teams were as busy as the new FFSC audit teams. The pilot season in the winter and spring of 2011 gave them the opportunity to put together the new version of the *Know Your Rights and Responsibilities* booklet, figure out how to present the training, train the trainers, and work through the logistics. Once the first full Fair Food season kicked off in the fall of that year, the education teams were working with close to thirty growers, visiting forty farms for more than seventy education sessions, and talking with 6,600 workers. By the completion of the third season, those numbers had risen to nearly ninety sessions, nearly fifty farms, and almost 8,000 workers. Perhaps equally impressive is that every worker in Florida's tomato fields, more than 33,000 people counting turnover, had received the rights and responsibilities booklet as part of their required training before getting to work.

But here's what you need to know. While the Fair Food Standards Council and the CIW's worker education teams were focused on implementation and on making the Fair Food Program real, the shouting, the marches, the clever, analytic, stick-in-the-eye articles on the CIW's website, the papier-mâché, the students and clergy with their poster paint, all the color and the noise of the Campaign for Fair Food were still going on. Without the campaign and the pressure from consumers denouncing tomatoes picked "from the hands of a slave" and demanding "We want our Food Fair!," there couldn't be a Fair Food Program.

To riff off of James Carville's insight of the 1990s, It's the market, stupid! Consumers, allies, students, church-goers, these were the combined force that Taco Bell, McDonald's, and Burger King couldn't stand bearing down on them before the tomato growers signed with the CIW. And in 2012, that force was still needed.

One target was right out of the Taco Bell playbook. The CIW hadn't stopped putting pressure on the fast-food chains. Chipotle was puzzling to outsiders. With its emphasis on quality sourcing and ethical treatment of animals, it was difficult for CIW's allies to understand why Chipotle would not sign onto a program calling for basic rights for farmworkers and a penny-per-pound increase in wages. With high expectations, the CIW had first approached Chipotle in the mid-2000s, even before McDonald's and Burger King had signed on. By the fall of 2012, the Fair Food Program had come to life, but still no Chipotle. The campaign found itself in Chipotle's hometown of Denver, where the firm was sponsoring a major festival featuring local food, chefs, and music but not, as the CIW pointed out, farmworkers. Gerardo Reyes was there as the face and voice of CIW's planned march and protest, reminding all who would listen of the discontinuity between Chipotle's motto of "food with integrity" and its refusal to sign on to the Fair Food Program. In the days before the kickoff of the festival, following a protest at Chipotle's headquarters, Gerardo explained in a TV interview the CIW's position. "For the first time, we created a whole new system to eliminate the abuses, to identify where abuses are going on and uproot them from the system. This is an opportunity for Chipotle to do the right thing. They claim that they sell food with integrity, and they are really focused on the sustainability part of that conversation as one of the main spokes-corporations. And what we are saying is, this is an opportunity for them to make it a reality."

Chipotle's communications director Chris Arnold responded that Chipotle had last rejected CIW's request because of concerns that Florida's growers had not signed the agreement and so Chipotle could not be sure of the quality of the tomatoes they would purchase through the program. By 2012, that was no longer an issue, but Arnold argued that since 95 percent of the Florida tomato growers were now part of the program, Chipotle knew the tomatoes they purchased from Florida were part of the Fair Food Program and "ethical." Chipotle provided their purchase records to the CIW and saw no need to sign the agreement (or pay the premium). Not surprisingly, Gerardo pointed out the free-rider problem. "It is true that 90 percent of the tomato industry is on board with us . . . all of them need the support of the corporations buying [tomatoes]. And the corporations need to pay a premium that addresses poverty wages, and that corporations need also to be able to cut purchases, if necessary, when there are abuses that are violated." Chipotle received the benefit of Fair Food tomatoes without paying the premium or providing the needed market power.

The prior years of protests, news coverage of the actions in Denver, and Gerardo's reminders about the disconnect between Chipotle's stated principles and their actions had their effect. The next day, October 4, 2012, it was all smiles at the table where Gerardo Reyes, joined by CIW's Oscar Otzoy, joined with Chris Arnold to sign the eleventh agreement with a Fair Food participating buyer. Standing behind the men was a small phalanx of student and faith-based campaign allies. Gerardo noted that farmworkers were now "finally recognized as true partners—every bit as vital as farmers, chefs, and restaurants—in bringing 'good food' to our tables." The fast-food people were getting on board. But the supermarkets would be another challenge altogether.

"Yes, CIW has had great success. But the enormous challenge they still face is the major supermarkets." It's the fall of 2011, just as the new Fair Food Standards Council is getting started, and David Wang is worried about what's next. "CIW has succeeded because it's been adaptable and creative. They've had extraordinary leaders in Laura [Germino] and Greg [Asbed] [and the] leadership of Lucas Benitez and Gerardo Reyes." But the power behind the Fair Food Program is the power of the market, and the fast-food chains "only account for 20 percent of the tomatoes. Eighty percent are still in the fields." The next step, said David, was for CIW "to get agreements from the grassroots national and regional chains. This is a much more difficult prospect."

The Coalition of Immokalee Workers got this. They knew the market. They knew the numbers. And the Campaign for Fair Food had been paying attention to supermarkets for at least the previous two years. But David had it right that grocery chains were a whole different animal than the fast-food giants. Yes, at the most basic level, they were simply much bigger. They could put overwhelming market power behind enforcement of the Fair Food Program. They could also provide the additional premium that would come close to doubling workers' wages. The market power of the supermarkets could support the CIW's expansion into produce beyond tomatoes. But their position in the economy and in the public life of citizens was very different than fast-food chains and would require a different approach.

The question was, how to put pressure on the supermarkets. The campus boycotts of Taco Bell and the Truth Tours to Chicago and McDonald's headquarters struck an emotional chord with the Coalition's student and faith-based allies: "Boot the Bell!" "Exploitation—Not Lovin' It." But protesting at a Kroger's or Safeway or Stop & Shop wouldn't have the same energy as the fast-food protests, in part because the supermarket corporations often own a number of grocery store brands. Kroger's owns Ralph's, Harris Teeter's, Fry's, and King Soopers. Ahold owns Stop & Shop and Giant, and Delhaize owns Food Lion and

Hannaford. For many supermarkets, their brands are tied more to "everyday low prices" than to sustainable food. CIW recognized that supermarkets also play a different role in people's lives than do fast-food restaurants. "It's really important not to ask people to boycott businesses where it is too hard to find a replacement." Laura Germino explains further, "Supermarkets are different from fast-food places. If you boycott Taco Bell, you can usually go to McDonald's across the street. There are few, or even only one, supermarkets in neighborhoods or towns, particularly in rural areas. It is much more costly to people to ask them to boycott a supermarket that may be their only nearby source of food." So protests may be less effective, and boycotts were off the table. Supermarkets were going to require a different strategy.

Before heading down this path, we should take a moment to reflect on something that happened in 2008, remarkable because a reader might quickly respond, "well, of course!" and dismiss the event. "Whole Foods Market Signs Agreement with the CIW to Support "Penny-per-Pound Tomato Program in Florida," is the headline for the joint press release by CIW and Whole Foods in early September 2008. Not long after, Whole Foods announced that they were bringing two of their organic tomato suppliers in Florida, Alderman and Lady Moon farms, into the initial Fair Food agreement. Without protests, without pressure, Whole Foods signed on and has been a leading supporter, really an enthusiastic supporter, of the CIW and the Fair Food Program ever since. "Well, of course!" you say. "Whole Foods is about sustainable food and it's good for their brand." Yes, this seems obvious enough, but Whole Foods has frustrated unions and their supporters in its resolute refusal to allow their employees to unionize. And, as the CIW found with Chipotle and as we'll see soon enough with another case, a brand proclaiming "responsibility" doesn't mean a company is going to take action and accept the limits and apparent costs of an agreement with the CIW. Jon Esformes hits on this point when comparing Whole Foods with some of the other Fair Food buyers: "I'm a big fan of Whole Foods. I know they make a lot of mistakes but the DNA of that company is real. I've gotten to know the senior managers on the buying side and they are the real deal. They're like the guys who play hacky-sack and then make it big and yet still play hacky-sack." In Jon's estimation, the Whole Foods crew isn't just protecting their brand. They're staying true to the company's original values.

That "of course" response turned out not to be accurate for another target supermarket in the Campaign for Fair Food. Whole Foods signed on in 2008, but we'll agree they are a special case. By the end of 2009, the campaign began to pay more attention to supermarkets in general. Thanksgiving of that year was declared "Supermarket Action Week" with Fair Food allies called upon to "shop and drop," delivering CIW's "manager's letter" to supermarkets including

Stop & Shop, Walmart, Winn-Dixie, Trader Joe's, and Publix. By the fall of 2010, just as Jon Esformes and Pacific were making it possible to make the Fair Food Program real, CIW announced on its website the formal kickoff of the "CIW Supermarket Campaign." The CIW once again revealed its talent for combining stark visuals with effective use of social media in its *One Penny More* video. As the video opens, we find ourselves joining a woman slowly cruising down the supermarket aisle, adding milk, bread, and chips to her cart, and accompanied by the kind of soothing music heard in elevators. As we turn into the produce aisle, celery and lettuce dissolve into long green rows of tomato plants in a farm field. Tomato workers move quickly, filling their buckets and tossing them up to the dumpers. We're met by Cruz Salucio, Leonel Perez, and Silvia Perez who explain to us the economics of tomato pricing and workers' wages, as the video moves back and forth between the fields and our shopper, each picking tomatoes. Their argument is simple. Supermarkets have tremendous market power. They push prices down. Tomato workers receive forty-five cents for each thirty-two-pound bucket of tomatoes, or 1.4 cents per pound. They are at risk of abuse and even modern-day slavery. In response, the Campaign for Fair Food is asking super-markets to pay a penny more per pound to provide the workers with something closer to a living wage. As the video ends, our shopper starts to check out, placing her bag of tomatoes on the belt. The message on the screen is "We're asking for a penny more per pound." The cashier weighs the tomatoes and they come to $3.69. The penny is added and scale shows $3.70. Point made.

As the campaign increased pressure on supermarkets including now Kroger, Giant, and Food Lion, there was one other chain that drew the "well, of course" response from those who thought about the question. Trader Joe's is often thought of in the same class of higher-end boutique supermarkets as Whole Foods. Fun, hip, Hawaiian shirts, and all about the exotic or at least interesting sources for its food. Bollywood popcorn, Somewhat Spicy Dill Kettle Cooked Potato Chips, Organic Grass Fed Beef, Wasabi Mayonnaise, Salted Caramel Cookies, and car-toons of "Trader Joe and his friends getting wiggy with it after reading the latest Fearless Flyer." Surely Trader Joe's would sign up for Fair Food.

Founded in Pasadena in 1967 by Joseph Coulombe, the original "Trader Joe," the stores kept it fun by making Hawaiian shirts their uniform by 1969 and installing maritime bells rung to get people's attention. By the 1970s, the stores were known for California wines, interesting customer newsletters, and a whole set of private labels including Trader Mings, Trader Jose, Trader Giotto, and Pilgrim Joe and an emphasis on interesting and innovative food from all over the world. In 1979, Joe Coulombe sold the chain just as it was expanding beyond California. The buyers, Theo Albrecht and his brother Karl, were part of the family that owned the Aldi chain in Germany, a chain of supermarkets known for bargain-basement prices. It is of note that these private companies were so well-known for their "extreme secrecy" that the bare-bones announcement of Theo Albrecht's death in 2010 was viewed as "unusual openness." And thus the evolution of a Trader Joe brand that was known for "innovative, hard-to-find, great-tasting foods" to include, unlike Whole Foods, pride in cutting costs and keeping prices low. The new Trader Joe's declared that they "bargain hard and then pass the savings on" and "buy in volume and contract early to get the best price."

Trader Joe's shared with its fast-food predecessors in the Campaign for Fair Food an inclination to dig in its heels when tomato workers tried to tell it what to do. What they also share, different from most of the other supermarket chains, was a high-profile brand attractive to younger people who might join the Student/ Farmworker Alliance or at least take part in a march for workers' rights. CIW upped the pressure on Trader Joe's in 2011 with a series of actions across the country: fifth-graders wrote letters to a Trader Joe's manager in Boston; a couple hundred people protested at a store in Oakland; actor Martin Sheen wrote to Trader Joe's CEO expressing his disappointment in the store he loved; and the CIW led a grand march to Trader Joe's headquarters in Monrovia, California. Tucked up against the San Gabriel Mountains, not far from Pasadena, Monrovia provided the setting for a march bearing all of CIW's signature moves. There were farmworkers in CIW and "Justice for Farmworkers" T-shirts leading the way, carrying a CIW banner. Students joined with church and synagogue members, wearing jeans and T-shirts, carrying signs and banging on drums as they marched down Monrovia's sunny and usually quiet streets. Signs and banners had the come-to-be-expected bold colors and creativity. Some were tomato bucket poster board hats, others called for an end to slavery in the fields, and a whole slew took advantage of the popular chain's name. "Seriously, Joe?" "Traitor Joe!" "Be a fair trader, yo!" CIW member Darinel Sales carried a full bucket of (red) tomatoes that was passed up and down the line of four hundred or so marchers, with old and young marchers alike posing for photos as they hefted the thirty-two pounds to their shoulders. Drums and songs kept the march going through Monrovia until it reached its conclusion at Trader Joe's headquarters. Standing at the campus entrance, the group was led in prayer from several faiths and a smaller group posted on the building's entrance a letter signed by a 100 rabbis calling for Trader Joe's to sign the Fair Food agreement. The marchers regrouped for a classic CIW popular education skit featuring a two-sided Trader Joe, one side smiling to the clients and the other a hard-nosed businessman. After more music the Monrovia action came to an end.

Gerardo Reyes, Lucas Benitez, Cruz Salucio, and other CIW staff were leading the actions. Behind the scenes, Greg Asbed and Steve Hitov were negotiating with

Trader Joe's. Interestingly, there is some indication that the negotiations were cordial, in part because by now Greg and Steve had a lot of experience negotiating with large corporations. The company made one last counterpunch the day of the Monrovia action, announcing that it had signed agreements with two growers who were part of the Fair Food Program and, although it would not sign an agreement with the CIW, was essentially in compliance. "Not going to cut it," was the CIW response. No audits, no verification of premium payments or their amounts, no commitment to cutting off growers who don't comply with the code of conduct; this is not going to work!

2011 turned to 2012 and the setting for an agreement between CIW and Trader Joe's was just right. Trader Joe's was about to open a new store, its first one in Florida. It's hard to imagine that Trader Joe's corporate leaders in Florida were unaware that the Naples location was just about thirty-five miles down Immokalee Road from the CIW's office. Either the company had already decided to come to an agreement with the CIW or decided that agreement was the price to pay for opening a store in one of the nation's wealthiest cities. As you've likely grown to expect, the CIW and their allies planned an enthusiastic welcome for their new neighbor. The day of Trader Joe's grand opening, February 9, tomato workers would bike the thirty-five miles from the CIW's office to the corner of Immokalee Road and Route 41 to greet the store's new customers and protest in front of the store. Two days later, on a Sunday, CIW planned a major protest to include all of its Florida allies from Interfaith Action, the Student/Farmworker Alliance, Florida immigrant rights groups, and the southwest Florida food crowd.

Call it off! On February 9, the CIW and Trader Joe's announced that they had come to an agreement and the supermarket chain with a reputation for fun, Hawaiian shirts, and ethical sourcing of its products would now be part of the Fair Food Program. Whether they were "all in" was subject to some discussion but Trader Joe's had signed and CIW had its second supermarket chain on board.

This brings us back to the earlier conversation with David Wang. Trader Joe's was another step forward but, as David Wang noted, "Whole Foods and Trader Joe's appeal to higher-end, educated customer bases. The large grocery stores have clientele that, in many cases, are struggling financially and are not necessarily eager to pay more for food so that people they don't know are paid more." This was the question for the CIW. How could they get the big supermarket chains into the Fair Food Program?

Two targets. Two companies with different organizational cultures and markets. Two very different strategies. The overwhelmingly big gun in the supermarket business, the largest retailer in the world, is Walmart. Around the time the CIW was declaring their supermarket campaign, Walmart's annual sales were over $120 billion. The next largest supermarket chain was Kroger at about $58 billion. (In comparison, Whole Foods Markets was just under $12 billion in 2012 sales and Trader Joe's was well below $9 billion.) As Greg Asbed notes, CIW knew from early in the supermarket campaign the potential power of Walmart's joining the Fair Food Program. "Walmart buys 25 percent of all groceries! . . . [And] Walmart is interesting. They basically state 'we are friends of the poor with our low prices, keeping money in their pockets.' But Walmart's problems in Mexico and Bangladesh belie that argument. Walmart is the largest buyer of tomatoes and they could use that power for good."

The second target of CIW's supermarket campaign was more personal for the farmworkers. Publix Super Markets is a chain born and raised in Florida, head-quartered in Lakeland, right in the heart of tomato country. The privately held company was founded by George W. Jenkins. Jenkins grew up in Georgia, working in his father's general store until he headed to Tampa, Florida, in 1925 and worked in a Piggly Wiggly grocery store. He left to open his own grocery store, Publix Super Market, in 1930, and soon new stores spread across Florida and up through the southeastern United States. Today there are more than a thousand Publix Super Markets with nearly $29 billion in sales in 2015. The company is privately held as an employee-owned stock program (ESOP) but the founding family holds four of nine seats on the Board of Directors and two family members are executive officers of the company. There is still very much the sense that this is George Jenkins' family's supermarket chain.

The Coalition of Immokalee Workers included Publix from the start of its push on supermarkets to sign Fair Food agreements. Publix is by far the dominant supermarket in Florida and may be the only available market for many of the workers and CIW's allies. To date, Publix has steadfastly refused to meet with the Coalition or consider joining the Fair Food Program. Even when the Florida Tomato Growers Exchange reached agreement with the CIW, Publix spokeswoman Shannon Patten made it clear that nothing had changed. "No, we are not signing on. It is not an issue that involves Publix." It's hard not to see that the animosity Publix holds for the CIW is strongly reminiscent of the view held by the Florida tomato growers prior to late 2010. The tractor apparently doesn't tell the supermarket how to run its business.

Publix's position is confounding when you learn more about the company. George Jenkins declared that he founded Publix in order build a store that was "different . . . [that would] respect the dignity of every individual . . . [and where] everyone would have a voice." Publix's corporate website has an entire section on "Publix Culture" with a headline "Respect Every Individual," and a moving video reflecting Jenkins' idea "if you want people to respect you or your company, you must first show respect for them." Publix trumpets its inclusive hiring, special initiatives on hiring physical challenged associates, and sharing the wealth as an employee-owned company. And Publix takes great pride in its community involvement in charity efforts, investments in community organizations, and an annual "Publix Serves Day" where Publix employees volunteer with community organizations.

The perspective of CIW members regarding Publix seems to be more one of deep frustration than animosity. Trying to decipher the conflict, Laura Germino comments that "Publix leadership and family ownership have economic power that goes far beyond the 'rural elite' of the growers and others who have made their fortune in Florida agriculture." She notes that the result is insularity but perhaps also there is an element of fear in Publix's reaction. CIW and the Fair Food Program have shifted the world that the Jenkins family has known.

Clashing perspectives combined with a "within the Florida family" element have encouraged escalating protests and ever deeper-dug-in heels, along with a bit of personal nastiness. In a story with the same tone as the Burger King incidents of spying on CIW, one of Publix's employees was caught following and filming people attending a 2009 action and then lied about not having any connection to the company. CIW and their supporters have found Publix's criticism of the CIW to be uniquely ideological, implying that the CIW is a "socialist" organization. And there seems to be a particularly difficult relationship between the CIW and Mark Codd, Publix's director of labor relations. In a story told both by author Barry Estabrook and pastor Clay Thomas, the pastor went into a Publix store not long after a CIW protest concluded. Thomas was wearing a CIW shirt but had not been part of the action. As he went to buy a sandwich, Mark Codd stopped him and told him to leave. Clay explained why he was there and headed to the deli section. Minutes later, the Sarasota police arrived, escorted Clay from the store, and told him he was banned from entering the store for a year. And it appears that Publix has refused to buy tomatoes from either Pacific Tomato Growers or Lipman (then Six L's) since they led the other growers in signing Fair Food Agreements with the CIW.

For its part, CIW has been relentless in its actions and use of social media to pressure Publix to sign. In 2009, the CIW unfavorably compared Publix to Whole Foods, with an accompanying photo of Six L's tomatoes being sold in a Publix store. The blog post held the company accountable for its supply chain (as the CIW had done with the fast-food chains) and tomatoes from one of the growers linked to the Navarrete slavery case. Lucas Benitez was particularly damning as he spoke to the *Fort Myers News-Press*. "In its commercials, Publix likes to cast itself as Florida's community grocer—the good neighbor. But how can you be a good neighbor when people are . . . forced to work as slaves and robbed of their hard-earned pay in your own backyard, and you turn a blind eye? Instead they continue to buy their tomatoes from one of the farms where workers held against their will picked tomatoes." October 2009 was declared "A month of Publix protests" with actions across southwestern Florida.

As of this writing, actions against Publix are a regular occurrence in the CIW's Campaign for Fair Food calendar. The most dramatic of these, the Fast for Fair Food, became the defining visual of the 2014 documentary *Food Chains*. Director Sanjay Rawal intercuts shots of the march to Publix's headquarters in Lakeland, Florida, and the six-day hunger strike held there by farmworkers and CIW allies with an explanation about the ever-growing market power of supermarket chains and their ability to push prices down, squeezing growers and keeping farmworkers at subpoverty wages. *Food Chains* opened at the Tribeca Film Festival, was screened at the Berlin Film Festival, and continues to be shown in screenings and discussions across college campuses, for church groups, and in events sponsored by "fair food" advocacy groups. The film is classic in its advocacy, combining powerful music with images of farmworkers heading to the fields or protesting at Publix's headquarters, and it is effective in explaining a market pressure not often recognized by the broader public but also not well known by those who argue for sustainable agriculture. In a later commentary, Lipman Produce's Kent Shoemaker makes the point that the film does not give full credit to the new collaboration between Florida's growers and the CIW, even though Jon Esformes is featured along with coproducer Eric Schlosser, Lucas Benitez, Gerardo Reyes, and Greg Asbed. The villain in *Food Chains* is Publix. Rawal shows Publix employees driving by the Fast for Fair Food protest each morning on their way to work, looking over at the farmworkers hunger striking so that, as Lucas declares with his son on his shoulders, "I am starving so that my son does not have to."

Publix devotes a page on its website to the campaign by the CIW and the company's position. "Publix remains the focus of a campaign by the Coalition of Immokalee Workers (CIW) who seeks to pressure us to become involved in the employment relationship between Florida farmers who grow tomatoes and the farmworkers they employ to harvest their product." In summary, Publix states that "we have consistently viewed this issue as a labor dispute, and our position remains the same today." Their argument is that a labor dispute is between an employer and its employees over wages, benefits, and working conditions. This dispute is not, Publix's argues, their business. With regard to the specific request for an additional penny per pound, Publix says the growers should simply put it into their pricing.

There are some inaccuracies in the case Publix makes. The Fair Food Program does not ask the buyers to pay workers directly but to pay the premium based on the amount of tomatoes it purchases. The premium is then passed through the supply chain to the growers, who pay the premium to the workers as a separate line item in their paychecks. The CIW has said that it would work with Publix as it works with other grocery stores to simplify the premium process, paying it to the growers as an identified element of the price per pound. More importantly, Publix is making the same argument originally made by the growers and then by the fast-food companies and Trader Joe's: the working conditions and poor pay of the farmworkers are not our responsibility. The CIW continues to counter with yes, this is the food chain that supplies you with the product you sell. You have used your market power to push prices down and we are now asking you to use your market power to ensure the basic rights of farmworkers to safe working conditions and fair pay.

But beyond the facts of the argument, it can be difficult to understand Publix's continuing opposition to the CIW and the Fair Food Program. Publix is the largest grocery store in Florida and is "home grown." It takes pride in being part of and actively supporting Florida's communities, where it is a consistent presence. It would seem that Publix could be an obvious ally of the tomato workers (many of whom shop at Publix) and support the Fair Food Program. The cost would be minimal and the public relations value immense. This is the logic that has caused David Wang and some of the growers to reach out to Publix executives behind the scenes. David is still baffled when describing an earlier effort to connect. "I tried to talk to them, you know, working through a relative of one of the founders. I'm a businessman and certainly not viewed as an extremist in any way. But the founding family still refused to meet with me. This is amazing given Publix is a Florida chain with its headquarters in Lakeland!" The actions and intransigence continue, but there have recently been signs of hope. Word has come that Publix is regretting they've taken such an uncompromising stand against the CIW. They understand the logic that their stance only hurts them but now cannot figure a way out. Whether Greg Asbed, Steve Hitov, or another representative of the CIW can help Publix find a face-saving way out remains to be seen.

It started a bit differently with Walmart. The CIW's strategy with this retail giant stands in stark contrast to the very public, very raw campaign against Publix. But again, the fight between the CIW and Publix, and the level of animosity and frustration in it, has the feel of a range war, a fight across neighboring fences, or even between two sides of a family. Walmart is a different kettle of fish.

"We really have a special opportunity tonight to learn about the food system and the possibilities of reforming it from the inside." It's Tuesday evening in early October 2011 and the auditorium is full as Berkeley students and faculty settle in for another session of Michael Pollan's course, Edible Education 101: The Rise and Future of the Food Movement. Tonight's class is a bit different. The guest speaker is not a chef, a farmer, or even Alice Waters. Instead, the topic is "Corporations and the Food Movement" and the speaker is Jack Sinclair, Walmart's executive vice president for their grocery division. Pollan continues, "Walmart is the largest buyer and seller of food in the United States . . . responsible for somewhere between one in four and one in five [dollars] spent on food in this country. Walmart essentially feeds a third of the country, and it is the bottom third demographically." Pollan then turns to the skepticism he expects from the audience. "What role can big corporations play . . . in reforming the food system?" Isn't the food movement about "setting up alternative food chains . . . organic agriculture, consumer supported agriculture . . . farmers markets? . . . Yet," Pollan points out, "democratizing the food movement, making healthy, sustainable food available to everyone, especially the poor, is a challenge the food movement hasn't yet met."

If the need to provide quality food for those who cannot afford to shop at Whole Foods or don't have access to farmers markets isn't compelling, Pollan makes an additional case for working with major food corporations. "The upside, if there is an upside, of having a highly concentrated food economy where a very small number of . . . corporations exert tremendous power, is that when they move, everything changes." He then gives the example of when McDonald's, under pressure from consumers and animal rights groups, "decided it would no longer tolerate the most brutal aspects of meatpacking . . . and the way the whole industry slaughtered animals changed virtually overnight. You don't have to love McDonald's to see how actively engaging with them might produce some positive results."

Turning to his guests, Pollan smiles, "Tonight we get to engage with another behemoth in the food and factory landscape, Walmart." Jack Sinclair joins Michael Pollan on the stage. His stature stands in contrast to Pollan's rangy height, but Sinclair is a bulldog of a man, and when in a crowd there's no doubt he's a man in charge. When he begins to speak, another distinctive characteristic jumps to the fore: a Scottish accent that would do Sean Connery proud. It's an accent grounded in youth and schooling in Scotland before Sinclair went off to one accomplishment after another in the grocery business: the UK's Fine Fare, Tesco, Safeway for more than a decade, and then to the largest of them all, Walmart, in 2008.

Engaging and open, Jack Sinclair comes across as knowing what he's talking about without radiating "corporate public relations." This is his business. And there is no doubt as to his knowledge or to his commitment to Walmart's mission, Sam Walton's philosophy since founding Wal-Mart in 1962: "A very simple philosophy of bringing low prices to as many people as he could" with the idea of "help[ing] people save money so they could live better." Sinclair focuses on how Walmart intends to "lead, use our size and scale to make a difference" and recognizes that "our greatest power is in our business." With particular regard to "the fundamental challenges [in the food industry] of obesity, hunger, and feeding a growing population" as well as concerns about sustainability, Walmart established in 2005 a set of "Sustainability Goals." These are: "To be supplied 100 percent by renewable energy; to create zero waste; to sell products that sustain people and the environment." In the year prior to Sinclair's joining Pollan for the Berkeley course, Walmart established a subset of goals specific to agriculture: "Support farmers and their communities; produce more food with fewer resources and less waste; sustainable sourcing of key agricultural products."

Michael Pollan picks up on Sinclair's themes in the discussion that follows the presentation. Both men focus on providing better quality and healthier food to Walmart's customers and to "all levels of the income ladder" as well as on supporting local farmers and reducing the price premium of organic food. They have just touched on the effect of "everyday low prices" on farmworkers and others who produce our food when Pollan raises the issue of the "high price of cheap food." Pollan notes the long-term costs of ranchers using pharmaceuticals to raise cheap meat and then looks back on his experience researching the feedlot and slaughter industries. Stopping by the local Walmart, "I went to the meat counter and they were selling a kind of [cheap] meat I'd never seen in my stores. . . . These were the people [working] in the slaughterhouse and this was the meat they could afford to buy." Pollan describes this as the "unvirtuous cycle" of low prices and low wages. Jack Sinclair recognized the problem and said that Walmart did not "want to provide cheap food, but to provide good food. We want to be able to give people a choice of good (actually good), better, and best quality." They were not there yet but were trying to get there.

Walmart really is often viewed as a "behemoth" and the center of the evil empire by those who profess their concern for sustainable agriculture, the treatment of animals, and a living wage. Concerns about the pay of Walmart's own employees have attracted attention in recent years, particularly with the rise of the $15 minimum wage debate that engulfed fast-food restaurants in 2015 and 2016. But there was much to think about in Jack Sinclair's presentation to the Berkeley audience. It had to have been revelatory to many, and Michael Pollan believed talking with Walmart was important if the "food movement" was to have broad effect.

It's a couple of weeks after Michael Pollan's class; late October and the Campaign for Fair Food's fight with Trader Joe's was coming to a head. Sitting in the parking lot of a church in Monrovia, not far from Trader Joe's headquarters, Greg Asbed gets a call from Michael Pollan. Even with their sustainability goals, support for small farmers, renewable energy, Walmart was still struggling with the poor pay and abuse of workers in their supply chain. That's the social responsibility issue Jack Sinclair didn't raise, possibly because things weren't looking so good. Greg recalls, "Michael had been talking to Jack Sinclair about how they could dig out of the hole they were in." If Walmart was interested in not only protecting its brand but starting to fix the treatment of workers, Pollan suggested "one of the things they could do is connect with CIW and the Fair Food Program as one of the most respected fair food/workers' right movements." And, he'd argue, the CIW and the Fair Food Program were among the few with a reputation for high integrity strong enough that Walmart wouldn't ruin it if they connected.

As the two men sit under unusually bright lights on opposite sides of a stage in Dallas, you might think that this is not their first conversation. It's "Engineering and Humanity Week" at Southern Methodist University and the topic is "The 21st Century Supermarket." Sanjay Rawal is well into making his documentary *Food Chains*. He's organized and now moderating this panel that includes, moving from left to right, Jack Sinclair, *Food Chains* coproducer Eva Longoria, Gerardo Reyes, and Greg Asbed. The lights are glaring but Jack Sinclair and Greg are both laughing. In fact, this was their first conversation and meeting. Michael Pollan had made the initial introduction between Walmart executives and the CIW and Walmart had begun researching the Fair Food Program. Sanjay realized that the SMU panel provided an opportunity for the CIW and Walmart to talk without "talking." Greg had a message to send to Walmart, but also to every one of the supermarket chains. The message was, at its simplest: times have changed. More specifically, "while the supermarket of the last century merely sold food, this century's shoppers are buying food plus the information behind the food— its nutritional value, its safety record, and, increasingly, the story of how the workers who produced the food were treated." As Greg explains, "we are now in the 'Information Age.' There is no returning to the 1960s model of supermarkets where no one knows what is going on behind the shelves." Making it personal, Greg remembers, "nobody knew the realities of the food chain, the worker situation or food safety issues, when we were growing up. My mother was a highly educated, enormously smart doctor of note and knew none of this. She cared about nutrition and what [we] ate, but not these other issues." The Information Age required supermarkets "to stop looking at issues of slavery and worker treatment as a public relations problem to cover up. . . . This is a human rights issue." The supermarkets, Greg encouraged, "that understand this new reality and get ahead of it first will thrive."

Behind the scenes, the discussions that began after the class presentation and phone calls of October 2011 were turning into negotiations. Their progress could be described as less "fits and starts" than a roller coaster of possibility and dismay.

The dynamic was different than for any of the other retail buyers Greg and Steve had sparred with; Walmart was negotiating with the CIW "because of the Fair Food Program, not because we were leading a campaign against them." Walmart was reaching out because their approach to social responsibility was not working. It was creating too many "externalities," to use Walmart's term, resulting in an unending cycle of public relations disasters. Greg's analysis was "Walmart had to move beyond putting out PR fires and get to the sources of the fires." Keeping with his message at the conference in Dallas, "Walmart had to recognize they were in the twenty-first-century information age; they can no longer hide these abuses."

The negotiations were sometimes a dance and sometimes closer to a boxing match. You might think the match decidedly uneven, with Walmart the heavyweight and the CIW climbing into the ring closer to the bantamweight class. But there are reasons you'd be wrong. There is no doubt as to Walmart's market power, particularly when it comes to pushing prices paid to their suppliers ever lower. But this was a different negotiation. As discussions transitioned to negotiations, Walmart knew of the CIW's successful implementation of the Fair Food Program. Walmart had initially contacted the Coalition because of the strength of its reputation. Learned negotiating tactics geared toward pushing prices down, perhaps closer to dictating than negotiating, weren't as useful in talks with the CIW. Walmart expressed a desire to adopt only some, but not all, of the components of the program, but the CIW remained committed to an all-or-nothing position. Let's not forget that members of the CIW had been negotiating with major corporations since the early days of the Taco Bell campaign. They believed in their approach and had the patience to let the negotiations play out, even if the possibilities of an agreement with the "behemoth" were otherwise tantalizing enough to jump at. Time and again, the negotiations accelerated and then drifted away.

Greg Asbed, Laura Germino, Steve Hitov—really, for that matter, all the CIW—had reasons to stand firm. Their approach was working precisely because it allocated responsibility among the various players, and each of the program's elements was essential to the philosophy, to the systemic view, the CIW had come to in the late 1990s. The food chain ran from the workers to the growers to the buyers, and it was the buyers that had the market power, and the brand vulnerability, to enforce the Fair Food Program. The CIW also argued that the buyers were responsible for their supply chains that had tolerated, or even led to, farmworker abuse and poverty. Greg hit the point hard. "You cannot declare the success of any social responsibility program if workers continue to earn compensation below poverty level. If a worker is on the edge of economic survival, it is extremely difficult for them to recognize their rights, report abuses, and stand up for themselves." Insisting on adoption of every aspect of the Fair Food Program was essential to the program's long-term success, perhaps even its survival. Walmart's market and financial power in the Fair Food Program would be an extraordinary victory, but not if the Coalition of Immokalee Workers negotiated away its principles and then lost its credibility, viewed by workers, allies, and other buyers as lackeys of the retail giant.

The pressure was on both the CIW and Walmart. David Wang thought the opportunity was too great to risk. As he told Greg and Laura, "If CIW came to an agreement with Walmart, it could be a model for the entire supermarket industry on compliance. Walmart would lead as the 'first in' and CIW would then be working for the entire grocery industry, not just Walmart." If the CIW, particularly Greg and Laura, took the "purist" position, they could lose the whole deal. As the CIW stuck to their guns, Walmart had its own pressures to deal with. They really were being hit with one public relations disaster after another. In December 2012, the *New York Times* reported that Walmart had been paying bribes in Mexico to manipulate building codes and decisions, including building a new facility "in an ideal location, just off this town's bustling main entrance and barely a mile from its ancient pyramids, which draw tourists from around the world." Reporters determined that the bribery was not an unfortunate reality of corrupt Mexican government, but instead that "Wal-Mart de Mexico was an aggressive and creative corrupter, offering large payoffs to get what the law otherwise prohibited" and had used bribery to get what it wanted for at least nineteen store sites. The month prior to the Mexican revelations, the clothing factory fire in Bangladesh killed hundreds, and in April 2013 the Rana Plaza factory collapsed, also in Bangladesh. Both of these were Walmart suppliers.

This gets us back to the roller coaster of negotiations. As Greg recalls, "It was frustrating because sometimes they were so close to an agreement, and then it would break down again." More than once, Sanjay Rawal and others involved in making *Food Chains* served as intermediaries, trusted by both the CIW and Walmart. Walmart's senior management, with Jack Sinclair leading a delegation of a dozen, all men in blue blazers except for the sole woman, ventured to Immokalee in June 2013, and following not long after was a delegation of Walmart's produce buyers. Walmart and the CIW had not yet worked out a deal, but even then the Walmart visitors were excited about being part of the discussions and the possibilities of the partnership and brought up the possibility of expanding the Fair Food Program not only beyond Florida but beyond tomatoes and into other produce. Time and again, they'd get so close and then the negotiations would fall apart. If there were four issues on the table, the CIW and Walmart would reach agreement on three but be at loggerheads on the fourth, and the negotiations would start all over again or simply go into a black hole.

It's worth mentioning the dog that did not bark. When negotiations broke down, in contrast to the campaigns against Trader Joe's and Publix or any of the fast-food chains, the Coalition never protested at Walmart stores. The CIW had long decided not to boycott grocery chains, but they never rallied their allies and painted colorful banners for marches or protests against the broader-based Walmart. This was partly because Walmart had come to the CIW rather than the Coalition going after them with a campaign. But it is also, as Laura Germino explained to David Wang, "because for most people, Walmart is more than just groceries. People shop there for all sorts of household items, clothes, etc. The CIW ran the risk of alienating customers if they had to walk through a picket over tomatoes to buy school supplies for their children."

Walmart, for its part, tried alternative strategies when negotiations weren't moving in their direction. They looked for another credible social responsibility program with which to work and even reached out to the Fair Food Program growers to try and come up with a program that excluded the CIW. Walmart representatives were part of social responsibility conferences with Verité and Oxfam but it was difficult for other organizations to make the case that they had succeeded where the CIW had not. By the fall of 2013, the CIW was entering the third full season of the Fair Food Program and had demonstrated real and measurable changes in the fields. Another year went by without a case of sexual assault or slavery in the Fair Food Program farms. And, as the Fair Food Standards Council gained the growers' trust, the growers were now seeing the benefits of the program. Growers could now say to Walmart, look, this program works.

The headlines in the *Latin Times* and other news outlets in the summer of 2013 shouted: "Mexican Authorities Rescue 275 Workers from 'Slavery' at Tomato Packing Camp." The Bioparques camp where tomatoes are sorted and packed for export was in Tolimán, in Mexico's western state of Jalisco. Workers were offered "housing, food, and attractive working conditions, offering them 100 pesos a day, and schools" for their kids, but when they arrived the conditions were "sub-human." Three families with children were living in rooms of fifty square feet. Water was rationed. Food was rancid and rotten. "And," described one victim, "if someone tried to escape . . . they were brought back and beaten." As the tragedy was uncovered, it was evident that the operation supplied major buyers from across the United States and that abuse of workers in Mexico was starting to get attention. The next year, in his groundbreaking series in the *Los Angeles Times*, "Product of Mexico," Richard Marosi publicly identified Bioparques as one of Walmart's suppliers, but the CIW had been aware of that fact all along.

Summer turned into fall 2013. Sanjay Rawal was wrapping up *Food Chains*. The film was intended for release early in the new year. Rawal knew the negotiations between CIW and Walmart weren't yet resolved. The question was how to end the film? Would he tie Walmart to the subpoverty wages and abuse of farmworkers in the United States and Mexico, joining Publix in fighting the CIW tooth and nail? Or would *Food Chains* recognize Walmart as a leader in the supermarket industry, supporting the CIW and the Fair Food Program?

There was little doubt that Walmart saw the need for improving and guaranteeing better pay and working conditions for the farmworkers in their supply chain. They also recognized the effectiveness of the Fair Food Program's monitoring and compliance of the code of conduct. It is also true that the headlines given to Bangladesh and Mexico were more red flags for the corporation. They had to do something and wanted to do something that worked. As Jon Esformes describes Walmart's decision at the end of 2013, "CIW was opening a door for [Walmart] to walk through." If Walmart did not, they faced the possibility of CIW actions bringing attention to "their relationships with abusive growers and suppliers."

The pressure was intense but the logic was clear. Walmart decided to move ahead and close the deal. They would comply with all elements of the CIW's program. Walmart would become not only a participant in, but a major supporter of, the Fair Food Program. Walmart and the CIW moved quickly, holding a private signing of the newest legally binding Fair Food agreement on December 20, 2013. The world's largest retail chain, the largest buyer of tomatoes, the behemoth, came to the table and stayed. Walmart was now part of the Fair Food Program.

"If someone had told me twenty years ago that we would be sitting with Walmart, with the growers, and a representative from the U.N., I would have said they were dreaming." Gerardo Reyes could easily have been speaking for nearly any member of the Coalition of Immokalee Workers. He later reminded us that "no other buyer of tomatoes has the buying power and influence that Walmart holds with it." Cruz Salucio made the official statement for the CIW. "We are truly pleased to welcome Walmart into the Fair Food Program. No other company has the market strength and consumer reach that Walmart has. Through this collaboration, not only will thousands of hard-working farm workers see concrete improvements to their lives, but millions of consumers will learn about the Fair Food Program and of a better way to buy fruits and vegetables grown and harvested here in the US."

The sense of victory and a game-changing agreement was not limited to members of the Coalition of Immokalee Workers. David Wang was truly amazed with Walmart's concession and the CIW and Walmart coming to terms for Walmart's full participation. He hosted a dinner to celebrate the signing and wrote a commentary recognizing this "landmark event" and the potential for Walmart and the CIW to both achieve "their broader vision, which, if implemented, could affect a far greater number of agricultural workers throughout America." Steven Greenhouse declared in the *New York Times*, "Perhaps the coalition's biggest success is luring Walmart, which joined the program in January without a fight. Walmart officials said they were looking for ethically sourced produce as well as a steady supply of tomatoes." He then quotes Jack Sinclair. "We try to sell safe, affordable, sustainable sources of food—that's the only way we will be able to grow the way we want in the future." A story in *USA Today* announced, "The nation's largest retailer became the most influential corporation to join the initiative promoted by a coalition of farmworker activists based in southwest Florida." Congratulations shot across social media including @KerryKennedyRFK (Robert F. and Ethel Kennedy's daughter) tweeting, "Huge news! @Walmart joins @CIW fair food program—monumental step forward." And Michael Pollan took care to congratulate both Walmart and the CIW for the work they had done. "Walmart's agreement with the Coalition of Immokalee Workers is a landmark for both the company and the Coalition. By agreeing to sign . . . the Fair Food Program, Walmart has demonstrated its commitment to take responsibility not just for the sustainability of its supply chain but for the welfare of the workers in that supply chain. Both parties to this agreement are to be congratulated. Let's hope that other retailers follow Walmart's lead."

The ceremonial signing and announcement took place on January 16, 2014, not coincidentally the Martin Luther King holiday, in a watermelon packing house shed on one of Lipman Produce's Immokalee area farms. Sanjay Rawal and the *Food Chains* crew were the only cameras documenting the ceremony. John Amaya and Tom Leech signed for Walmart, joined by Lucas Benitez, Gerardo Reyes, and Nely Rodriguez signing for the CIW. Joining the CIW members and allies were Reggie Brown from the Florida Tomato Growers Exchange and Alexandra Guáqueta, chairwoman of the UN's Working Group on Business and Human Rights. A large group of farmworkers watched the ceremony on a large-screen TV back in the CIW's offices. The significance of the signing was felt by those in the audience as well as the CIW and Walmart representatives at the table. Laura Germino recalls the moment, remembering in particular "an amazing interaction with one of the growers, an Italian-American man who grew up in Philly. At the Walmart signing, he started talking about what an important moment it was. He said 'all of us know this is a time for dreams as we head into this special weekend.' Everyone was looking around and trying to figure out what he was talking about. Was there a wedding or other event this weekend? Then we realized he was referring to Martin Luther King Day, celebrated on the long weekend Monday. It was an incredible moment."

Before the ceremony, the CIW hosted a broad-based discussion with its members, senior leadership from Walmart, and members of the UN working group.

But even before then, now that there was agreement, Walmart's senior management seemed truly moved by what had happened. Just a week or two after the signing, Greg remarked, "Ever since they signed this deal, the Walmart leadership and staff have been overjoyed. . . . They are excited and happy to be part of this effort, the Fair Food Program." A couple of days after the private signing, Laura and Greg were Christmas shopping in Laura's hometown. Laura remembers, "Walmart people were calling and e-mailing, saying this was the best thing they had ever done in their professional lives [and] this was the best Christmas gift ever." In the days before the January public announcement and signing, Walmart brought "tons of people" to Immokalee. It was as though, Greg explained, "They had spent their entire careers at Walmart with the fundamental value that low prices meant good value and would improve people's lives." This was, in fact, just what Jack Sinclair had highlighted as Sam Walton's vision when talking to Michael Pollan's class. "But with this agreement, they've realized that there is more to it than that. . . . Value can have a different meaning and they were changing the lives of those in their supply chain. Since then, people at Walmart have mentioned that it can take a long time for Walmart to make a change, like turning a battleship. But once committed, they are all in."

WHAT DIFFERENCE?

Driving down the Delmarva peninsula, locally known as the Eastern Shore, you start in Delaware, cut through a piece of Maryland, and then, a little further north than you might have expected, you find yourself in the American South. Churches everywhere: Baptist, Methodist, and even a Catholic church or two. Evangelical churches in storefronts or an abandoned garden center. Only signs for Virginia peanuts and blue crab let you know you're not in Georgia or at least the Carolinas. "Metompkin Seafood Market—fried fish, soft crab sandwiches, fried oysters." Time for lunch. It's already hot, and the dog sleeping under the pickup truck in the driveway has figured that out, barely lifting his head as you pull in. Back on the road, passing small wooden houses, space between them but pressed up hard against the highway, revealing memories of quieter days and smaller roads. A large Tyson chicken processing plant and then Perdue. To the right and to the left there are great stretches of farm fields; lots of corn but also the potatoes the region was once known for. As you get closer to the southern end of the peninsula, you start to see Latino stores and Mexican restaurants, a telling clue as to who is doing a lot of the work. Not many tomato farms along Route 13, but turn off the highway, follow the dirt roads, and you're there.

Traffic is light and there's time to think. It's been a good story: Greg Asbed, the neuroscience major, rethinks the meaning of "human rights" after time with Haitian communities and uses both sets of lessons with the CIW to develop the strategy that upends the traditional approach to fighting for workers' rights. Lucas Benitez emigrates from rural Guerrero, Mexico, and, after taking his first stand brandishing a tomato stake, joins with the other cofounders of the Coalition of Immokalee Workers and becomes a leader in this revolutionary creation of farmworkers' rights. Laura Germino draws on six generations of Florida roots and experience with the good intentions and slim results of farmworker aid projects to relentlessly (and courageously) uncover and track down modern-day slavery operations in Florida's fields and swamps, teaching sheriffs, prosecutors, and federal agencies how to go after a scourge most thought was long gone. After standing on principle and finding himself without a home or food, Gerardo Reyes discovers he is a natural leader and brings a voice and intelligence to the workers of the Coalition. Using the humility, insight, and the strength to do what's right gained from his battle with addiction, fourth-generation farmer Jon Esformes forges an unprecedented partnership between growers and farmworkers. And at the right time, in the right place, Judge Laura Safer Espinoza realized she really had prepared her whole career to lead the Fair Food Standards Council.

Watching the fields and scattered houses roll by, you might be turning over in your head what you've seen. The names and faces keep coming, so many others who have been part of this story. Immokalee's farmworker community is the starting point, the motivation intrinsic to each. CIW members have shared and analyzed their experience in Florida's fields, marched in protest of abuse and low wages, risked their lives to rescue others from slavery, raised and answered the question of why farmworkers are poor, encouraged allies, targeted Taco Bell, defeated McDonald's, inspired the code of conduct, developed and conducted worker education sessions, and each and every day provided tens of thousands of Fair Food Program monitors in the rows, on the buses, and in the dorms and trailers and apartments that are their homes during the season. Nely Rodriguez speaking out for women in the fields. Silvia Perez and Wilson Perez leading worker education teams. Cruz Salucio's voice reaching farmworkers in their trailers bringing reminders of home and the possibility of a better future.

The Immokalee community gradually expanded, welcoming those who were willing to stand with farmworkers. The students, clergy, and other allies of the Coalition extended their reach and profile. Steve Hitov provided legal counsel with FRLS and then joined Greg in negotiating with one corporate giant after another. Sean Sellers and the investigators of the Fair Food Standards Council threw themselves into keeping track of the details to ensure growers and crew leaders complied with the code of conduct. And, of course, Pacific, Lipman, Harlee, Compass, Walmart, and Whole Foods—the tomato growers and corporations—who, after decades of conflict, joined in this improbable alliance with farmworkers to transform the fields and workers' lives.

The story is a good one, but that gets us to the questions that are the crux of the matter. Let's start with the bottom line: What lasting difference have the Coalition of Immokalee Workers and the Fair Food Program actually made?

Answering the question about the effect of the CIW and the Fair Food Program should be fairly straightforward. The first question is: What did the CIW set out to do and have they achieved it? Are farmworkers paid more? Is it safe to work in the tomato fields? Do farmworkers have "a seat at the table?" Let's keep it simple. Yes. Yes. And yes. Those are the first-order answers, but clearly there is more to this. We'll begin by digging into the situation of farmworkers on Fair Food Program farms. What has been the effect of the Fair Food Program? And then we'll step back and look at the effects of the program on the other two partners in this new collaboration: growers and buyers. Finally, we must ask, as the CIW has tackled the persistent and complex problem of agricultural labor, a problem that has troubled the United States for most of its history, has the CIW affected public policy itself, the work of the government?

Are farmworkers paid more? Let's start with the centerpiece of the Campaign for Fair Food: payment of the Fair Food premium of a penny per pound by participating tomato buyers. If all the buyers for a given grower were in the Fair Food Program, this would be a thirty-two-cents-per-bucket increase, or about a 50 to 70 percent increase, depending on the piece rate, per bucket price, for tomatoes. While essentially all Florida (and East Coast) fresh tomato growers are in the program, that is not yet true for buyers. With Ahold and Walmart participating, Fair Food Program buyers are about 50 percent of the fresh tomato market. All the workers are receiving the premium but the percentage increase varies, perhaps between 25 and 50 percent. The percentage of a grower's buyers participating in the Fair Food Program, the percentage of sales in a given week that are to participating buyers, and how much a worker picked that week all contribute to variability in the percentage increase coming from the premium. What we do know is that since 2011 the penny-per-pound premium has resulted in payments to workers of more than $25 million.

There's variability in the amount of increase workers see from the Fair Food premium, but they've seen an immediate increase from perhaps the most worker-driven requirement of the code of conduct. Eliminating the *copete*, or "cupping," of tomato buckets is effectively another 10 percent raise. Eliminating the *copete* means that a bucket of tomatoes is a bucket of tomatoes and no more. The code also ensures that workers are paid when they work. The Fair Food Program has largely eliminated wage theft. Growers now directly employ farmworkers, use paychecks (or even debit cards) rather than cash, require signatures for paychecks, and, if needed, may remove crew leaders from the pay process. Workers are guaranteed at least minimum wage for every hour they work and are paid for every hour they are at work, clocking in as soon as they arrive on the farm and clocking out just as they leave. Sitting at a gas station or on the bus waiting for the dew to dry is no longer an uncompensated part of a worker's day. Earlier, we heard from Judge Laura Safer Espinoza that complaint line calls had shifted from violence or fear to "last check" calls—workers who were moving north and hadn't received their last paycheck from the farm they were leaving—and even these have significantly decreased. By the end of the 2014–2015 tomato season, the Fair Food Program reported that "less than 15% of valid complaints this season concerned failure to provide proper compensation, down from 40% last season."

The last piece contributing to an increase in farmworkers' pay gets back to a demand of the CIW's first strike in the Pantry Shelf parking lot. Tomato harvesting, like much produce harvesting, is still primarily a piece-rate compensation system. Workers are paid for what they pick. The bucket rate for the large, green "rounds" tomatoes is now between fifty and sixty cents, according to Laura Safer Espinoza, with most growers paying between fifty-five and sixty cents. It depends on where you are in the season, the availability of workers, and the grower's interest in retaining workers at the end of a season. It takes longer to pick a bucket of grape or cherry tomatoes, so the bucket rate may be higher or the grower may pay an hourly wage plus a bucket rate. For much of the 1980s and through the first decade of the 2000s, the rate was closer to forty to forty-five cents. The ceiling on wages that held for about thirty years has increased by at least 30 percent since the growers signed on to the Fair Food Program. Answering our question: workers are paid, are paid for every hour of work, and are paid 80 to 100 percent more.

The data also give us a first cut at answering this question: Are farmworkers now safe in the tomato fields? The code of conduct and the Guidance Manual require "zero tolerance for forced labor, child labor, violence, and sexual assault." We've seen from the Ramos, Navarrete, and other cases that modern day-slavery has been alive and well in American agriculture. Sexual assault is even more common in agriculture, the United States included. When Silvia Perez first came to Immokalee in the 1990s, "there were so few women, there may be three to four women in a work crew," which increased their vulnerability to sexual abuse and made it virtually impossible to complain about sexual harassment because they would likely lose their jobs. The 2012 Human Rights Watch report "Cultivating Fear" highlighted numerous examples of assaults and widespread harassment and the reasons immigrant workers in the United States are particularly vulnerable to both. The following year, PBS *Frontline* released "Rape in the Fields," a full-length documentary on the rampant sexual violence against women farmworkers across the United States. A farmworker recounts in a 2014 Al Jazeera America report how "a contractor or supervisor . . . would take women to a private place, to the edge of the field, and we understood that sexual assault is what is happening." For all of these zero-tolerance violations of the code of conduct, the situation has changed dramatically since the implementation of the Fair Food Program. As of the end of 2015, there had been no cases of forced labor on participating farms since the program was first piloted in the 2010–2011 season. There were no reported cases of child labor, violence, or sexual assault in the 2013 through 2015 seasons.

Our attention is captured by consideration of these extreme abuses, but the CIW has long recognized that lower-level harassment and abuse provided the environment for such extremes. The code and the Fair Food Program are intended not to support more prosecutions for violence and slavery but, as emphasized by Laura Germino, to "eliminat[e] the conditions that allow violence and slavery to exist." Leonel Perez reiterates the importance of going after the preconditions for the extremes: "Back before the [Fair Food] program, when there were more abuses, it was very easy for the situation to escalate into violence. The program is intended to prevent anything from becoming a bigger case of violence."

So ensuring that work in the fields is safe requires not just zero tolerance for these extremes but addressing the lower-level harassment and abuse that have long characterized agricultural work. Long-time farmworkers who came to Florida before the implementation of the Fair Food Program well remember what their lives were like only a few years ago. An older worker spoke with Fair Food Standard Council investigators Paola Ferst and Victor Yengle during a recent farm audit. After a few minutes of conversation, you'd guess that the T-shirt he's wearing is a deliberate choice, showing as it does a graphic of red, yellow, brown, and black human figures holding hands and reaching across the globe, even with its anachronistic announcement of an international college counseling organization's 2000 summer camp. "Yes," he grinned when Victor noted the day's heat, "it is hot but God would not give us more heat than we can bear! It is a beautiful day." Victor asked about what it was like harvesting tomatoes before the Fair Food Program. "Oh, it was brutal! We had to line up in the rows five minutes before picking could start. The whistle blew and you had to crouch down and start picking. If you stood up, you were yelled at. We had to sneak out of the rows to pee or to drink water. If you complained, you were beaten right in the fields."

New York Times reporter Steven Greenhouse tells a similar story after talking with another experienced worker. Angelina Velasquez told Greenhouse of days starting with boarding a crew leader's bus at 5:00 a.m., sitting for hours on the bus until the dew dried, and then picking tomatoes while "crew leaders often hectored and screamed at the workers, pushing them to fill their 32-lb buckets ever faster . . . pick[ing] without rest breaks, even in 95-degree heat."

Writing about the progress in Florida's tomato fields, Greenhouse continues, "but those abusive practices have all but disappeared." The farmworkers in Fair Food Program fields now both tell and demonstrate a new story of striking contrast to this recent history. The older worker talking with Victor broke into a smile recounting the changes he had seen. "I expected it was just talk but [they] did it! I am very happy." Victor headed off to join the other FFSC auditors but turned his head after hearing shouting from several workers. They were pointing back into the field, and a young man came out of the tomato row in jeans and the unofficial uniform of T-shirt, long-sleeves, and baseball cap, stepping through the red and green grape tomatoes that carpet the ground between the plants. "I need to talk with you. That new bus driver, Fabio, he uses harsh language and he rushes us." Victor had seen Fabio earlier in the morning, walking the fields. A big man, appearing even taller because of his large straw hat, he had the air of the young and the officious, ensuring that the others could see his walkie-talkie. He was not of them . . . Victor listens to the young man and promises to get back to him. Later, reflecting on what had happened, Victor pointed out the difference between the world lived not very long ago by the older worker and the new world on the Fair Food farms. "The fact that this worker felt comfortable yelling to us and talking with us in front of everyone, that's great! I gave him my personal cell phone number and I'll follow up to see if the situation gets better."

Getting at the underlying causes of extreme abuse is more difficult with sexual harassment of women farmworkers, in part because it can come not only from supervisors or crew leaders, but from coworkers. Steve Hitov recognizes that it is in part "the nature of the work and the roughness of the environment plus many [workers] come from cultures where sexual harassment is not encouraged but it is often tolerated." And there are also complications of family connections within work crews. Lina is a lovely woman from Veracruz. She's going to visit her sister in Houston so she can catch up with her nieces and have them help her with her English. Out in the fields, she's covered from head to toe: denim shirt, pink scarf around her neck, and a baseball cap with a bright yellow and gray checked shirt over top to keep off the sun. The fields are safer but it's hard to avoid harassment. "The men use hard language and tell coarse jokes." Has she reported this to anybody? "No. Many people on the crew are related so it won't help."

If sexual assault and sexual harassment are, as described by Jon Esformes, "the dark underbelly of American agriculture," the Fair Food Program has been identified as the only bright light. PBS described the program as "an innovative program . . . that helps prevent abuses," and the producer of the PBS documentary described the FFP as standing alone with its "proactive policies, the participation of workers, and the economic incentives placed on anti-harassment policies." The Fair Food Program uses a combination of the "Know Your Rights and Responsibilities" pamphlet and worker education sessions to let women know their right to work without harassment and to let men know such behavior is disrespectful and inappropriate and will not be tolerated. When investigating incidents or conducting an audit, the investigators talk to both women and men about what is going on. They've learned the key question to ask the male workers is "would you want your wife (or sister or daughter) working here?" Worker education team members and the FFSC's investigators have noticed that some of the men have been embarrassed by what is said to women in the fields and welcome the change in what's viewed as appropriate behavior.

Some of the challenge has come from a complete lack of appropriate training materials for agriculture. Virtually all the growers in the Fair Food Program now have company-led training on preventing sexual harassment and discrimination for both workers and supervisors. Most workplaces in the United States require some sort of anti-sexual-harassment training in agriculture, at least for their managers and supervisors. Beyond the CIW's worker education material and the training provided by the FFP growers, there have been but a few other attempts at this kind of training, even for farm supervisors. Liz Esformes laughs with frustration when she describes the HR department at Pacific Tomato Growers' effort to set up a company training program using standard HR resources. "You've seen the sexual harassment videos! They're from the 1960s and show people in offices and a woman in a June Cleaver dress with a man making sly remarks. None of this was relevant to agriculture and the fields."

Funded by a Department of Justice grant, the CIW, the Fair Food Standards Council, and Pacific Tomato Growers are working with VIDA Legal Assistance and Futures without Violence to develop training materials that are relevant and useful for farmworkers and supervisors. This, Laura Safer Espinoza declares, is "a first of the kind program to develop an anti-sexual-violence/sexual-harassment curriculum for agricultural workers." Pacific's East Coast farms have been the sites for piloting the new curriculum. Unlike training currently in place with Fair Food Program growers and in a few cases in California, these are not one-to two-hour sessions but, as FFSC's Lindsay Adams describes, "classroom-style, multiday training for management." The collaboration has developed versions appropriate for farm management, crew leaders, supervisors, all the way to the "dumper" level for those taking the buckets from the harvesters, as well as the workers. "CIW produced the video, wrote the script, and were the actors." They and the FFSC then team taught the curriculum to all the farm management in Pacific's Palmetto, Florida, facilities. Training of supervisors, crew leaders, and workers—simultaneously in English, Spanish, and Haitian Creole—took place in training sheds on the farms.

Do Fair Food farmworkers now have safe working conditions? Slavery, gun violence, and sexual assault have been eliminated. Verbal abuse and sexual harassment are no longer acceptable and continue to be reduced. The FFSC and the CIW have successfully resolved 1,700 complaints (most within less than a month) and the worst actors in the tomato industry have been weeded out. What about the more mundane aspects of agricultural labor that are not at the extremes of abuse but nonetheless affect the health and safety of all farm-workers? It's long been common in the agricultural industry to use pesticides and other chemicals without regard to farmworker safety. Workers might be caught in the spray or simply be harvesting produce from plants drenched in chemicals. Long hours in the direct sun, lack of clean water (or even any water), and no toi-lets were all simply part of the job in Florida and throughout the United States. Today, if you visit a Fair Food Program farm, you will see shade, clean water, and toilet facilities near where the workers are harvesting. If you're lucky, you'll be where the M&C Villagomez harvesting crew is working. It's midafternoon and music is playing from the flatbed trucks where the dumpers work, a rap version of *Walk this Way* competes with more traditional music from northern Mexico. On the back of the truck there are two large yellow coolers with ice water, much needed as you escape the overwhelming smell of green that closes in on you in the heat between the rows. Time for a quick break and you head over to the four portable toilets near the red and white Villagomez bus. Given the heat, there's a bit of hesitation as you open the door to head into the sunbaked stall. Stepping in, there's an overall sense of . . . cleanliness! Sparkling comes to mind and that scent . . . I think it is Fabuloso! Turns out there are two attendants for these toilets and Mrs. Villagomez takes some pride in their cleanliness. She makes a point of the attendants using Fabuloso, the cleaning liquid that says "clean" to all who have grown up in Mexico.

Even if you are not with the Villagomez crew, the Fair Food Program requires moveable shade, water, and toilets nearby. All the farms meet some or all the requirements, although availability of shade structures for all workers at all times continues to be a challenge that is a particular point of emphasis for the FFSC monitors. Crew leaders receive "spray maps" each morning so that they know where chemicals will be used and can avoid those areas. All workers are given guidance on what to wear to protect themselves from the sun and are provided protective gloves to avoid inadvertent exposure to pesticides or chemical fertil-izers. Laura Safer Espinoza says the idea of these plans was a difficult concept for some of the growers and crew leaders. She tells of an incident during the first few years of the Fair Food Program, when a dumper was unhappy with how a worker had filled his tomato bucket. Throwing the bucket at him, the dumper broke the man's eye socket. The crew's health and safety "plan" was to leave the man on the side of the road to "wait for help" that never came. Not surprisingly, in addition to firing the violent dumper, the FFSC's corrective action plan for the grower required the company to immediately develop and implement a comprehensive health and safety plan and train its entire staff on it. "This has been a new concept . . . and so the FFSC audits this by interviewing crew leaders. If there are eight crew leaders and eight different answers as to what they'll do if someone is hurt, this is not a good sign." There should be a plan for treating an injured worker, including how to get the worker to a clinic for medical attention. And yes, workers may stop work if they are concerned about their safety. They will not be paid for the time they are not working, but supervisors may not retaliate if they do so, and growers must educate the workers in how to do their jobs safely.

Shade, water, and toilets in the fields. Health and safety plans to protect workers. These are measurable improvements in working conditions. Add these to the reduction and even elimination of the physical threats and abuse of male and female workers, and our answer to the second question is yes, farmworkers are safer, in fact safe, when working on Fair Food Program farms.

"The tractor doesn't tell me how to run my farm," was the growers' response when the Coalition called for "a place at the table" in the late 1990s. This, then, was the CIW's third and most audacious objective. The Fair Food Program is grounded in farmworkers sharing the table with growers and corporations. A permanent, and real, seat at the table begins with the CIW's fourteen agreements with major retail buyers requiring the buyers to purchase tomatoes only from growers in compliance with the code of conduct. This is what gives the Fair Food Program the power of market consequences to compel compliance with the code's human right standards. Looking further, farmworkers are embedded in every aspect of the program. The code of conduct is drawn from workers' concerns and experiences. The working group that developed the detailed guidance to implement and enforce the code and the Fair Food Program includes farmworkers and growers. Monitoring of compliance with the code is significantly done by the farmworkers.

To see this transformation in the relationship between workers and growers, the place to start is at a smaller table, this one in a conference room at Pacific Tomato Growers' Immokalee offices. Alejandrina Carrera and her coworker Abel have joined Liz Esformes, Sarah Goldberger, Angel Garcia, and Jessica Abrigo. Even with the bulk of the long-sleeve white men's shirt, bandanna around her neck, and baseball cap, Alejandrina is a small woman, although her physical size belies her presence once the conversation gets going. Alejandrina and Abel are Health and Safety Committee members from their work crews. They've both been with Pacific for more than fifteen years, but Alejandrina is the veteran on the committee. Abel just joined. It's early in the season and so the crews are still small, laying plastic, planting seedlings, and staking tomatoes.

The Fair Food Program requires growers to establish Health and Safety Committees made up primarily of farmworkers and usually including members of the company's HR department. The CIW's intent is to establish "a channel of communication between the field-level workforce and management relating to a broad range of health and safety issues." This has been the slowest of the code of conduct's requirements for the growers to fully implement, because it is, in fact, the tractor telling the farmer how to run his farm. It's also been a challenge for farmworkers since it requires, as Laura Germino points out, "trust in the growers" to engage in the committee's work. Changing their relationships with farm managers is difficult for the committee members. Other crew members are often suspicious of what they're up to or envious that they are getting paid for time away from the fields. Peer pressure affects all of us, and it can take some strength for committee members to stay engaged and not drop off. Alejandrina said one of the toughest things about being on the committee is "learning how to communicate effectively with coworkers." Abel shares the same frustrations, "Some of the crew members make jokes about us and are resistant. They weren't aware of Pacific's commitment to this."

At the monthly meetings, farmworkers raise concerns and work with management to find solutions. Full compliance with the code requires a committee of at least five farmworker members, with a representative selected by the workers from each crew. Committee members should be "qualifying" workers, those not in supervisory positions and therefore eligible to receive the Fair Food premium. The FFSC expects all workers on a crew to know who their Health and Safety Committee representatives are (at Pacific, Alejandrina and Abel wear yellow T-shirts and white baseball caps declaring "PTG: Grupo de Salud Y Seguridad"), and it expects farm management to announce the monthly committee meetings. Committee members are paid for their time "at a rate above minimum wage." By the end of 2015, 30 percent of participating growers had fully complied and an additional 55 percent were working toward full compliance. The shortfall is often because growers have included qualifying and nonqualifying (supervisory) workers as representatives. The remaining 15 percent of growers had not yet established committees.

For the farmworkers, Health and Safety Committees have provided entirely new, direct access to the farm and company managers. But the same holds true for the managers; they now have a direct channel of communication with those working at the day-to-day operational level of their farms. Like the complaint lines, the growers are learning about problems, often before they can escalate, reducing risk but also improving operations. Laura Safer Espinoza has seen that "a lot of the growers get surprising feedback. One company got feedback on a danger when workers are hammering stakes, staking tomatoes. Some of the workers were doing this without proper training, particularly if they came from other farms. They've also had feedback about sexual harassment occurring."

"We go to the fields and talk to our people [on the crews] and about whatever needs they have related to health and safety." Alejandrina gives us a feel for the committee's work. "The crews know we are the people they can come to and that we will report back to management, Jessica [Abrigo], and Angel [Garcia]. We have concerns about cuts, water, the quality of the water, PPE [personal protective equipment], whether the bathrooms are clean and in good condition, whether there is someone in the field to provide first aid help if help is needed."

Abel joins in: "We are always concerned about water quality and cups!" This turns out to be a big issue—the quality of drinking water and ice—and it's an issue that has shown the value of the Health and Safety Committee not only to the workers but to Pacific's managers. Pacific Tomato Growers was providing water before the Fair Food Program. But there had been issues in Immokalee with the quality of the water some of the farms were using. Alejandrina explains, "The truck drivers and crew leaders, they got water from whatever place. Now we know where the water comes from and that it is safe." "But there was still a problem," Abel continues. "The water was clean but the crew leaders got ice and put it in the trucks using shovels. They threw it on the coolers and dirt would get into the coolers." It turns out that most farms around Immokalee get their water from the same place. The crew leaders go there because the place gives them free ice along with the water, ice shoveled up and thrown into the water coolers. Pacific's operational and HR managers thought they were providing clean water and had no idea this was going on. The workers had all worked on other farms and knew the risks from contaminated water. Once they found out what was going on, Pacific installed a state-of-the-art water filtration system that even the managers now use for water and ice.

The workers on the Health and Safety Committee have helped the company improve the effectiveness as well as the safety of the farms' operations. Farm work is a dangerous occupation and injuries are common. Committee members get advance word out to the other farmworkers of risks, avoiding problems. For example, says Abel, workers want to fix machinery that jams. "The company has taught us that we are not the mechanics. If a machine jams or breaks, we should not try and fix it ourselves. Call the supervisor or the mechanic. You can get hurt trying to help." Demonstrating once again that small things matter when it comes to effecting real change, farmworkers bring a different expertise than the managers. For example, when transplanting tomatoes, growers use a mechanical planter that burns out the holes. Workers follow behind, putting the tomato plants in the hole and filling in the dirt. The holes are hot enough to burn workers' hands. After a woman was severely burned and had to file for workers' compensation, the Health and Safety Committee helped Pacific's farm managers develop a new planting process and new training for farmworkers and the supervisors for the planting.

We've looked at the basic data and heard from the workers. Farmworkers in the tomato fields are paid more and they're safer. They have a secure place at the table. The CIW has demonstrably achieved its objectives. But there's more to measuring the effectiveness of the CIW and the Fair Food Program. What has been the effect on the other members of this new partnership, the growers and the buyers? The apt analogy for the growers is perhaps a profound shift in the tectonic plates of agricultural workers and employers. It begins with the first requirement of the code. Sean Sellers explains. "The requirement that the workers be recognized as employees of the growers has a very strong psychological effect on the growers; these are our employees and this cannot be denied. The code says, 'These are YOUR workers and you are responsible for their pay, training, health and safety.' If you didn't know the history of the industry and the particulars of the work environment, you may not understand why this approach, rather than contract labor, is essential." Remember, says Sean, "Ag was subcontracting before subcontracting was cool."

On the ground, growers and their managers have seen benefits unimagined when they signed with the CIW in 2010. The first is improvements in some of the farms' operations, not only from the Health and Safety Committees but through the complaint line and audits and resulting corrective action plans. These mechanisms have given the growers, particularly senior managers, additional sets of eyes and ears monitoring daily operations. Asked about how Pacific has benefited from worker involvement in operations, Liz Esformes replies, "They tell us what is going on from a perspective we would never know. . . . We are better at what we do. We were good. Now we are better." Farm operations manager Miguel Talavera agrees. "The Coalition has helped us get better at what we're trying to do. . . . When we decided to make the agreement with the Coalition, I was completely against it. We weren't doing anything wrong and didn't need to change. And change is hard! Now, I am one of the biggest supporters of the partnership with the Coalition." Pacific Tomato Growers is not alone in seeing these positive effects. Lipman's CEO Kent Shoemaker has written about the benefits of the Fair Food Program on the Florida tomato industry. "The CIW has engaged our farmworkers in a meaningful way. . . . Lipman was one of the earliest supporters of the

Fair Food Program. . . . That's not to say there isn't room for improvement [but] we continue to implement changes that are revolutionizing the industry and bettering workers' lives." And Harllee Packers has found it useful to use worker education teams and discussions to resolve worker complaints about operational details during the harvest.

The second positive effect from the growers' perspective has been increased stability and experience in their workforce. Lucas Benitez has seen a remarkable change in the makeup of the agricultural workforce in Florida's tomato industry. "There are more permanent workers. In the past, at the end of the year there would be six thousand W2s for fifteen hundred positions. Now, W2s are reduced by 50 percent. There are more established workers as people see their jobs like a normal job, not jumping from job to job, eager to get out of Immokalee. When I arrived in Immokalee, the workers were 90 percent single men. Now there are absolutely more women. Thanks to the changes from the Fair Food Program, new generations of kids are born in the US whose parents work in the fields. The kids finish high school and work in the fields [and earn a living]. Last season, there were three sisters who are now women. I remember them as kids. They recognize 'Mr. Lucas' and remember going to the strike. These three sisters . . . I'm happy because their mother suffered harassment but they do not. They have better treatment and more respect. Finally, farm labor is an American job."

What the growers were unlikely to have imagined when they signed on to the Fair Food Program is a third benefit that comes directly from the move to a collaborative relationship with the CIW. Produce is a hard business. Most of the major growers make money, but, as we've seen, margins are low and the market can change quickly and dramatically. Too much or too little water, freezes, food poisoning scares, all can ruin a crop or the market for Florida tomatoes. But in recent years, the threat to tomato growers has come from Mexico. Accusations, with some evidence, of Mexico dumping tomatoes in the United States market to build market share have become common. Mexican growers have to comply with US food safety requirements but there has only recently been attention paid to worker abuse and wage theft on Mexican farms. Growers have found in the CIW and the Fair Food Program an unexpected ally against the market threat from Mexico, particularly in flooding the market with cheap tomatoes. Greg Asbed, joined by other CIW members, has been vocal in making the case to the US Department of Commerce that Mexico is unfairly competing against Florida growers who are now treating farmworkers with respect and ensuring safe working conditions. Similarly, Florida growers now benefit from the Fair Food label that differentiates their tomatoes from other commodity tomato growers (particularly from Mexico) in Whole Foods, Walmart, Ahold grocery chains, and a growing number of independent stores. Listening to their customers, these brands have come to believe that verifiable social responsibility can bring a competitive edge. Similarly, Jon Esformes declares, "Pacific is competing on social responsibility. We'll sell tomatoes to people who care about these issues." And, of course, perhaps the most powerful benefit to the growers is the one that compelled them to sign in the first place and ensures their continuing compliance with the code: access to the market. Fourteen of the world's largest buyers of US fresh tomatoes participate in the Fair Food Program. The sanction is a powerful one. Buyers will not purchase tomatoes from growers outside, or suspended from, the program. But the incentives are equally strong. Participating growers have access to a vast, semiprotected market for their product. The power of the purchase order indeed!

Okay. The growers have seen a benefit from the Fair Food Program in their operations. But there's a third partner in this collaboration: the buyers themselves. Fourteen buyers have signed Fair Food agreements with the Coalition. The agreements vary somewhat, depending on when they were signed, but all must comply with basics: paying the Fair Food premium for tomato workers, buying Florida tomatoes only from those growers that participate in the Fair Food Program, and refusing to buy tomatoes from those growers that are not in compliance (or working with the FFSC to come into compliance) with the code of conduct. The buyers are the "market consequence," the stick behind the Fair Food Program that pressured tomato growers to sign on and change their behavior. And the stick of market consequences has made it possible for growers to change their behavior and then see the benefits of having done so.

Like the growers, there's a range of participation and enthusiasm for the Fair Food Program among the participating buyers. There is correlation, even if not necessarily causation, between those companies that were actively targeted by the CIW's Campaign for Fair Food and those that don't promote the Fair Food Program on their website or elsewhere, and vice versa. Yum! Brands, McDonald's, and Burger King all have social responsibility sections on their websites, but the emphases are on their corporate codes of conduct and, not surprisingly, more focused on food safety, animal rights, and sustainable farming. Trader Joe's doesn't bring the topic up much at all. Jill Manata is McDonald's vice president for global public affairs and CSR engagement (although "engagement" may be a bit of a stretch). In conversation, Manata did all she could to indicate there was nothing special about the CIW or the Fair Food Program and it had no real effect on the company. She explained, "McDonald's is not really the best buyer to talk with since it was an early agreement and a different agreement for the others. McDonald's priority was to recognize and work within established relationships and the 'relationship chain' within the supply chain. . . . We do encourage our suppliers to take a lead on these types of things . . . and it is in our interest to always work with responsible suppliers. . . . We have no strong view on the [Fair Food] program or its success [and] McDonald's continues to look at its relationship with suppliers." But, to be fair, Manata did not think any other social responsibility programs were notably good or effective. The best ones, she thought, are those "that have multistakeholder situations and lots of perspectives and solution. . . . Programs that value and bring in suppliers and producers make the path a lot easier." Her concern was that social responsibility movements "don't realize the relationship structure. They overestimate what we can do. . . . We have to work with suppliers and be respectful of the relationship. . . . [Even with] cage-free eggs and antibiotic-free beef, all of the announcements were us with our suppliers . . . [and] we had lots of conversations with them about what could we do, and what can we get done." The tension appeared to be in McDonald's not wanting to be held responsible for what was going on several levels below in the supply chain. And it is this responsibility that is exactly the point of the Campaign for Fair Food.

There is another end of this spectrum. There you'll find corporations that are "all in" and have found the CIW and the Fair Food Program congruent with their organizational values. It's not surprising that Whole Foods is a strong supporter, but it's too easy for either the reader or the CIW to take their support for granted. As Jon Esformes points out, Whole Foods is a company "where their culture internally is even stronger than they communicate externally. Just a bunch of people doing what's right." Time and again, Whole Foods has led the way as the first grocery chain to sign a Fair Food agreement, first to display the Fair Food label, and willing to buy produce outside of tomatoes that is grown and harvested consistent with the code of conduct.

Maisie Ganzler recounts Bon Appetit's (and her) path to throwing themselves full-force into the Fair Food Program. "I grew up in Santa Cruz [California] and had driven through the fields of Watsonville many times. . . . I hadn't understood the conditions they worked under." Ganzler is Bon Appetit's chief strategy and brand officer. The company is an "institutional caterer" providing food services to corporations, private colleges and universities, and specialty venues like music centers. They have gained a reputation over the years for providing higher-end food and a strong commitment to social responsibility.

"In the early 2000s, a group in Oregon, PCUN [Pineros y Cempesions Unidos del Noroeste, a farmworkers union], approached Bon Appetit about boycotting NORPAC, a vegetable processor. They showed us photos and videos of farmworker living conditions and documented farmworker mistreatment. It is through this that Bon Appetit learned about farmworker mistreatment. We were the first to sign onto the NORPAC boycott." Bon Appetit's CEO, Fedele Bauccio, seized onto the bigger issue. "Fedele asked, 'how could Bon Appetit help improve farmworkers' living and working conditions?'" The answer did not come quickly. Maisie continues, "Every six months or so we'd have a meeting to talk about possibilities. We used a scale to report on the initiatives we were working on. . . . Red meant we wanted to do something but were not yet. Farmworkers were in the red category for years."

But then "we got a letter from the Coalition of Immokalee Workers and the path was clear. We scheduled a visit to Immokalee for April 2009. In March 2009, Barry Estabrook's article [in *Gourmet* magazine] came out. We started getting e-mails from some of our chefs asking about our tomatoes. . . . I was on a panel at Washington University in St. Louis and a student brought up the Coalition. I was happy to say that we already had a trip scheduled to Immokalee." The Bon Appetit delegation in that first visit to Immokalee included Maisie, CEO Fedele Bauccio, and Francisco Alvarez, a Bon Appetit chef from California. They were "already primed and knew this was something we wanted to do." The delegation was so enthusiastic about the visit and moving forward that when Chef Alvarez ran into Lucas Benitez in the airport, "it was like seeing a celebrity. Francisco went up to Lucas and told him he had read all about Lucas and the CIW." Building on its relationship with the CIW, Bon Appetit signed on to the Fair Food Program and has continued its commitment to farmworker issues, eventually supporting new initiatives including Oxfam America and its Equitable Food Initiative.

Cheryl Queen is the vice president for communications and corporate affairs for the Compass Group USA. Deeply committed to the Fair Food Program, Queen is instantly recognizable with her short blond hair and bold jackets when she speaks on responsible and sustainable supply chains at conferences and workshops across the country and internationally. Compass is the largest contract food service group in the world, owning a number of catering and institutional food organizations, including Bon Appetit. Compass promotes their relationship with the Coalition of Immokalee Workers and participation in the Fair Food Program on their website, and through Cheryl Queen, Compass has also become a frequent voice in support of the program and responsible sourcing. Speaking at the United Nations Forum on Business and Human Rights, sharing a stage with Gerardo Reyes at the FoodCon2016 conference, or as a featured speaker at the Responsible Sourcing Summit, Queen has made it clear that "we're very proud to support the work of the Coalition" and that "the Fair Food Program is a proven model for change in U.S. agriculture." Compass worked with the CIW, providing the corporate perspective as they worked through the details needed to turn the Campaign for Fair Food into the Fair Food Program. To this day, Cheryl Queen represents corporate buyers on the Fair Food Standards Council Board of Directors. As described by Queen, the value of this partnership to Compass goes beyond brand protection. "[T]he Fair Food Program . . . serves as another way to eliminate risks in the supply chain [and] our partnership with the Coalition has proven to be meaningful to our guests and just as importantly, to our own associates. We see that reflected in recruitment, engagement, and retention."

Walmart has led the way for CIW partnerships with major retailers. The immediate benefit to Walmart, as we've seen, was brand security in their supply chain and a direct counter to a steady drumbeat of reports on Walmart connections to suppliers denounced for factory and farmworker abuse and below-poverty pay. But there has also been a positive effect that is still fulfilling its potential, not only protecting Walmart's brand but strengthening it through supporting and extending the Fair Food Program to other regions and produce.

The next big target for the CIW was Ahold, one of the largest grocery chains in the world and the owner of Giant, Peapod, Stop & Shop, and, with its merger with Delhaize, Food Lion and Hannaford chains in the United States. While Greg Asbed and Steve Hitov negotiated behind the scenes, Lucas Benitez and the CIW applied lower-key but persistent pressure on Ahold through the campaign. No protests or marches, but a steady stream of articles from the Coalition. The characteristic tenacity of the campaign was demonstrated by the CIW, most particularly Lucas, regularly showing up at Ahold annual shareholder meetings. Asking questions from the floor, cornering Ahold's CEO to explain the Fair Food Program and the farmworkers' request, Lucas made the CIW's point. At the April 2015 meeting the tone and tenor changed. In his address to shareholders, Ahold CEO Dick Boer talked about the changing demands of grocery customers. "We are seeing a shift in what our customers want. They want responsibly sourced and healthy food. They want to know where the products come from." Increasingly, Ahold recognized that "[a]s a large employer, as a producer and a customer . . . we see a role for ourselves in tackling a number of major challenges in society, including health, food security, diversity, responsible consumption and production." Boer reported on Ahold's progress in a number of "Responsible Retailing" objectives, and then he focused on sourcing of Ahold's products. "We analyze the supply chain, farmer to customer, and continuously take steps to ensure food safety, sustainable production and good working conditions." And then it comes, after at least five years of pressure, "I am very pleased to report at this meeting that Ahold USA has joined the Coalition of Immokalee Workers' (CIW) Fair Food Program, dedicated to delivering responsibly sourced tomatoes and improving the lives of farm workers in the U.S." In fact, the deal was not quite done. There were still details to work out but serious negotiations were underway.

On July 29, 2015, CIW and Ahold USA announced that the company was officially part of the Fair Food Program. Ahold USA's chief operating officer James McCann commented, "The Fair Food Program is a time-tested leader in improving the lives of agricultural workers, and we have observed the Program's success over the past several years." The negotiations were not easy, summed up by Steve Hitov as, "yeah, it was a bit like giving birth to an elephant (which of course makes the Walmart agreement like giving birth to a dinosaur), but it came out well." Ahold USA was the first major grocery chain to sign on to the Fair Food Program. Even without the Delhaize merger, the numbers were impressive. With the 750 grocery stores then owned by Ahold USA, the number of participating grocery stores increased by about 75 percent, providing fifty million additional customers with access to Fair Food tomatoes. In combination with Walmart, Whole Foods, Trader Joe's, and Fresh Market, one-third of the US supermarket industry was part of the Fair Food Program. The pattern continued, with each Fair Food agreement evolving from the ones before. In particular, in addition to paying the premium and agreeing to purchase only from participating growers, Ahold USA agreed to provide annual funding to the Fair Food Standards Council and actively promote Fair Food tomatoes in their stores and online. Beyond the specifics of the agreement, the CIW's real hope is that Ahold USA will be, as described by Barry Estabrook, "the first domino among the supermarket chains," beginning with the Delhaize Group chains. "We believe," explained Gerardo Reyes, "[Ahold USA's] leadership will send an invaluable message to the rest of the grocery industry that social responsibility is greatly strengthened when workers, suppliers, and retailers work together toward a more modern, more humane agricultural industry." The additional power the Ahold USA agreement brings to the Fair Food Program, strengthening the market consequences and opportunities for participating growers, was evident from the start. As is true with Walmart, whether Ahold will use that power to support expanding the Fair Food Program is an opportunity that will play out over time.

One of the compelling aspects of the Coalition of Immokalee Workers and the Fair Food Program is that the CIW imagined, developed, implemented, and achieved measurable success without government involvement. The CIW has succeeded where laws, regulation, and the courts had not, creating the profound change the cofounders of the CIW believed essential to ensuring farmworkers' human rights of fair pay and safe working conditions, not to mention recognition of the role farmworkers play in the food chain. Even in the Coalition's antislavery work, discovery and initial investigations have been accomplished by Laura Germino, Lucas Benitez, Romeo Ramirez, Nely Rodriguez, and other CIW members, then joined by law enforcement and the federal government. The Coalition recognized that change in the fields had to come from outside of traditional government mechanisms, and the Campaign for Fair Food and the Fair Food Program have been their nongovernmental solution to the persistent and complex problems in US agricultural labor. What was perhaps unexpected is that the CIW's decidedly nongovernmental approach has, over time, had a significant effect on legislation, policy, and the government's work.

The most powerful effect has been in raising the visibility of modern-day slavery in the US agricultural industry and then developing, implementing, and training others to combat human trafficking. As described earlier, Laura Germino and the CIW uncovered the human trafficking and slavery operations of Miguel Flores and Sebastian Gomez in the early 1990s, eventually leading to their conviction in 1997. The initial reaction of law enforcement and Department of Justice officials was disbelief, and it took some time before they could effectively investigate and prosecute these cases. The scale and brutality of the Flores case led to the federal Department of Justice, the FBI, and the Border Patrol as well as local law enforcement in Collier County, Florida, to develop their human trafficking investigative capabilities. More importantly, the Flores case was the first modern-day agricultural trafficking case to gain national attention and was thus a landmark case. The CIW's work led directly to establishment of the federal Worker Exploitation Taskforce and, most importantly, the passage of the Victims of Trafficking and Violence Protection Act in 2000, the first antislavery legislation since 1865. The law provided definitions, charges, and penalties for sex and labor slavery cases in the United States. In 2010, the legislation was updated, again informed by the CIW's antislavery expertise, which provided clarifications of the conspiracy statute and expanding responsibility for trafficking beyond traffickers to those who benefit financially (e.g. growers and factory owners) from trafficking, an expansion that Lucas Benitez argued for in his 2008 testimony before the Senate. US laws and the justice system have, therefore, benefited from the on-the-ground work of those who might have been their clients.

In 2003, the CIW's Lucas Benitez, Romeo Ramirez, and Julia Gabriel received the Robert F. Kennedy Human Rights Award for the CIW's antitrafficking work, the first US organization to receive the recognition. At the ceremony commemorating the 2010 release of the Tenth Trafficking in Persons Report, then secretary of state Hillary Clinton spoke of the evolution of the United States' antitrafficking strategy. Secretary Clinton declared that the new strategy emphasized "prevention, protection, prosecution" as well as "partnership." Attention to prevention comes out of the CIW's insisting that the objective must be eliminating the conditions in which modern-day slavery flourishes, not just being better at prosecutions. During the ceremony, ambassador Lou C.deBaca made clear Laura Germino and the CIW's leadership of antitrafficking efforts in the United States and the Department's strategy when presenting her with the TIP Heroes award. "[W]e talk about a multi-sectoral approach, tapping NGOs, law enforcement, labor inspectors and the survivors themselves. And the pioneer of that approach here in the United States is Laura Germino. In the early 1990s, Laura began to not just give a voice to escaped slaves, but traveled to Washington on her own dime to hold the federal government accountable to investigate and prosecute these cases. . . . [T]he Coalition of Immokalee Workers and Laura Germino have always been there. They've been important partners and, more importantly, an independent and pressing voice as they uncover slavery rings, tap the power of the workers, and hold companies and governments accountable."

Recognition of the CIW's antislavery work has continued, including receiving the Presidential Award for Extraordinary Efforts to Combat Trafficking in Persons in 2015, but even more important is the training that Laura Germino, as part of the Freedom Network Training Institute, developed and conducts for law enforcement, including the FBI and international agencies, on the signs of human trafficking, interview and investigation techniques, and protection of victims. Like the investigations the CIW has conducted for more than twenty years, Laura's training program and consulting move well beyond advocacy to on-the-ground action and implementation. Similarly, Laura and the CIW have also provided guidance to the Department of Health and Human Services and White House antitrafficking efforts on services for victims of human trafficking, serving on the technical working group convened by DHHS.

As the Fair Food Program has come to life and its effect in the fields have become real, the CIW has started to have significant influence on government policies and actions in areas beyond antislavery and antitrafficking. Dr. David Weil became the administrator of the Department of Labor's Wage and Hour Division in 2014 after several years of serving as an advisor to the division and the larger department. An economist, he joined the division with a strong reputation in public and labor policy. Mike Rios has worked with and for Weil across the years. A "game changer" is how Rios describes Weil's effect on the division's perspective and strategy. Weil has moved to a "strategic enforcement approach rather than whack-a-mole." Under Weil's leadership, the Wage and Hour Division has shifted to an approach directly influenced by the CIW, "trying to change not just one grower but an industry's way of doing things."

The CIW has, says Rios, "changed the way we think . . . moving up the [supply] chain and addressing issues present [throughout] the supply chain, not just down at the bottom." This new perspective, beginning to look at the larger system beyond workplace violations, goes beyond wages and hours. In 2016, the department issued a press release announcing that Red Diamond, a major vegetable producer, was paying a $1.4 million fine for wage and labor violations. For the first time, the department's statement named Publix Super Markets as one of Red Diamond's customers, linking agricultural labor to the buyer at the top of the food supply chain. In a sign for the future, the Department of Labor's Bureau of International Labor Affairs (ILAB) is now, according to Rios, "looking at establishing something that is 'CIW-ish' in the projects they fund in other countries."

The CIW's influence is also seen in the work of the federal Equal Employment Opportunity Commission. The EEOC's Select Task Force on the Study of Harassment in the Workplace highlighted the CIW's "radically different accountability mechanism." The task force noted that large corporate buyers "such as McDonald's and Wal-Mart, have begun to hold their tomato growers accountable by buying tomatoes only from those growers who abide by a human rights based Code of Conduct, which, among other elements, prohibits sexual harassment and sexual assault of farmworkers." The EEOC took in the program in its entirety, explaining that "the companies agreed to the program because of consumer-driven market pressures, and most of the agricultural companies [growers] . . . entered the program . . . because of the resulting financial pressures." The report continues, noting the importance of worker-to-worker education programs, the complaint system, and corrective action plans.

Farmworkers are not only paid for all their work, but they are paid more. Farmworkers are safe in the fields from violence and physical danger. They have access to shade, water, and toilets. Farmworkers are now part of the decision making with growers for those issues that affect their livelihood and safety and are the first-line monitors for compliance with the code of conduct. Improbable goals in 1993, yet each has been achieved on Fair Food farms.

What the CIW might not have foreseen in those early years were the benefits that have come to growers and buyers, the other partners in this new collaboration. What might have been just as surprising for this workers' group that stepped in where federal, state, and local governments had failed is that the concept, structure, design, and implementation of CIW's Fair Food Program and anti-slavery strategy and tactics would influence government legislation, policy, and action. The question we must now ask is why? Why have the Coalition of Immokalee Workers and the Fair Food Program been successful when government programs and other social responsibility initiatives have failed?

Lucas Benitez and Jon Esformes at the press conference announcing that
Pacific Tomato Growers had signed on with the CIW (2010)

Con Copete/Sin Copete, the Fair Food Program's revolution in a tomato bucket.
For years, workers were forced to overfill buckets and were not paid for the
extra pounds on top (the *copete*). Under the Fair Food Program, this practice
of systematic wage theft was eliminated, resulting in an effective wage
increase of roughly 10 percent and eliminating a major cause of violence in
the tomato fields.

Fair Food Standards Council monitor Victor Yengle interviews a farmworker during an audit on Virginia's Eastern Shore (2016)

Fair Food Program card provided to every worker on participating farms; farmworker rights and the twenty-four-hour complaint line phone number

Farmworker rights include access to shade, water, and toilets. The Fair Food Standards Council monitor Lindsay Adams interviews a crew leader on Virginia's Eastern Shore (2016).

Clean and cold water

Cruz Salucio and Nely Rodriguez lead a worker education session in South Carolina (2016)

Silvia Perez (standing, holding papers and facing the camera) leading a worker education session in Virginia (2016)

Leonel Perez speaking at a Campaign for Fair Food action against Wendy's in New York City (2016)

CIW and Walmart sign the Fair Food agreement with Walmart representatives John Amaya and Tom Leech and CIW's Lucas Benitez and Gerardo Reyes (left to right) in January 2014

CIW receives the 2015 Presidential Medal for Extraordinary Efforts Combatting Modern-Day Slavery. Jon Esformes, CIW member Catalina Ramirez, Lucas Benitez, Compass's Cheryl Queen, Laura Germino, Laura Safer Espinoza, Greg Asbed (2015)

Dawn in the tomato fields (2016)

DESIGNED FOR THE FUTURE

Why has this worked? Why has *this* effort to bring fair pay, safe working conditions, and basic human rights to farmworkers succeeded when so many social movements and social responsibility programs have succeeded in raising issues but not in achieving real change? Once we can answer this question, we can then look to the future. Where does the Fair Food Program go next? Is it a model not only for agricultural labor in the United States but for low-wage workers—clothing manufacturing, electronics production, as well as agriculture—around the world? Could the CIW and the Fair Food Program be an example of a larger phenomenon, a changing policy-making environment where governments still matter but where nonprofits, nongovernmental organizations, and even the private sector are not just influencing public policy but increasingly making and implementing it?

First, let's go to the headlines from 2016: "Six Accuse Clewiston Farm of Human Trafficking, Say They Were Forced to Work, Threatened with Guns." "Mexican Men Living in Homestead Indicted for Conspiracy to Provide, Obtain Forced Labor." The more things change, the more they remain the same. Why have the Coalition of Immokalee Workers and the Fair Food Program been successful in achieving their objectives for farmworkers? The CIW's success has not been because their work has been part of a trend in agricultural labor across the world, or even in the United States. Farmworkers in America are still faced with low pay, wage theft, abuse, sexual harassment, and, yes, even slavery. The first headline is from the 2014–2015 case of C&C Agricultural Farms. The mailing address is Clewiston, Florida, but the fields are located in what's known as Devil's Grove, the remote area northeast of Immokalee and south of Lake Okeechobee. Seven workers, including two women, were part of Reyes Tapia-Ortiz's crew. Forced to work ten- to twelve-hour days in the fields followed by three to eight hours in the packing house, they were not paid for all the hours they worked and even then often not paid minimum wage. Tapia-Ortiz used the classic (and illegal) wage theft technique of subtracting "cost" from the workers' wages for expenses such as drinks and transportation to and from the fields. Tapia-Ortiz sexually harassed and groped at least one of the women workers. When she protested, Tapia-Ortiz had her boyfriend falsely arrested and he was ultimately deported. The crew's workers came from Immokalee, Clewiston, and elsewhere in Florida. When they protested or tried to leave, the crew leader threatened them with guns and deportation and threatened in Spanish that he could "kill a worker and simply leave the body in a ditch." The crew leader carried weapons in the field and threatened the workers if they were not picking fast enough. The workers eventually settled with the C&C owners in 2015 and the federal court awarded a default judgment against Tapia-Ortiz for violations of the Trafficking Victims Protection Reauthorization Act, the Migrant and Seasonal Agricultural Worker Protection Act, and the Fair Labor Standards Act. In February 2017, the courts awarded $3.5 million in statutory damages to those victims who had stuck with the case for nearly four years, money they will be unlikely to ever see.

Perhaps not surprisingly at this point in the story, the CIW found out about the abuse at C&C through farmworkers who had worked on Fair Food farms. Not long after, Laura Germino and the CIW were involved in another Florida case, but this time the calls came in through the Fair Food Standards Council hotline. After five years without a similar case, when modern-day slavery raised its ugly head once again on a Fair Food farm, it was shocking. But the system worked. As soon as the FFSC received calls from a witness and then a victim of the forced labor operation at farms in Homestead, Florida, they notified the CIW. The FFSC dove into its own investigation. There was no doubt; the complaints were valid. Within just a few days of the first call, the FFSC referred the case to law enforcement. Soon after, the Department of Justice issued a press release from the US Attorney's Office in the Southern Florida District. Agustin Mendez-Vazquez and his son Ever Mendez-Perez were indicted for "utiliz[ing] physical force, threats of physical force, threats of deportation, and debt bondage to maintain control over other migrant workers. Workers under the defendants' control were beaten if they did not work every day; were subjected to harassment and abuse; and were required to relinquish large portions of their paychecks—sometimes entire paychecks—to the Mendezes." Both men ultimately pled guilty and in January 2017 Agustin was sentenced to seventy-two months in prison and his son to a year. The Fair Food Standards Council suspended the grower, DiMare Homestead, from the Fair Food Program.

Of course these cases are the extreme of violations of farmworker rights; but they're not rare. Lesser violations abound outside the Fair Food Program, in strawberries, okra, peppers, and even in tomatoes on farms outside of the Fair Food Program, like the Red Diamond Farms (also known as Tomato Thyme) case mentioned earlier. And there are ongoing cases, prosecuted or not, in strawberries and other crops throughout Florida.

Abuse of agricultural labor is not, of course, reserved for Florida. New cases arrive with depressing frequency, up the East Coast, in Georgia, and in Virginia, outside of the Fair Food Program. Farmworker issues including reliable and easily accessible access to shade and water, farmworker housing (or the lack of it in wealthy areas such as Napa Valley), and low pay are a continuing characteristic of agricultural life in California. Journalists such as the *Los Angeles Times'* Richard Marosi have brought attention to issues of farmworker abuse, child labor, and poor pay in Mexico. Steven Greenhouse, until recently of the *New York Times*, has highlighted the success of the CIW and the Fair Food Program while reporting on the early but not yet conclusive steps of other groups taking on agricultural labor issues. Particularly in his reporting on the continued tragedy of factory workers in Bangladesh, Greenhouse has highlighted the failure of advocacy and corporate social responsibility efforts to make progress. The Coalition of Immokalee Workers' success in making real, sustainable change in the lives of farmworkers has not been because farmworkers' lives are getting better in general across the United States. The CIW and the Fair Food Program have succeeded in making demonstrable progress in one of the most persistent and complex societal problems in our nation's history. We've seen the data and evidence of change in farmworkers' lives and the unexpected benefit to growers and buyers. So why *has* the CIW succeeded while many others have not?

Answering this question brings us to insights about not only the CIW but more broadly in achieving solutions to long-standing social problems. The effectiveness of the CIW and the Fair Food Program brings to light five insights that make it possible to go after systemic, deeply rooted issues long impervious to traditional, government-based solutions. The first of these is that real change, sustainable change, cannot be led or forced from the outside. The second is that to "change the system," you have to understand the system from one end to the other. Third is the distinctive ability of the Coalition of Immokalee Workers to tell a coherent, consistent, and, most of all, compelling story. The fourth is the piece often left behind by advocates and policy makers alike: implementation

matters! Finally, real systemic change is about people as much as policy or organizations; people with courage, objectivity, creativity, and persistence.

Real and Sustainable Change Cannot Be Led or Forced from the Outside

The problem of agricultural labor is not new in the United States. Throughout
its history, our nation has struggled, for cultural and economic reasons, with
the role and place of agricultural labor, even into the twenty-first century. In the
face of a vacuum of successful government protections, advocacy groups have
sprung up to represent agricultural workers. Many of these groups have taken a
legalistic approach, building cases to fight individual violations. In Florida, the
primary organization representing the legal rights of workers was Florida Rural
Legal Services. The organization filed complaints with the Department of Labor
or charges against work crew leaders and the growers for individual legal violations of minimum wage laws or wage theft. But the Department of Labor was
slow to respond to such complaints, and wins in court were difficult, given the
migrant population and a shortage of concrete evidence.

More recently, corporate social responsibility (CSR) programs have become
popular as major corporations have responded to consumer concerns about mistreatment of—often outsourced—workers producing T-shirts, computers, etc.
These CSR programs often include a corporate statement of standards for the
treatment of workers and audits from international organizations such as Verité,
SGS, or Asia Inspection. The effectiveness of these programs has been repeatedly
brought into question, as in the case of the collapse of factories in Bangladesh
weeks after a passed audit, or the persistent noncompliance by plants and workers in Asian microchip and electronic manufacturing firms.

A defining strength of the Coalition of Immokalee Workers and the eventual
Fair Food Program is that workers, not an outside party, led the effort to change
their working conditions. This, then, is the first insight: Real and sustainable
change cannot be led or forced from the outside. The Coalition was founded
by the community of tomato and other produce workers in Immokalee, and its
membership remains as founded, with the addition of workers from new produce farms as the program expands. This was not organization, or even advocacy,
from outside the Immokalee community. From its earliest days, the Coalition
emphasized workers educating other workers about their circumstances and their
causes. Leadership has been broad and inclusive, which is essential given that this
is a migrant workforce with tens of thousands of new workers each season. The
code of conduct is a set of standards and requirements drawn directly from the
workers' experiences in the fields. When it came time to enact the program, CIW

members and growers together refined the code and were able to successfully implement it because it addressed the root causes of abuse and the realities of operating a farm. Finally, the growers' compliance with the code is monitored substantially by the workers themselves through the complaint process and enforced by market sanctions established in binding legal agreements won by the workers with more than a dozen leading retail food companies.

To Change the System, You Have to Understand the System from End to End

The traditional approach to most advocacy efforts is to focus attention immediately above the abused party. Animal rights advocates target the farmers who raise chickens or the slaughterhouse that processes meat. Unions target employers, whether they are car manufacturers or grape producers. Protests are usually focused on the direct employer rather than across an industry.

The Coalition's signal insight as the twentieth century became the twenty-first was recognizing that the growers—the apparent "enemy"—actually had little room to maneuver with regard to paying workers more. The CIW developed an understanding of the food system, which provided our second insight: To change the system, you must understand the system from end to end. Workers harvested tomatoes. Growers sold tomatoes to repackers or directly to retail corporations. The purchasing power and substantial margin were at the top of the food chain. The growers were being pushed from above by the fast-food chains and grocery chains that used their market power to push prices lower. They were also pushed from below by the rising costs of the petroleum-based inputs they needed to grow tomatoes in Florida. The market power of the major corporations could be both pressured and leveraged. The major retail corporations had the resources to pay the workers more, with minimal effects on costs. They also had a vulnerability: the critical asset of their brands. Produce "from the hands of a slave," no matter how cheap, hurt the bottom lines of Taco Bell, Burger King, and Trader Joe's when the CIW allied with consumers. Through understanding the food chain in its entirety the CIW was able to harness the power of the market to pressure the Florida tomato industry to comply with the code of conduct and increase farmworker pay.

The system-level perspective has continued to be a strength of the Fair Food Program as it has moved from an idea to a real program. The comprehensiveness of the approach—from a worker-driven code of conduct to the worker and grower collaboration in detailed operational guidance; worker-to-worker training; formal audits and investigations supported by a worker-triggered complaint system; and the power of market-based sanctions—is only possible when considering the supply chain as a whole. The results are farmworkers who take pride in their work, growers who respect farmworkers' contributions, and corporate buyers that take responsibility for their supply chain.

The Power of a Cohesive, Consistent, and Compelling Story

Our third insight is the importance of well-crafted storytelling. The CIW's story is compelling in part because of its remarkable consistency. The clarity of the story grabs listeners and is easy to understand. Its organic nature, from the experience of the farmworkers themselves, results in the same story from every member of the CIW staff, colored with their own personal insights. It is reinforced through popular education that provides context and language to CIW members. This story comes to life through many voices. "We are all leaders" continues to play out with an extensive number of CIW members speaking for the organization but also for the other workers.

The Coalition has leveraged meager financial resources and rich human resources to capture the attention of allies and consumers. Colorful and often dramatic protests and marches were amplified by Greg Asbed in his early use of the nascent Internet. Students, faith-based groups, and other allies were led by the workers in getting out the CIW's themes—"just one penny more," "from the hands of a slave"—and slogans that were directed at specific targets—"Say it ain't so, Joe"—and got a laugh from observers. Giant puppets, a papier-mâché Statue of Liberty, tomato buckets passed along the line of marchers; these all used drama and "showmanship" to tell the CIW and farmworkers' story.

The ability to tell a story played out on Capitol Hill or in news interviews, but some of the most effective and sophisticated storytelling was directed at those journalists, corporate representatives, and faith organizations that visited Immokalee. "Our experience of being in Immokalee [in 2009] and meeting the Coalition was unlike anything we expected," reported Compass Group's Cheryl Queen in her firsthand account of the CIW's hosting of her company's first visit. "We saw tomato fields, we walked the streets of Immokalee and saw the poverty and hardship first hand. We heard stories from the workers about conditions. . . . We sat in an Immokalee-style meeting surrounded by workers, families, and children and we shared our conversation—in English and Spanish. . . . The circumstances in Immokalee were so compelling and the ask was relatively small." Maisie Ganzler from Bon Appetit picks up on an important aspect of these Immokalee conversations: "CIW handles translation better than anyone else we deal with. [When we met with people in Immokalee,] each person had their own translator and so you had a conversation with multiple people, rather than one person listening, summarizing, and translating for the group. This approach respected individual voices of everyone and was a more personal conversation, even with a language barrier." It's important to remember that this is not a visit to a major corporation with public relations staff directing interactions with men in suits. CIW's community organizing and development of farmworkers' understanding of their situation and role in the food system makes it possible for CIW members to tell a compelling story time and again.

Implementation Matters!

Ten years after the launch of the Campaign for Fair Food, with the Coalition, commercial buyers, and growers in agreement, the door was open for the extraordinary change we see today. Before anyone could walk through that door, however, what had been the idea of the Campaign for Fair Food had to become an enacted and enforceable Fair Food Program. Why does implementation matter? Isn't it enough that this group of workers in central Florida won victories over major corporations and gained the acquiescence of the tomato growers after two decades of battling? In short, no. Implementation is simply getting things done, making an idea real. Implementation is where the advocates and journalists can sometimes turn aside, moving on to the next story or the next cause. The details needed for the endgame is where most ideas, policies, and programs fail. Getting things done is central to this story because to achieve the systemic change necessary to eliminate the causes of worker abuse, the program had to work, its success measured by metrics of real and enduring change in the fields.

The difficulty of implementing new public policy and legislation, turning ideas into concrete actions, is usually underestimated by advocates, policy makers, and policy researchers alike. Whether it is enacting the mental health reform legislation of the 1960s, building new and effective Special Operations Forces in the 1990s, or establishing the health insurance exchanges of the Affordable Care Act in this decade, new laws are often imprecise or vague. Policies and programs from outside the government, such as those promoted by major corporations like Nike or McDonald's, are not immune to these problems. Examples of ineffective corporate social responsibility programs include J.C. Penney and Benetton's standards for their suppliers in Bangladesh or Safeway and Walmart's standards and monitoring of suppliers in Mexico. Each of these cases is an example of how skipping over implementation considerations in developing policy or law results in unintended consequences or even outright failure.

The Fair Food Program ran the risk of ineffectiveness too. What has been distinctively different about the Coalition of Immokalee Workers' approach has been their persistence in taking their system-level perspective to the structure and elements of the Fair Food Program. The Coalition paid the same attention to making the Fair Food Program real—who, what, and how—as they did to planning the Campaign for Fair Food. That they've done so should not be a surprise given that this is a worker-driven social responsibility program. Workers designing a program to protect their own rights are going to be certain that the mechanisms built into the program to ensure compliance in fact work. The *appearance* of compliance isn't going to cut it.

The first step to getting past appearance and making this all work was recognizing that they would need to change their relationship with participating buyers and growers from one of confrontation to collaboration. The CIW refers to those they are campaigning against, or negotiating with, as "future partners." This framing influences all of CIW's actions in the campaign phase, whether with Trader Joe's, Taco Bell, or Wendy's. The second step was working with the growers to develop the details needed for implementing the code of conduct. The third step was establishing the Fair Food Standards Council. Defining and building a new organization might seem like an uninteresting bureaucratic exercise, but the FFSC is distinctive in its independent role of auditing, investigating complaints, and strengthening the tomato industry by advising on best practices. This is not a government organization and so it is constrained only by the code of conduct and the Guidance Manual in its jurisdiction or speed of action. The FFSC stands on the foundation of worker-to-worker education on farmworker rights and the power of sanctions and incentives drawn from the market and participating buyers. The fourth step was integrating the workers throughout the program with worker-to-worker education and the complaint line. End-to-end indeed.

Intentional Systemic Change Requires People Who Have Courage, Objectivity, Creativity, and Persistence

In answering the question of why the Fair Food Program worked when so many other social responsibility programs did not, we cannot leave out people who have made this happen. Greg Asbed and Laura Germino brought to Immokalee the idea of taking a community-driven approach to claiming farmworker rights, in direct contrast to the individual, legalistic strategy common in farmworker advocacy and legal aid organizations. Greg Asbed, Lucas Benitez, Cristal Pierre, and other workers from Haiti and Central America who cofounded the Coalition brought to the community popular education and leadership development techniques from the Caribbean, Central America, and South America. Laura Germino has faced down threats from crew leaders to do the painstaking and soul-wrenching work of uncovering and investigating slavery cases. Gerardo Reyes joined the cofounders and other CIW members in stepping back, looking outside the farm gate, and developing an entirely new strategy that used the power, resources, and connections of the food system as whole. Steve Hitov used a lifetime of legal experience and dedication to fighting for the poor, represented CIW pro bono for seven years, then joined Greg in negotiating with some of the world's largest corporations. Each has been devoted to pursuing the Coalition's objectives of fair pay, safe working conditions, and recognition of farmworkers as the first major element of the food chain.

These individuals have committed not only their labor but their ideas and creativity. The ideas were novel and original: worker-driven social responsibility, a system-level perspective on the supply chain, and then implementation of a distinctly comprehensive program. A notable characteristic of the CIW and the Fair Food Program has been its embrace of data and analysis. This is personified in Greg but is a characteristic of members of the CIW and FFSC's staff members. Lucas and Gerardo have been front-and-center leading and inspiring other workers and new allies, developing strategies for marches, and as powerful voices of the CIW. Greg has built and developed the intellectual foundation and systematic structure of the broader worker-driven social responsibility model. Laura Germino has established protocols and training for US and international slavery investigations and prosecution. Each has persisted even as they have been faced with indifference from producers, buyers, and consumers; an often critical lack of funding; and not infrequently physical danger.

Humility and courage are defining characteristics of tomato grower Jon Esformes. Jon's remarkable intelligence and business skills are now buttressed by a profound belief in the basic humanity and dignity of every person. This belief, and Jon's persistent lack of interest in what others think of him, led Jon to break with the other Florida growers, and the ties that had bound the growers together for generations, to sit down and talk with Greg and Lucas. A few weeks after that first cup of coffee, Jon and Pacific Tomato Growers signed the Fair Food agreement. Within a month, in November 2010, the Florida Tomato Growers Exchange, representing 90 percent of Florida's tomatoes, had little choice but to also sign with the Coalition.

It should not come as a surprise that implementation of the Fair Food Program has required not only new skills but new leaders. Since 2011, Laura Safer Espinoza's experience as a judge has been invaluable in leading the establishment of the Fair Food Standards Council. Her steadiness in standing down growers and supervisors who were waiting for the Fair Food Program to fail has brought a new element to further strengthen the CIW's Fair Food Program.

A challenge in writing about the Coalition of Immokalee Workers and the Fair Food Program is that this is current history and analysis. The CIW and the Fair

Food Program are still moving, evolving, and expanding. In March 2017, the Return to Human Rights Tour was the largest march in the past ten years of the Campaign for Fair Food, providing new energy to the year-long boycott of Wendy's in the face of the chain's refusal to sign on to the Fair Food Program. New corporate agreements, expansion into new crops, involvement in emerging slavery cases, and the growing influence of the CIW's worker-driven social responsibility model continue. The last question to address is, of course, the hardest to answer since it is about the future. We know what has happened and its effect. We have insight and conclusions as to why the Fair Food Program has worked. But, what *is* its future? Is the Fair Food Program a model not only for agricultural labor but for industrial and other low-wage labor? Is the CIW's worker-driven social responsibility a model not just for the next decade but for the next fifty years? And is the success of the CIW in addressing the problem of agricultural labor a signal of a policy-making environment that has expanded beyond governmental solutions?

Before we head off to a future of new scale and scope, let's look at where the current Fair Food Program is heading. The door to expansion opened when the CIW and Walmart signed and announced their new Fair Food agreement in January 2014. Together, they declared, "Walmart will work with CIW [to] [e]xpand the Fair Food Program beyond Florida to its tomato purchases from participating Florida-based growers with operations outside the state; . . . [and w]ork over time to expand the Fair Food Program to other crops beyond tomatoes in its produce chain."

The expansion of the Fair Food Program gets us back to Route 13 on Virginia's Eastern Shore. Pink and red crepe myrtles cut through the glaring sun as you head to Pacific and Lipman's tomato fields. Geographical expansion was the natural first step in expanding the program since the tomato harvest heads up the East Coast—Georgia, South and North Carolina, Virginia, Maryland, and New Jersey—when the Florida season ends. The tomato production expertise of the worker education teams and the Fair Food Standards Council investigators was as relevant in Georgia as it was in Florida, and the growers would remain the same. The new elements were new managers and supervisors and a small percentage of work crews who live full-time in the expansion regions or, like the Puerto Rican crew that worked on the Eastern Shore, traveled each year to work for a few months and then head home. Local crews often do the preharvest preparation work and the postharvest clean up. Harvest crews are usually based in Florida, moving up the East Coast following the season.

From Laura Safer Espinoza's perspective, "the [tomato] expansion has been organic, moving naturally into a national program. The growers involved in the [initial] expansion come through the Walmart agreement. They supply Walmart in Florida and now must have all of their farms outside of Florida come into compliance to continue supplying Walmart." FFSC investigator Matt Wooten reiterates the point. "Companies knew the expansion was coming and many had rolled their Florida practices up north, so there were relatively few problems. The seven participating growers in the first expansion season the summer of 2015 were nearly all Walmart suppliers, but soon after, several additional corporate buyers agreed to participate in the expansion."

The CIW and the FFSC were able to quickly design the system and work out the schedule to support the expansion up the East Coast at the end of the Fair Food Program's fourth full season in summer 2015. The harvest season in the other states is short and sweet, running four to six weeks as compared to Florida's six months, and so the timing of worker education team sessions and audits was a fast-moving choreography.

In Virginia, by the second year, the FFSC audit teams had the logistics of expansion down. The coffee from the Holiday Inn Express on Route 13 jolts the team awake. They're standing in the early morning dark, relaxed as they go through the day's schedule with a senior regional farm manager and wait for the workers to arrive. The workers at the farms the FFSC is auditing today attended the CIW worker education session held just a week or two ago. The education and audits are deliberately timed this way, moving up the East Coast following the crop. "The goal," says Matt Wooten, "is if you work in the fields you should see the partnership between the grower and the CIW and the Fair Food Program as broad and strong. The CIW comes in and then the FFSC, and the growers and supervisors are supporting the team, helping in whatever way needed." With the expansion, Matt continues, "the program feels very big to the workers because it has all of these connecting pieces." Workers will see CIW and FFSC team members in every state where they harvest tomatoes." And the perception of breadth and strength is reinforced as the Fair Food Program applies uniform standards across the large growers' operations, regardless of state. Safety protocols; easily accessible water, shade, and toilet facilities; pay procedures; and access to the complaint line—the standards of the code of conduct—are applied at every farm.

Back in Florida, that "bigness" comes from extending the program to new crops. A press release tells us: "Whole Foods Market expands partnership with Coalition of Immokalee Workers: First retailer to introduce Fair Food Program certified strawberries." Whole Foods announced its expanded partnership in May 2016 and, perhaps not surprisingly, it would be buying the Fair Food strawberries from Jon Esformes and Pacific Tomato Growers. But expanding the Fair Food Program into new crops is more complicated than staying in tomatoes and heading north. One of the reasons for the effectiveness of the code of conduct and the Guidance Manual is because of the deep expertise that the workers and the CIW have in the growing and harvesting of tomatoes. While many of the tomato workers also work in other produce, the CIW must develop institutional expertise in these crops within the code and in the Fair Food Standards Council. As with the original code, the workers themselves provide the field expertise that is the foundation of this institutional knowledge. Farmworkers regularly move from tomatoes to strawberries, and many of the other crops being considered for expansion—peppers, cucumbers, blueberries—are often grown on the same Fair Food farms. And expansion into a new crop gives the CIW the opportunity to rework the code, keeping its foundational tenets but clarifying and strengthening it to reflect what has been learned as the Fair Food Program has matured.

A bigger issue, however, is getting the same market power that McDonald's, Taco Bell, and other commercial buyers provide in tomatoes into new produce markets. Each market and network of suppliers is different, depending on the number of producers, the timing of the seasons, and the volume buyers purchase. The first step was taken by Whole Foods.

Jon leans back in the booth at Lenny's Deli in Los Angeles. He had just come back from taking a smoke break, the red and white Marlboro hard pack placed on the Formica table. Jon focuses in on the case for Pacific moving into strawberries: "We're growing them on the same farm as tomatoes, near Palmetto [Florida]. . . . We've always looked at the berry business as a natural expansion. We have a land base and it came down to some economic decisions as to how we can expand and how we can increase the utility of our workforce."

Absolutely. Jon's not in business to lose money. He made an economic case for expanding into a new crop. But there is also, as the Department of Labor's Mike Rios makes clear, something about strawberries. "Strawberries have been a dug-in, entrenched industry . . . a dark spot for years, compliance wise." Looking back, Mike rues the Wage and Hour Division's difficulty in getting strawberry growers to comply with even the most basic of labor requirements: "It has been a struggle. Plant City [Florida] is the center for strawberries. All, underline all, strawberries nationwide you buy in this country between January and March or April, they come from Plant City. It's a very small town. The growers know what they've got and they can do what they want." But things are about to change. "Jon Esformes is now going into strawberries. . . . The fact that Jon has planted his flag in the middle of the strawberry industry, with the CIW and the Fair Food Program, has changed the game." There's real excitement in Mike's voice now. "It has been a real struggle for Wage and Hour to get compliance but now [we] have a plan for strawberries. . . . The fact is that now that Jon Esformes, the Fair Food Program, and the Coalition are in town will actually help Wage and Hour."

The CIW and the FFSC continue to receive a lot of phone calls from farmworkers harvesting strawberries because it's common for workers to move from tomatoes over to strawberries, where the pay can be better or during the slow times in tomato production. Since the tomato workers are trained in the Fair Food Program, they know their rights, they know the number of the FFSC hotline, and they've taken on the responsibility of monitoring and reporting violations of those rights. For example, in early 2014, the CIW received calls reporting a severe case of abuse of farmworkers in the strawberry harvest. This was a case with guns in the fields and beatings of workers. But in this case, the workers not only called the FFSC, they took videos with their phones of what was going on. There it was; crew leaders spraying chemicals where workers are eating lunch, crew leaders and field supervisors beating workers and then shouting at the other workers to get back to work and threatening anyone thinking of reporting the incident.

And so strawberries were at the top of the list when the CIW was thinking about expanding into new crops. Jon did the economic analysis. But there was also Jon's impatience with other growers' not recognizing that times have changed, or at least need to change. Cradling his coffee mug as he considers the question, Jon responds, "So, it was a natural expansion [for Pacific]. But I was also getting pissed off that no one in the strawberry business would join with the CIW and the Fair Food Program." When Mike Rios heard the news, he warned Laura Germino, "I know that you're ready for a big fight" but at the same time he was optimistic about the possibilities. Jon was not fazed by the possibilities. Whole Foods has been behind him all along and Walmart has reached out. Some of Pacific's managers received phone calls from the strawberry growers, but, Jon reported, "I can tell you that no one in my company quit over our going into strawberries. I think everyone walked a little taller because we continue to do the right thing and fight for the dignity of our workers, and hopefully make some money!"

As Jon staked a claim in strawberries, the CIW worked with growers and buyers to determine the next steps in crop expansion and to encourage moving forward. Walmart had agreed to work with the CIW on expanding to other crops but the nature of the market and market share was such that expansion required more negotiations with suppliers. As Jon has shown, the easiest way to expand into new crops has been with growers willing to do so and buyers interested in a source of abuse-free produce. By 2016, Lipman Produce led the way with bell peppers, bringing their Florida production into the Fair Food Program. Since peppers and other crops such as cucumbers are often grown on the same farms as tomatoes, the CIW is negotiating with Fair Food growers and buyers to move the program forward. This same model shows promise as the CIW thinks through the possibility of expanding the Fair Food Program into Texas.

What are the obstacles and challenges the CIW faces as it looks to the possibility of becoming the national standards, monitoring, and enforcement system for farm labor across American agriculture? The first challenge is expanding the strength of the current program's harnessing of market power to encourage and even force growers into the Fair Food Program. The second set of concerns comes with threats, or perceived threats, from outside the CIW and the Fair Food Program. Finally, we head back to the on-the-ground reality of implementation, effecting change, with the third set of challenges.

We've already seen the challenge of building market power needed to expand the Fair Food Program geographically and into new crops. Tomatoes offered a unique market because the US source of winter or out-of-season tomatoes is deeply concentrated in Florida and its long growing season, and the fast-food buyers purchased vast quantities of them. Walmart has been willing, even eager, to support these moves into new crops, but it has conflicting pressures coming in some part from wanting to maintain a broad-based supply network. Walmart signed with the CIW after Pacific and the Florida Tomato Growers Exchange had signed Fair Food agreements. Virtually all the Florida tomato growers were in the program and it was easy to expand the program north using these same growers. Walmart might be less willing to require Fair Food Program participation from suppliers in a new crop until there are some number of growers ready to do so. Recognizing that concern, Walmart, along with Whole Foods, could give preference to Fair Food–participating growers that expand into new crops (e.g., Pacific with strawberries and Lipman with peppers). Their market power combined with the differentiation of Fair Food–certified products is an incentive for other participating growers to expand or for new growers to join.

The picture is mixed in getting buyers beyond Whole Foods and Walmart to support expansion. As of early 2017, Fair Food agreements signed by the fourteen major corporate buyers in the program were specific to tomatoes. Walmart left the door open for expansion to other crops and Whole Foods has encouraged expansion. But what about the other buyers? As discussed earlier, buyers targeted by the Campaign for Fair Food such as Yum! Brands, McDonald's, and Trader Joe's seem unlikely to expand voluntarily. Those buyers that came voluntarily into the program, such as Compass Group and Bon Appetit, welcome expansion into new crops but don't have the market power to pressure growers. The additional market power may come from supermarket giant Ahold-Delhaize. Ahold indicated in their initial announcement upon joining the program that they might welcome further expansion, and they have continued to promote Fair Food tomatoes in their stores. Ahold-Delhaize is not a Walmart behemoth, but, particularly when combined with Whole Foods and other grocery partners, could be part of a combination that offers a powerful market to Fair Food–participating growers. It is not, in fact, necessary that every buyer be part of the Fair Food Program or that every buyer actively support expansion of the program. What matters most of all is that there is enough market share controlled by participating buyers to create an incentive for growers to join the program.

The most compelling reasons for Walmart, Ahold, or new major corporate buyers (to include Amazon after its 2017 Whole Foods purchase) to extend or sign on to the Fair Food Program are the continuing abusive working conditions characteristic of American agriculture, not to mention of international suppliers in Mexico and beyond. These conditions put corporate food service and food retailer brands at risk. Tempting as less demanding certification programs might be, the Fair Food Program now has a lengthy track record of effectively eliminating farmworker abuse and quickly identifying and resolving problems that are inevitable in major agricultural operations. As the CIW's monitoring and complaint system expands, particularly if the complaint hotline is available to more farmworkers, new cases of abuse will arise and will keep the pressure on buyers. Returning to the system-level perspective, growers themselves can provide corporate buyers the carrot to the hotline's stick. When Pacific or Lipman expand the Fair Food Program to new crops, they offer corporate buyers a demonstrated, effective, certified source of produce. And the buyers' take-up of this certified produce again acts as an incentive for major growers. Growers like Pacific and Lipman have the capacity and capital to expand, just as the major buyers have the market power to pressure (or entice) growers. If buyers want to protect their brands by purchasing Pacific or Lipman's strawberries or peppers, both companies will buy and plant more acres. Steve Hitov explains that large growers like Pacific "can make it work financially by cornering the market with Whole Foods and other buyers who want to buy Fair Food Program strawberries. [Jon] just keeps buying up land and growing more strawberries and taking more of the market." Growers who have been refusing to join the Fair Food Program, or even talk to the CIW, will see that they are losing market in a low-margin business. And participating buyers can apply direct pressure on new growers because even as they want to protect their brands, they don't want the risk of a single supplier.

A sticking point for the buyers not addressed in these expansion scenarios is the penny-per-pound premium. The idea of fair pay has been central to the CIW since its founding, and the penny-per-pound premium combined with the CIW's antislavery work compelled allies and consumers alike to support the farmworkers. The premium is highly complicated in its execution and remarkably simple in its intent. The mechanics of paying the premium have been complicated in significant part because the original idea was to have buyers passing a penny-per-pound directly to the workers rather than leaving it to growers to raise the price of their tomatoes and pay farmworkers more. We've seen that buyers pay something close to one and a half cents more per pound to cover the administrative costs to the growers and, as Matt Wooten explains, "there are four different mechanisms or reporting frameworks for tracking the penny . . . [in order] to accommodate the different supply chains of the buyers." Payment of the premium has often been the declared primary obstacle for corporate buyers to join the program.

It would, perhaps, as David Wang once urged, be easiest for the CIW to agree to put the premium "in the price" that growers charge for their produce. The risk on a practical level to the CIW and the growers is that the buyers could decide to negotiate with other suppliers to purchase cheaper tomatoes, strawberries, or peppers. The bigger issue, however, is tied into the simplicity of the idea of the premium. The CIW has argued that rather than providing farmworkers a range of public- or private-sector supports such as housing, SNAP (food stamps), or food banks, just pay people more so that they can afford good lives. "If you believe," argues Steve Hitov, "that subpoverty wages are a human rights violation, it makes the issue of the premium critical." The Campaign for Fair Food resulted from the CIW's analysis and conclusion that the top of the supply chain has an economic responsibility to the workers at the bottom of the supply chain. The CIW argues that the fundamental principle of the penny-per-pound premium is the explicit connection, and accountability, of the buyers to the workers. If the Fair Food Program loses this explicit recognition, you lose some of the advantage of the market as the most effective driver for enforcement. Given that the premium is at the heart of the Campaign for Fair Food, it is not enough for buyers to purchase Fair Food produce. They need to be full participating members paying the premium, although ideally with a simplified execution mechanism.

If incentives and pressuring growers and buyers is a continuation of what the CIW has done for more than fifteen years, there are signs of a potential external threat to the CIW's expansion of the Fair Food program. This threat is perhaps an unsurprising result of the CIW's success both in pressuring major corporations and in changing pay, working conditions, and traditional relationships with growers. This threat comes from international corporations concerned about the Fair Food Program radically changing longtime practices and cost structures in the agricultural industry. The first signal of this type of external threat raised its head in 2013, when Del Monte (specifically, Fresh Del Monte Produce) bought more than 7,000 acres of agricultural land in Florida from East Coast Brokers and Packers, a tomato grower that went out of business. They purchased another 2,600 acres the following March. Del Monte joined the Fair Food Program in 2014, perhaps due to pressure from Walmart, or perhaps with a more strategic intent: to break the program up from the inside.

Del Monte's vice president Paul Rice declared, "We are pleased to join the Fair Food Program and continue our commitment to strong ethical sourcing standards which ensure that the products we sell are produced in a way that provides fair treatment for workers in our supply chain." Unfortunately, Del Monte's track record with treatment of workers was not as strong as this statement would indicate. Not long after joining the Fair Food Program, Del Monte Fresh ran into compliance issues and sued the CIW and the Fair Food Standards Council when the FFSC moved to suspend the company. Del Monte was able to bring significant legal resources against the CIW and FFSC, and it is difficult not to wonder if this conflict was Del Monte's intent all along. The CIW and FFSC eventually had pro bono legal support, but the stress in time and resources on these small staffs was tremendous. In the end, the CIW and FFSC won the battle when Del Monte Fresh settled moments before heading into court. Del Monte Fresh is now in compliance with the code of conduct and as of 2016 is a Fair Food participating grower. The suit does, however, indicate that the success of the Fair Food Program and its potential to disrupt and change agricultural labor in the United States and beyond makes it a target for large agricultural corporations, particularly those with overseas holdings and the financial means to feel inspired to go after the CIW and FFSC.

The last category of challenges is that which affects all successful start-ups: resources and leadership succession. Funding for the Coalition and then the Fair Food Program has been a concern throughout. For much of the CIW's history, foundations including Kellogg, Kresge, and the Foundation for a Just Society have provided invaluable support. Oxfam provided support until it changed its strategic approach and led the founding of the Equitable Food Initiative partnership. A few individual donors have made substantial contributions, and as the CIW's network of allies came to life in the late 1990s, they have provided volunteers or funded staff positions. The FFSC is, as Laura Safer Espinoza describes it, "the gas guzzler of the Fair Food Program. What we do is really labor-intensive and requires people with certain skills sets. The pay isn't lavish, but it is better pay than the CIW staff, with benefits, etc." But the CIW itself has been operating on a shoestring since Greg, Lucas, and Laura cofounded it. As of 2016, the FFSC's budget was just over $1 million and the CIW's operating budget about $600,000. Salaries, tied to the current rate for what workers are paid in the field, are about half the CIW's budget, followed closely by travel. The problem became far more pressing when the CIW moved from focusing largely on the Campaign for Fair Food to the expanded portfolio of implementing the Fair Food Program and advising others on establishing worker-driven social responsibility programs.

Looking forward, the CIW has pursued and experimented with new funding mechanisms and sources in addition to continuing foundation support. Most concrete are new agreements like those with Ahold-Delhaize and Fresh Market supermarket chains, which include financial support for the Fair Food Standards Council, requirements that the CIW intends to include in future buyer agreements.

The debut of the "Fair Food" label in the fall of 2014 opened up a potential source of new revenue for the CIW. The label's release built on the momentum that began with the Walmart signing ceremony in January, continued with the US premier of *Food Chains* in April, and was followed by recognition of the CIW by the Roosevelt Institute and then the Clinton Global Citizen Award. The label's design is a bit Socialist Heroic, in bold green with a woman farmworker, tomato bucket on her shoulder, at the focal point, "Fair Food" across the top, and the legend "Consumer Powered, Worker Certified" across the bottom. Greg Asbed was delighted with the design: "We think of it as Rosie the Riveter meets the Chiquita Banana lady. The ideas behind the label are that we have a 'worker certified' label and standards; there is a female because that is where the most amazing changes have occurred; personal freedom . . . where men and women are treated well." First out of the box were Jon Esformes' tomatoes proudly displayed with the Fair Food label in Whole Foods, followed soon after by Compass as another early adopter of the label. By the end of 2015, Ahold carried out their commitment to promote the Fair Food Program and Fair Food label with bold Fair Food label displays next to the tomatoes in the produce sections of Giant and Stop & Shop and glossy photo spreads in their customer magazine.

The label follows the growth in organic, local food, or "Fair Trade" labels on food and coffee but is distinctive in its focus on the workers and in the market consequences for growers who violate the code of conduct. Eric Schlosser makes this point: "Everyone who eats fruits and vegetables should care about the farmworkers who harvest these foods. Our good health depends upon their hard labor. The organic label is wonderful, but it only describes how the food was produced. And local agriculture is important, too, but it doesn't guarantee that workers are treated fairly. . . . The Fair Food label lets you know that when you buy that tomato, you're helping people, not subjecting them to misery." The label has been used by Whole Foods, Compass, and the Ahold-Delhaize stores and the growers to promote the program and differentiate the product from other commodity tomatoes. New revenue will come if the CIW uses the label to develop licensing fees from retailers or growers, similar to Fair Trade and Rainforest Alliance. Broad use of the Fair Food label is up against two challenges. The first is technical: ensuring clarity that the label certifies the fair treatment of farmworkers, not issues such as food safety. The second challenge, however, is one that Jon Esformes identifies when talking about his use of the Fair Food label. It's possible "that consumers have 'label fatigue.' There's so much going on in a store in terms of claims by all these different organizations. . . . Unless it is with a chain like Whole Foods that really means what they say and is supporting it by giving it premier floor space, the label won't have a strong effect." Jon is concerned that "we're all a lot more excited by the label than any consumer or any store that wants to market to consumers. Pacific uses it on any East Coast products that a particular retailer wants us to. . . . Whole Foods, they're all about it. Trader Joe's hasn't asked me to put it on any produce."

Including independent and small chain grocery stores in the Fair Food Program is another possibility for generating new revenue to sustain the program. As discussed earlier, the original Fair Food model was aimed at massive markets dominated by major corporations: fast-food chains and supermarkets. As Greg reminds us, "pennies matter at that scale and the buyers' commitments give the program market power for enforcement." But many smaller chains or stores, or even restaurants, have expressed an interest in becoming part of the program. The CIW might do so by developing a "Fair Food Program sponsor" program with a small yearly fee. Most recently, the CIW announced the "Fair Food Sustainer Program" as a structured and deliberate individual membership program.

What the CIW has not done as of this writing is what might seem obvious: charge the growers to at least partially cover the costs of the monitoring, audits, and investigations. Initially, the CIW in particular had concerns about conflicts of interest. If the program was dependent on fees paid by the growers, would the FFSC be reluctant to suspend or even put on probation a grower? More recently, the CIW has expanded the argument against charging growers. To do so, Greg Asbed explained, "[would be] one more example of pushing costs down the chain to the growers, not up the chain to the top [buyers]." Both arguments are consistent with the CIW's stated principles but the latter is notable for the evolution of the relationship between the farmworkers and the growers, both now finding themselves closer to each other than to the buyers at the top.

There is a continuing tension with the CIW and the Fair Food Program between building on unique and demonstrated success and having the resources to do so. Not dissimilar to a Silicon Valley start-up, the CIW needs financial resources and human resources to build and expand the program. Exploring potential sources for long-term, sustaining revenue is important for the CIW to both expand and maintain its independence. In the near- to mid-term, a few more rounds of venture capital investment, most likely from philanthropic support from foundations and individuals, is essential and should have a high social payoff in transforming the fields. Financial resources are not, however, the only challenge when looking at the human resources and capital needed to build for the future, the last significant challenge to the future of the CIW and the Fair Food Program.

As Greg Asbed notes, "There continues to be an inherent conflict between expansion and maintaining integrity in the program." Some of this tension can be solved with resources; increased funding makes it possible to hire more staff for both the CIW and FFSC, fund operations, and support outreach including mentoring other organizations and participating in national and international forums. Some of the human capital concerns, as discussed earlier, are in building expertise as the Fair Food Program moves into new crops, but the farmworkers themselves mitigate that concern. A different type of challenge is staffing the Fair Food Standards Council. The combination of skills required for success—analytic education and mindset, physical strength, fluency in Spanish, maturity to handle conflict in the fields, and the ability to connect with workers and managers—are challenging enough. But an unexpected difficulty has been attracting applicants to Florida and the southeastern United States. Expressing frustration, Laura Germino remarks, "We need competent people willing to live in places other than New York City, Washington, DC, or Boston. For 'socially-minded' people, it is easier to get them to live and work in rural Morocco than in rural North Carolina. HR is really the limiting factor for expansion. The Fair Food Program is one of the most exciting, one of the most effective social responsibility programs in the world, but it is difficult to find competent people to staff the FFSC."

More resources will help the FFSC and CIW hire more people, but they may not get at the fundamental human capital issue that faces start-ups and non-profits alike: Who will lead when it comes time for the founders to step down? Greg, Lucas, and Laura are the three remaining cofounders who imagined, created, and established the community organization that became the Coalition of Immokalee Workers. Steve's creativity has been critical to their success in winning negotiations with major corporations. Gerardo picked up the CIW's banner and has become an articulate and compelling spokesman for the farmworkers' sacrifice and struggle, joining in to develop and evolve the CIW's strategy. And Judge Laura has brought to the FFSC a jurist's mind and an arbitrator's understanding. There are three reasons to believe that the Fair Food Program and the campaign will find its way out of "the founder's dilemma" and grow in the future. The first is that the design and coherence of the Fair Food Program and the concept of worker-driven social responsibility are detailed and robust while still flexible enough to expand and be applied to new labor areas. The extraordinary nature common to successful founders can be replaced by good and talented people focused on building on this foundation and expanding the reach of the CIW and the Fair Food Program. The second reason for optimism is the institutionalization of the FFSC's work through the refinement of the code of conduct, the documented procedures for audits and investigations, and the underlying database, as well as a steady stream of articles and speeches on worker-driven social responsibility (WSR).

The third reason to believe in the strength of the future CIW is that the CIW continues to do the community organizing and development work that is its foundation. The CIW still leads popular education and training for farmworkers and CIW allies, and education activities have only expanded as the Fair Food Program has moved to other states and new crops. It's important to note that definition of "membership" in the CIW has evolved as the Fair Food Program has expanded. Leonel Perez notes that workers far beyond Immokalee now know about the Coalition and their rights. "Many workers don't live near Immokalee and so they can't participate in CIW meetings . . . but they continue to look after their community." Greg Asbed expands on Leonel's observation: "The first and most important engagement came when we implemented the Fair Food Program. We engage every person in the fields through education sessions, talking to auditors, with the live and active complaint line. . . . Every worker is participating [in the Fair Food Program] all the time, every day." The second level of farmworker engagement continues to be with the CIW in Immokalee. Active members still attend the Wednesday meetings, Grupo de Mujeres, and Saturday movie nights. The third level of engagement, and the most likely source of future CIW staff members and voices, is the Central Comité. There, CIW members and staff members develop the strategy for the season's actions and the campaign. A significant part of this continuing community engagement is the essence of building human capital present since CIW's founding: "*Todos somos lideres.*" We are all leaders. The CIW has long taken a broad view of leadership. Rather than emphasizing elected leaders or representatives, all those interested in leading are provided training and the opportunity to lead wherever their strengths take them. Farmworkers who had the courage to enter the tomato fields have had the intelligence and communication skills to lead the Campaign for Fair Food and have inspired others to follow. The CIW has never been constructed around a single charismatic leader. There have been many voices of the CIW, some externally focused and some leading from within. Most of the CIW's decision making is still accomplished through Wednesday meetings and the Central Comité. Lucas, Greg, Gerardo, Cruz, Nely, and Leonel continue to train those who come behind them. And the same principle is applied to those who will follow Judge Laura at the FFSC.

If coming up with the idea for worker-driven social responsibility and the creativity of the Campaign for Fair Food requires "extraordinary talent," Lucas, Greg, Laura, and Gerardo must do what all founders and early employees of a start-up must do. They must continue to mentor and strengthen the good and talented people who will take on formal and informal leadership roles in the CIW and the Fair Food Standards Council. At the same time, they must begin to look for the new "extraordinary" talent that can see beyond where the CIW and the FFP are now to what they could be in the future.

Before answering the question of whether the Fair Food Program is a model for the future, we need to know whether the program is truly unique or if there are other alternative models. Beyond the corporate social responsibility models that the worker-driven social responsibility model is intended to replace, there are a number of other social responsibility organizations and programs in the United States. Many of these organizations have advocacy and legal representation missions, in some cases similar to Florida Rural Legal Services and now often including a component of educating workers about their legal rights. An example of this type of program is Farmworker Justice. It's been around a decade longer than the CIW and is now a subsidiary of the National Council of La Raza, a US Hispanic civil rights organization. Farmworker Justice advocates for immigration and labor issues, as well as health initiatives, and occupational health and safety. The organization is primarily an outside advocacy organization, rather than being led and run by workers. Its emphasis is on advocacy, lobbying, legal representation, education programs on labor and immigration law and healthcare resources, and facilitating connections for workers to needed services.

The Farm Labor Organizing Committee (FLOC) is strongly union-oriented, which is appropriate given its founding in the late 1960s and its ongoing affiliation with the AFL-CIO. Within this framework, it has focused on bringing workers into union contracts, including a 2003 contract that included workers, growers (the North Carolina Growers Association), and an agricultural manufacturer (the Mount Olive pickle producer). FLOC has specifically reached out to H2A workers (international "guest workers" within the United States) and farmworkers in Mexico who travel to the United States to work on farms in North Carolina. FLOC was an ally in a 2015 strike by berry pickers in Baja California, a strike that led to a pay raise for the workers.

One of the most high-profile farmworker initiatives is the Equitable Food Initiative (EFI), a collaboration initially among Oxfam America, the United Farmworkers, other farmworker unions and civil society groups, and Costco, now operating independently of Oxfam. EFI focuses on issues of food safety, social responsibility in produce supply chains, and pest management. EFI's origins go back at least to 2007–2008. Oxfam America had long supported farmworker initiatives, including the CIW. In the mid-2000s, it made a strategic shift from supporting others to establishing its own effort. Oxfam came together with its partners to ask how to go beyond symbolic victories and achieve concrete changes on the ground. In addition to farmworker organizations including Oregon's Pineros y Campesinos Unidos del Noroeste (PCUN), United Farm Workers, and FLOC, the group reached out to major retailers. As Peter O'Driscoll, EFI's executive director, tells it, many of these retailers were companies the farmworker unions had questioned in the past, asking, "Why don't you do more to ask suppliers to improve working conditions and wages?" This time, what became EFI changed the question: "The agricultural industry isn't working well for workers.

There are substandard wages, poverty, and dangerous working conditions. How is the system working for you? And what keeps you up at night." This was the first step toward building the partnership between workers, retailers, and growers that has become the foundation of the EFI. The retailers quickly identified food safety in the supply chain as a nightmare-inducing concern, but also the labor abuse newly brought to the public's attention by the CIW beginning in the 1990s and more recently through journalists like the *Los Angeles Times'* Richard Marosi and his "Product of Mexico" series. From there on out, the emphasis has been on collaboration. As O'Driscoll explains, "we say to our partners: We can all agree that food safety is an issue. We can all agree that abusive farm labor is a problem. Can we bring together all of our separate interests to address these issues in a way that creates value for all stakeholders?"

After "two to three years of discussion among strange bedfellows," the Equitable Food Initiative came to life in 2012. Peter O'Driscoll had a strong record in nonprofits and NGOs focused on the global food system and the effect of industry consolidation and globalization on small farmers and farmworkers. Oxfam hired him to lead the new initiative with a partnership that now includes farmworker organizations, growers, and major buyers Costco, Whole Foods, and Bon Appetit. EFI's standards cover food safety, farm labor, and pest management. Food safety standards address strategies to limit the spread of foodborne illness, with a focus on worker education and access to hygienic facilities. Pest-management standards address the protection of workers from exposure to hazardous chemicals and promotion of integrated pest-management strategies to reduce pesticide use. Labor standards include worker safety, compensation, and the right to organize and free association. Workers are trained not only to follow best food safety practices but to identify potential problems. In return, workers receive "above-average pay" and the growers have seen increased worker retention. Costco's participation from the program's initiation, joined now by Bon Appetit and Whole Foods Market, provides a market for certified produce.

O'Driscoll recognizes that "yes, food safety got the attention of the retailers but EFI has insisted on the interrelatedness of all three elements." EFI's program is based on the idea that the people doing the work have the insight and knowledge to do the right thing. To give a specific example from food safety, O'Driscoll uses the strawberry harvest. "Farmworkers field pack directly from the plant into the [plastic] clam shell. Then it is sent to the distributor. So, the last hand that touched the strawberry before you open the clamshell is the hand of the farmworker. If the worker doesn't have access to sanitary facilities, they can't clean their hands. Jewelry such as wedding rings are very important to farmworkers. But they collect bacteria under the rings. If workers don't know not to wear jewelry in the fields, they can introduce bacteria into berries and into the clamshell."

Worker education addresses food safety issues as well as worker safety issues in the field, including pesticide use.

O'Driscoll says that the foundational premise of the EFI is that there must be a return on investment for every sector in the partnership. The intent is for buyers to get a safe and ethical supply chain. Growers gain a market and efficiencies that come from implementing the standards and engaging the skills of their workers. O'Driscoll identifies the "thorniest challenge" in the program as the return to workers. Workers benefit from a safer working environment and the very real qualitative value of having a voice in farm operations. Farmworkers join supervisors and farm management on fifteen- to eighteen-member leadership teams at each farm (or grouping of farms). These teams have the primary responsibility for implementation and verification of the EFI standards, with an emphasis on conflict resolution, problem solving, and evaluation. The thorny part gets to the economic return for workers if there is value created throughout the supply chain from the EFI program.

In July 2013, the EFI standards were formally published on the web. "It was," explains O'Driscoll, "two to three years of work, under the initial expectation that EFI would be a primarily domestic program. So the economic return for workers was initially conceived as an increase over the national minimum wage of $7.25, which led to an agreement on $9.05," or 125 percent of the US federal hourly minimum wage. EFI viewed this as a floor, not a ceiling, but the landscape changed as EFI became an international program and as California and other states increased their minimum wages. The EFI wage standard was quickly out of date. As a result, in March 2016, a notable gathering of about seventy-five people was held at Costco's facilities, including representatives from across the groups on EFI's Executive Board: buyers, growers, and thirty-five farmworkers who had been participating on leadership teams on the farms of seven producers. The result was an unexpected consensus that EFI should not just talk about "wages" but instead look at total compensation including health care and other benefits. The EFI standards are, as of early 2017, being rewritten to reflect a commitment to increase and improve compensation. The next question, according to O'Driscoll, is "How?" "How to increase compensation?" EFI is working with partners, with a nod to the CIW's 'penny-per-pound" premium and the Fair Trade premium, to institute a percentage premium retail buyers will pay on the produce they purchase. O'Driscoll quickly notes that even when the idea is a good one, "the devil is in the details." How does EFI capture and measure the "farmgate price" known as freight on board? How do they calculate the percentage, measure the premium, and, most importantly, track it back to the workers? How do we ensure the premium is consistent and equitable across produce types and regions? And, most importantly, how does EFI get the premium back to the workers? As the CIW found with the Fair Food Program, none of these questions is easy to answer and the answers are even harder to execute. EFI is working with Costco, Whole Foods, and several growers to pilot the program.

The EFI program is still relatively new, starting as a pilot with a single California berry grower. As of early 2017, eighteen farms operated by six suppliers had received EFI certification, with twelve more in the certification process. EFI began in California but now has initial presence in three US states, eight Mexican states, and two provinces in Canada. If the return to workers is thorny, the briar patch is, of course, ensuring compliance with the standards. The on-farm leadership teams provide greater presence than relying solely on external audit teams. Workers are trained to identify food safety and pest-management issues. The challenge for EFI, as it is for any program, is the need for a combination of reporting, investigation, and resolution of issues, backed by effective sanctions. EFI is evaluating the use of phone-based apps for reporting. The issue of sanctions is trickier in a voluntary program.

Most of these initiatives have elements in common with the Fair Food Program or the Campaign for Fair Food, beginning with concerns about the pay and treatment of agricultural labor. The UFW began its work in the 1960s and FLOC in the 1980s. As CIW was well aware of the origins of these farmworker groups—and their successes and failures—the evolution of older organizations and the newer supply-chain-oriented groups like the EFI have been significantly influenced by the CIW's work. Peter O'Driscoll gives the CIW full credit for identifying and pursuing the largely unknown reality of modern-day slavery in Florida and the southeastern states. He, like many in farmworker advocacy organizations, uses language that reflects the tremendous progress since the CIW's founding in the early 1990s, progress that has in many ways redefined the vocabulary now used to discuss farmworker rights and an ethical supply chain. A focus on the supply chain, worker-led programs, brand risk, and worker-developed solutions all echo the CIW's language and ideas over the past twenty-five years. The Equitable Food Initiative and the Farm Labor Organizing Committee recognize the importance of the supply chain from worker to grower to manufacturer to buyer. Farmworker Justice has long understood that farmworker rights go beyond fair pay and include safe working conditions. But although workers on EFI farms participate with farm managers on leadership committees, most agricultural and farmworker justice programs are driven from the top through corporate buyer and grower interest in food safety, driven by unions organizing for workplace agreements, or are operating primarily as external advocacy groups without extensive operational programs. And none have developed the robust monitoring, complaint, investigation, and resolution system of the Fair Food Program.

The Fair World Project makes exactly this point. The distinctive nature and success of the Fair Food Program in comparison to other farmworker programs is noted in its 2016 evaluation of seven such programs, *Justice in the Fields*. The Fair World Project is a nonprofit "which seeks to protect the use of the term 'fair trade' in the marketplace," essentially evaluating organizations that have some sort of "fair trade" label and certification. The report gives the highest recommendation to the CIW's Fair Food Program. The Fair Food Program gets particularly strong marks for the combination of audits, worker-to-worker education, and the twenty-four-hour complaint line. The Fair World Project's strongest praise is for the Fair Food Program's "market mechanism for enforcement" that goes far beyond the other programs' "incentive of use of a label" and a primary sanction of loss of certification that may have "little or no impact on sales." The "immediate loss of valuable markets" is the sanction for growers that are not compliant with the CIW's code of conduct.

James Brudney comes to a similar conclusion from a different perspective. Writing about voluntary or corporate social responsibility standards, Brudney concludes that "[t]he Fair Food Program is substantially more successful than other corporate compliance programmes in the labour standards area." He identifies distinctive aspects that have led to this success including workers defining the issues; workers having multiple mechanisms for reporting violations and being protected in doing so; an "immediate meaningful impact for failure to comply"; and the Fair Food Program holding brands accountable for their supply chains.

Equitable Food Initiative is an example of an approach to social responsibility known as a "multistakeholder initiative." Jennifer Gordon has written extensively on immigrant workers and labor organizing, most notably *Suburban Sweatshops: The Fight for Immigrant Rights*. Recognizing the vagueness of the term, she says multistakeholder initiatives usually "bring together businesses . . . global brands with names most people recognize . . . and combine them with non-profit and religious organizations and sometimes with governments." Multistakeholder initiatives have come to replace stand-alone corporate standards or codes of conduct. The idea of multistakeholder initiatives is appealing: buyers and producers, and ideally including workers, coming together to improve safety, working conditions, or pay. The CIW and its Campaign for Fair Food called for just such a collaboration beginning in the early 2000s. The difference between most of these initiatives and the CIW's effort is that, unlike the Fair Food Program, multistakeholder initiatives are usually voluntary and their standards are not legally enforceable. For the Fair Food Program, the CIW's agreements with participating buyers are legally binding, like any contract. Buyers may not buy from growers who are not in compliance with the code of conduct. It is then the power of the market that keeps the growers in compliance. The code sets out standards of conduct, and if a grower doesn't meet those standards, it gets suspended. When the grower gets suspended, the participating buyers will not (because of the contractual requirements) buy from that grower. These market consequences are real and immediate for those growers that do not come into compliance. For most, if not all, other farmworker programs, the primary sanction for factories or growers that fail to comply with the standards is losing their certification, a sanction that is weakened in the confusion that comes from a growing number of seals of approval or labels. Gordon concludes, "while the rhetoric of MSIs is strong . . . overall studies have found repeatedly that the standards that MSIs have set are not reflected in meaningful changes on the ground." It is important to note that Gordon's work has been in the apparel industry in Asia. What remains to be seen is the effectiveness in the food supply chain of the MSI approach of newer programs like EFI, not to mention the difference in effectiveness between US-based operations and those in Mexico. The question remains open as to whether it is possible to have an effective voluntary certification partnership or if the EFI and others will need to move to more binding agreements with its buyers along the lines of the Fair Food Program?

Mike Rios at the US Department of Labor also sees the CIW as distinct from other social responsibility or farmworker initiatives. Asked if there were other groups like the Coalition in effect or approach, Mike jumped to answer. "Zero. There is nothing like it. Some folks are trying to implement something like the Fair Food Program. There are other advocacy groups. . . . But the comprehensiveness of the CIW program? No. Not even close." What about corporations that have up-close experience with not only the Fair Food Program but with other food system social responsibility programs, including those headlined by corporate standards? Jill Manata, McDonald's vice president for corporate social responsibility, was careful, offering "no strong view on a program or its success" although she did mention that McDonald's moved away from the early grower-led SAFE standards program "when the CIW started moving forward." Bon Appetit's chief strategy and brand officer Maisie Ganzler is encouraged by the promise of the EFI and notes that there are social responsibility programs in the areas of environment and public health, such as Seafood Watch, that have been effective in using consumer pressure to change the behavior of large corporate buyers. But "these efforts are mostly about raising issues with producers and the government. . . . [And even though] the Equitable Food Initiative has been effective on the farms where it has been piloted, it is nowhere near as mature as the CIW and the Fair Food Program." Pausing, Ganzler considers and then responds: "For pure social responsibility, the longest track record and the most effective has been the CIW." And Compass Group's Cheryl Queen makes a similar estimation.

DESIGNED FOR THE FUTURE

"The Fair Food model works. It is worker-led responsibility within a system that carries market-driven consequences. I expect to see more companies and retailers join the Fair Food Program because it serves as another way to eliminate risk within their supply chain."

Community organization, antislavery program, consumer-supported worker campaign, the Fair Food Program.... With each step, the CIW has created a new ring on a tree, supporting each other to thus far produce remarkable strength. The question is, where does this go? Is the next ring a national and even global worker-driven social responsibility (WSR) model for labor rights, for workers' human rights? Can the WSR model, supported by the earlier tree rings, provide a model for the future of agricultural labor specifically and low-wage labor more broadly? Certainly the United Nations Working Group of the Human Rights Council believes in this possibility. The working group visited the United States in the spring of 2014 to investigate issues of "human rights and transnational corporations and other business enterprises." More specifically, the group looked at implementation by the US federal government of the international "Guiding Principles on Business and Human Rights; issues relating to respect for internationally recognized labour standards . . . and on challenges, gaps, and opportunities and good practice in implementing the Guiding Principles for businesses operating in particular contexts and in particular sectors, such as the extractive, finance, and information and communication technology sectors."

The report's conclusion gives the reader a sense of the surprise and concern of the working group after its interviews with company representatives, civil society organizations, managers, and workers throughout the United States. The conclusion notes that the US government is making progress toward the international guiding principles, but has significant room for improvement. The working group pays particular attention to agricultural laborers because they are excluded from the federal National Labor Relations Act. The working group also expressed surprise over "the hostility, particularly with respect to labour rights, of many business representatives to the notion that business enterprises have distinct responsibilities with regard to human rights." As a result, the working group emphasized, "[t]he Guiding Principles . . . reaffirm the expectation that business complies with national law, but where the regulatory framework is either absent, insufficient or not enforced, business cannot assume that legal compliance alone is commensurate with meeting their responsibility to respect human rights."

The working group did find a ray of hope in what was otherwise a dark visit. The working group met with, or researched, several "multistakeholder" initiatives to address labor rights in the supply chain. It found these ineffective in terms of worker access to remedies for violations of labor rights, the ability to identify violations, or effective grievance processes. The bright spot for the working group was the CIW and the Fair Food Program. Citing the combination of worker education sessions, the code of conduct, the use of the FFSC as a third-party monitor, and the legally binding nature of the Fair Food agreements, the working group declared the Fair Food Program "a groundbreaking model for promoting labor rights . . . which go[es] beyond existing legal requirements." The UN Human Rights Council and its working group strongly believes "that the ultimate responsibility remains with the Government to ensure that . . . labour rights are protected," but "in the absence or failure of those State mechanisms, the Fair Food Program provides a model of a market-based approach to the protection of human rights in corporate supply chains that ensures a substantive role for the rights holders themselves in monitoring and enforcement of their own rights."

What the UN working group missed is that the CIW is leading the way in a policy-making environment that has changed. Today, governments, of course, still matter. International organizations have an important role as well. But increasingly, nongovernmental organizations, nonprofits, and even the private sector are not only influencing policy but are making and implementing what has traditionally been viewed as "public policy." The CIW and the Fair Food Program have pushed this idea and action even further, since the FFSC monitors and enforces the public policy of the code of conduct and the market provides sanctions for violation of this new policy. The CIW demonstrates how nongovernmental organizations, particularly in a partnership between workers, industry, and the market, can create, implement, and execute public policy in areas where government solutions may not be possible. The Fair Food Program is not an interim program until government catches up, as framed by the UN working group. Nor is it an unfortunate result of a "failed state." It is instead a success that shows the need for, and the power of, novel solutions in those policy areas where the nature of government may mean the solution cannot come through government mechanisms. Governments do many things well, but they cannot solve every societal problem. In the case of labor abuse, governments require, by law and legitimacy, legislated and regulated process. The government must use the court system to fight abuse. If it takes six months or a year—or, in the case of forced labor in Devil's Grove, four years—the victims may eventually benefit from the judgment and payment. But all the coworkers, particularly women, don't see the abuser held accountable. They still believe they have to, in the words of Steve Hitov, "check their dignity at the farm gate." The Fair Food Program has established a process that can move quickly so that all workers see the consequences of violating farmworkers' human rights. Increasingly, it is becoming evident that programs like the Fair Food Program can be complementary to, and collaborative with, government programs such as the Department of Labor's Wage and Hour Division or the Department of State's human trafficking work. But programs like the Fair Food Program can also pave the way for government programs that lack not only resources but on-the-ground knowledge and persistent presence that comes from in the fields and on factory floors. The Fair Food Program is a trail-blazing example of a nongovernmental solution to a persistent and complex public policy problem. With each success, the program signals a sea change in "policy solutions" that could inspire other such creative and system-level approaches to solving other persistent and seemingly intractable public policy issues, such as low-wage labor, poverty, and educational outcomes.

How could the CIW's worker-driven social responsibility (WSR) model expand in the agricultural sector and beyond? For the CIW and the Fair Food Program, the most immediate challenges to expansions are described above. Human and financial resources are essential for staffing and leading the CIW and the Fair Food Standards Council. Corporate buyers are essential to the market power behind the Fair Food Program. Buyers provide both incentives through guaranteed or preferred market space as well as the sanctions to ensure compliance. Expansion into new crops is possible as growers see the marketing advantage encouraged by buyers and as large buyers including Walmart and Ahold-Delhaize see both the social good and brand protection in extending the program to new produce. Whole Foods has a distinct role as it leads the way in considering the fair treatment of farmworkers, along with organic food and animal welfare, in a sustainable food chain. As it continues to build buyer support, convey value to growers, and strengthen its resource foundation, the CIW will continue to expand the Fair Food Program into new states and new crops.

Beyond its own immediate efforts, the CIW is achieving scale and broadened scope through the formalization and dissemination of the WSR model. Greg Asbed has led the further development and refinement of WSR, writing and speaking widely on the concept and how the CIW has made it real, and spearheading the establishment of the WSR Network (WSR-N). Interestingly, it is possible that the power of WSR is significantly rooted in the very globalization that is often the target of groups supporting the CIW and other social responsibility efforts. "Multinational corporations" means that it doesn't matter if no one in India or Bangladesh cares about the abuse of workers. Consumers in the United States and Western Europe do. These consumers can put pressure on the corporations regardless of where they are located. The WSR model can protect workers' human rights and protect the brands that buy the goods they produce. In addition to fifteen years or more writing commentary for the CIW website, Greg, sometimes joined by Sean Sellers, has been published in a number of online news and commentary outlets, as well as in local and national newspapers ranging from the *Tampa Bay Times* to the *Los Angeles Times*. Similarly, Greg, Lucas Benitez, Laura Germino, Gerardo Reyes, and Laura Safer Espinoza are frequent speakers at international conferences including the United Nations Forum on Business and Human Rights, the Organization for Security and Cooperation in Europe (OSCE), and national events including the Washington Post Future of Food Conference, the Southern Methodist University annual Engineering and Humanity Conference, and discussions in association with recognition such as the James Beard Leadership Awards, the Clinton Global Citizen Award, and the Roosevelt Four Freedoms Awards.

Beyond articles, speeches, and awards, the CIW's WSR model has had visible influence. Recognition of supply-chain relationships beyond worker-employer and the power of the market have already been mentioned in the EFI and FLOC initiatives. Farmworker leaders in the strike against fruit growers in Mexico explicitly cited their experience with the CIW as invaluable in giving voice to the workers and shaping their protests. In Texas, the construction industry has been influenced by the CIW. There, Workers Defense Project fights unsafe working conditions, poor pay, and an exceptionally high death rate for largely immigrant construction workers. The result is the "Better Builder" standards and the city of Austin granting tax credits and a swifter permit review to developers who comply with the program. CIW's WSR model is cited, along with the Worker Rights Consortium, as a significant influence in the Bangladesh Accord developed to increase the safety of garment workers in Bangladesh factories. The most explicit influence, and even direct consulting from the CIW, can be seen in the Migrant Justice movement in Vermont. Founded by Vermont dairy workers, the group has declared a "Milk with Dignity Campaign" and is calling for collaboration between workers, dairies, and corporate buyers to ensure fair pay for dairy workers, safe working conditions, and reasonable working hours.

CIW's worker-driven social responsibility approach and antislavery work continue to gain traction and attention internationally. The group serves on the advisory board, along with organizations from Brazil, Indonesia, and Ghana, for the European Union's Horizon 2020 project to end forced labor in European supply chains as part of the globalized production of goods. Dr. Fabiola Mieres, a lead researcher for this project, highlights the worker monitoring aspect of the Fair Food Program as well as the move from contract labor to direct hire of farmworkers by the growers as particularly powerful elements of the WSR model. In addition to establishing the Freedom Network for conducting training for US and international law enforcement agencies, Laura Germino is increasingly bringing expertise and leadership to the problem of international slavery and trafficking. In 2015, Laura brought together two dozen "anti-slavery and anti-trafficking advocates, practitioners, researchers, and organizers" calling on the Obama administration to "take action to protect vulnerable communities within the declared 'Islamic State of Iraq and the Levant' ('ISIL'), including Yezidis, Christians, and Shia Muslims." She is an active participant in the Trafficking and Victim Protection task force of the Organization for Security and Cooperation in Europe (OSCE).

We'll return to Greg Asbed to consider the CIW and the influence of the Fair Food Program, antislavery efforts, and WSR. Greg goes back to the football he loves as an analogy: "In the NFL, they talk about coaching trees, like the [Bill] Parcells coaching tree or the Bill Walsh coaching tree. Those trees didn't come into focus in the midst of Parcells's coaching career; it's only after the second Super Bowl [victory] . . . that people say, 'this is clearly a coaching tree, a proven approach with offspring' and they give it a name." The CIW and the Fair Food Program have more than five years of proven results in the tomato fields of Florida and the East Coast, with first steps taken into new crops. Worker pay has increased because of the elimination of wage theft, payment for every hour worked, and corporations taking responsibility for their supply chains with the penny-per-pound premium. Working conditions are safe and without violence, sexual harassment is no longer tolerated, and the conditions that have allowed slavery to thrive have been eliminated. As farmworkers have taken their place at the table, growers have benefited from a stronger, more stable work force and a marketing advantage for their product. And corporate buyers, the original target of the Campaign for Fair Food, have benefited from a supply chain that is transparent and accountable to both workers and buyers. This is a proven body of work.

But let's seize the opportunity and push further. The Coalition of Immokalee Workers have succeeded not simply where many other well-intentioned initiatives and programs have yet to make sustained, significant, measurable progress. The Coalition of Immokalee Workers has succeeded where more than 150 years of government and legislative solutions have failed. Chattel slavery, immigrant labor, prison labor, debt peonage; our country has not shone at its brightest in the persistent and complex policy problem of agricultural labor. Led from the inside, by the farmworkers and their community, the CIW and its Campaign for Fair Food and the resulting Fair Food Program have succeeded not only in transforming tomato fields, but in how we view the relationship between workers, producers, corporate buyers, and consumers. This system-perspective, looking outside the farm gate and understanding the supply chain from end to end, provides the insight that holds buyers at the top of the supply chain accountable for those that put food or clothes or computers on our tables. The people who had the vision to establish and build the CIW had the intelligence to provide ideas that are revolutionary in the change they demand combined with the willingness to grind out the details needed to effect that change. And they did so by creating a narrative that was compelling in both its vision and its logic.

Yes, the CIW's comprehensive approach—rings of a tree that not only increase in strength but strengthen each other—is a model for agricultural labor in this country. But it goes beyond that. The CIW did not ask the government to "take care of workers." Overturning conventional wisdom, the CIW and the farmworker community did not view themselves as "liabilities to be managed by the government" but as human beings already demonstrating their strength and potential in their work. The fingers of both his hands pressing into the table with the strength of his statement, Gerardo Reyes is emphatic in his clarity. "We were not 'given' our rights. It is not even 'we took our rights.' Instead, we *created* our rights." Working outside of traditional government structures, leveraging the power of the market to create and enforce the human rights of farmworkers, the CIW's Fair Food Program is a model for eliminating abuses that have long plagued our industrial supply chains. Where there are consumers, there are pressures on corporate buyers. But where there are workers with a recognized value in the supply chain, there is also the possibility of a partnership that benefits workers, producers, and buyers alike. "I think it is very simple," says Lucas Benitez. "We are proud of our job and we [the workers] need people like Jon [Esformes] and his company to provide jobs for us so that we feed our families. And they, the growers, need us to get their product out. It's quite simple. We need each other and we need to work together."

A Note on Sources

This book is the telling and analysis of current history. The Coalition of Immokalee Workers, the Fair Food Standards Council, and the Fair Food Program are living, breathing, and evolving institutions. Because of this, the sources for much of what I've written are interviews, e-mail exchanges, and site visits. The richness of this story results from the insights, time, and patience of those who were willing to share their story with me. I am deeply appreciative. Most interviews were in person, although some were over the phone. I transcribed the interviews by hand. I strove to keep any quotations as accurate as possible. In some cases, I made minor edits to increase clarity. In many cases, I interviewed people multiple times or asked follow-up questions through a series of e-mails. While I have notes from each separate interview or exchange, to simplify the citations in the published book, where the source of the material (or quote) was evident, I did not use a separate citation. The exception is if there is additional clarifying material or comment in the endnote. The list below provides the names and affiliations of those I interviewed and the time period over which the interviews occurred.

Jessica Abrigo. Pacific Tomato Growers. Fall 2015, 2016

Lindsay Adams. Fair Food Standards Council audit team. Summer 2016

Lupita Acquila. FFSC. Spring 2013

Michelle Asuncion. FFSC audit team. Summer 2016

Greg Asbed. Coalition of Immokalee Workers. Interviews and e-mails 2011–2017

Kathryn Babineau. FFSC audit team. Summer 2016

Lucas Benitez. CIW. 2011–2016

Rabbi Mark Borovitz. Beit T'Shuva. Fall 2014

Derek Brinks. FFSC audit team. Summer 2016

Alejandra Carrera. Pacific Tomato Growers. Fall 2015

Noelle Damico. National Economic & Social Rights Initiative (NESRI). 2011, 2015

Jon Esformes. Pacific Tomato Growers. 2014–2017

Liz Esformes. Pacific Tomato Growers. Fall 2015, 2016

Laura Safer Espinoza. Fair Food Standards Council. Interviews and e-mails, 2012–2017

Paola Ferst. FFSC audit team. Summer 2016

Maisie Ganzler. Chief strategy and brand officer, Bon Appetit. Fall 2015

Angel Garcia. Pacific Tomato Growers. Fall 2015, 2016

Laura Germino. CIW. 2011–2017

Sarah Goldberger. Pacific Tomato Growers. Fall 2015

Luis Gomez. FFSC. Spring 2013

Steve Hitov. CIW. 2011–2017

Adele Jamieson. Senior director, Office of the Chairman, McDonald's
    Corporation. Fall 2015

Brian Kudinger. CIW. Worker education team. Fall 2015

Jill Manata. Vice president, Global Affairs and CSR Engagement,
    McDonald's Corporation. Fall 2015

Emanuel Martinez. Pennsylvania Student Power Network, Student/
    Farmworker Alliance. Fall 2015

Patrick Mason, Professor, Department of Economics, Florida State
    University. Summer 2016

Sandra Mendoza. FFSC. Spring 2013

Diana Moreno. FFSC. Spring 2013

Veronica Musi. FFSC. Spring 2013

Peter O'Driscoll. Executive director, Equitable Food Initiative.
    December 2016–March 2017

Leonel Perez. CIW. Fall 2015

Silvia Perez. CIW. Fall 2015

Wilson Perez. CIW. Worker education team. Fall 2015

Sanjay Rawal. Director, *Food Chains*. Fall 2016

Gerardo Reyes. CIW. 2011–2016

Miguel "Mike" Rios. Regional enforcement coordinator, Wage and Hour
    Division, US Department of Labor. 2015–2016

Abel. Pacific Tomato Growers. Fall 2015

Harriet Rossetto. Beit T'Shuvah. Fall 2014

Cruz Salucio. CIW. Worker education team. Fall 2015

Sean Sellers. FFSC, CIW, Student/Farmworker Alliance. 2011–2015

Miguel Talavera. Pacific Tomato Growers. Fall 2015

David Wang. 2009–2016

Matt Wooten. FFSC. 2014, 2016

Victor Yengle. FFSC audit team. Summer 2016

Notes

CHARACTERS

ix *Taco Bell, McDonald's, and Walmart* For decades, "Wal-mart" was the official spelling of the company's name. In recent years, the company has rebranded, using "Walmart." I will use the same for consistency (see https://www.walmart.com/).

PROLOGUE

1   *lives in virtual slavery* Estabrook, "Politics of the Plate."
2   *working with the Coalition . . . for years* David Wang, interview, March 12, 2009, in-person discussion; interview, April 27, 2015.
3   *picked by a slave* As quoted by Laura Germino. Laura Germino, telephone interview, June 22, 2011. A variation of this quote is also found in Powell, "Eric Schlosser Would Rather." As reported, Schlosser said, "If there are organic tomatoes being picked by indentured servants, I'd rather not have the organic tomato." Schlosser's wake-up call to consumers came with *Fast Food Nation* in 2000, followed by 2003's *Reefer Madness* and its chapter on strawberry workers in California.
4   *worst . . . to the best* I am quoting myself here as I first publicly made this observation in Steven Greenhouse's April 25, 2014, article, "Florida Tomato Fields, a Penny Buys Progress," in the *New York Times*. This book is the result of analyzing how this progress came about.
4   *fields of the South* Hurt, *American Agriculture: A Brief History*.
4   *in 1848* Southern Poverty Law Center, "A Brief History of Guestworkers in America."
4   *workforce in California* Guerin-Gonzales, *Mexican Workers and the American Dream*; Hurt, *American Agriculture: A Brief History*.
4   *picked up the slack* Rothenberg, *With These Hands*.
5   *harvested by Mexican immigrants* Schlosser, *Reefer Madness*. Schlosser provides an excellent short history of agricultural labor in California, pp. 88–90. According to the National Agricultural Workers Survey of 2001–2002, 79 percent of farmworkers were born in Mexico and in the 2013–2014 survey, that percentage was 67 percent (see US Department of Agriculture, National Agricultural Workers Survey, 2015). More comprehensive histories include Daniels, *Bitter Harvest*; Rothenberg, *With These Hands*; Hurt, *American Agriculture: A Brief History*; Majka and Majka, *Farmworkers, Agribusiness, and the State*. An excellent book focused on farmworkers in the Hudson River Valley but including an overview of "agricultural exceptionalism" in US labor law is Margaret Gray's *Labor and the Locavore*.
5   *told they owed* Bales and Soodalter, *The Slave Next Door*, chap. 1.
5   *during the harvest season* Ibid.
6   *One dies, get another* A truly remarkable book, Oshinsky, *Worse Than Slavery*, pp. 55–57.
6   *in the groves or work camps* Ibid., pp. 71–76; King, *Devil in the Grove*, pp. 76–80.
7   *increasingly industrialized economy* Sinclair, *The Jungle*; Lange and Taylor, *An American Exodus*, originally published in 1939 and including photos taken in the early 1930s; Evans, *American Photographs*, 1938.

7   *employed as an agricultural laborer* National Labor Relations Act, pp. 151–69; Bales and Soodalter, *The Slave Next Door*, chap. 3; Ganz, *Why David Sometimes Wins*.

7   *delivery or storage for markets* US Department of Labor, Fair Labor Standards Act of 1938.

7   *do not require overtime pay* US Department of Labor, "History of Changes to the Minimum Wage Law."

7   *rather than in the fields* Bales and Soodalter, *The Slave Next Door*, chap. 3; Miguel "Mike" Rios, interview, December 11, 2015.

7   *taxes into these systems* Oxfam America, "Like Machines in the Fields."

7   *chemical poisoning* Estabrook, *Tomatoland*; Bales and Soodalter, *The Slave Next Door*.

8   *Now, we just rent them* CBS-TV, "Harvest of Shame."

8   *mostly young immigrant men* Rothenberg, *With These Hands*; Patrick Mason, phone interview, August 16, 2016.

CHAPTER 1. TO BEAT ONE OF US IS TO BEAT US ALL!

10   *Pantry Shelf parking lot* Jefferson, "Alienation," p. 55.

10   *overpriced market* Descriptions of places, unless otherwise noted, come from the author's observations.

10   *working that day* Jefferson, "Alienation," p. 55.

11   *improve the lives of farmworkers* Greg Asbed and Laura Germino, interview, November 3, 2015, their home in Labelle, Florida, the coffee shop in Labelle, and running errands in Laura's car.

12   *Harvest of Shame* Steve Hitov, CIW general counsel, interview, September 18, 2015, Ted's Bulletin, breakfast restaurant/coffee shop, Washington DC.

12   *Legal Services Corporation in 1966* Sellers, "Del Pueblo, Para El Pueblo," p. 60.

12   *half the state* Jefferson, "Alienation," pp. 55–56; Greg Asbed, interview, November 4, 2015, CIW offices, Immokalee; Soohoo, Albisa, and David, *Bringing Human Rights Home Volume 2*, p. 12.

13   *not-too-distant past* Laura Germino, interview, November 3, 2015; "Obituary: Mary Audrey Roseborough."

13   *Spanish was invaluable* Laura Germino, interview, November 3, 2015; Jefferson, "Alienation," 1993.

13   *if you dared complain* Jefferson, "Alienation," 1993.

14   *each in turn* Descriptions of characters in this book come from the author's observations.

14   *Before heading to Brown* Author interviews; Grace, "Justice in the Fields."

15   *in graduate school* see Fuller Funeral Home, Naples, FL, Obituary for Norig Garo Asbed; "Obituary for Ruth-Alice Asbed"; Greg Asbed and Laura Germino, interview, January 31, 2014; Grace, "Justice in the Fields."

15   *hardened in every way* Edgerrin James with Dan Le Batard, "Straight Up," *ESPN the Magazine*, September 4, 2000.

16   *over 100 degrees* Asbed and Sellers, "The High Cost of Anti-Immigrant Laws," *The Nation*, October 11, 2011.

17   *in the early 1980s* Wasem, "U.S. Immigration Policy on Haitian Migrants," pp. 1–4; Soohoo, Albisa, and David, *Bringing Human Rights Home. Volume 2*, pp. 6–7.

17   *achieved some success* Laura Germino, interview, November 3, 2015; Lucas Benitez, interview, Immokalee; Soohoo, Albisa, and David, *Bringing Human Rights Home. Volume 2*; Sellers, "Del Pueblo, Para El Pueblo," pp. 61–65; Lucas Benitez, Laura Germino, Greg Asbed, interview, Immokalee, September 15, 2011.

17   *of Papay, or MPP* Sellers, "Del Pueblo, Para El Pueblo," p. 63; Greg Asbed and Laura Germino, interview, November 3, 2015. Greg Asbed, e-mail, January 16, 2017.

18 *Felipe Miguel* Greg Asbed, interview, November 4, 2015; Sellers, "Del Pueblo, Para El Pueblo," p. 65.

18 *where this would go* Greg Asbed, interview, November 4, 2015; Lucas Benitez, interview, Immokalee; Sellers, "Del Pueblo, Para El Pueblo."

18 *their movie nights* Sellers, "Del Pueblo, Para El Pueblo," p. 61; Greg Asbed, interview, November 4, 2015.

19 *wretched and expensive housing* Sellers, "Del Pueblo, Para El Pueblo," p. 65.

20 *financial investment* Laura Germino, interview, November 3, 2015; Sellers, "Del Pueblo, Para El Pueblo," p. 65.

20 *workers in Immokalee* Lucas Benitez et al., interview, Immokalee; Soohoo, Albisa, and David, *Bringing Human Rights Home. Volume 2.*

20 *as human beings* Soohoo, Albisa, and David, *Bringing Human Rights Home. Volume 2*, pp. 12–13.

21 *farmworkers in Florida* Steve Hitov, interview, September 2015; Soohoo, Albisa, and David, *Bringing Human Rights Home. Volume 2*, pp. 12–13.

21 *and Latin America* Laura Germino and Greg Asbed, interview, April 30, 2013; Soohoo, Albisa, and David, *Bringing Human Rights Home. Volume 2*, pp. 7–8; Estabrook, *Tomatoland*, p. 118–119.

21 *problems they faced* Lucas Benitez et al., interview, Immokalee; Estabrook, *Tomatoland*, pp. 118–19; Soohoo, Albisa, and David, *Bringing Human Rights Home. Volume 2*, pp. 7–8; Sellers, "Del Pueblo, Para El Pueblo," pp. 66–67.

22 *collective destiny* Lucas Benitez et al., interview, Immokalee, September 15, 2011; Laura Germino and Greg Asbed, April 30, 2013; Soohoo, Albisa, and David, *Bringing Human Rights Home. Volume 2*; Sellers, "Del Pueblo, Para El Pueblo," p. 67. Quote is from Sellers.

22 *provoked discussion* Laura Safer Espinoza et al., interview, December 19, 2012; Soohoo, Albisa, and David, *Bringing Human Rights Home. Volume 2*, pp. 7–13.

22 *examining the system* Sellers, "Del Pueblo, Para El Pueblo," p. 68. Quote is as told to Sellers.

23 *new ideas* Solnit, "Taco Bell Boycott Victory."

23 *could train others* Soohoo, Albisa, and David, *Bringing Human Rights Home. Volume 2*, pp. 7–13.

24 *actions in response* Ibid., p. 7.

24 *from Collier County* Bowe, *Nobodies.*

25 *earning $80* Soohoo, Albisa, and David, *Bringing Human Rights Home. Volume 2*, pp. 13–14

25 *in the 1970s* Ibid., pp. 13–14.

25 *Take it or leave it* Lucas Benitez et al., interview, Immokalee; Soohoo, Albisa, and David, *Bringing Human Rights Home. Volume 2*, pp. 13–15. Greg Asbed, e-mail, January 16, 2017. See also Estabrook, *Tomatoland*, pp. 99–100.

25 *their participation* Soohoo, Albisa, and David, *Bringing Human Rights Home. Volume 2*, pp. 13–15.

26 *returned to the fields* Lucas Benitez et al., interview, Immokalee; Sellers, "Del Pueblo, Para El Pueblo," p. 82; Soohoo, Albisa, and David, *Bringing Human Rights Home. Volume 2*, pp. 13–15.

26 *$4.50* Lucas Benitez et al., interview, Immokalee.

26 *The Coalition of Immokalee Workers* Description of banner from author's visits and the explanation and translation from Greg Asbed. From Greg Asbed and Laura Germino, e-mail, March 15, 2015.

26 *under its new name* Laura Germino and Greg Asbed, interview, November 3, 2015; Sellers, "Del Pueblo, Para El Pueblo," p. 72.

27   *not drink water!* Lucas Benitez et al., interview, Immokalee; Sellers, "Del Pueblo, Para El Pueblo," p. 2.

27   *fear on that one* Lucas Benitez et al., interview, Immokalee; Bowe, *Nobodies.*

27   *parking lot as usual* Lucas Benitez et al., interview, Immokalee; Bowe, *Nobodies.*

28   *many of the houses* Lucas Benitez et al., interview, Immokalee; Benitez, interview, Immokalee; Bowe, *Nobodies;* Sellers, "Del Pueblo, Para El Pueblo." There are variations on this story, with the number of patrol cars ranging from fifteen to twenty-eight and the police including just the sheriffs or additional police from neighboring municipalities. They are consistent in overall perspective. I have primarily used Lucas Benitez's recounting in September 2011 and November 2015, filling in with Asbed in Soohoo and Sellers.

28   *protest Edgar's beating* Lucas Benitez, interview, Immokalee; Soohoo, Albisa, and David, *Bringing Human Rights Home. Volume 2.* The exact shout and translation comes from Soohoo.

29   *determination grows* Holden, "Research and Evaluation Report."

29   *debt bondage* As quoted in: Soohoo, Albisa, and David, *Bringing Human Rights Home, Volume 2,* p. 15.

CHAPTER 2. "BANG YOUR HEAD AGAINST THE WALL LONG ENOUGH . . ."

30   *Coalition of Immokalee Workers' offices* Gerardo Reyes, interview, November 5, 2015, Roma in Cubano restaurant, Immokalee, FL. Most of the story of Gerardo Reyes's arrival in Immokalee comes from the November 2015 interview, unless otherwise noted.

31   *common in tomatoes* Kilborn, "Tomato Pickers' Hope"; pinhooker is not used only in harvesting produce. An interesting example, also from Florida, is found in horse racing. In an article about Triple Crown winner American Pharoah, it turns out that the horse's owner's father "Luke McKathan eventually returned to Florida and became a pinhooker, buying horses as wenlings or yearlings, raising and training them himself, and then selling them at auction or privately, long before they hit the racetrack." Drape, "An Early Glimpse of Magic."

31   *tomato crates* Gerardo noted in an aside that many people were transported to the fields that way in the 1990s and that it still happens today outside of tomatoes.

33   *Immokalee's fields* Gerardo Reyes, interview; Gerardo Reyes and Marquis; Green, "Crop of Abuse"; CIW, "Slavery in the Fields."

33   *responded with silence* Sellers, "Del Pueblo, Para El Pueblo," pp. 83–84.

33   *those who protested* Long, "Hunger Strike Feeds on Despair"; Sauer, "Growers Insist Wages Are Good."

33   *decade that followed* Soohoo, Albisa, and David, *Bringing Human Rights Home. Volume 2,* pp. 16–17.

34   *different companies* Ibid., pp. 16–17; Sellers, "Del Pueblo, Para El Pueblo," pp. 83–84.

34   *religious groups* Greenhouse, "Going Hungry to Make a Point."

34   *outside of Immokalee* The *Fort Myers News-Press*'s Amy Bennett Williams regularly covered the Coalition's activities, slavery cases, and the Florida growers throughout the 2000s into the implementation of the Fair Food Program after 2010.

34   *Fort Myers News-Press* Sellers, "Del Pueblo, Para El Pueblo," pp. 84–86. Sauer, "Growers Insist Wages Are Good"; Long, "Hunger Strike Feeds on Despair."

34   *$8.50 an hour* This same argument about the high potential pay of farm workers shows up again in the testimony of the Florida Tomato Growers Exchange's executive vice president Reggie Brown before a Senate committee in 2008. The senators were not convinced by the argument.

34 *highest bidder* Sauer, "Growers Insist Wages Are Good."

35 *run his farm!* US Senate, Committee on Health, Education, Labor, and Pensions, *Examining Ending Abuses*; quote from Lucas Benitez's testimony; Krueger, "Striking for Pay."

35 *January 18, 1998* Soohoo, Albisa, and David, *Bringing Human Rights Home. Volume 2*, p. 17; Sellers, "Del Pueblo, Para El Pueblo," pp. 84–86.

35 *California, to Sacramento* Ganz, *Why David Sometimes Wins.*

35 *raised right hand* Soohoo, Albisa, and David, *Bringing Human Rights Home. Volume 2*; Sellers, "Del Pueblo, Para El Pueblo," p. 87; CIW, December 2012, announcement of spring action with march to Publix headquarters but also includes information on 2000 march for dignity.

36 *hunger strike* Soohoo, Albisa, and David, *Bringing Human Rights Home. Volume 2*, pp. 17–18.

37 *workers [participating]* Quote from Lucas Benitez; Krueger, "Striking for Pay."

37 *2000 compared to 1996* Steve Hitov, interview, September 2015. Steve Hitov and Greg Asbed made clear that reducing direct violence in the fields was a significant improvement.

37 *December 1999* Sellers, "Del Pueblo, Para El Pueblo," p. 86.

38 *from a lynching* Green, *Ely: An Autobiography.*

38 *filled the county* King, *Devil in the Grove*, p. 61, for "lawanorder." King's book is a remarkable, Pulitzer prize-winning account of this case.

38 *blood to attend* "The Press: Look at Your Own Child"; Berry, "Suspicion of 'Nigra' Blood"; Maxwell, "Jim Crow Conflict"; Laura Germino, interview, November 3, 2015.

38 *Laura, Pilin, and Greg* Bales and Soodalter, *The Slave Next Door*, particularly pp. 55–59; Laura Germino, e-mail, January 16, 2017; Bowe, *Nobodies*; CIW, "Slavery in the Fields and the Food We Eat"; US Senate, Committee on Health, Education, Labor, and Pensions, *Examining Ending Abuses and Improving Working Conditions for Tomato Workers*, Senate Testimony of Lucas Benitez, p. 14. Note: The story of the Flores case is covered in several sources. The material is from these sources unless otherwise noted.

40 *"modern-day slavery" look like* Several sources including Bales and Soodalter, *The Slave Next Door*, pp. 54–67; Laura Germino, e-mail, January 16, 2017.

40 *law-enforcement agencies* Bales and Soodalter, *The Slave Next Door.* This book is a well-researched and thoughtful resource for learning more about the nature, history, and evidence of "modern-day slavery."

40 *ground zero for modern-day slavery* US Senate Committee on Health, Education, Labor, and Pensions, *Examining Ending Abuses and Improving Working Conditions for Tomato Workers*, April 15, 2008, Mary Bauer testimony; Bales and Soodalter, *The Slave Next Door*, p. 51.

40 *country and state* Damico, "Eyes Wide Open."

40 *under Federal law* US Senate Committee on Health, Education, Labor, and Pensions, *Examining Ending Abuses and Improving Working Conditions for Tomato Workers*, April 15, 2008, Lucas Benitez testimony, p. 15.

41 *minimizes any liability* Ibid. Detective Charlie Frost testimony. At the time of Frost's testimony before the Senate subcommittee, antitrafficking legislation passed in 2000 required "actual knowledge [as] the standard of proof." Prior to 2000, and at the time of the Flores case, even this standard didn't exist. The revised federal antitrafficking legislation passed in 2010, based significantly on the CIW's work, relaxed the standard of proof for liability. The Fair Food Program, discussed later in this book, pushed this even further.

41   *threats of violence* Bales and Soodalter, *The Slave Next Door*, pp. 51–52.

41   *face of abuse* Ibid., pp. 23, 51.

41   *Flores was in jail* Ibid., pp. 51–54; CBS-TV, "CBS Reports: Legacy of Shame."

41   *Julia Gabriel* Bales and Soodalter, *The Slave Next Door*, pp. 57–58.

42   *Flores's work crews* Ibid., pp. 54–58.

42   *robberies and drugs* Wilson, *Bureaucracy*. Author James Q. Wilson discusses the strengths and weaknesses of strong organizational cultures, such as that found in the FBI. A particular weakness is "selective attention" and the inability to take on new tasks. Wilson also wrote extensively about the FBI in his book *The Investigators*; Bales and Soodalter, *The Slave Next Door*, pp. 58–59; Laura Germino, notes from conversation, June 22, 2011.

42   *those he spoke with* Bales and Soodalter, *The Slave Next Door*, pp. 57–58.

42   *Flores and the others* US Department of State, "Trafficking in Persons Report."

43   *little to help the case* CBS-TV, "CBS Reports: Legacy of Shame."

43   *entirely different person* Laura Germino and Susan Marquis; CBS-TV, "CBS Reports: Legacy of Shame."

43   *to southwest Florida* Bales and Soodalter, *The Slave Next Door*, pp. 49–50.

43   *to change a flat tire* Greene, "Crop of Abuse"; Greene, "Brutal Farm Labor Bosses Punished." The *Palm Beach Post* story identified Francisco and Antonio's cousin, but Gerardo Reyes confirmed the relationship as uncle and nephew Reyes and Marquis. "Five Recent Cases."

43   *owned by the Cuellos* Bales and Soodalter, *The Slave Next Door*, p. 49; Gerardo Reyes, interview.

43   *frequent visitors* Greene, "Crop of Abuse"; "Five Recent Cases"; Greene, "Brutal Farm Labor Bosses Punished."

43   *$700 smuggling fee* Greene, "Crop of Abuse."

44   *recounted Antonio* Greene, "Brutal Farm Labor Bosses Punished."

44   *One afternoon* Bales and Soodalter, *The Slave Next Door*, pp. 49–50.

44   *coyote fee back* Greene, "Crop of Abuse."

44   *tomato fields* US Department of Justice, "Two Men Plead Guilty."

44   *sentenced to two years* "Five Recent Cases"; Estabrook, *Tomatoland*, pp. 85–87; Bales and Soodalter, *The Slave Next Door*, pp. 49–50.

44   *Congress in 2000* Bales and Soodalter, *The Slave Next Door*, pp. viii–ix, 58. This act was reauthorized in 2008 with expanded definitions and increased punishment for human trafficking and benefiting from human trafficking.

44   *found the victims* Ibid., p. 59.

44   *Trafficking in Persons Report* US Department of State, "Trafficking in Persons Report."

45   *21st century headline news* Laura Germino to Humantraffickingsearch.net, March 11, 2015, arguing that success is "prevention" not "prosecution." http://humantrafficking search.net/wp/do-successful-prosecutions-constitute-success-in-the-fight-against-modern-day-slavery/.

45   *truth to what he says* CBS-TV, "The Growing Demand for 'Fair Food.'"

45   *considered alternatives* Laura Germino and Greg Asbed, interview, November 3, 2015; Gerardo Reyes, interview; Lucas Benitez and Greg Asbed, interview by Sanjay Rawal, 2014, film and audio.

46   *National Labor Relations Board* Soohoo, Albisa, and David, *Bringing Human Rights Home. Volume 2*, p. 18.

46   *talk with the Coalition* My analysis, but a related analysis is in ibid.

46   *$5.15 an hour* Florida Dept. of Economic Opportunity, "Florida Minimum Wage History."

47   *$96 to $120* Laura Germino, interview, November 3, 2015; David Wang, telephone conversation. David Wang provided a detailed description of his discussions with Laura Germino, Greg Asbed, and Lucas Benitez on the idea for a penny-per-pound surcharge. Greg Asbed later provided more detail on the logic behind the idea.

47   *because there are none* Liz Esformes et al., interview, October 29, 2014. Tavaras quote is from this visit to Pacific Tomato Growers; Estabrook, *Tomatoland*, pp. 129–30.

47   *the large retail buyers* Lucas Benitez et al., interview, Immokalee; Laura Germino and Greg Asbed, interview, November 3, 2015; Estabrook, *Tomatoland*.

48   *no grower can* Note: In addition to the conversation David Wang describes, CIW was talking to growers outside of the tomato industry and getting similar information. Greg Asbed was less definitive than David Wang about this discussion; Laura Germino, interview, November 3, 2015.

49   *power to change our lives* Greg Asbed in Laura Germino, interview, November 3, 2015, and in Greg Asbed, e-mail, January 17, 2017.

50   *the leverage for the CIW* Soohoo, Albisa, and David, *Bringing Human Rights Home. Volume 2*; Laura Germino, interview, November 3, 2015.

50   *begin as early as age two* Schlosser, *Fast Food Nation*, pp. 43, 239.

CHAPTER 3. CAMPAIGNING FOR FAIR FOOD

52   *Walmart, and the like* Penn Live, "At a Glance"; "Top 100 Chains." The largest grocery chains by sales in the United States are Kroger, Safeway, and then the Ahold US chains that include Giant and Stop & Shop. The largest fast-food chains by sales in the United States are McDonald's, Subway (Starbucks), Burger King, Wendy's, and Taco Bell.

53   *and early 1970s* Although this book is not a history or analysis of unions, there are numerous books on Cesar Chavez and the United Farm Workers I'd recommend, such as Marshall Ganz, *Why David Sometimes Wins* (2009), Miriam Pawel's *The Union of Their Dreams* (2009), and *The Crusades of Cesar Chavez* (2014).

53   *also their vulnerability* See discussion in chapter 4 regarding how Greg and the CIW came to this realization and then saw that Eric Schlosser had reached the same conclusion from a different starting point.

53   *labor and sweatshops* Examples of food poisoning damaging a corporate brand include Jack in the Box and e. coli in 1993; e. coli and Taco Bell in 2006; and, more recently, Chipotle in 2015. Protests against Nike's use of cheap labor and sweatshops developed in the 1990s and came to a head in the mid-2000s, just as CIW was reconsidering their strategy.

54   *against doing it* Laura Germino and Susan Marquis, e-mail, September 1–3, 2015. Quote is from Greg Asbed.

54   *in the late 1990s* Lucas Benitez, interview, Immokalee. Quote and description of Mr. Taco are from this interview. Laura Germino, interview with Laura Germino and Greg Asbed, November 3, 2015; Taco Bell, "Yo Quiero Taco Bell."

55   *far beyond Immokalee* Smith, "Growing Pains."

57   *leaders of the campaign* Soohoo, Albisa, and David, *Bringing Human Rights Home. Volume 2*, p. 21.

57   *lead their fight* Ibid., p. 21; Sellers, "Del Pueblo, Para El Pueblo," p. 98.

57   *fighting for their rights* Soohoo, Albisa, and David, *Bringing Human Rights Home. Volume 2*, p. 21.

58   *spirit, and consciousness* Ibid., p. 21.

58   *The Long Tail* Greg Asbed, interview, November 4, 2015; Anderson, *The Long Tail*, originally published in 2004 as a long article in *Wired* magazine.

58   *into the campaign* See www.ciw-online.org.

59   *anarchists to archbishops* Sellers, "Del Pueblo, Para El Pueblo," p. 99, quote from Kristi Laughlin.

59   *led the parishioners* Lucas Benitez et al., interview, Immokalee. Quote is from Noelle Damico.

59   *at the local Taco Bell* Sellers, "Del Pueblo, Para El Pueblo," p. 97.

60   *alongside the tomato workers* Damico, "Eyes Wide Open."

60   *situation of the tomato farmworkers* Lucas Benitez et al., interview, Immokalee. Quote from Noelle Damico.

60   *with the Coalition of Immokalee Workers* Laura Safer Espinoza and Sean Sellers, interview, November 3, 2015, Sarasota, Florida. Sean Sellers' story of becoming involved with CIW and then moving to Immokalee to lead the Student/Farmworker Alliance is largely from this interview, with some material (noted) coming from Sellers, "Del Pueblo, Para El Pueblo."

61   *the New Yorker* Bowe, "Nobodies."

61   *had featured the CIW* The *National Geographic* article *21st-Century Slaves* appeared in 2003.

61   *Human Rights Award* Robert F. Kennedy Center for Justice and Human Rights, 2016.

61   *volunteer with the CIW* Laura Espinoza and Sean Sellers, interview, November 2015; Sellers, "Del Pueblo, Para El Pueblo," pp. 111–12.

62   *protests against Nike* Soohoo, Albisa, and David, *Bringing Human Rights Home. Volume 2*, p. 20; Sellers, "Del Pueblo, Para El Pueblo," pp. 111–12.

62   *recognition and memories* This has happened with the author a half-dozen times or more when testing out the ideas of this book.

62   *branded products* Student/Farmworker Alliance, "Who We Are."

62   *youth culture* Klein, *No Logo*.

63   *Wendy's headquarters* Emanuel Martinez, interview, October 28, 2015. I met Emanuel when giving a talk at the University of Pennsylvania in October 2015.

63   *offices in Immokalee* Ibid.; Student/Farmworker Alliance, "80 Students and Young People Gather."

63   *life in Immokalee* Ibid.

64   *twenty-five years later* Ibid.; Emanuel Martinez, phone conversation.

64   *supporting groups* CIW, "Florida Farmworkers Cross Country"; CIW, "Coalition of Immokalee Workers 2005 Taco Bell Truth Tour."

64   *supporting the CIW* Sellers, "Del Pueblo, Para El Pueblo," pp. 111–13; Soohoo, Albisa, and David, *Bringing Human Rights Home. Volume 2*, p. 20.

64   *Conference on Global Justice* CIW, "Coalition of Immokalee Workers 2005 Taco Bell Truth Tour," 2005.

64   *CIW for social responsibility* CIW, "Taco Bell Agreement Analysis."

65   *Miami Workers Center* Sellers, "Del Pueblo, Para El Pueblo," 2009, pp. 96–97.

65   *consider CIW's demands* Two of these were the case of Michael Lee, who used drugs, alcohol, and guns to lure and then enslave US citizens from homeless shelters in Miami and the case of Ramiro and Juan Ramos who had more than seven hundred workers in forced labor.

65   *not going to let it go* Lucas Benitez, interview, Immokalee.

67   *other fast-food corporations* Sellers, "Del Pueblo, Para El Pueblo," pp. 116–17.

67   *farmworkers' rights* CIW, "Taco Bell Agreement Analysis."

67   *a need for reform* Ibid.

67   *firm's code of conduct* Ibid. Quotes and factual statements are from the joint CIW-Yum! press release and report on the press conference and agreement found in CIW, "Taco Bell Agreement Analysis."

68   *take much longer* This analysis comes out of six years of discussion with CIW members and Fair Food Standards Council staff, as well as reading about the Fair Food Program and strengths and weaknesses of other standards and compliance programs. A comparison of standards and compliance systems is found in chapter 8.

69   *human rights in the field* CIW, "Coalition of Immokalee Workers 2005 Taco Bell Truth Tour."

69   *the food it sold* CIW, "Chicago Thanksgiving Day Parade."

69   *the House of Blues* CIW, "McDonald's Tangled Web"; CIW, "PACK YOUR BAGS."

69   *Florida-based tomato industry* CIW, "McDonald's USA and Its Produce Suppliers."

70   *New York Times* Doyle, "Activists Out Burger King"; Williams, "Burger King Exec"; Schlosser, "Burger with a Side of Spies."

70   *Subway in 2008* CIW, "Subway Signs Agreement"; Steve Hitov, interview, December 2015; Greg Asbed, interview, April 22, 2015.

71   *against these corporations* Cruz Salucio and Nely Rodriguez, interview by unknown, November 20, 2012; Nely Rodriguez, video interview by Prometheus Radio.

72   *working in the fields* Cruz Salucio, interview. Gabriel's story is featured in the Modern Day Slavery Museum and on the CIW website.

72   *Geneva, Switzerland* CIW, "CIW 2007 Truth Tour"; CIW, "Interview with CIW member," includes information on Romeo Ramirez; Estabrook, *Tomatoland*, p. 84.

72   *with the megaphone* Gerardo Reyes-Chavez, interview.

73   *food chains that supported them* Reyes-Chavez, "Making Corporations Pay."

73   *against slavery with CIW* CIW, "McDonald's Tangled Web."

73   *Wendy's fast-food chain* CIW, "A Powerful Voice."

73   *domestic abuse at home* WGCU-TV, "Makers."

73   *pesticides and herbicides* Lantigua, "Why Was Carlitos Born This Way?"

73   *who works in the fields* WGCU-TV, "Makers."

74   *continue to suffer* CIW, "CIW's Nely Rodriguez."

74   *migrant worker housing* Greenhouse, "Homeless Harvest."

74   *2007 book by the same name* Bowe, "Nobodies"; Bowe, *Nobodies*, 2007.

74   *Christian Science Monitor* Greene, "Crop of Abuse"; Jonsson, "In Florida's Tomato Fields."

74   *the chain's capitulation* Schlosser, *Fast Food Nation*; Schlosser, *Reefer Madness*; Schlosser, "Burger with a Side of Spies."

74   *supermarket chains* Rawal, *Food Chains*.

75   *agricultural labor in 2008* US Senate, Committee on Health, Education, Labor, and Pensions, *Examining Ending Abuses*, 2008.

75   *and Dick Durbin* Senator Durbin was not a member of the committee but was actively involved in issues of low-wage workers. It is of interest that Senators Hillary Clinton and Barack Obama were members of this committee but were both running for president during the time of this hearing.

75   *Senator Sanders* During the 2016 presidential primary, the CIW released a "special commentary" praising both Sanders and Clinton for their support of the CIW and the Florida farmworkers. The commentary followed the release by Bernie Sanders on March 5, 2016, of a campaign ad on his holding of these hearings. The ad ran in Florida, in Spanish, just prior to the Florida primary.

76   *Brown argued otherwise* US Senate, Committee on Health, Education, Labor, and Pensions, *Examining Ending Abuses*, pp. 46–47.

76   *the Fair Food Program* Ibid., p. 63.

76   *I can't hear you* Ibid., pp. 39–47.

76   *declined to participate* Ibid., p. 40.

76   *employment with the corporate buyers* Ibid., pp. 41–47.

77   *mystifying* Ibid., pp. 71–73.
77   *Association and others* Ibid., pp. 46–47.
77   *widespread and getting worse* Ibid., p. 4.

CHAPTER 4. HAS ANYONE TALKED WITH THESE GUYS?

83   *driving a shopping cart* Jon Esformes, interview, June 3, 2014. The material on Jon Esformes's life and struggle with addiction comes largely from a series of interviews with the author in 2014–2015. Additional personal material comes from a series of interviews conducted by Sanjay Rawal in preparation for a tribute to Jon's work prepared for Beit T'Shuvah.

84   *they had been selling* Ibid.; Esformes et al., notes from Pacific Tomato Growers visit; DiMartino, "Nathan Esformes."

84   *New York, and Boston* Jon Esformes, interview, June 3, 2014. A book recommended by Jon Esformes that provides both a remarkable tale and insight into the immigrants that built the produce industry in the United States is Cohen, *The Fish That Ate the Whale*.

85   *end my life* Rabbi Mark Borovitz and Jon Esformes, interview by Sanjay Rawal 2014, film and audio, Los Angeles Beit T'Shuvah.

85   *take him in* Ibid.

85   *every human being* Rabbi Mark Borovitz, Harriet Rossetto, and Jon Esformes, interview, September 11, 2014; Jon Esformes, interview, June 3, 2014.

85   *but now thrives* Harriet Rossetto's memoir *Sacred Housekeeping* and Rabbi Mark Borovitz's memoir *The Holy Thief* provide much of the background on Beit T'Shuvah and their relationship, as well as being fascinating reads. Rossetto and Mandelbaum, *Sacred Housekeeping*; Borovitz and Eisenstock, *The Holy Thief.*

85   *"helped" her look for it* Jon Esformes, interview, June 3, 2014; Rossetto and Mandelbaum, *Sacred Housekeeping.*

85   *help me do it better* Jon Esformes, interview, June 3, 2014. Quote is per Jon Esformes but the story is found in both the author's interview with Esformes and in Rossetto and Borovitz's memoirs.

85   *back from the edge* Rabbi Mark Borovitz, Harriet Rossetto, and Jon Esformes, conversation notes; Rabbi Mark Borovitz and Jon Esformes, interview for Jon Esformes tribute.

86   *I get out of here* Rabbi Mark Borovitz and Jon Esformes, interview for Jon Esformes tribute.

86   *my head and heart* Ibid.

86   *as human beings* Ibid.

86   *different place on it* Rabbi Mark Borovitz, Harriet Rossetto, and Jon Esformes, conversation notes; Rabbi Mark Borovitz and Jon Esformes, interview for Jon Esformes tribute.

86   *bottle of booze* Jon Esformes, interview, June 3, 2014.

86   *and last residency* Ibid.; Rabbi Mark Borovitz and Jon Esformes, interview for Jon Esformes tribute; Jon Esformes, phone interview, March 5, 2017.

86   *to a life of service* Rabbi Mark Borovitz, Harriet Rossetto, and Jon Esformes, conversation notes; Rabbi Mark Borovitz and Jon Esformes, interview for Jon Esformes tribute.

87   *roots in the grower community* Ibid.; "Billy Heller Promoted"; Jon Esformes, phone interview, March 2017.

88   *deal to form an alliance* Jon Esformes, phone interview, March 2017.

88   *$100 million* Jon Esformes, interview, June 3, 2014; Estabrook, *Tomatoland.*

88   *winter tomatoes* Steve Hitov, interview, December 2015.

88   *had long been entrenched* Jon Esformes, phone interview, March 2017.

88 *says we're human* Rabbi Mark Borovitz and Jon Esformes, interview for Jon Esformes tribute.

89 *December 7, 2007* I can no longer get the original *Naples Daily News* article from December 7, 2007, but have several references to it.

89 *they tried to escape* Batista, "FL: Family Accused of Enslaving Workers in Immokalee"; Williams, "Immokalee Family Sentenced."

89 *federal and state prosecutors* CIW, "Anti-Slavery Program"; CIW, "Slavery in the Fields."

89 *investigations at the time* Williams, "Immokalee Family Sentenced."

89 *hunger strike in 1997* Long, "Hunger Strike Feeds on Despair"; Sauer, "Growers Insist Wages Are Good"; Sellers, "Del Pueblo, Para El Pueblo."

89 *SAFE, program* Reiss, "Growers Seeking Safe Haven."

90 *Florida produce suppliers* Ibid.

90 *outfit like the CIW* Ibid.

90 *Miami Herald and other press* CIW, "Fresh Allegations."

90 *sense of irony* Greg Asbed, interview, November 4, 2015.

90 *who held them in Immokalee* Estabrook, *Tomatoland*.

90 *twelve years in prison* Williams, "Immokalee Family Sentenced."

91 *to prevent labor abuses* Ibid.

91 *$100,000 fine for those who did so* See Greenhouse, "Tomato Pickers' Wages," for more on the FTGE's argument; "Victory a Long-Time Coming."

91 *Fair Food Program was building* For a list of all who signed the Fair Food agreement and when, see Fair Food Program "Partners."

92 *Fair Food agreements* Williams, "Florida Growers Group Changes Stance."

92 *signed with the Coalition* Ibid.

92 *no interest in working together* The account of this story comes from Lucas Benitez and Greg Asbed.

93 *independence of crew leaders* This account comes from several interviews with Jon Esformes, Greg Asbed, and Steve Hitov.

94 *chief operating officer* "Billy Heller Promoted"; McClure, "Pacific Tomatoes Taps COO."

94 *Florida Tomato Growers Exchange* Kaufmann, "The Wall Comes Tumbling Down."

94 *he was going to carry it out* Jon Esformes, phone interview, March 2017.

94 *then the lawyers can talk* Interviews with Lucas Benitez, Greg Asbed, Jon Esformes, and Steve Hitov.

95 *their own corporate counsel* Instead, Jon and Billy hired a Washington D.C.–based law firm—"the most left-wing firm we could find"—to negotiate the confidentiality agreement with the CIW. Jon Esformes, phone interview, March 2017.

95 *joined by phone* Jon Esformes, interview, June 3, 2014; Lucas Benitez, interview, Immokalee; Laura Germino, interview, November 3, 2015; Steve Hitov, interview, December 2015; Jon Esformes, interview, March 2017. There is some confusion about who was at this first meeting between Jon Esformes and the Coalition, but there is certainty that Jon, Greg Asbed, and Lucas Benitez were in the room and Steve Hitov was on the phone.

95 *within the same industry* Lucas Benitez and Greg Asbed, interview for Jon Esformes tribute.

95 *good for business* Lucas Benitez, interview, Immokalee.

96 *the course of many years* Lucas Benitez and Greg Asbed, interview for Jon Esformes tribute; Greg Asbed in Laura Germino, interview, November 3, 2015.

96 *never went back to the trenches* Lucas Benitez and Greg Asbed, interview for Jon Esformes tribute.

96   *agreement with the Coalition of Immokalee Workers* Laura Germino, interview, November 3, 2015; Lucas Benitez et al., interview, Immokalee; Rabbi Mark Borovitz, Harriet Rossetto, and Jon Esformes, conversation notes; Kaufmann, "The Wall Comes Tumbling Down"; CIW, "Lucas Benitez of the CIW Speaks."

97   *their barbecues* Jon Esformes, interview, June 3, 2014.

97   *Heller was in the audience* Kaufmann, "The Wall Comes Tumbling Down"; Rabbi Mark Borovitz, Harriet Rossetto, and Jon Esformes, conversation notes.

97   *wait until tomorrow* Kaufmann, "The Wall Comes Tumbling Down."

97   *out of the business* "When Working Conditions Are Ripe for Change."

97   *signed at the end of 2010* Lucas Benitez et al., interview, Immokalee; Lucas Benitez and Greg Asbed, interview for Jon Esformes tribute.

98   *the denial was broken* Greg Asbed in Lucas Benitez, et al., interview, Immokalee, September 2011.

99   *Coalition, and Reggie Brown* Description is from a photo of the event. Williams, "Tomato Struggle Over."

99   *for the 21st century* The actual joint statement is found on the CIW's website in the archives. Estabrook, "A Sweet Deal for Tomato Workers"; CIW, "Historic Breakthrough in Florida's Tomato Fields."

CHAPTER 5. EYES WIDE OPEN

100   *Navarrete slavery case* Damico, "Eyes Wide Open."

103   *soon to become Lipman* "Six Ls Packing Company Rebrands." Max Lipman, his sons and sons-in-law founded Six L's in 1950. Max had moved to Florida after working as a pushcart vendor in New York City. The last remaining founder, Bill "Mr. Bill" Lipman, died in May 2011 during the pilot year of the Fair Food Program. Kent Shoemaker rebranded the company "Lipman Produce" in September of the same year. See Koger, "Bill Lipman."

103   *that could be executed* CIW, "Historic Breakthrough in Florida's Tomato Fields."

103   *divided into two sections* The code referenced in the discussion below is from April 2011 (the most current code is online at http://www.fairfoodstandards.org/resources/fair-food-code-of-conduct/). The code continued to evolve over the implementation of the Fair Food Program. The version as of summer 2016 has a different structure, refined and additional requirements, and a section on "Joining the Fair Food Program," which includes policy on rejoining the program after a grower has been suspended. There is a further discussion of the evolution of the code in chapter 9.

104   *suspension would follow* CIW, "Fair Food Code of Conduct; Version 1."

104   *has changed the industry* Lucas Benitez and Greg Asbed, interview for Jon Esformes tribute. Note that the interviews conducted by Sanjay Rawal were transcribed from audio recordings.

104   *grower Jimmy Grainger* "Six Ls Packing Company Rebrands"; Koger, "Bill Lipman"; Ohlemeier, "Lipman Family Cos. Hires Sysco Veteran." Like Pacific, Six L's was transforming as a company in the wake of the Navarrete slavery case and the agreement with CIW. The last Lipman family CEO, Larry, stepped down in January 2011 and Toby Purse was named interim CEO. Kent Shoemaker was hired from Sysco to become the grower/packer's CEO effective September 2011. Shoemaker then brought in another outsider to become CFO and Toby Purse moved to chief administrative officer and then chief farming officer. The company rebranded as Lipman in the fall of 2011.

104   *from time to time* Greg Asbed, e-mail, July 1, 2016; Steve Hitov, e-mail, June 25–27, 2016; Jon Esformes, interview, June 3, 2014. There is some variation in memories as to who was in the original working group, but it changed slightly over time, according to the issues being discussed. Hitov, interview by Susan Marquis, July 26, 2016.

104 *October 2010* Jon Esformes, interview, June 3, 2014. Pacific rejoined the FTGE sometime after 2014. See the Florida Tomato Committee website, Grower Resources and the listing of annual reports. Jon Esformes and Billy Heller appear as members for district 3 beginning with the 2013–2014 report. https://www.floridatomatoes. org/grower-resources/.

105 *about the program's benefits* Shoemaker, "Tell the Complete Story."

105 *in front of these issues* Jon Esformes, interview, June 3, 2014; Ohlemeier, "Lipman Family Cos. Hires Sysco Veteran"; Shoemaker, "Tell the Complete Story."

106 *for every ten picked* Germino and Asbed, interview, Immokalee, April 2013; Leonel Perez, interview, November 4, 2015. Also (as explained in Steve Hitov, interview, July 2016), growers were paid by weight, not by volume, and so cupping of the tomato buckets also increased their profits.

106 *dumped on the ground* Because of food safety regulations, tomatoes dumped on the ground couldn't be put back in the bucket and sold.

106 *paid for the uncompensated pounds* CIW, "Fair Food Code of Conduct; Version 1."

106 *avoids all disputes* Germino and Asbed, "Discussion Section 1." Clarification from Greg Asbed, e-mail, January 17, 2017.

106 *they could work with* Steve Hitov, interview, July 2016.

107 *other members for specific issues* A pattern that continues to this day in 2017.

107 *thirty-two requirements or standards* CIW, "Fair Food Code of Conduct, Version 1."

107 *buckets by [farm] workers* Farmworkers that are eligible for the penny-per-pound premium and whose rights are the primary focus of the code of conduct are referred to as "Qualifying Workers" in the Guidance Manual. See CIW, "Guidance for Implementation."

107 *check mark on the bucket* Two large versions of these photos are on the wall of the CIW's offices. An amusing short video on "Copete: Know Your Rights" can be seen on YouTube (see CIW, "Copete: Know Your Rights"). Finally, if you'd like to know even more about filling tomato buckets, there is a photo comparing the 2008 pre–Fair Food Program and 2011 post–Fair Food Program buckets later in this book.

107 *control their time cards* CIW, "Guidance for Implementation, p. 3.

108 *pick up food and drinks* Ibid., p. 3.

108 *who have to carry it out* Ibid., p. 1.

109 *for their suppliers* See Nike, "Nike Aims to Transform Manufacturing"; Wendy's, "Responsibility Overview"; Sears Holding Company, "Human Rights Policy." From the Sears Holding Company website: "SHC is committed to working with and encouraging all of our partners to uphold the principles as described in the International Labor Organization's (ILO) Declaration on Fundamental Principles and Rights at Work."

109 *pay and working conditions* Clifford and Greenhouse, "Fast and Flawed Inspections."

109 *or European settings* Brudney, "Decent Labour Standards."

109 *deception to fool inspectors* Ibid.; Jamieson and Hossain, "Bangladesh Collapse"; Jamieson, "Safety Inspections By Social Audit Firms."

109 *2,500 more* Clifford and Greenhouse, "Fast and Flawed Inspections"; Goldie, "As Bangladesh's Garment Industry Booms."

109 *didn't have safety standards* Ali Manik and Yardley, "Building Collapse in Bangladesh."

110 *largest garment exporters* Clifford and Greenhouse, "Fast and Flawed Inspections."

110 *over just a few years* Ibid.; Jamieson and Hossain, "Bangladesh Collapse."

110 *earlier in the story* See www.verite.org; www.sgsgroup.us.come; www.accountability. org; www.us.bureauveritas.com; Hale and Held, *Handbook of Transnational Governance*, pp. 243–44, 339–43; Jamieson and Hossain, "Bangladesh Collapse."

110 *paying for the service* Clifford and Greenhouse, "Fast and Flawed." An investigation by reporters Stephanie Clifford and Steven Greenhouse highlighted Levi's and Patagonia as requiring "rigorous—and costly—audits."

110 *more than 260 people* Jamieson and Hossain, "Bangladesh Collapse"; Walsh and Greenhouse, "Inspectors Certified Pakistani Factory."

110 *that FLA had missed* Tam, "Fair Labor Association." The actual EPI briefing paper is Nova and Shapiro, "Polishing Apple."

111 *ends up a racket* Clifford and Greenhouse, "Fast and Flawed Inspections"; Jamieson and Hossain, "Bangladesh Collapse."

111 *five commercial auditing companies* Quote is from Steve Hitov, phone conversation, June 2015. CIW first reached out to the auditing companies in preparation for the 2009 initial pilot of what later became the Fair Food Program. There were briefly three growers (Lady Moon and Alderman as very small niche growers plus East Coast Growers, a larger grower that came in with the Fair Food agreement signed by Compass and its subsidiary, Bon Appetit.) This initial program ended with the Florida Tomato Growers Exchange ban on cooperation.

112 *talk to everyone* Laura Safer Espinoza, Randall Sean Sellers, and FFSC staff, in-person visit to FFSC, Sarasota, Florida, April 29, 2013. FFSC staff: "Verité states with pride that they 'must interview 10–15% of workers,'" but one of Verité's audit reports does state that in their audit of the Rosita Knitwears factory in Bangladesh, there were 2,000 production workers and their audit team interviewed 32 (see Verité, "Comprehensive Factory Evaluation Report"). The Department of Labor Wage and Hour Division usually interviews 20 percent of workers in their audits (see Hoffman, "Are You Ready").

113 *experience to consult* Judge Laura Safer Espinoza, "The Purpose Prize 2015 Narrative Application," unpublished, 2015 (see Encore.org, "Laura Safer Espinoza").

113 *about thirty growers* Fair Food Standards Council (FFSC), "Fair Food Program 2013 Annual Report," p. 33.

113 *enforcement . . . made them so* Laura Safer Espinoza, "The Purpose Prize 2015 Narrative Application," unpublished, 2015.

CHAPTER 6. FORGING THE PATH BY WALKING IT

114 *Florida's west coast* Biographical notes on Judge Laura Safer Espinoza come from several interviews as well as her narrative application for the 2015 Purpose Prize and the press release and video interview that accompanied her recognition with that prize (see Encore.org, "Laura Safer Espinoza"); Espinoza and Sellers, interview, November 2015; Laura Safer Espinoza, Randall Sean Sellers, and FFSC staff, in-person visit to FFSC, Sarasota, Florida, April 29, 2013; Espinoza, "The Purpose Prize 2015 Narrative Application"; Laura Safer Espinoza et al., conversations with CIW and David Wang.

114 *across the country* Laura Safer Espinoza et al., conversations with CIW and David Wang; Espinoza, "The Purpose Prize 2015 Narrative Application"; Encore.org, "Laura Safer Espinoza."

115 *surroundings of our home* Espinoza, "The Purpose Prize 2015 Narrative Application."

115 *deep-rooted problems* Ibid.

115 *might be useful* Laura Safer Espinoza, Randall Sean Sellers, and FFSC staff, in-person visit to FFSC, Sarasota, Florida, April 29, 2013; Espinoza and Sellers, interview, November 2015; Espinoza, "The Purpose Prize 2015 Narrative Application."

116 *never before existed* Fair Food Standards Council (FFSC), biography, executive director Laura Safer Espinoza; Fair Food Standards Council (FFSC), job description, human rights attorney.

116 *even have a resume* Espinoza, "The Purpose Prize 2015 Narrative Application."

116 *who listened respectfully* Ibid.

116 *And she said yes* Laura Safer Espinoza and Sean Sellers, interview, November 2015.
117 *had prepared me well* Espinoza, "The Purpose Prize 2015 Narrative Application."
117 *but she's a judge* Laura Safer Espinoza, Randall Sean Sellers, and FFSC staff, in-person visit to FFSC, Sarasota, Florida, April 29, 2013.
117 *shoestring budget* Encore.org, "Laura Safer Espinoza."
117 *the parent organization* FFSC audit team, interview, July 27–28, 2016.
118 *excellent communicators* CIW farmworker education team, interview, November 4, 2015, observations and in-person discussions, Bradenton, Sarasota, Immokalee, Florida; Laura Safer Espinoza, phone conversation, December 12, 2014.
122 *Fair Food Standards Council comes in* The FFSC also monitors corporate buyer compliance with the code to include appropriate payment of the Fair Food penny-per-pound premium and purchasing Florida (and now East Coast) tomatoes from the Fair Food Program's "participating buyers." CIW farmworker education team, interview, November 4, 2015, observations and in-person discussions, Bradenton, Sarasota, Immokalee, Florida; also, see Fair Food Standards Council Annual Reports.
122 *violations of the code* There are circumstances where the CIW conducts the investigations, but those are discussed later in this chapter.
122 *corporate buyers and growers* Espinoza, "The Purpose Prize 2015 Narrative Application."
123 *at the job site* CIW, "Guidance for Implementation of the Fair Food of Conduct."
123 *75 percent or more of the workers* CIW farmworker education team, interview, November 4, 2015, observations and in-person discussions, Bradenton, Sarasota, Immokalee, Florida.
123 *safety of the housing* The FFSC only has the ability to enforce basic standards of housing quality and safety in grower-owned or controlled farmworker housing.
124 *led by Matt Wooten* Unless otherwise noted, descriptions of the field audits come from personal observation (FFSC audit team visit to Pacific Tomato Growers).
127 *apply to agricultural workers* Miguel Rios, Department of Labor, Wage and Hour Division, interview.
127 *appeal for me* Ibid.
127 *voice messaging system in English* Bowe, *Nobodies*, pp. 54–55.
127 *has traditional hours* In 2016, the Department of Labor Wage and Hour Division listed seven district offices in Florida. The listing is in English. It includes local addresses and phone numbers as well as the national hotline 1-866-4-USWAGE. The national hotline is toll-free (see US Department of Labor, "U.S. Wage and Hour Division District offices").
128 *when they are closed* The author called the various numbers to see what would happen. When calling after hours, there is an option to press "3" for languages other than Spanish that sends you to the district office voice mail, in English, and then provides office hours.
128 *even in the Tampa office* Miguel Rios, e-mail, August 20–22, 2016.
128 *fear of retribution* CIW, "Guidance for Implementation."
128 *Fair Food Standards Council* Ibid.
129 *database includes reports* The database was built on the SalesForce platform and then significantly customized by Sean Sellers (Laura Safer Espinoza and Sean Sellers, e-mail, June 16, 2015).
130 *within two working days* The Guidance Manual for the code of conduct has a detailed protocol and flow chart for handling complaints. CIW, "Guidance for Implementation."
130 *code violation or not* CIW, "Guidance for Implementation."

132 *compliance with the code* Ibid.
132 *just outside of Miami* Amanda Batchelor, "Mexican Men Living in Homestead Indicted"; Fair Food Standards Council (FFSC), "Participating Growers."; CIW, "Fair Food Standards Council Unearths Forced Labor."
134 *collaboration needed for success* CIW, "CIW Training Video for Fair Food Code of Conduct."
134 *great deal in the Fair Food Program* CIW, "Know Your Rights and Responsibilities."

CHAPTER 7. "VALUE" CAN HAVE A DIFFERENT MEANING

139 *tomatoes into May* Unless otherwise cited, discussions with Miguel Talavera, Liz Esformes, and Sarah Goldberger are from Esformes et al., notes from Pacific Tomato Growers visit. Acreage was clarified by Jon Esformes in a March 5, 2017, phone interview.
140 *Banana King* Cohen, *The Fish That Ate the Whale.*
140 *agricultural sciences* Zamorano Pan-American Agricultural School (see http://www.zamorano.edu).
140 *of the tomato industry* DiMartino, "Nathan Esformes."
143 *into an escrow account* Espinoza, et al., Fair Food Standards Council interview, Sarasota, April 29, 2013; Fair Food Standards Council, *Fair Food Program 2013.*
144 *standards from the Guidance Manual* Fair Food Standards Council, Fair Food Program Annual Reports; Espinoza, et al., Fair Food Standards Council interview, Sarasota, April 29, 2013; Espinoza, phone interview, June 5, 2015.
144 *visits to the growers to investigate* Fair Food Standards Council, Fair Food Program Annual Reports.
144 *success by both sides* The ability to resolve a complaint without a formal investigation and finding is also highlighted in each of the Fair Food Program/Fair Food Standards Council annual reports, e.g., 2015 Annual Report, p. 35.
145 *basic rights and reporting violations* Fair Food Standards Council, "Fair Food Program 2015 Annual Report."
145 *with physical contact* The full list of Article I violations is use of forced labor, systemic use of illegal child labor, use or threat of physical violence, use or display of weapons of any kind, sexual harassment that involves physical contact. CIW, "Guidance for Implementation," p. 13. As discussed in chapter 6, suspension is immediate for forced labor or child labor. For the other Article I violations, the grower must immediately terminate the perpetrator or the grower will be suspended.
145 *just a few weeks* Ibid., p. 16.
145 *probation during the same period* Fair Food Standards Council, "Fair Food Program 2015 Annual Report," p. 45.
147 *before getting to work* Fair Food Standards Council, "Fair Food Program 2015 Annual Report."
148 *treatment of animals* See Chipotle Mexican Food website: www.chipotle.com.
148 *food with integrity* From a Chipotle promotional video for the Denver festival as shown in *Democracy Now!,* "Seeking Living Wage."
148 *make it a reality* Ibid.
148 *or pay the premium* Ibid. (phone interview with Chris Arnold).
148 *abuses that are violated* Ibid. (interview with Gerardo Reyes).
149 *'good food' to our tables* CIW, "Chipotle Signs Agreement."
149 *more difficult prospect* David Wang, conversation, November 18, 2011. David Wang touched on this same topic in June 2011, identifying the grocery chain percentage of the tomato market as being between 70 and 75 percent; interview and notes from phone conversation, June 2011.

149 *previous two years* CIW, "National Supermarket Week."

149 *doubling workers' wages* The "penny-per-pound" or Fair Food premium is only paid for tomatoes sold to participating buyers. In 2011, those buyers were most of the major fast-food chains (Yum! Brands, McDonald's, Burger King), major food service companies (Compass, Bon Appétit, Sodexo, Aramark), and Whole Foods as the only grocery chain. Together, they accounted for between 25 and 30 percent of the tomato market. Partners are updated regularly on the Fair Food Program website (see Fair Food Program, "Partners").

149 *grocery store brands* A recent flurry of mergers also makes it difficult to tell who the players are or where to focus the protest. Safeway merged with Albertson and Ahold merged with Delhaize in 2015. Strom and Bray, "Ahold-Delhaize Deal." Note that in 2017, Amazon purchased Whole Foods.

150 *than to sustainable food* Lately, there has been some discussion as to the effectiveness of this business strategy. Ibid.; Matthews, "10 Ways Walmart Changed the World."

150 *early September 2008* CIW, "Whole Foods Markets Signs."

150 *into the Fair Food agreement* Whole Foods, "Florida Tomato Growers, Whole Foods Market Sign."

150 *employees to unionize* See for example, Philpott, "Employees Are 'Bitter.'" Michelle Chen references Whole Foods' "love-hate relationship with customers who've gotten hooked on its cornucopia of guilty-liberal indulgences." See Chen, "Surprise."

151 *One Penny More video* CIW, *One Penny More* (CIW video). Cruz Salucio, Leonel Perez, and Silvia Perez are the primary spokespersons in the video.

151 *interesting sources for its food* Anyone who has spent time perusing a Trader Joe's flyer knows what it's like to get caught up in the possibilities of a shopping adventure (e.g., http://www.traderjoes.com/fearless-flyer).

151 *latest Fearless Flyer* See http://www.traderjoes.com/fearless-flyer/article/3120.

151 *original Trader Joe* "Theo Albrecht Dies at 88."

152 *unusual openness* Ibid.

152 *unlike Whole Foods* I will not make the "Whole Paycheck" joke here.

152 *to get the best price* Trader Joe's, "Our Story."

152 *in Monrovia, California* CIW, "Boston 5th Graders"; CIW, "Martin Sheen"; Gerber, "Hundreds March to Trader Joe's."

152 *action came to an end* Gerber, "Hundreds March to Trader Joe's."

153 *essentially in compliance* CIW, "Trader Joe's: We'll Be Fair"; CIW, "CIW Response."

153 *not going to work* CIW, "CIW Response."

153 *nation's wealthiest cities* King and Logan, "Income Gap Alive and Well"; Victoria Winkler, "Here Are The 10 Richest Cities In Florida."

153 *Florida food crowd* CIW, "Trader Joe's Set to Open."

153 *subject to some discussion* The press release of the CIW/Trader Joe's agreement was notable in its brevity: a bland quote from Gerardo Reyes, no quote from Trader Joe's management, and a description of Trader Joe's (provided by the company) as simply that "with the opening of the Naples, Florida location, Trader Joe's operates 367 neighborhood grocery stores across the nation." CIW, "Welcome Aboard."

154 *well below $9 billion* Food Dive, "The Top 10 U.S. Retailers for Food"; Market Watch, "Whole Foods Market Inc. Annual Financials." It is tremendously difficult to find the financial information for Trader Joe's. https://en.wikipedia.org/wiki/Trader_Joe%27s.

154 *$29 billion in sales in 2015* The history of George W. Jenkins and Publix is from the Publix website (see Publix, "History").

154 *executive officers of the company* Morningstar, "Publix Super Markets Insiders"; Publix, "Publix Announces Fourth Quarter."

154 *to sign Fair Food agreements* CIW, "A Tale of Two Groceries."

154 *issue that involves Publix* Williams, "Tomato Struggle Over."

155 *show respect for them* Publix, "About Publix."

155 *volunteer with community organizations* Ibid.

155 *connection to the company* CIW, "Unsettling Experience."

155 *entering the store for a year* Estabrook, "Publix Still Claiming"; Cox, "Minister Kicked Out of Publix."

155 *signing with the CIW* Confidential source. In an interesting exchange, Lipman CEO Kent Shoemaker responded with a letter to the editor of the *Miami Herald* in response to comments Eva Longoria had made promoting the film she co-produced, *Food Chains.* Shoemaker first clarified that Florida's tomato growers were strong supporters of the Fair Food Program after signing on in 2010. In the same letter, Shoemaker defended Publix's refusal to work with the CIW, stating, "When it comes to farmworkers' rights, Publix Super Markets is not the problem. . . . I believe it has been forced into a defensive stance because of the offensive statements and actions being directed at them." Shoemaker, "Tell the Complete Story."

155 *Navarrete slavery case* CIW, *A Tale of Two Groceries,* June 8, 2009. http://www.ciw-online.org/blog/2009/06/tale_of_two_groceries/.

156 *against their will picked tomatoes* Ibid. The original article from the *News-Press* is no longer available. The article was quoted extensively on the CIW website.

156 *across southwestern Florida* CIW, "And So It Begins."

156 *farmworkers at subpoverty wages* Rawal, *Food Chains.*

156 *Gerardo Reyes, and Greg Asbed* Shoemaker, "Tell the Complete Story."

156 *my son does not have to* Rawal, *Food Chains.*

156 *remains the same today* Publix, "About Publix."

156 *into their pricing* Ibid.

157 *price per pound* Presbyterian Mission Agency, "CIW Responds to Publix's Publicly Stated Concerns," 2012.

157 *Future of the Food Movement* Quotes and other material from Michael Pollan and Jack Sinclair are from a video of the Edible Education class (see Sinclair, Ellison, and Pollan, "Edible Education 101."

158 *Walmart, in 2008* Ibid.; Bloomberg, "Executive Profile: Jack L. Sinclair."

159 *restaurants in 2015 and 2016* For example, see Elias Isquith, "A less friendly, less comforting place"; O'Connor, "Walmart Hikes Hourly Pay"; Fight for $15, "Fight for $15.

159 *from Michael Pollan* Sanjay Rawal, interview, October 9–10, 2016.

160 *The 21st Century Supermarket* Southern Methodist University, Engineering and Humanity Week.

160 *the food were treated* CIW, "Left Behind."

160 *first will thrive* Greg Asbed and Laura Germino, notes on conversation, January 31, 2014; CIW, *Left Behind: 21st Century Supermarket,* May 8, 2012. http://www.ciw-online.org/blog/2012/05/left_behind/.

162 *nineteen store sites* Barstow and von Bertrabdec, "How Wal-Mart Used Payoffs."

162 *were Walmart suppliers* Clifford and Greenhouse, "Fast and Flawed Inspections"; Ali Manik and Yardley, "Building Collapse in Bangladesh."

163 *Tomato Packing Camp* Iaconangelo, "Mexican Authorities Rescue 275 Workers"; Agence France Presse, "Mexico Rescues 275 Workers."

163 *brought back and beaten* Agence France Presse, "Mexico Rescues 275 Workers."

163 *aware of that fact all along* Marosi, "Desperate Workers."

164 *Walmart holds with it* As quoted from an article from *Take Part.* See CIW, "American History Happens."

164 *harvested here in the US* CIW, "Coalition of Immokalee Workers Announces Walmart."

165 *workers throughout America* David Wang, notes from conversation, January 31, 2014; Wang, "A Simple Lesson."

165 *without a fight* One imagines that Greenhouse meant without "a CIW campaign" and was unaware of the intense back and forth between CIW and Walmart over just more than two years.

165 *we want in the future* Greenhouse, "In Florida Tomato Fields."

165 *based in southwest Florida* Schneider and Lee, "Wal-Mart Joins Farmworker Pay Initiative."

165 *monumental step forward* See https://twitter.com/KerryKennedyRFK; CIW, *The World Responds to the Walmart Agreement*, June 20, 2014. http://www.ciw-online. org/blog/2014/01/walmart-american-history/.

165 *follow Walmart's lead* CIW, *The World Responds to the Walmart Agreement*, June 20, 2014. http://www.ciw-online.org/blog/2014/01/walmart-american-history/.

165 *TV back in the CIW's offices* Ibid.

CHAPTER 8. WHAT DIFFERENCE?

169 *$25 million* As of April 25, 2017, per Laura Safer Espinoza, e-mail exchange.

169 *another 10 percent raise* Fair Food Standards Council, "Fair Food Program 2015 Annual Report," p. 26.

169 *directly employ farmworkers* Fair Food Standards Council, "Fair Food Program 2015 Annual Report," pp. 15–16. By the 2013–2014 season, a special group of tomato workers known as "pinhookers," who pick tomatoes that have ripened on the vine or the few remaining tomatoes at the end of the season, are now included as fully registered, direct-hire employees.

169 *from the pay process* CIW, "Guidance for Implementation"; Fair Food Standards Council, "Fair Food Program 2015 Annual Report," pp. 17–18; CIW farmworker education team, interview, November 4, 2015, observations and in-person discussions, Bradenton, Sarasota, Immokalee, Florida.

170 *every hour they are at work* With the exception of agreed-upon breaks such as when a worker stops because of concerns for his or her safety.

170 *uncompensated part of a worker's day* FFSC audit team visit to Pacific Tomato Growers; FFSC, "Fair Food Program 2015 Annual Report," pp. 25–26; CIW, "Guidance for Implementation"; CIW farmworker education team, interview, November 4, 2015, observations and in-person discussions, Bradenton, Sarasota, Immokalee, Florida.

170 *down 40% last season* Fair Food Standards Council, "Fair Food Program 2015 Annual Report."

170 *plus a bucket rate* FFSC audit team visit to Pacific Tomato Growers.

170 *likely lose their jobs* Silvia Perez. See Khokha, "Silenced By Status."

170 *vulnerable to both* Human Rights Watch, "Cultivating Fear."

171 *across the United States* PBS-TV, *Frontline*, "Rape in the Fields."

171 *sexual assault is what is happening* Bapat, "Effort to Protect Farmworkers."

171 *2010–2011 season* Fair Food Standards Council, "Fair Food Program 2015 Annual Report." p. 49.

171 *slavery to exist* Germino, CIW website. Perez.

172 *in 95-degree heat* Greenhouse, "In Florida Tomato Fields."

172 *underbelly of American agriculture* PBS-TV, *Frontline*, "A Voice for Workers." In addition, PBS *Frontline* produced a full-length documentary called "Rape in the Fields" following a year-long study of sexual violence against women farmworkers. See PBS-TV, *Frontline*, "Rape in the Fields."

172 *helps prevent abuses*" PBS-TV, *Frontline*, "A Voice for Workers."

173 *both workers and supervisors* Fair Food Standards Council, "Fair Food Program 2015 Annual Report."

173 *even for farm supervisors* Some farms in California were offering two-hour training sessions to supervisors.

173 *VIDA Legal Assistance* VIDA Legal Assistance is a South Florida nonprofit supporting immigrant victims of abuse. See Voices for Immigrant Defense & Advocacy (VIDA), "Mission Statement."

174 *have been weeded out* The number of complaints is as of April 2017. Laura Safer Espinoza, e-mail exchange, April 24, 2017.

174 *emphasis for the FFSC monitors* FFSC audit team visit; Fair Food Standards Council, "Fair Food Program 2015 Annual Report."

174 *chemical fertilizers* CIW, "Guidance for Implementation," pp. 6–7, 29–35; FFSC Audit Team, interview, Eastern Shore, July 27–28, 2016. Individuals interviewed are listed in the note on sources.

175 *her coworker Abel* Abel was not available to sign the release form and so I will refer to him only by his first name. Unless otherwise noted, the discussion with Alejandrina and Abel is from interviews at Pacific Tomato Growers farms in Immokalee, Florida, October 29, 2014. Individual interviewed are included in the note on sources.

176 *health and safety issues* Fair Food Standards Council, "Fair Food Program 2015 Annual Report," p. 36.

176 *effectively with coworkers* This is likely the same problem that most corporate senior managers would identify as well!

176 *not yet established committees* Fair Food Standards Council, "Fair Food Program 2015 Annual Report," pp. 36–37.

179 *bettering workers' lives* Shoemaker, "Tell the Complete Story."

179 *have become common* Reed, "How SWFL's Tomato Industry Is Changing"; Estabrook, *Tomatoland*; Jon Esformes, interview; Laura Germino and Greg Asbed, notes from coffee.

179 *safety on Mexican farms* Marosi, "Desperate Workers on a Mexican Mega-Farm"; Marosi, "Hardship on Mexico's Farms."

179 *safe working conditions* Greg Asbed, "Threat of a New 'Harvest of Shame'"; Interviews with the worker education team occurred in Bradenton and Immokalee, Florida, November 4-–5, 2015. Individuals interviewed are included in the note on sources; CIW, "Hu Proposal Part II."

180 *people who care about these issues* McMillan, "Fair-Food Tomatoes"; Michael Holtz, "Human Trafficking"; Jon Esformes, phone interview, March 5, 2017.

180 *purchase order indeed* Greg Asbed used this phrase in accepting the James Beard Foundation's Leadership Award on October 17, 2016.

180 *agreements with the Coalition* Fair Food Standards Council, "Participating Buyers."

180 *topic up much at all* McDonald's, "Sustainability/Sourcing: Good Sourcing"; Yum! Brands, "Ethical Sourcing and Supply"; Burger King, "Burger King: Corporate Responsibility"; Trader Joe's, "Our Story."

180 *public affairs and CSR engagement* CSR is "corporate social responsibility."

180 *In conversation* Jill Manata, Adele Jamieson, and McDonald's Corporation, telephone interview, September 24, 2015.

181 *what can we get done* Ibid.

181 *consistent with the code of conduct* CIW, "Whole Foods Markets Signs Agreement"; CIW, "Fair Food Program Label"; Whole Foods, "Whole Foods Market Expands Partnership."

182 *Estabrook's article [in Gourmet magazine] came out* Estabrook, "Politics of the Plate."

182 *Equitable Food Initiative* Bon Appetit financially supported Oxfam America's March 2011 report, "The Inventory of Farmworker Issues and Protection in the U.S."

The Equitable Food Initiative is now separate from Oxfam America. See Greenhouse, "Farm Labor Groups Make Progress."

182 *including Bon Appetit* Compass Group, "Compass Group and the Coalition"; Cheryl Queen, Linked-In profile.

182 *and responsible sourcing* Compass Group, "Compass Group and the Coalition"; Rawal, *Food Chains.*

182 *change in U.S. agriculture* CIW, "The Fair Food Program Is a Proven Model"; Underwriters Laboratories, "The Seventh Responsible Sourcing Summit."

183 *Board of Directors* Fair Food Standards Council, "Fair Food Program 2015 Annual Report."

183 *recruitment, engagement, and retention* CIW, "The Fair Food Group Is a Proven Model." CIW online, http://www.ciw-online.org/blog/2015/05/compass-expansion-2/ 2015.

183 *chains in the United States* In July 2016, Ahold merged with Delhaize. Ahold and Delhaize reached agreement on the merger in June 2015, prior to the announcement of the agreement with the CIW. Ahold Delhaize, "Ahold Delhaize Successfully Completes Merger"; Ahold Delhaize, "About Us"; Strom and Bray, "Ahold-Delhaize Deal."

183 *shareholder meetings* CIW, "The Three Lies CEOs Tell Themselves"; PRNewswire, "Ahold USA Joins the Coalition."

183 *products come from* Boer, "Ahold CEO Dick Boer."

184 *negotiations were underway* CIW, "Big News Out of Ahold's Shareholder Meeting."

184 *officially part of the Fair Food Program* PRNewswire, "Ahold USA Joins the Coalition."

184 *industry was part of the Fair Food Program* Estabrook, "Major Grocery Chain Agrees."

184 *Delhaize Group chains* Ibid.

184 *humane agricultural industry* PRNewswire, "Ahold USA Joins the Coalition."

185 *develop their investigative capabilities* See earlier discussions in chapter 4 as well as Bales and Soodalter, *The Slave Next Door*, pp. 50–61; and US Senate, Committee on Health, Education, Labor, and Pensions, *Examining Ending Abuses and Improving Working Conditions for Tomato Workers*, 2008, testimony of detective Charles Frost.

185 *before the Senate* Bales and Soodalter, *The Slave Next Door*, pp. 58, vii–xii; Estabrook, *Tomatoland*, p. 85; Sellers, "Del Pueblo, Para El Pueblo," p. 23; US Senate, Committee on Health, Education, Labor, and Pensions, *Examining Ending Abuses and Improving Working Conditions for Tomato Workers*, April 15, 2008; CIW, "Hu Proposal Part II."

185 *Trafficking in Persons Report* This was the first trafficking in persons (TIP) report to include the United States not only as a recipient of human trafficking but as a source country for trafficking. See US Department of State, "Remarks on the Release."

186 *better at prosecutions* Ibid.

186 *governments accountable* Ibid.

186 *Trafficking in Persons in 2015* Kerry, "Remarks at the White House Forum."

186 *protection of victims* US Department of State, Trafficking in Persons Report: Heroes. 2016. "Laura Germino, United States of America, Class of 2010"; Laura Germino, "Session 2."

186 *convened by DHHS* CIW, "Hu Proposal Part II."

187 *down at the bottom* Mike Rios, Department of Labor, Wage and Hour Division, interview; US Department of Labor, "Dr. David Weil, Administrator."

187 *the food supply chain* US Department of Labor, Wage and Hour Division, "Vegetable Supplier to Major Grocery Chains Assessed."

187 *corrective action plans* US Equal Employment Opportunity Commission (EEOC), "EEOC Select Task Force."

CHAPTER 9. DESIGNED FOR THE FUTURE

194   *threatened with guns* Perez, "Six Accuse Clewiston Farm of Human Trafficking."

194   *obtain forced labor* Batchelor, "Mexican Men Living in Homestead Indicted," March 2016.

195   *body in a ditch* Perez, "Six Accuse Clewiston Farm of Human Trafficking"; Perez, "Farm Workers Settle Lawsuit"; *John Doe, Jane Doe v. Reyes Tapia-Ortiz and Carlos A. Rodriguez.*

195   *unlikely to ever see* *John Doe, Jane Doe v. Reyes Tapia-Ortiz and Carlos A. Rodriguez*; "Florida Court Orders Crew Leader."

195   *case to law enforcement* CIW, "Fair Food Standards Council Unearths."

195   *to the Mendezes* US Department of Justice, US Attorney's Office, Southern District of Florida, "Two Mexican Nationals Charged with Conspiracy"; US Department of Justice, US Attorney's Office, South District of Florida, "Two Mexican Nationals Sentenced to Prison."

196   *from the Fair Food Program* CIW, "Fair Food Standards Council Unearths"; Fair Food Standards Council (FFSC), "Participating Growers."

196   *crops throughout Florida* "When Working Conditions Are Ripe for Change"; Jon Esformes, interview. Both sources reference a recent case of abuse and gun violence at a strawberry grower; some of these workers have joined Jon Esformes/Pacific Tomato Growers' new strawberry operation; US Department of Labor, Wage and Hour Division (WHD), "Vegetable Supplier to Major Grocery Chains Assessed."

196   *outside of the Fair Food Program* FFSC audit team visit to Pacific Tomato Growers.

196   *agricultural life in California* North, "California Heat Puts Farm Workers at Risk." Contrasts with the Florida tomato fields situation after FFP implementation; Rawal, *Food Chains.*

196   *poor pay in Mexico* See Marosi's remarkable four-article series "Product of Mexico": "Hardship on Mexico's Farms," "Desperate Workers on a Mexican Mega-Farm"; "Company Stores Trap Mexican Farmworkers"; and "In Mexico's fields, Children Toil."

196   *efforts to make progress* For example, Greenhouse, "In Florida Tomato Fields"; Clifford and Greenhouse, "Fast and Flawed Inspections"; Greenhouse, "Farm Labor Groups Make Progress."

199   *the ask was relatively small* CIW, "The Fair Food Program Is a Proven Model."

203   *sign on to the Fair Food Program* CIW, "Save the Date!"

203   *in its produce chain* CIW, "Coalition of Immokalee Workers Announces Walmart to Join."

203   *then head home* FFSC audit team visit to Pacific Tomato Growers.

204   *participate in the expansion* Fair Food Standards Council (FFSC), *Fair Food Program 2015 Annual Report*; Laura Safer Espinoza and Sean Sellers, interview, November 2015; FFSC audit team visit to Pacific Tomato Growers.

204   *East Coast following the crop* True to form, the FFSC ran a controlled experiment to test the effectiveness of different audit strategies. The FFSC compared audit results when done before worker education session versus when done after the education session. Every point of the audits was higher when audits were done after the education sessions. Greg Asbed, interview, November 4, 2015.

204   *certified strawberries* "Whole Foods Expands Partnership."

206   *negotiations with suppliers* Laura Safer Espinoza and Sean Sellers, interview, November 2015.

206   *production into the Fair Food Program* Fair Food Standards Council (FFSC), "Participating Growers."

206   *Fair Food Program into Texas* Discussions with CIW members, April 2017.

207 *vast quantities of them* The unique characteristics of the Florida tomato market are identified by a number of people ranging from Barry Estabrook to Jon Esformes to Peter O'Driscoll of the Equitable Food Initiative. These unique characteristics were clearly important to the CIW's early victories, but a similar concentration of producers is also seen in strawberries and in much US-grown winter produce.

209 *driver for enforcement* This argument comes out of a range of discussions and readings including Soohoo, Albisa, and David, *Bringing Human Rights Home Volume 2*; FFSC audit team visit to Pacific Tomato Growers; Jon Esformes, interview; Steve Hitov, interview, July 2016.

209 *went out of business* Bouffard, "Fresh Del Monte Produce."

209 *the following March* Ohlemeier, "Del Monte Expands Tomato Production."

210 *in our supply chain* "Del Monte Joins the CIW's Fair Food Program."

210 *statement would indicate* Pfeifer, "Del Monte to Pay $1.2 Million"; Feinstein, "Del Monte to Settle."

210 *Fair Food participating grower* Fair Food Standards Council (FFSC), "Participating Growers"; Laura Safer Espinoza and Sean Sellers, interview, November 2015.

210 *provided invaluable support* Foundations have included the Kellogg Foundation, the Kresge Foundation, and the Foundation for Just Society, among others. CIW, "Hu Proposal Part II"; CIW, "W. K. Kellogg Foundation 2015–2018 Grant Application."

210 *Equitable Food Initiative* Laura Germino, mail exchange with Susan Marquis, January 11, 2017; Peter O'Driscoll, interview, December 23, 2016, and January 6, 2017.

210 *closely by travel* Laura Safer Espinoza and Sean Sellers, interview, November 2015; CIW, "IRS Form 990." In 2014, CIW raised about $1.9 million and the Fair Food Standards Council $1 million in contributions and grants.

210 *future buyer agreements* PRNewswire, "Ahold USA Joins the Coalition"; CIW, "Fresh Market Signs."

211 *Clinton Global Citizen Award* Williams, "CIW Debuts Fair Food Label."

211 *soon after by Compass* CIW, "Fair Food Program Label"; Jonsson, "In Florida's Tomato Fields."

211 *customer magazine* CIW, "The Fair Food Label Is in the Produce Aisle."

211 *subjecting them to misery.* McMillan, "Fair-Food Tomatoes."

212 *Fair Food Sustainer Program* CIW, "CALL TO ACTION."

215 *workers to needed services* Farmworker Justice, "Advocacy and Programs"; Farmworker Justice, "2015 Annual Report"; US Environmental Protection Agency (EPA), "Grant Awards Database."

215 *pay raise for the workers* Singh, "How Migrant Farmworkers," July 2015.

215 *pest management* Equitable Food Initiative (EFI), "Equitable Food Initiative."

215 *go back at least to* Peter O'Driscoll, interview, January 6, 2017.

216 *increased worker retention* Strom and Greenhouse, "On the Front Lines."

216 *market for certified produce* Ibid.; Hornick, "Equitable Food Initiative."

217 *published on the web* Current standards can be found at Equitable Food Initiative (EFI), "Certification Documents."

218 *in the certification process* Greenhouse, "Farm Labor Groups Make Progress"; Hornick, "Equitable Food Initiative Faces the Skeptics," *Packer*, September 27, 2016.

218 *two provinces in Canada* Mike Hornick, "Equitable Food Initiative."

218 *over the past twenty-five years* For example, see Fair World Project, "Justice in the Fields"; "Mind Over Matters."

219 *Justice in the Fields* Fair World Project, "Justice in the Fields."

219 *label and certification* Fair World Project, "Introduction."

219 *compliant with the code of conduct* Fair World Project, "Justice in the Fields," p. 17. It's likely that all the organizations in the report would take issue with some aspect of the analysis. In part, this is because the report appears to value standards over effect. The other recommended program is the Agricultural Justice Project. The program has "high standards in most areas" including requirements for organic production, but it is a tiny program that has certified two co-ops, three small farms, and a butcher/grocery store. If the intent is to improve farmworkers' lives and benefit a significant number of workers, it is difficult to determine that a program is effective if it cannot apply and implement standards and their enforcement at some scale.

219 *accountable for their supply chains* Brudney, "Decent Labour Standards"; Jennifer Gordon, "Roles for Workers and Unions."

219 *sometimes with governments* Open Society Foundations, "The Problem with Multi-Stakeholder Initiatives."

220 *meaningful changes on the ground* Jennifer Gordon, "Roles for Workers and Unions," p. 4, citing studies on the Forest Stewardship Council and the Bangladesh factory tragedies in 2012 and 2013. Clarification of the legal aspects of the Fair Food agreements comes from Steve Hitov, e-mail, January 8, 2017.

221 *within their supply chain* CIW, "The Fair Food Program Is a Proven Model."

221 *communication technology sectors* United Nations, Human Rights, Office of the High Commissioner, 2014 Visit to the United States, cover page of addendum.

221 *National Labor Relations Act* Ibid., p. 22.

221 *to respect human rights* Ibid., p. 22–23.

222 *effective grievance processes* Ibid., pp. 13–14.

222 *enforcement of their own rights* Ibid., p. 14.

223 *the goods they produce* National Economic & Social Rights Initiative (NESRI), "Worker-Driven Social Responsibility Collaborative"; National Economic & Social Rights Initiative (NESRI), "Sean Sellers." The WSR-N is housed in the National Economic & Social Responsibility Initiative (NESRI). Thanks to Steve Hitov for the discussion of the potential power of WSR in a globalized economy.

224 *to the Los Angeles Times* Asbed and Sellers, "The Fair Food Program"; Asbed, "Threat of a 'New Harvest of Shame.'"

224 *shaping their protests* Marosi, "Baja Labor Leaders"; Singh, "How Migrant Farmworkers Are Cross-Pollinating Strategies."

224 *comply with the program* Mertens, "Tomato Pickers Win Higher Pay."

224 *workers in Bangladesh factories* Worker-driven Social Responsibility Collaborative, https://www.nesri.org/programs/worker-driven-social-responsibility-collaborative.

224 *reasonable working hours* Greenhouse, "Farm Labor Groups Make Progress"; NESRI (National Economic & Social Rights Initiative), e-mail, December 30, 2015.

224 *globalized production of goods* Dr. Fabiola Mieres of Durham University, UK, is the lead for the forced labor in the supply chain research (see Durham University, Durham, UK, "Staff Profile: Dr. Fabiola Mieres"); Laura Germino, e-mail, August 15, 2016.

224 *elements of the WSR model* Mieres and McGrath, "Addressing Forced Labour."

225 *Yezidis, Christians, and Shia Muslims* CIW, Laura Germino, and antislavery organizations, letter to President Obama, November 12, 2015.

225 *Cooperation in Europe (OSCE)* Laura Germino, "Trafficking for Labour Exploitation in the Agricultural Sector," Speech at the Organization for Security and Co-operation in Europe (OSCE) Seminar THB, April 27–28, 2009.

226 *to be managed by the government* McGurn, "Playing the Music of Capitalism."

226 *we need to work together* Lucas Benitez and Greg Asbed, interview for Jon Esformes tribute.

Bibliography

Agricultural Justice Project. "Certified Farms and Businesses." https://www.agricultural justiceproject.org/en/learn-more/.

Ahold Delhaize. "About Us." https://www.aholddelhaize.com/en/about-us/.

——. "Ahold Delhaize Successfully Completes Merger, Forming One of the World's Largest Food Retail Groups." July 25, 2016. https://www.aholddelhaize.com/en/media/media-releases/ahold-delhaize-successfully-completes-merger-forming-one-of-the-world-s-largest-food-retail-groups/.

"Ahold USA Joins the Coalition of Immokalee Workers' Fair Food Program." PRNewswire, July 29, 2015.

Ali Manik, Julfikar, and Jim Yardley. "Building Collapse in Bangladesh Leaves Scores Dead." *New York Times,* April 24, 2013. http://www.nytimes.com/2013/04/25/world/asia/bangladesh-building-collapse.html?pagewanted=all&_r=1.

Anderson, Chris. *The Long Tail.* Westport, CT: Hyperion Press, 2006.

Asbed, Greg. "Coalition of Immokalee Workers: '¡Golpear a Uno Es Golpear a Todos!' To Beat One of Us Is to Beat Us All." In *Bringing Human Rights Home. Volume 2: Portraits of the Movement, Bringing Human Rights Home,* edited by Cynthia Soohoo, Cynthia, Catherine Albisa, and Martha F. David. Westport, CT: Praeger Publishers.

——. "Threat of a New 'Harvest of Shame.'" *Tampa Bay Times,* September 2, 2012. http://www.tampabay.com/opinion/columns/threat-of-a-new-harvest-of-shame/1249082.

Asbed, Greg, and Sean Sellers. "The Fair Food Program: Worker-Driven Social Responsibility for the 21st Century." *Moyers and Company,* May 29, 2014. http://billmoyers.com/2014/05/29/the-fair-food-program-worker-driven.

——. "The High Cost of Anti-Immigrant Laws." *The Nation,* October 11, 2011.

Bales, Kevin, and Ron Soodalter. *The Slave Next Door: Human Trafficking and Slavery in America Today.* Berkeley: University of California Press, 2009.

Bapat, Sheila. "Effort to Protect Farmworkers from Sexual Assault Gaining Momentum." *Al Jazeera America,* April 17, 2014. http://america.aljazeera.com/articles/2014/4/17/farmworkers-sexualassault.html.

Barstow, David, and Alejandra Xanic von Bertrabdec. "How Wal-Mart Used Payoffs to Get Its Way in Mexico." *New York Times,* December 17, 2012. http://www.nytimes.com/2012/12/18/business/walmart-bribes-teotihuacan.html.

Batchelor, Amanda. "Mexican Men Living in Homestead Indicted for Conspiracy to Provide, Obtain Forced Labor." *Local10.com.* March 18, 2016. http://www.local10.com/news/mexican-men-living-in-homestead-indicted-for-conspiracy-to-provide.

Batista, Elysa. "Family Accused of Enslaving Workers at Immokalee Work Camp." *Naples Daily News,* December 7, 2007. http://www.alipac.us/f12/fl-family-accused-enslaving-workers-immokalee-camp-87870/.

Berry, Steve. "Suspicion of 'Nigra' Blood Racked Family Lake County Racial Case Captured National Attention." *Orlando Sentinel,* February 10, 1991. http://articles.orlandosentinel.com/1991-02-10/news/9102100121_1_platt-mount-dora-mccall.

"Billy Heller Promoted by Pacific Tomato Growers." *Produce News,* March 28, 2006. http://www.theproducenews.com/category-list/9-story-cat/1159-1047.

Bloomberg. "Executive Profile: Jack L. Sinclair." 2015. http://www.bloomberg.com/research/stocks/people/person.asp?personId=8304707&ticker=WMT.

Boer, Dick. "Ahold CEO Dick Boer Addresses Annual General Meeting." 2016. https://www.aholddelhaize.com/en/media/media-releases/ahold-ceo-dick-boer-addresses-annual-general-meeting-2016/.

Borovitz, Mark, and Alan Eisenstock. *The Holy Thief: A Con Man's Journey From Darkness to Light.* New York: HarperCollins Publishers, 2004.

Bouffard, Kevin. "Fresh Del Monte Produce Buys 7,200 Acres of Tomato Fields." *Ledger* (Lakeland, FL), October 7, 2013. http://www.theledger.com/article/20131007/NEWS/131009420.

Bowe, John. "Nobodies: Does Slavery Exist in America?" *New Yorker*, April 21, 2003.

——. *Nobodies: Modern American Slave Labor and the Dark Side of the New Global Economy.* New York: Random House, 2007.

Brudney, James J. "Decent Labour Standards in Corporate Supply Chains: The Immokalee Workers Model." In Joanna Howe and Rosemary Owens, eds. *Temporary Labour Migration in the Global Era: The Regulatory Challenges*, pp. 351–76. Oxford: Hart Publishing, 2016.

Burger King. "Burger King: Corporate Responsibility." 2016. https://www.bk.com/corp-respon.

CBS-TV. "CBS Reports: Legacy of Shame." July 20, 1995.

——. "The Growing Demand for 'Fair Food.'" August 9, 2015. http://www.cbsnews.com/news/the-growing-demand-for-fair-food/. Video available at https://www.youtube.com/watch?v=b6s4YAOISns.

——. "Harvest of Shame." November 25, 1960.

Chen, Michelle. "Surprise: Whole Foods Is Not the World's Greatest Employer." *The Nation*, November 14, 2014. https://www.thenation.com/article/surprise-whole-foods-not-worlds-greatest-employer/.

CIW. "A Tale of Two Groceries," June 8, 2009. http://www.ciw-online.org/blog/2009/06/tale_of_two_groceries/.

——. "American History Happens in a Watermelon Shed." January 20, 2014. http://www.ciw-online.org/blog/2014/01/walmart-american-history/.

——. "And So It Begins." October 17, 2009. http://www.ciw-online.org/blog/2009/10/and-so-it-begins/.

——. "Anti-Slavery Program." 2012. http://www.ciw-online.org/slavery/.

——. "Big News Out of Ahold's Shareholder Meeting in Amsterdam, with More to Come." April 17, 2015. http://www.ciw-online.org/blog/2015/04/ahold-big-news.

——. "Boston 5th Graders to Trader Joe's: You 'might have snazzy Hawaiian shirts and tasty snacks.' December 14, 2011. http://www.ciw-online.org/blog/2011/12/workmans_circle/.

——. "CALL TO ACTION: Become a Founding Member of the Fair Food Sustainer Program!" September 14, 2016. http://www.ciw-online.org/blog/2016/09/fair-food-sustainer/.

——. "Chicago Thanksgiving Day Parade with Rolando the Clown." November 24, 2006. http://www.ciw-online.org/blog/2006/11/rolando_on_parade/.

——. "Chipotle Signs Agreement with CIW to Join Fair Food Program." October 4, 2012. http://www.ciw-online.org/blog/2012/10/chipotle_agreement_news/.

——. "CIW 2007 Truth Tour; Making Fast Food Fair." 2007. http://www.ciw-online.org/2007truthtour/schedule.html.

——. "CIW, Compass Group, East Coast Announce 'sweeping changes to benefit tomato harvesters' at Press Conference in DC!" September 25, 2009. http://www.ciw-online.org/blog/2009/09/compass_agreement/.

——. "CIW Response to Trader Joe's Announcement of Oct. 21, 2011." October 26, 2011. http://www.ciw-online.org/blog/2011/10/ciw_response_to_tj_1021/.

——. "CIW Training Video for Fair Food Code of Conduct" ("Tus Derechos Responsabilidades bajo el Programa por Comida Justa"). 2011. https://www.youtube.com/watch?v=UU4mPKxu_Uo. Also available at https://www.lexiconoffood.com/files/ciw-training-video-fair-food-code-conduct.

——. "CIW's Nely Rodriguez Recognized for Leadership." November 30, 2012. http://www.ciw-online.org/blog/2012/11/ciws-nely-rodriguez-recognized-for-leadership/.

——. "Coalition of Immokalee Workers 2005 Taco Bell Truth Tour." 2005. http://www.ciw-online.org/tz_site-revision/breaking_news/2005dailyupdates.shtml.

——. "Coalition of Immokalee Workers Announces Walmart to Join Groundbreaking Fair Food Program." January 16, 2014. http://www.ciw-online.org/blog/2014/01/walmart-press-release/.

——. "Coalition of Immokalee Workers: McDonald's Truth Tour 2006: The Real Rights Tour!" 2006. http://ciw-online.org/2006truthtour/dailyupdates.html.

——. "Copete: Know Your Rights Training Video from the Fair Food Program." April 17, 2014. https://www.youtube.com/watch?v=aAMIYcMv4Gg.

——. "Fair Food Code of Conduct; Version 1," edited by CIW general counsel Steve Hitov. http://www.fairfoodprogram.org/.

——. "The Fair Food Label Is in the Produce Aisle—and On the Air—in Stores Now!" December 15, 2015. http://www.ciw-online.org/blog/2015/12/ahold-fair-food-labels/.

——. "Fair Food Program Label Finds its First Home at Whole Foods!" December 2, 2014. http://ciw-online.org/blog/2014/12/first-label/.

——. "The Fair Food Program Is a Proven Model for Change in US Agriculture." May 13, 2015. http://www.ciw-online.org/blog/2015/05/compass-expansion-2/.

——. "Fair Food Standards Council Unearths Forced Labor Case on FFP Farm." April 6, 2016. http://www.ciw-online.org/blog/2016/04/ffsc-unearths-forced-labor-case/.

——. "Florida Farmworkers Cross Country, Take Fight for Human and Civil Rights to Fast-Food Giant Taco Bell, Feb 25-Mar 10." 2004. http://ciw-online.org/tz_site-revision/breaking_news/2004pressrelease.shtml.

——. "Fresh Allegations of 'Human Slavery' Emerge from the Tomato Fields of Immokalee." December 10, 2007. http://www.ciw-online.org/blog/2007/12/no_slave_labor/.

——. "Fresh Market Signs Fair Food Agreement with CIW!" January 8, 2015. http://www.ciw-online.org/blog/2015/01/fresh-market-signs/.

——. "'A Giant step forward for farmworkers!' . . . Ahold, Parent Company to Giant, Stop & Shop, and Peapod, Joins Fair Food Program!" July 29, 2015. http://www.ciw-online.org/blog/2015/07/ahold-agreement/.

——. "Guidance for Implementation of the Fair Food Code of Conduct." 2014. Unpublished internal document.

——. "Historic Breakthrough in Florida's Tomato Fields." November 16, 2010. http://www.ciw-online.org/blog/2010/11/ftge_ciw_joint_release/.

——. "Hu Proposal Part II." September 2013. Unpublished internal document.

——. "Interview with CIW Member Wins First Round in Nationwide Human Rights Video Contest!" September 8, 2010. http://www.ciw-online.org/blog/2010/09/ushrn_video_award/.

——. "IRS Form 990 from 2014 Tax Return for CIW and Fair Food Standard Council." 2014. https://www.guidestar.org/profile/65-0641010; http://www.guidestar.org/profile/45-2982573.

——. "Know Your Rights and Responsibilities under the New Fair Food Agreement." 2012. Pamphlet.

——. "Left Behind." May 8, 2012. http://www.ciw-online.org/blog/2012/05/left_behind/.

——. "Lucas Benitez of the CIW Speaks." October 3, 2010. http://www.ciw-online.org/blog/2010/10/benitez_on_pacific_ciw_agreement/.

——. "March on Trader Joe's Headquarters Monrovia, CA October 21, 2011." October 21, 2011. http://www.ciw-online.org/blog/2011/10/march_on_monrovia/.

——. "Martin Sheen Pens Powerful Letter to Trader Joe's CEO." January 9, 2012. http://www.ciw-online.org/blog/2012/01/martin-sheen-pens-powerful-letter-to-trader-joes-ceo/.

——. "McDonald's Tangled Web." March 14, 2006. http://www.ciw-online.org/blog/2006/03/tangled-web/.

——. "McDonald's USA and its Produce Suppliers to Work with the Coalition of Immokalee Workers." April 9, 2007. http://www.ciw-online.org/blog/2007/04/ciw_mcdonalds_release/.

——. "National Supermarket Week of Action a Wrap." November 27, 2009. http://www.ciw-online.org/blog/2009/11/national-supermarket-week-of-action-a-wrap/.

——. "On the Elimination of the Required Overfilling of Buckets through the CIW's Fair Food Code of Conduct." April 30, 2011. http://www.ciw-online.org/blog/2011/04/bucket_overfilling/.

——. *One Penny More* (CIW video). 2010. https://www.youtube.com/watch?v=VURs-rsi_KQ.

——. "PACK YOUR BAGS, WE'RE HEADING TO CHICAGO!" April 1, 2007. http://www.ciw-online.org/blog/2007/04/pack-your-bags-were-heading-to-chicago/.

——. "A Powerful Voice for Dignified Wages and Working Conditions in the Fields of Florida. CIW Staff Lupe Gonzalo Honored as Mother, Community Leader!" May 16, 2013. http://www.ciw-online.org/blog/2013/05/lupe-honored/.

——. "Save the Date! Return to Human Rights Tour Announce for March 16–29." December 6, 2016. http://www.ciw-online.org/blog/2016/12/return-to-human-rights-tour/.

——. "Slavery in the Fields and the Food We Eat." 2013. http://ciw-online.org/wp-content/uploads/12SlaveryintheFields.pdf.

——. "Subway Signs Agreement with the Coalition of Immokalee Workers (CIW) to Improve Tomato Harvester Wages, Working Conditions in Florida." December 2, 2008. http://www.ciw-online.org/blog/2008/12/ciw_subway_joint_press_release/.

——. "Taco Bell Agreement Analysis." March 10, 2005. www.ciw-online.org/blog/2005/03/agreement-analysis.

——. "The Three Lies CEOs Tell Themselves about Social Responsibility (That Only They Believe), Brought to You by Royal Ahold!" April 27, 2013. http://www.ciw-online.org/blog/2013/04/the-three-lies-ceos-tell-themselves-about-social-responsibility.

——. "Trader Joe's Set to Open First Florida Store . . . on Immokalee Road!" January 11, 2012. http://www.ciw-online.org/blog/2012/01/immokalee_rd_tjs/.

——. "Trader Joe's: We'll Be Fair. Trust Us." October 24, 2011. http://www.ciw-online.org/blog/2011/10/trader-joes-well-be-fair-trust-us/.

——. "Unsettling Experience at Last Weekend's Publix Actions Becomes Issue in Publix Campaign." October 23, 2009. http://www.ciw-online.org/blog/2009/10/unsettling-experience-at-last-weekends-publix-actions-becomes-issue-in-publix-campaign/.

——. "Welcome Aboard . . . Trader Joe's and CIW Sign Fair Food Agreement!" February 9, 2012. http://www.ciw-online.org/blog/2012/02/tj_agreement/.

——. "Whole Foods Markets Signs Agreement with CIW." September 10, 2008. http://www.ciw-online.org/blog/2008/09/wf_ciw_press_release/.

——. W. K. Kellogg Foundation 2015–2018 Grant Application. 2014. Unpublished internal document.

Clifford, Stephanie, and Steven Greenhouse. "Fast and Flawed Inspections of Factories Abroad." *New York Times*, September 1, 2013. http://www.nytimes.com/2013/09/02/business/global/superficial-visits-and-trickery-undermine-foreign-factory-inspections.html?_r=0.

Cohen, Rich. *The Fish That Ate the Whale: The Life and Times of America's Banana King*. New York: Farrar, Strauss and Giroux, 2012.

Compass Group. "Companies." 2016. http://www.compass-usa.com/companies/.

——. "Compass Group and the Coalition of Immokalee Workers (CIW) Announce Sweeping Changes to Benefit Tomato Harvesters." September 25, 2009. http://www.compass-usa.com/press-releases/coalition-immokalee-workers-ciw/.

——. "Food Chains." 2014. http://www.compass-usa.com/food-chains/.

Cox, Billy. "Minister Kicked Out of Publix in Wake of Labor Dispute." *Sarasota Herald-Tribune*, September 11, 2012. http://www.heraldtribune.com/article/20120911/ARTICLE/120919929?p=1&tc=pg.

Damico, Nicole. "Eyes Wide Open." 2010. Unpublished.

Daniels, Cletus. *Bitter Harvest: A History of California Farmworkers, 1870–1941*. Ithaca, NY: Cornell University Press, 1981.

"Del Monte Joins the CIW's Fair Food Program." *Produce News*, April 8, 2014. http://www.producenews.com/more-what-s-new/12710-del-monte-joins-the-wic-s-fair-food-program.

Democracy Now! "Seeking Living Wage and Humane Conditions, Immokalee Workers Bring Fair Food Struggle to Chipotle." October 3, 2012. https://www.democracynow.org/2012/10/3/seeking_living_wage_and_humane_conditions

DiMartino, Christina. "Nathan Esformes, Partner in Pacific Tomato Growers, Dies at 83." *Produce News*, October 7, 2015. http://www.producenews.com/more-people-articles/people/17098-industry-veteran-nathan-j-esformes-dies-at-83.

Doyle, Leonard. "Activists Out Burger King Dirty Tricks Operation." *Independent*, May 9, 2008. http://www.independent.co.uk/news/world/americas/activists-out-burger-king-dirty-tricks-operation-825097.html.

Drape, Joe. "An Early Glimpse of Magic, American Pharoah Dropped Jaws Long Before He Hit the Racetrack." *New York Times*, April 18, 2016. http://www.nytimes.com/2016/04/18/sports/horse-racing/american-pharoah-triple-crown-baffert-mckathan.html.

Durham University, Durham, UK. "Staff Profile: Dr. Fabiola Mieres." 2016. https://www.dur.ac.uk/geography/staff/geogstaffhidden/?id=13327.

Encore.org. "Laura Safer Espinoza, Executive Director, Fair Food Standards Council, Purpose Prize Winner 2015." 2015. http://encore.org/purpose-prize/laura-safer-espinoza/.

Equitable Food Initiative (EFI). "Certification Documents" including "EFI Standards, Guidance and Interpretations." 2016. http://www.equitablefood.org/standards.

——. "Equitable Food Initiative." 2016. http://www.equitablefood.org.

Espinoza, Laura Safer. "The Purpose Prize 2015 Narrative Application." Unpublished. 2015.

Estabrook, Barry. "Major Grocery Chain Agrees to Sign On to Fair Labor Program for Tomato Workers." 2015. http://civileats.com/2015/07/29/major-supermarket-chain-behind-giant-food-stop-n-shop-agrees-to-sign-on-to-fair-labor-program-for-tomato-workers/.

——. "Politics of the Plate: The Price of Tomatoes." *Gourmet*, March 2009.

——. "Publix Still Claiming Workers Don't Deserve a One-Cent Raise." 2012. http://www.takepart.com/article/2012/11/21/2012-year-farm-workers-can-be-thankful.

——. "A Sweet Deal for Tomato Workers: Coalition of Immokalee Workers and Florida Tomato Growers Exchange Reach Landmark Labor Agreement." 2010. http://politicsoftheplate.com/?p=680.

——. *Tomatoland: How Modern Industrial Agriculture Destroyed Our Most Alluring Fruit.* Kansas City, MO: Andrews McMeel Publishing, 2011.

Evans, Walker. *American Photographs.* New York: Museum of Modern Art, 2012 (75th Anniversary Edition, replicating the original publication of 1938).

Fair Food Program (FFP). "Partners." 2015. http://www.fairfoodprogram.org/partners/.

Fair Food Standards Council (FFSC). "Biography, Executive Director Laura Safer Espinoza." 2017. http://www.fairfoodstandards.org/about/judge-laura-safer-espinoza/.

——. "Fair Food Code of Conduct." 2015. http://www.fairfoodstandards.org/resources/fair-food-code-of-conduct/.

——. *Fair Food Program 2013 Annual Report.* Sarasota, FL: Fair Food Standards Council, 2013. http://fairfoodstandards.org/cms/wp-content/uploads/2015/08/13SOTP-Web.pdf.

——. *Fair Food Program 2014 Annual Report.* Sarasota, FL: Fair Food Standards Council, 2014. http://fairfoodstandards.org/cms/wp-content/uploads/2015/08/14SOTP-Web.pdf.

——. *Fair Food Program 2015 Annual Report.* Sarasota, FL: Fair Food Standards Council, 2015. http://fairfoodstandards.org/15SOTP-Web.pdf.

——. "Job Description, Human Rights Attorney." 2017. http://www.fairfoodstandards.org/careers/human-rights-attorney/.

——. "Participating Buyers." 2016. http://www.fairfoodstandards.org/resources/participating-buyers/.

——. "Participating Growers." 2016. http://www.fairfoodstandards.org/resources/participating-growers/.

Fair World Project. "Introduction." 2016. https://fairworldproject.org/about/introduction/.

——. "Justice in the Fields: A Report on the Role of Farmworker Justice Certification and an Evaluation of the Effectiveness of Seven Labels." 2016. http://fairworldproject.org/wp-content/uploads/2016/10/Justice-In-The-Fields-Report.pdf.

Farmworker Justice. "2015 Annual Report." 2015. https://www.farmworkerjustice.org/sites/default/files/FarmworkerJustice2015AnnualReport_email.pdf.

——. "Advocacy and Programs." 2016. https://www.farmworkerjustice.org/advocacy-and-programs.

Feinstein, Gary. "Del Monte to Settle Underpayment Lawsuit for $7.5 Million." *Hanford Sentinel*, February 14, 2015. http://hanfordsentinel.com/news/local/del-monte-to-settle-underpayment-lawsuit-for-million/article_42a42826-0042-5337-86d3-57d21a4999ce.html.

Fight for $15. "Fight for $15: About Us." 2016. http://fightfor15.org/about-us/.

"Five Recent Cases with Slavery Convictions." *Palm Beach Post*, December 7, 2003. http://www2.palmbeachpost.com/moderndayslavery/reports/peonageblurbs 1207.html.

"Florida Court Orders Crew Leader to Pay U.S. $3.5m in Forced Labor Damages," February 27, 2017. www.freshfruitportal.com.

Florida Department of Economic Opportunity. "Florida Minimum Wage History 2000 to 2013." 2012. http://www.floridajobs.org/minimumwage/Florida MinimumWageHistory2000-2013.pdf.

Food Dive. "The Top 10 U.S. Retailers for Food and Beverage Sales Right Now." September 10, 2013. http://www.fooddive.com/news/the-top-10-us-retailers-for-food-and-beverage-sales-right-now/169323/.

FoodCon 2016. "FoodCon 2016 Agenda." 2016. http://foodcon2016.com/agenda/.

Fuller Funeral Home, Naples, Florida. "Obituary for Norig Garo Asbed." October 1, 2015. http://www.fullernaples.com/obituaries/Norig-Asbed/#!/Obituary.

Ganz, Marshall. *Why David Sometimes Wins: Leadership, Organization, and Strategy in the California Farm Worker Movement*. Oxford: Oxford University Press, 2009.

Gerber, Marisa. "Hundreds March to Trader Joe's Headquarters in Monrovia to Demand a One Penny Per Pound Raise for Florida Farm Workers." *Orange County Weekly*, October 21, 2011. http://www.ocweekly.com/restaurants/hundreds-march-to-trader-joes-headquarters-in-monrovia-to-demand-a-one-penny-per-pound-raise-for-florida-farm-workers-6629869.

Germino, Laura. "Do Successful Prosecutions Constitute Success in the Fight against Modern-Day Slavery?" March 11, 2015. http://www.humantraffickingsearch. net/wp1/do-successful-prosecutions-constitute-success-in-the-fight-against-modern-day-slavery.

——. "EU Horizon 2020 Project." August 15, 2016. Unpublished.

——. "Session 2: Identification of Cases of Trafficking for Labour Exploitation in the Agricultural Sector." In "A Summary of Challenges on Addressing Human Trafficking for Labour Exploitation in the Agricultural Sector in the OSCE Region." Office of the Special Representative and Co-ordinator for Combating Trafficking in Human Beings, pp. 13–14. April 27–28, 2009. http://www.osce. org/cthb/37937?download=true.

——. "Trafficking for Labour Exploitation in the Agricultural Sector." Speech at the Organization for Security and Co-operation in Europe (OSCE) Seminar THB. April 27–28, 2009. http://www.osce.org/what/trafficking/62945?download=true.

——. "Legacy of Shame." August 30–31, 2015. Unpublished.

——. "Slavery." September 1–3, 2015. Unpublished.

Goldie, Jeremy. "As Bangladesh's Garment Industry Booms, Workers Struggle for Better Conditions." *Global Envision*: Exploring Market-Driven Solutions to Poverty. March 30, 2016. http://www.globalenvision.org/2016/03/30/bangladeshs-garment-industry-booms-workers-struggle-better-conditions.

Gordon, Jennifer. "Roles for Workers and Unions in Regulating Labour Recruitment in Mexico." In Joanna Howe and Rosemary Owens, eds. *Temporary Labour Migration in the Global Era: The Regulatory Challenges*, pp. 320–50. Oxford: Hart Publishing, 2016.

Grace, Stephanie. "Justice in the Fields." *Brown Alumni Magazine*, January–February 2016.

Gray, Margaret. *Labor and the Locavore: The Making of a Comprehensive Food Ethic.* Berkeley: University of California Press, 2014.

Green, Ely. *Ely: An Autobiography.* Athens: University of Georgia Press, 2004.

Greene, Ronnie. "Brutal Farm Labor Bosses Punished, But Not Growers Who Hire Them." *Miami Herald,* September 1, 2003. http://www.fachc.org/pdf/mig_ Brutal%20farm%20labor%20bosses%20punished,%20but%20not%20 growers%20who%20hire%20them.pdf.

——. "Crop of Abuse." *Miami Herald,* August 31, 2003. http://www.miamiherald.com/ news/state/article1927844.html.

Greenhouse, Steven. "Farm Labor Groups Make Progress on Wages and Working Conditions." *New York Times,* July 3, 2015. http://www.nytimes.com/2015/ 07/04/business/economy/farm-labor-groups-make-progress-on-wages-and- working-conditions.html?hpw&rref=business&action=click&pgtype=Home page&module=well-region&region=bottom-well&WT.nav=bottom-well&_r=1.

——. "Going Hungry to Make a Point; A Fast for Poor Laborers Is a Sign of New Inter- est in an Old Technique." *New York Times,* March 31, 2000. http://www.nytimes. com/2000/03/31/nyregion/going-hungry-make-point-fast-for-poor-laborers- sign-new-interest-old-technique.html.

——. "Homeless Harvest: A Special Report: As Economy Booms, Migrant Workers' Housing Worsens." *New York Times,* May 31, 1998. http://www.nytimes.com/ 1998/05/31/us/homeless-harvest-special-report-economy-booms-migrant- workers-housing-worsens.html.

——. "In Florida Tomato Fields, a Penny Buys Progress." *New York Times,* April 25, 2014. http://www.nytimes.com/2014/04/25/business/in-florida-tomato-fields- a-penny-buys-progress.html?_r=0.

——. "Tomato Pickers' Wages Fight Faces Obstacles." *New York Times,* December 24 2007. http://www.nytimes.com/2007/12/24/us/24tomato.html?pagewanted= print&_r=0.

Guerin-Gonzales, Camille. *Mexican Workers and The American Dream: Immigration, Repatriation, and California Farm Labor, 1900–1939.* New Brunswick, NJ: Rutgers University Press, 1994.

Hale, Thomas, and David Held. *Handbook of Transnational Governance: Institutions and Innovations.* Cambridge: Polity, 2011.

Henry, Rabbi Sharyn. "Sleeping Through the Tempest: A Wake Up Call from Jonah." A Sermon for Yom Kippur, 5772. 2011. http://www.truah.org/9-issuescampaigns/ slavery-a-human-trafficking/209-sleeping-through-the-tempest-a-wake-up- call-from-jonah.html.

Hitov, Steve. "Ahold Agreement." August 3, 2015. Unpublished.

——. "Checking In." June 25–27, 2016. Unpublished.

——. "Fair Food Agreement Template." December 2–3, 2011. Unpublished.

Hoffman, Lorraine. "Are You Ready for a Department of Labor Audit?" *Seattle Business: The Magazine,* no date. http://www.seattlebusinessmag.com/business- corners/are-you-ready-department-labor-audit.

Holden, Daphne. "Research and Evaluation Report: The Coalition of Immokalee Workers." Mertz Gilmore Foundation, 2008.

Holtz, Michael. "Human Trafficking: 6 Solutions That Are Working." *Christian Science Monitor,* January 25, 2016. http://www.csmonitor.com/World/2016/ 0125/Human-trafficking-6-solutions-that-are-working/Fair-food-labeling- for-US-produce.

Hornick, Mike. "Equitable Food Initiative Faces the Skeptics." *Packer,* September 27, 2016. http://www.thepacker.com/news/equitable-food-initiative-faces-skeptics.

Howe, Joanna, and Rosemary Owens, eds. *Temporary Labour Migration in the Global Era: The Regulatory Challenges.* Oxford: Hart Publishing, 2016.

Human Rights Watch. "Cultivating Fear: The Vulnerability of Immigrant Farmworkers in the US to Sexual Violence and Sexual Harassment." May 15, 2012. https://www.hrw.org/report/2012/05/15/cultivating-fear/vulnerability-immigrant-farmworkers-us-sexual-violence-and-sexual.

Hurt, R. Douglas. *American Agriculture: A Brief History*. West Lafayette, IN: Purdue University Press, 2002.

Iaconangelo, David. "Mexican Authorities Rescue 275 Workers from 'Slavery' at Tomato Packing Camp." *Latin Times*, June 12, 2013. http://www.latintimes.com/mexican-authorities-rescue-275-workers-slavery-tomato-packing-camp-133131.

Isquith, Elias. "'A less friendly, less comforting place': Steve Greenhouse on the End of an Era in Labor Reporting." *Salon*, January 8, 2015.

James, Edgerrin, with Dan Le Batard. "Straight Up." *ESPN the Magazine*, September 4, 2000.

Jamieson, David. "Safety Inspections by Social Audit Firms For U.S. Companies Called 'Facade' by Labor Groups." *Huffington Post*, April 23, 2013. http://www.huffingtonpost.com/entry/safety-inspections-social-audit-afl-cio_n_3134930.

Jamieson, David, and Emran Hossain. "Bangladesh Collapse Shows Safety Audit Shortcomings." *Huffington Post*, May 4, 2013. http://www.huffingtonpost.com/2013/05/04/bangladesh-collapse-safety-audit_n_3211091.html.

Jefferson, Jon. "Alienation: Is There a Legal Solution to the Immigration Mess?" *American Business Association (ABA) Journal* 79:54 (1993).

John Doe, Jane Doe v. Reyes Tapia-Ortiz and Carlos A. Rodriguez. Case No: 2:14-cv-206-FtM-38MRM. U.S. District Court, Middle District of Florida, Fort Myers Division. https://dockets.justia.com/docket/florida/flmdce/2:2014cv00206/296363.

Jonsson, Patrik. "In Florida's Tomato Fields, a Fight for Ethical Farm Labor Grows." *Christian Science Monitor*, November 16, 2015. http://humantrafficking.csmonitor.com/fight-for-fair-food-labels.

Kaufmann, Greg. "The Wall Comes Tumbling Down." *The Nation*, October 18, 2010. https://www.thenation.com/article/wall-comes-tumbling-down-2/.

Kerry, John. Remarks at the White House Forum on Combatting Human Trafficking in Supply Chains. January 29, 2015. https://www.state.gov/secretary/remarks/2015/01/236950.htm.

"Mind Over Matters." Sustainability Segment, interview with Peter O'Driscoll and Guadalupe "Lupe" Gamboa. KEXP-FM (Seattle, Washington). July 30, 2012. http://feeds.kexp.org/kexp/mindovermatterssustainability. Podcast available at http://podbay.fm/show/450970411/e/1343631600.

Khokha, Sasha. "Silenced By Status, Farm Workers Face Rape, Sexual Abuse." National Public Radio, *All Things Considered*. November 5, 2013. http://www.npr.org/2013/11/05/243219199/silenced-by-status-farm-workers-face-rape-sexual-abuse.

Kilborn, Peter T. "Tomato Pickers' Hope of a Better Life Becomes Victim as Industry Steps In." *New York Times*, May 9, 1991. http://www.nytimes.com/1991/05/09/us/tomato-pickers-hope-for-better-life-becomes-victim-as-industry-steps-in.html?pagewanted=print.

King, Gilbert. *Devil in the Grove: Thurgood Marshall, the Groveland Boys, and the Dawn of a New America*. New York: Harper Perennial, 2012.

King, Ledyard, and Casey Logan. "Income Gap Alive and Well in Southwest Florida." *Fort Myers News-Press*, January 28, 2015. http://www.news-press.com/story/news/2015/01/28/income-gap-alive-southwest-florida/22487609/.

Klein, Naomi. *No Logo: Taking Aim at the Brand Bullies.* New York: Picador, 2000.

Koger, Chris. "Bill Lipman, Last of Six L's Founders, Dies." *Packer*, May 20, 2011. http://www.thepacker.com/fruit-vegetable-news/Bill-Lipman-last-of-the-Six-Ls-founders-dies-122332679.html.

Krueger, Curtis. "Striking for Pay, Pride." *St. Petersburg Times*, December 19, 1999. http://www.sptimes.com/News/121999/news_pf/State/Striking_for_pay_pride.

Lange, Dorothea, and Paul Taylor. *An American Exodus: A Record of Human Erosion.* New York: Reynal and Hitchcock, 1939.

Lantigua, John. "Why Was Carlitos Born This Way?" *Palm Beach Post*, March 16, 2005. http://www.palmbeachpost.com/news/carlitos/.

Long, Bryan. "Hunger Strike Feeds on Despair; the Impasse Between the Coalition of Immokalee Workers and the Tomato Growers Strikes at the Heart of a Town Dependent on Agriculture." *Sarasota Herald-Tribune*, January 3, 1998.

Majka, L. C., and T. J. Majka. *Farmworkers, Agribusiness, and the State.* Philadelphia: Temple University Press, 1982.

Market Watch. "Whole Foods Market Inc. Annual Financials." No date. http://www.marketwatch.com/investing/stock/wfm/financials.

Marosi, Richard. "Baja Labor Leaders Learned Tactics from Their Efforts in the U.S." *Los Angeles Times*, March 28, 2015. http://www.latimes.com/world/mexico-americas/la-me-baja-labor-leaders-20150329-story.html.

——. "Company Stores Trap Mexican farmworkers in a Cycle of Debt." *Los Angeles Times*, December 12, 2014. http://graphics.latimes.com/product-of-mexico-stores/.

——. "Desperate Workers on a Mexican Mega-Farm. 'They treated us like slaves.'" *Los Angeles Times*, December 10, 2014. http://graphics.latimes.com/product-of-mexico-labor/.

——. "Hardship on Mexico's Farms, a Bounty for U.S. Tables." *Los Angeles Times*, December 7, 2014. http://graphics.latimes.com/product-of-mexico-camps/.

——. "In Mexico's Fields, Children Toil to Harvest Crops That Make It to American Tables." *Los Angeles Times*, December 14, 2014. http://graphics.latimes.com/product-of-mexico-children/.

Marquis, Susan. "Wal-Mart Chooses Fairness, Giving Farmworkers a Boost." *Orlando Sentinel*, February 6, 2014. http://www.rand.org/blog/2014/02/wal-mart-chooses-fairness-giving-farmworkers-a-boost.html.

Matthews, Christopher. "10 Ways Walmart Changed the World: Everyday Low Prices." *Time*, June 29, 2012. http://business.time.com/2012/07/02/ten-ways-walmart-changed-the-world/.

Maxwell, Bill. "Jim Crow Conflict Clouded the Point." *St. Petersburg Times*, February 14, 2001. http://www.sptimes.com/News/021401/Columns/Jim_Crow_conflict_clo.shtml.

McClure, Bob. "Pacific Tomatoes Taps COO." *Packer*, May 17, 2011. http://www.thepacker.com/fruit-vegetable-news/pacific_tomato_growers_taps_coo_122091339.html.

McDonald's. "Sustainability/Sourcing: Good Sourcing." 2016. http://corporate.mcdonalds.com/mcd/sustainability/sourcing.html.

"Mexico Rescues 275 Workers from 'Slavery' at Tomato Plant in Toliman." *Agence France Presse.* August 12, 2013. http://www.huffingtonpost.com/2013/06/12/mexico-workers-slavery-toliman_n_3427120.html.

Mertens, Richard. "Tomato Workers Win Higher Pay. Can Other Workers Use Their Strategy?" *Christian Science Monitor*. March 9, 2017. http://www.csmonitor.com/Business/2017/0309/Tomato-pickers-win-higher-pay.-Can-other-workers-use-their-strategy

Mieres, Fabiola, and Siobhan McGrath. "Addressing Forced Labour in Fragmented Chains of Production." *Open Democracy*, March 4, 2015. https://www.opendemocracy.net/beyondslavery/fabiola-mieres-siobh%C3%A1n-mcgrath/addressing-forced-labour-in-fragmented-chains-of-produc.

McGurn, William. "Playing the Music of Capitalism." *Wall Street Journal*, July 10, 2016. http://www.wsj.com/articles/playing-the-music-of-capitalism-1436568716.

McMillan, Tracie. "Fair-Food Tomatoes: What Are They and Are They Worth It?" *EatingWell*, July–August 2015. http://www.eatingwell.com/food_news/green_sustainable/fair-food_tomatoes_what_are_they_are_they_worth_it.

Morningstar. "Publix Super Markets Insiders: Board of Directors." 2015. http://insiders.morningstar.com/trading/board-of-directors.action?t=0P0000 CO34&culture=en-US.

Moshenberg, Dan. "For Women Farmworkers of Immokalee NOW IS THE TIME!" March 21, 2014. http://www.womeninandbeyond.org/?p=10701.

National Economic & Social Rights Initiative (NESRI). "Help Grow Worker-Driven Social Responsibility Efforts." December 30, 2015. Unpublished.

——. "Sean Sellers: Director of Strategic Partnerships at the Worker-Driven Social Responsibility Network." 2016. https://www.nesri.org/about/staff/sean-sellers.

——. "Worker-driven Social Responsibility Collaborative." 2016. https://www.nesri.org/programs/worker-driven-social-responsibility-collaborative.

National Labor Relations Act. 29 U.S.C 151–69. https://www.nlrb.gov/resources/national-labor-relations-act.

Nike. "Nike Aims to Transform Manufacturing." 2016. http://about.nike.com/pages/transform-manufacturing.

North, Anna. "California Heat Puts Farm Workers at Risk." *Taking Note: The Editorial Page Editor's Blog*. September 3, 2015. http://takingnote.blogs.nytimes.com/2015/09/03/california-heat-puts-farm-workers-at-risk/?_r=1.

Nova, Scott, and Isaac Shapiro. "Polishing Apple: Fair Labor Association Gives Foxconn and Apple Undue Credit for Labor Rights Progress." Economics Policy Institute, Briefing Paper #352, November 8, 2012. http://www.epi.org/files/2012/polishing-apple-fla-foxconn-apple-undue.pdf .

"Obituary: Mary Audrey Roseborough." *Daytona Beach News-Journal*, May 3, 2011. http://www.legacy.com/obituaries/news-journalonline/obituary.aspx?n=mary-audrey-roseborough&pid=150801506.

"Obituary for Ruth-Alice Davis Asbed." *P&S Journal* (Columbia Medical School, College of Physicians and Surgeons Journal) 18:1 (Winter 1998). http://www.cumc.columbia.edu/psjournal/archive/archives/jour_v18n01_0029.html.

O'Connor, Clare. "Walmart Hikes Hourly Pay To $10 Minimum For Most Workers." *Forbes*, January 20, 2016. http://www.forbes.com/sites/clareoconnor/2016/01/20/walmart-hikes-hourly-pay-to-10-minimum-for-most-workers/#e5eb56d26afc.

Ohlemeier, Doug. "Del Monte Expands Tomato Production in Florida, Again." *Packer*, March 4, 2014. http://www.thepacker.com/fruit-vegetable-news/Del-Monte-expands-tomato-production-in-Florida--again-248443841.html.

——. "Lipman Family Cos. Hires Sysco Veteran as CEO." *Packer*, May 17, 2011. http://www.thepacker.com/fruit-vegetable-news/foodservice/lipman_family_cos_hires_sysco_veteran_as_ceo_122002324.html.

Open Society Foundations. "The Problem with Multi-Stakeholder Initiatives."
    June 11, 2014. https://www.opensocietyfoundations.org/events/problem-
    multi-stakeholder-initiatives.
Oshinsky, David M. *"Worse than Slavery": Parchman Farm and the Ordeal of Jim Crow
    Justice.* New York: Free Press, 1996.
Oxfam America. "Like Machines in the Fields: Workers' Rights in American
    Agriculture." March 2004. https://www.oxfamamerica.org/static/oa3/files/like-
    machines-in-the-fields.pdf.
Pawel, Miriam. *The Crusades of Cesar Chavez: A Biography.* New York: Bloomsbury
    Press, 2014.
———. *The Union of Their Dreams: Power, Hope, and Struggle in Cesar Chavez's Farm
    Worker Movement.* New York: Bloomsbury Press, 2009.
PBS-TV. *Frontline,* "Rape in the Fields." June 25, 2013. PBS online. http://www.pbs.
    org/wgbh/frontline/film/rape-in-the-fields/.
PBS-TV. *Frontline,* "A Voice for Workers." June 25, 2013. PBS online. http://www.pbs.
    org/video/2365031701/.
Penn Live. "At a Glance: 8 Largest Grocers in the U.S." 2015. http://www.pennlive.com/
    midstate/index.ssf/2015/06/8_largest_grocers_in_the_us.html#0.
Perez, Maria. "Farm Workers Settle Lawsuit over Labor Violations, But Want Case
    Reopened against Recruiter." *Naples Daily News,* March 18, 2015. http://archive.
    naplesnews.com/news/crime/farm-workers-settle-lawsuit-over-labor-violations-
    but-want-case-reopened-against-recruiter-ep-998822-335544361.html.
———. "Six Accuse Clewiston Farm of Human Trafficking, Say They Were Forced to
    Work, Threatened with Guns." *Naples Daily News,* August 31, 2014. http://
    archive.naplesnews.com/news/local/six-accuse-clewiston-farm-of-human-
    trafficking-say-they-were-forced-to-work-threatened-with-guns-ep--337087911.
    html.
Pfeifer, Stuart. "Del Monte to Pay $1.2 Million to Settle Worker-Discrimination
    Lawsuit." *Los Angeles Times,* November 18, 2013. http://articles.latimes.com/
    2013/nov/18/business/la-fi-mo-del-monte-to-pay-12-million-to-settle-
    humantrafficking-lawsuit-20131118.
Philpott, Tom. "Employees Are 'Bitter' as Whole Foods Chops Jobs and Wages." *Mother
    Jones,* October 3, 2015. http://www.motherjones.com/tom-philpott/2015/09/
    whole-foods-bob-mackey-job-wage-cuts-unions-wall-street.
Powell, Bonnie Azab. "Eric Schlosser Would Rather Chew on a Wooden Podium than
    Cloned Meat." January 23, 2008. http://www.ethicurean.com/2008/01/23/
    schlosser-2/.
Presbyterian Mission Agency. "CIW Responds to Publix's Publicly Stated Concerns."
    2012. https://pma.pcusa.org/ministries/fairfood/ciw-responds-publixs-publicly-
    stated-concerns/.
"The Press: Look at Your Own Child." *Time,* December 13, 1954.
Publix. "About Publix." 2015. http://corporate.publix.com/about-publix.
———. "History." 2015. http://corporate.publix.com/about-publix/culture/history.
———. "Publix Announces Fourth Quarter and Annual Results for 2014." March 2,
    2015. http://www.publixstockholder.com/stockholders/financial-information-
    and-filings/financial-news-releases/publix-announces-fourth-quarter-and-
    annual-results-for-2014.
———. "Publix Announces Fourth Quarter and Annual Results for 2015." March 1,
    2016. http://www.publixstockholder.com/stockholders/financial-information-
    and-filings/financial-news-releases/publix-announces-fourth-quarter-and-
    annual-results-for-2015.

———. "Put It in the Price: Publix's Position on the CIW Campaign." 2015. http://corporate.publix.com/about-publix/newsroom/put-it-in-the-price.

Queen, Cheryl. Linked-In profile. 2015. https://www.linkedin.com/in/cheryl-queen-199baa3.

Rawal, Sanjay, dir. *Food Chains.* 2014. http://www.foodchainsfilm.com/.

Reed, Anne. "How SWFL's Tomato Industry Is Changing." *News-Press,* April 10, 2015. http://www.news-press.com/story/money/2015/04/10/tomatoes-swfl-static-sales-changing-market/25582733/.

Reiss, Cory. "Growers Seeking SAFE Haven." *The Ledger,* January 26, 2006. http://www.theledger.com/apps/pbcs.dll/article?p=1&tc=pg&AID=/20060129/NEWS/601290370/1039.

Reyes-Chavez, Gerardo. "Making Corporations Pay." TEDx Fruitvale Harvesting Change. 2011. https://www.youtube.com/watch?v=N6fly-p3hu0.

Robert F. Kennedy Center for Justice and Human Rights. Robert F. Kennedy Human Rights Award Winners. 2016. http://rfkhumanrights.org/who-we-are/awards/rfk-human-rights-award/human-rights-award-winners/?edit_off.

Rossetto, Harriet, and Reeva Hunter Mandelbaum. *Sacred Housekeeping: A Spiritual Memoir.* Bloomington, IN: AuthorHouse, 2012.

Rothenberg, Daniel. *With These Hands: The Hidden World of Migrant Farmworkers Today.* New York: Harcourt Brace & Company, 1998.

"Ruth-Alice Davis Asbed, MD. Health Official, Dies." *Washington Post,* July 16, 1993. http://www.washingtonpost.com/archive/local/1993/07/16/ruth-alice-davis-asbed-md-health-official-dies/47dc4f79-3116-411e-8962-86eb1b01ac98/.

Salucio, Cruz, and Nely Rodriguez. "Coalition of Immokalee Workers Talks about Radio Conciencia." November 20, 2012. https://www.youtube.com/watch?v=14APjPC7IWw.

Sauer, Matthew. "Growers Insist Wages Are Good." *Sarasota Herald-Tribune,* January 3, 1998. https://news.google.com/newspapers?nid=1755&dat=19980103&id=5UAgAAAAIBAJ&sjid=cH0EAAAAIBAJ&pg=7023,2580629&hl=en.

Schlosser, Eric. "Burger with a Side of Spies." *New York Times,* May 7, 2008. http://www.nytimes.com/2008/05/07/opinion/07schlosser.html?_r=2&oref=slogin&.

———. *Fast Food Nation: The Dark Side of the American Meal.* London: Penguin Books, 2001. http://jhampton.pbworks.com/w/file/fetch/51769044/Fast%20Food%20Nation.pdf.

———. *Reefer Madness: Sex, Drugs, and Cheap Labor in the American Black Market.* Boston: Houghton Mifflin, 2003.

Schneider, Mike, and Wilfredo Lee. "Wal-Mart Joins Farmworker Pay Initiative in Florida." *USA Today,* January 16, 2014. http://www.usatoday.com/story/money/business/2014/01/16/wal-mart-joins-initiative-on-farmworker-pay-in-fla/4535805/.

Sears Holding Company. "Human Rights Policy." 2016. https://searsholdings.com/docs/corporate-responsibility/Human-Rights-Policy.pdf.

Sellers, Randall Sean. "'Del Pueblo, Para El Pueblo': The Coalition of Immokalee Workers and the Fight for Fair Food." MA thesis, University of Texas at Austin, 2009. http://citeseerx.ist.psu.edu/viewdoc/download?doi=10.1.1.471.7557&rep=rep1&type=pdf.

Shoemaker, Kent. "Tell the Complete Story About Florida's Tomato Industry." *Miami Herald,* November 30, 2014. http://www.miamiherald.com/opinion/letters-to-the-editor/article4208162.html.

Sinclair, Jack, Jib Ellison, and Michael Pollan. "Edible Education 101: Corporations and the Food Movement." October 4, 2011. https://www.youtube.com/watch?v=O2Kwa1pjV3w.

Sinclair, Upton. *The Jungle.* Mineola, NY: Dover Publications, 1906.

Singh, Sonia. "How Migrant Farmworkers Are Cross-Pollinating Strategies and Winning." July 6, 2015. http://www.labornotes.org/2015/07/how-migrant-farmworkers-are-cross-pollinating-strategies-and-winning.

"Six Ls Packing Company Rebrands, Changes Name to Lipman." *Produce News*, 2011. http://producenews.com/list-all-categories2/6553-six-ls-packing-changes-its-name-to-lipman.

Smith, S. E. "Growing Pains: Why Labor Is the Real Food Movement We Should Be Paying Attention To." *Bitch*, January 15, 2014. http://ciw-online.org/wp-content/uploads/BitchMagazine_GrowingPains.pdf.

Solnit, David. "Taco Bell Boycott Victory—A Model of Strategic Organizing: An Interview with the Coalition of Immokalee Workers." August 1, 2005. http://www.leftturn.org/taco-bell-boycott-victory%E2%80%94-model-strategic-organizing-interview-coalition-immokalee-workers.

Soohoo, Cynthia, Catherine Albisa, and Martha F. David, eds. *Bringing Human Rights Home. Volume 2: Portraits of the Movement, Bringing Human Rights Home.* Westport, CT: Praeger Publishers.

Southern Methodist University. Engineering and Humanity Week (April 15–20, 2012) program. https://www.smu.edu/News/2012/engineering-humanity-week-13april2012.

Southern Poverty Law Center. "A Brief History of Guestworkers in America." 2013. http://www.splcenter.org/publications/close-to-slavery-guestworker-programs-in-the-united-states/a-brief-history-of-guestwork.

Strom, Stephanie, and Chad Bray. "Ahold-Delhaize Deal Would Create One of Largest Grocery Chains in U.S." *New York Times*, June 24, 2015. http://www.nytimes.com/2015/06/25/business/dealbook/supermarkets-ahold-delhaize.html?_r=0.

Strom, Stephanie, and Steven Greenhouse. "On the Front Lines of Food Safety." *New York Times*, May 24, 2013. http://www.nytimes.com/2013/05/25/business/a-program-to-combat-food-contamination.html?_r=1.

Student/Farmworker Alliance. "80 Students and Young People Gather in Immokalee for #Encuentro2015." September 23, 2015. http://www.sfalliance.org/news/2015/9/23/80-students-and-young-people-converge-in-immokalee-for-annual-gathering-15-actions-ignite-nationwide-for-schoolingwendys-week-of-action.

——. "Who We Are." 2015. http://www.sfalliance.org/who-we-are/.

Taco Bell. "Yo Quiero Taco Bell." 1997. https://www.youtube.com/watch?v=M8sZ1DWsAHE.

Tam, Donna. "Fair Labor Association Too Easy on Apple, Foxconn, Study Says." *CNET*, November 7, 2012. http://www.cnet.com/news/fair-labor-association-too-easy-on-apple-foxconn-study-says/.

"Theo Albrecht Dies at 88; German Billionaire Was Co-owner of Trader Joe's." *Los Angeles Times*, July 29, 2010. http://articles.latimes.com/2010/jul/29/local/la-me-theo-albrecht-20100729.

Trader Joe's. "Our Story." 2016. http://www.traderjoes.com/our-story.

"Top 100 Chains: U.S. Sales." *Nation's Restaurant News.* 2012. http://nrn.com/us-top-100/top-100-chains-us-sales.

US Department of Agriculture. National Agricultural Workers Survey. 2015. http://www.doleta.gov.

US Department of Justice. "Two Men Plead Guilty in Southwest Florida Slavery Ring." May 26, 1999. https://www.justice.gov/archive/opa/pr/1999/May/216cr.htm.

US Department of Justice, US Attorney's Office, Southern District of Florida. "Two Mexican Nationals Charged with Conspiracy to Provide and Obtain Forced Labor." March 18, 2016. https://www.justice.gov/usao-sdfl/pr/two-mexican-nationals-charged-conspiracy-provide-and-obtain-forced-labor.

———. "Two Mexican Nationals Sentenced to Prison for Participating in Forced Labor Scheme. Press release, January 9, 2017. https://www.justice.gov/usao-sdfl/pr/two-mexican-nationals-sentenced-prison-participating-forced-labor-scheme-0.

US Department of Labor. "Dr. David Weil, Administrator, Wage and Hour Division." 2015. https://www.dol.gov/whd/about/org/dweil.htm.

———. Fair Labor Standards Act of 1938. 29 U.S.C. 201, June 25, 1938. https://www.dol.gov/whd/regs/statutes/FairLaborStandAct.pdf.

———. 1988. "History of Changes to the Minimum Wage Law." Adapted from *Minimum Wage and Maximum Hours Standards Under the Fair Labor Standards Act*, 1988 Report to the Congress under Section 4(d)(1) of the FLSA. https://www.dol.gov/whd/minwage/coverage.htm.

———. "U.S. Wage and Hour Division District Offices." 2016. https://www.dol.gov/whd/america2.htm#Florida.

US Department of Labor, Wage and Hour Division (WHD). "Vegetable Supplier to Major Grocery Chains Assessed over $1.4 Million in Civil Money Penalties After Two-Year Federal Investigation." May 12, 2016. https://www.dol.gov/newsroom/releases/whd/whd20160512.

US Department of State. "Laura Germino, United States of America, Class of 2010. Working With the Coalition of Immokalee Workers, Laura Germino Began Fighting against Modern-Day Slavery in the Tomato Picking Industry." Trafficking in Persons Report: Heroes. 2016. http://www.tipheroes.org/laura-germino/.

———. "Remarks on the Release of the 10th Annual Trafficking in Persons Report." June 14, 2010. https://www.state.gov/secretary/20092013clinton/rm/2010/06/143113.htm.

US Environmental Protection Agency (EPA). "Grant Information for Healthy Fields – Healthy Kids." Grant Awards Database. 2016. http://yosemite.epa.gov/oarm/igms_egf.nsf/3b85f9fbd4a5e54b85256fb60070e5a2/fa6dbc34c2a9c55585257d6f0071e6de!OpenDocument&Highlight=0,Farmworker,Justice.

US Equal Employment Opportunity Commission (EEOC). "EEOC Select Task Force on the Study of Harassment in the Workplace, Report of Co-Chairs Chai R. Feldblum & Victoria A. Lipnic." 2016. https://www.eeoc.gov/eeoc/task_force/harassment/.

US Senate, Committee on Health, Education, Labor, and Pensions. *Hearing of the Committee on Health, Education, Labor, and Pensions: Examining Ending Abuses and Improving Working Conditions for Tomato Workers.* April 15, 2008.

Underwriters Laboratories (UL). "The Seventh Responsible Sourcing Summit: Refocusing the Lens on Human Rights." January 10, 2012. http://www.csrwire.com/press_releases/33586-The-Seventh-Responsible-Sourcing-Summit-Refocusing-the-Lens-on-Human-Rights.

United Nations, Human Rights, Officer of the High Commissioner. Visit to the United States: Report of the working group on the issue of human rights and transnational corporations and other business enterprises. 2014. http://ap.ohchr.org/documents/dpage_e.aspx?si=A/HRC/26/25/Add.4.

Verité. "Comprehensive Factory Evaluation Report of Rosita Knitwears (PVT.), LTD." April 9, 2012. http://www.globallabourrights.org/documents/Verite-Comprehensive-Factory-Eval-Rpt-Rosita-Knitwears.pdf.

"Victory a Long-Time Coming for FL Tomato Pickers." *Tampa Bay Times*, October 15, 2010. http://www.tampabay.com/opinion/editorials/victory-long-time-coming-for-florida-tomato-pickers/1128359.

Voices for Immigrant Defense & Advocacy (VIDA). "Mission Statement." 2016. http://www.vidalaw.org/index.php?area=mission.

Walsh, Delcan, and Steven Greenhouse. "Inspectors Certified Pakistani Factory as Safe Before Disaster." *New York Times*, September 19, 2012. http://www.nytimes.com/2012/09/20/world/asia/pakistan-factory-passed-inspection-before-fire.html?_r=0.

Wang, David. "A Simple Lesson About the Power of Collaboration." *Public Administration Review* 74:4 (2014). doi:10.1111/puar.12253. http://online library.wiley.com/doi/10.1111/puar.12253/full.

Wasem, Ruth Ellen. "U.S. Immigration Policy on Haitian Migrants." Congressional Research Service, May 17, 2011. https://fas.org/sgp/crs/row/RS21349.pdf.

Wendy's Company. "Responsibility Overview." 2015. https://www.wendys.com/en-us/about-wendys/responsibility-overview.

WGCU-TV (PBS). "Makers: Women Who Make Southwest Florida: Nely Rodriguez." April 3, 2013. http://wgcumakers.org/nelyrodriguez/.

"When Working Conditions Are Ripe for Change." *Reveal News*, December 21, 2015. http://reveal.prx.org/2015/12/when-working-conditions-are-ripe-for-change/.

Whole Foods. "Florida Tomato Growers, Whole Foods Market sign Agreement Supporting Coalition of Immokalee Workers." June 4, 2009. http://media.wholefoodsmarket.com/news/florida-tomato-growers-whole-foods-market-sign-agreement-supporting-coaliti.

——. "Whole Foods Market Expands Partnership with Coalition of Immokalee Workers." March 22, 2016. http://media.wholefoodsmarket.com/news/whole-foods-market-expands-partnership-with-coalition-of-immokalee-workers.

Williams, Amy Bennett. "Burger King Exec Uses Daughter's Online ID to Chide Immokalee Coalition." *Fort Myers News-Press*, April 28, 2008. http://www.commondreams.org/news/2008/04/28/burger-king-exec-uses-daughters-online-id-chide-immokalee-coalition.

——. "CIW Debuts Fair Food Label Nationwide." *Fort Myers News-Press*, October 24, 2014. http://www.ciw-online.org/blog/2014/10/label-media/.

——. "Florida Growers Group Changes Stance on Tomato Pickers' Pay." *Fort Myers News-Press*, February 17, 2010. http://flcitrusmutual.com/render.aspx?p=/news/newspress_tomato_021710.aspx.

——. "Immokalee Family Sentenced for Slavery; Each Navarrete Boss Gets 12 Years in Prison." *Fort Myers News-Press*, December 20, 2008. http://www.sanders.senate.gov/newsroom/must-read/immokalee-family-sentenced-for-slavery-each-navarrete-boss-gets-12-years-in-prison-ft-myers-news-press.

——. "Tomato Struggle Over After Immokalee Coalition Signs Historic Deal." *Fort Myers News-Press*, November 16, 2010. http://webcache.googleusercontent.com/search?q=cache:Y9Bz7ewGUKEJ:www.verite.org/es/news/tomato_struggle_over_after_coalition_signs_historic_deal+&cd=14&hl=en&ct=clnk&gl=us.

Wilson, James Q. *Bureaucracy: What Government Agencies Do and Why They Do It.* Vol. 227. New York: Basic Books, 1989.

Winkler, Victoria. "Here Are The 10 Richest Cities In Florida." August 24, 2015. http://www.onlyinyourstate.com/florida/richest-towns-fl/.

Yum! Brands. "Ethical Sourcing and Supply." 2017. http://www.yum.com/responsibility/food/ethical-sourcing-supply-chain/.

Zamorano Pan-American Agricultural School. www.zamorano.edu, 2017.

Note: All website addresses have been accessed or verified during the week of January 9, 2017.

Index

Page numbers in italics refer to figures.